DIVERSITY MATTERS

RACE, ETHNICITY, & THE FUTURE OF CHRISTIAN HIGHER EDUCATION

SECTION EDITORS / ALLISON N. ASH & ALEXANDER JUN
KATHY-ANN HERNANDEZ / REBECCA HERNANDEZ
MICHELLE LOYD-PAIGE / PETE MENJARES

GENERAL EDITOR / KAREN A. LONGMAN

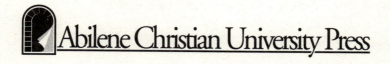
Abilene Christian University Press

Diversity Matters
Race, Ethnicity, and the Future of Christian Higher Education

Copyright © 2017 by Karen A. Longman

ISBN 978-0-89112-454-2

Printed in the United States of America

CIP data available through the Library of Congress.

Cover and interior text design by ThinkPen Design, LLC

For information contact:
Abilene Christian University Press
ACU Box 29138
Abilene, Texas 79699
1-877-816-4455
www.acupressbooks.com

18 19 20 21 22 / 7 6 5 4 3 2

Contents

Foreword

A FIERCE RESOLVE TOWARD UNIFYING GRACE

Shirley V. Hoogstra, JD
President, Council for Christian Colleges & Universities

I am more convinced than ever that Christ-centered colleges and universities are uniquely positioned to model and lead the crucial discussion on matters of diversity.

There are several reasons I believe this. First, Christian colleges may struggle like other sectors of higher education, yet these institutions are anchored in a biblical theology of sin and failure, of grace and second chances. We believe the power of the Holy Spirit will empower such discussions and lift up the broken-hearted. We are guided by the story of our Creator's commitment to his people. We are grounded in God's love, and we are not alone in our journey.

Second, those working in Christian higher education understand the theological imperative of viewing diversity as a gift to be celebrated through our common commitment to Christ and his kingdom. Though we might come from different denominations and experiences, we share a bold and historic belief that unites us: Christ crucified and resurrected.

In my own learning over the past twenty years—which unfortunately includes stumbling and silence when a strong voice was needed—I have felt the grace of my sisters and brothers of color as they educated me. They have loved me and challenged me . . . and loved me some more until I understood the issues, at least better, even if not perfectly. Why did they do it? Because they believed as I do in this unifying gospel message that motivates us to encourage and equip leaders for diversity across our campuses. The "Excellence Imperative," as I call the CCCU diversity work, has been at the forefront of my presidency. This "imperative" also distinguishes our mission and positions us to respond to those around us.

And yet, we are not where we want to be. As we consider how best to serve and equip our students, knowing the challenges we face in our twenty-first century world for both the church and academy, we as Christ-followers are called to the hard conversations around issues of culture, privilege, and race. Such discussions are not easy, but they are happening: in the CCCU's Leadership

Development Institutes, in CCCU diversity conferences, and in other professional development conferences that emphasize diversity imperatives for all of our leaders. Likewise, through articles in the CCCU *Advance* magazine, specific networking opportunities within and beyond our institutions, and intentional relationship building, diversity becomes ever more deeply embedded in our core commitments. From each conversation and conference, each article and relationship, I am all the more confident that God will lead us into creative and strategic responses during this period of time when cities, countries, and the entire world long for grace. Our culture and our mission require such engagement. The collection of voices expressed throughout this book brings us closer to such engagement.

Another reason I believe Christian higher education is uniquely positioned for such leadership is that—as you will see in the chapters that follow—scholars and leaders on our campuses share a desire to honor God. Our discussions and efforts are anchored in the character of the Triune God—Father, Son, and Holy Spirit—whose very being expresses the beauty of diversity in community. Yes, we approach this topic with a sense of urgency, yet we do so believing that it is a reflection of personal faith and institutional excellence, both of which define Christian higher education. We acknowledge the findings of research replete with examples that the best teams and the most effective leadership comes when multiple points of view have a voice in the planning, learning, and implementation of organizational mission. And we admit that such effectiveness doesn't happen accidently or independently. It is intentional, born of our collective pursuit of excellence, and out of obedience *to* God while fulfilling our calling *from* God.

Inherent in any discussion on diversity, then, is genuine humility, evidence of which you will see in the following pages. Each honest admission, each anecdote, insight, and recommendation, is wrapped in the posture of humility, an integral quality for leaders. In this regard, the description of a "level five" leader by Jim Collins, in his book *Good to Great*, comes to my mind; such leaders are individuals who blend "extreme personal humility" with what Collins refers to as "fierce resolve" to do whatever needs to be done.[1] Because the authors in the following pages spend themselves in the work of diversity every day, their credibility and authority model this kind of "fierce resolve" of excellence for us. Their words also humble us as we learn from them, respecting and appreciating the value of their diverse contributions to the advancement of Christian higher education.

As a result, I believe there is rich fodder here for moving forward. In the book's first section, under the direction of CCCU Diversity Fellow and respected senior leader Pete Menjares (Vanguard University), four institutional case studies show us how campuses have adjusted to a changing and diverse world. No change is easy, and sometimes the resistance in these case study institutions has brought as much discomfort and reluctance as conviction and self-reflection. Even the term *diversity* can be difficult to embrace, since differences of ethnicity, race, social background, religion, economic status, gender, and worldview often intersect. Leaders on these campuses, though, have brought together teams of people—fellow leaders and practitioners—who convey a humble awareness and confidence that their perspective is necessary for the greater good.

Hearing the voices and stories of leaders of color who have stayed in their predominately white campuses offers exactly what the next section subtitle conveys: "Lessons in Resiliency and Leadership from Long-Term CCCU Diversity Professionals." With guidance from Michelle Loyd-Paige of Calvin College, these authors describe from their own experiences the practical strategies they discovered while persisting in kingdom work. Such insights could have far-reaching implications for our colleges and universities, especially as our ever-changing culture affects the composition of our campuses.

Scholars Alexander Jun (Azusa Pacific University) and Allison Ash (Wheaton College) and their colleagues next paint a stark, sometimes uncomfortable, yet essential picture of what it means to be "white allies" in the work of social justice. Advocacy efforts, suggest the authors, are like diversity and not so easily prescribed. Neither are curricular and cocurricular initiatives, as described by diversity leader Rebecca Hernandez (George Fox University) and her team of chapter authors. In this fourth section of the book, a variety of programs and strategies demonstrate how a commitment to diversity work can take root and flourish in key places such as faculty development and chapel programming, and can also spring up from the commitment of individuals who have passion, expertise, and any other sphere of influence. Each new step, each activity, speaker program, or training session, requires the noble and ongoing work of relationship building across areas of campus if differences are to be celebrated.

In the book's final chapters, we have the benefit of hearing from the voices and perspectives of eight emerging leaders within the CCCU who participated in a recent Multi-Ethnic Leadership Development Institute that focused, in part, on the concepts of mentoring and sponsorship. The messages conveyed in these chapters reinforce for us the care and commitment that must be honored if we are to successfully navigate professional roles, leadership development, family responsibilities, and life's various transitions. Each stage in this journey is unique. Each takes time and support if the common good is to be achieved.

In many ways, every chapter in this important collection—patiently shepherded by long-time diversity visionary Karen Longman (Azusa Pacific University)—reminds us of the great and difficult privilege it is to represent God's kingdom, not unlike the Apostle Paul's challenge to the Romans:

> For just as each of us has one body with many members, and these members do not all have the same function, so in Christ we, though many, form one body, and each member belongs to all the others. We have different gifts, according to the grace given to each of us. If your gift is prophesying, then prophesy in accordance with your faith; if it is serving, then serve; if it is teaching, then teach; if it is to encourage, then give encouragement; if it is giving, then give generously; if it is to lead, do it diligently; if it is to show mercy, do it cheerfully. (12:4–8 NIV)

Diversity Matters celebrates the gifts of our many and varied differences, because we belong to one another as the body of Christ. It invites us into those necessary conversations that will move our institutions forward while honoring what the CCCU founders knew all along: that spiritual insight, biblical truth, and sustaining faith as the hallmarks of our academic pursuits are best expressed in the many voices of God's people. At the heart of Christian higher education is a moral underpinning that comes from a community life of faith in the One whose life, death, and resurrection has shaped cultures long before our campuses existed.

Finally, I am convinced of our unique opportunity within the movement of Christian higher education, because as *The Message* paraphrases Paul's words in Romans 8, God gives us hope with a tender message of love and faithfulness, even though the reconciling work is and will be difficult:

> God knew what he was doing from the very beginning. He decided from the outset to shape the lives of those who love him along the same lines as the life of his Son. The Son stands first in the line of humanity he restored. We see the original and intended shape of our lives there in him. After God made that decision of what his children should be like, he followed it up by calling people by name. After he called them by name, he set them on a solid basis with himself. And then, after getting them established, he stayed with them to the end, gloriously completing what he had begun. (8:29–30)

It is only because of Christ's promise to complete the good work he has begun in us that we can dedicate ourselves to the "Excellence Imperative" each day we are given the opportunity. I am grateful for each writer in this important book, and I want to extend a word of special thanks to the section leaders who went above and beyond the call of duty to ensure that each chapter in their respective sections represented a well-coordinated contribution to the project overall. I am grateful for my friend, Karen Longman, and her careful and patient guidance as the editor of this important collaborative project. Also, sincere thanks to Jo Kadlecek, formerly with Gordon College and now living in Australia, for her excellent work in editing several of the chapters early in the process. And to the staff at Cedar Springs Christian Retreat Center in Sumas, Washington, for their prayers of support for this project and for hosting a writers' retreat in June 2016 that allowed focused time for the writers to begin their collaborative work. Finally, I am grateful for the commitment, support, and partnership of Abilene Christian University Press in helping the Council for Christian Colleges & Universities advance this essential discussion through the following pages.

May this book give each reader a "fierce resolve" toward unifying grace. To God be the glory.

NOTE

1   Jim Collins, *Good to Great* (New York: HarperBusiness, 2001), 21.

Introduction

DIVERSITY IN THE CCCU: THE CURRENT STATE AND IMPLICATIONS FOR THE FUTURE

Pete C. Menjares, PhD

CCCU Senior Fellow for Diversity, Vanguard University of Southern California

A college is a school, and as such, it places disciplined study at the center of its project. But the lure of shalom will direct and energize it. The goal of the Christian college, so I have begun to think, is to promote that mode of flourishing which is shalom.
—Nicholas Wolterstorff, *Educating for Shalom: Essays on Christian Higher Education*[1]

What we should dream of is making our campuses joyful, pioneering communities of interethnic justice and healing, as well as launching pads for social change efforts in the broader local, national, and global communities.
—David P. Gushee, *A Biblical Vision for Intercultural Competencies*[2]

Early in the fall 1995 semester, I was invited by the leadership of the School of Arts and Sciences at the university where I was employed to deliver a talk to the faculty on the problem of racism in the classroom. I was surprised to receive this invitation since I was new to my role and still settling into my first teaching post, while also completing my doctoral studies at the University of Southern California in Los Angeles. And though I was flattered by the invitation to address this important topic with my faculty colleagues, there were numerous questions welling up in me that I felt needed to be answered before I could accept the invitation. Some of those questions were: Why was I being invited to speak? Were there no other experts available or willing to speak? Was there a race problem on campus? If so, where did my white colleagues stand on the issue? I did not get many answers to my immediate questions and I was admittedly apprehensive, but after giving the invitation further thought and prayer, I agreed to speak to the faculty at the next school-wide meeting, scheduled for Tuesday morning, October 3rd.

As the room proceeded to fill, one senior member of the faculty asked me if he could keep a transistor radio and earphones on hand since there was going to be a significant news announcement made within the hour. Being focused on my presentation, and perhaps due to some of the nervousness, I agreed and then proceeded to give my talk. After defining several terms, I turned my attention to what racial discrimination might look like in a classroom setting. At that point my colleague raised his hand and asked if he could speak. Having gained the attention of the entire room, he proceeded to report that a verdict had been reached and that the jury comprised of nine African Americans, two whites, and one Latino had found O. J. Simpson not guilty of the double murder for which he was being tried, thus ending one of the most dramatic and race-infused murder trials in US history.

For those of us living and working in the Los Angeles area at the time, the O. J. Simpson trial became a part of our lives as it was recapped nightly on the local news with the drama of a Hollywood soap opera. The racial undertones associated with the trial were also significant for a city still recovering from the devastation of the 1992 riots that had been sparked by the acquittal of four white police officers who were videoed beating an unarmed African American named Rodney King. Needless to say, the news of the O. J. Simpson verdict left the faculty stunned and silent as many believed he would be found guilty. I paused at the podium, let the news sink in, and then moved from the topic of racism in the classroom to the broader topic of race in society, higher education, and the church. In the twenty-one-plus years following this initiatory event, I have continued to engage the subject of race in Christian higher education on campuses around the country . . . and it has not always been easy.

INTRODUCTION

I have more than two decades of personal experience in the Council for Christian Colleges & Universities (CCCU) as an ethnic minority in predominantly white evangelical colleges and universities as a professor, administrator, and CCCU Senior Fellow for Diversity. During this period, I have had hundreds of conversations with students, faculty, staff, and administrators from across the council on matters of diversity and racial reconciliation in Christian higher education. These individuals have shared openly with me their perspectives and experiences, both positive and negative, and much of what I have heard and learned is reflected in this chapter.

My goal here is to paint an honest picture of the current state of diversity in the CCCU. I provide an overview of the current demographic, social, and cultural contexts that serve as the backdrop to the changing face of faith-based higher education; I then detail how diversity is impacting the people, culture, and programming of our Christian colleges and universities. I also address the necessity of a biblically based and holistic approach to diversity that should guide our endeavors. In concluding the chapter, I identify five areas that I believe must be attended to if Christian higher education is to have a viable future in a diverse and complex higher education landscape.

DIVERSITY IN THE CCCU

Current demographics suggest that, as diversity scholar Daryl G. Smith recently stated, "Today, diversity is no longer a projection—it is a reality."[3] For more than two decades, social scientists and educators have forecasted a demographic shift in the United States that would inevitably have a direct impact on the enrollments of colleges and universities. Continued growth in the racial/ ethnic minority and immigrant populations have contributed to this shift. Consequently, it is now estimated by the US Census Bureau that the United States will have a majority-minority population by the year 2044.[4] This demographic shift also parallels changes in the American religious landscape as the percentage of white mainline Protestants and white evangelical Protestants, since 1988 and 2008, respectively, has declined.[5]

The changing demographics in the white evangelical Protestant population is having a direct impact on evangelical Christian higher education, given the related decline in this pool of prospective students who have historically chosen to attend our colleges and universities. In turn, there has been a demonstrable increase in the number of students from historically underrepresented backgrounds and underserved communities enrolling at historically majority white Christian institutions. This reality is registering on the minds of institutional leaders throughout the CCCU and has elevated the urgency of the "diversity" conversation on many campuses; this conversation is currently being framed as a matter of "institutional survival" across the council.[6] The shift in demographics has signaled that times have changed for predominantly white evangelical Christian colleges and universities, and that "business as usual" can no longer be considered a viable strategy if our institutions are to remain relevant and flourishing in these changing times.

A KAIROS MOMENT

Diversity is changing Christian higher education, and I believe this change is for the good. The current wave of diverse students enrolling is impacting virtually every area of campus life and organizational functioning. Diverse students are infusing new cultural norms, perspectives, and experiences that are challenging long-held traditions, historic boundaries, and the comfort zones of existing people and structures, while also enriching the overall educational experience. They are also introducing faith traditions, worship styles, and religious practices that are new to predominantly white evangelical Protestant institutions in ways that are both refreshing and a challenge to the status quo. Diversity is broadening the academy in dynamic ways, which will only add to the educational value of a Christian college degree as that fact is recognized, affirmed, embraced, and leveraged for the benefit of all members of these learning communities.

From the perspective of faith, the current influx of diverse students is being recognized by many educators across the CCCU as a "Kairos moment," a time when God is moving significantly in human history, and it is critical that we recognize this seismic shift as orchestrated by God.[7] The kingdom of God is composed of people from the east and west and north and south (Luke 13:29). One could say, therefore, that CCCU member and affiliate institutions are looking more like the kingdom than ever before. Thus Christian higher education today is being reimagined to keep in step with the "new thing" God is doing at present (Isa. 43:19). CCCU leaders are also seeking to discern what these changes mean for the mission of Christ-centered education, given the enormity of problems presenting themselves nationally and internationally.

A Time of Lament

Over the course of my career in Christian higher education, I have witnessed progress toward a better understanding and appreciation of diversity at many institutions in the CCCU. At the time of this writing, however, the nation is experiencing very serious challenges in race relations in the broader society, the political arena, and in higher education. Many North Americans have been disturbed over the numbers of unarmed African American men and youth being killed by law enforcement; the recent long and discouraging political process that lacked civility, and some prominent acts of domestic terrorism. In the aftermath, deep and significant divisions between individuals and communities have been exposed and the nation is seeking to recover.

On college and university campuses, students of color and white allies have protested the current state of things, orchestrated demonstrations, signed petitions, and made demands on administrators to act on their stated commitments to diversity in clear and demonstrable ways, while also ensuring accountability going forward. Demands for greater student diversity, a more diverse and interculturally competent faculty, a more diverse curriculum, and improved campus climates are factors generally found at the top of the list, and Christian higher education is not without its challenges in these regards.

In January of 2016, *The Chronicle of Higher Education* published an article entitled "Evangelical Colleges' Diversity Problem." In this article, the author noted the significant strides in campus diversity that have been made but also asserts that there are challenges ethnic and racial minority students and faculty experience at predominately white Christian institutions, such as having a sense of being different or not fitting in on many of these campuses. Additionally, the article observed that racial tensions sometimes stem from differences in expressions of faith and worship styles, where the predominantly white way is perceived as the norm.[8]

My own encounters with campus leaders around the country bear witness to the experiences of the students and faculty described in the article. Additionally, my interactions with diversity personnel invariably lead to serious conversations about the causes of and solutions to the racial divide that continues to persist in society, the church, and Christian higher education. The frequency and cyclical nature of the problems raises concerns about the permanence of the progress that has been made in recent decades, with these concerns often giving way to grief and lament. Indeed, this is a time of lament for many racial and ethnic minorities and among white allies on our campuses. While some of the assertions of the *Chronicle* article could be questioned, it did serve as a vivid reminder that we in Christian higher education have unfinished work to do in order to create the kinds of welcoming spaces in which all students, staff, and faculty can flourish.

DIVERSITY AND ITS IMPACT

Increased diversity in the CCCU is evident, especially among students. What is also evident is the impact student diversity is having on institutions and the students there, namely faculty, staff, and administrators. Several strategic areas where diversity is having a noticeable effect are highlighted in the following section.

Enrollment Growth

As noted in Table 1.1, there was a demonstrable increase in the number of students from diverse backgrounds enrolling at CCCU institutions during the decade that stretched from 2004 to 2014. In fact, the proportion of nonwhite students in 2014 was 28 percent, up from 19 percent in 2004. The proportion of students from American Indian/Alaska Native backgrounds declined slightly during the same decade (–0.03 percent), but there were increases in the percentage of students from Asian/Native Hawaiian/Pacific Islander backgrounds (+0.89 percent), black/African American (+2.43 percent), and Hispanic/Latino students (+3.58 percent). During the same period, these campuses experienced a decrease in the percentage of white students (–9.36 percent). Further, a disaggregated analysis of the student population at sixty member institutions with the greatest diversity reflected that fifty-two institutions had at least 28 percent or greater diversity, twenty-one schools had greater than 40 percent diversity, and ten campuses had a notable majority-minority enrollment of more than 50 percent diversity in 2014.[9]

Faculty Diversity

Table 1.2 reveals that the 2014 percentage for ethnically diverse faculty (full- and part-time) stood at 9.95 percent, up slightly from 8.3 percent in 2007. The ethnic distribution as of 2014 reflected American Indian/Alaska Native at 0.31 percent, Hispanic/Latino at 2.49 percent, Asian/Native Hawaiian/Pacific Islander at 2.95 percent, and black/African American at 4.20 percent. The ethnic diversity of the faculty stands in contrast to that of students, which is not surprising given that the pool from which students are drawn is greater than the pool for faculty, there are fewer positions for faculty to occupy on these campuses than there are for students, and faculty are replaced far less frequently than students. Accordingly, although the increase in faculty diversity is relatively modest in comparison to students, the needle has moved.

Diverse Leadership

Women and minorities are currently significantly underrepresented in senior leadership roles on CCCU campuses, although considerable progress has been made over the past two decades to advance more women into leadership, in part due to the effectiveness of the CCCU's Women's Leadership Development Institutes and Women's Advanced Leadership Institutes.[10] An analysis of women holding vice-president or higher leadership roles in CCCU institutions between 1998 and 2010 indicated that 91.5 percent of those holding senior roles in 1998 were men; by 2010, that percentage had shifted to 83.2 percent; and as of June 2015, the proportion was 79.8 percent. Still, less than a third (31 percent) of the CCCU's 120 member institutions had more than one woman holding a vice-president or higher position.[11]

In addition to the Mixed-Cohort (i.e., men and women) Leadership Development Institutes that have been offered since 1998, the CCCU launched biannual Multi-Ethnic Leadership Development Institutes in 2011. The institutes offer a broad leadership curriculum taught by resource leaders throughout the council, and the series has been intentional about engaging topics related to diversity and inclusion in higher education administration from a faith perspective. The impact of these institutes cannot be overstated, as they have involved more than four hundred emerging leaders, representing more than ninety campuses. From these participants, over fifty "graduates" are serving in cabinet-level leadership, including thirty-three chief academic officers and thirteen presidents. Intentional leadership development efforts are bearing fruit, and time will tell what impact this initiative will have on populating the senior leadership ranks with leaders of color in the presidency and other cabinet-level roles.

Students of Color

Students represent the greatest area of growth in diversity for the CCCU. As noted in Table 1.1, the proportion of nonwhite students across the member campuses stands at 28 percent, yet despite the progress that has been made in this area, students of color remain the numerical minority on most campuses. As a result, students have expressed difficulty "fitting in," feeling pressured to assimilate into the dominant (white) campus culture. However, as representation by students of color increases, they are making their voices heard. Many have expressed frustration with the slow progress being made, the repeated microaggressions that they experience, and the continual need to educate others about their race or culture. Because the need to support their social, cultural, and religious identities is real, diverse students want professors who share their ethnic/racial characteristics and who understand and can identify with their sociocultural contexts. They also want their faculty to be culturally literate, advocates for racial equity, and able to address the microaggressions directed toward them. Many diverse students also express a desire to see their white peers engaged in racial matters and diversity conversations, and to assume a posture of cultural humility toward those in the cultural minority.

Diverse Staff

Faculty, staff, and administrators of color have experiences on predominantly white Christian campuses similar to those experienced by students of color. As noted earlier, as of 2014, only 9.95 percent of the faculty in the CCCU was nonwhite. This being the case, faculty of color in the CCCU are even more of a minority than are students; often, they are the only persons of color in their department or academic division. Many of these professionals want to see intentional and concrete efforts taken on the part of their institutions to increase diversity in faculty and staff ranks, to provide opportunities for professional development, and for mentoring by senior leaders of color. They also express a desire to network with peers of color for soul care, sociocultural support, affirmation, and professional collaboration.

Chief Diversity Officers (CDO)

CDOs and Multicultural Affairs staff are the professionals in the "diversity trenches" who often find themselves preventing or solving crises, carrying heavy workloads, and wearing many hats in their attempt to live up to the demands of their job to support students of color, educate white students and staff, and hold their institutions accountable. I know many of these individuals personally, and they are some of the most gifted and dedicated people in the Christian college movement. Most of them are also ethnic/racial minorities, and they carry the "double burden" of being one of the only professionals of color on their campuses; as such, they are often implicitly expected to serve as role models for students and as spokespersons for their racial or ethnic group. Thus, these professionals speak of the need for personal and professional sustainability given the weight of responsibility demanded by their roles. Many of these individuals also feel underresourced and frequently speak of the need for additional staff, budget, programming, and space to do their jobs well and with excellence.

Presidents

The responsibilities of leadership weigh heavily on presidents, and decisions about where to invest their limited time and executive resources is a daily preoccupation. Presidents have extraordinarily complex jobs, and they spend a significant amount of their time raising funds for capital projects and other university needs. Crisis management is also a regular concern for many presidents who would rather spend their time building meaningful relationships with students and nurturing their campus communities. As campuses become increasingly diverse, there are related expectations for the president to not only care about racial matters, but also be personally committed to the "multicultural journey," and serve as an advocate for racial justice by leveraging the presidential platform to build a more equitable learning community while also holding others accountable to do their part.

Boards of Trustees

As a former university president and current trustee, I have spent a significant amount of time in the boardroom. I have a deep appreciation for the work of trustees and the enormous responsibility they shoulder to steward the mission, resources, and people of the institution in the higher education environment of today. These accomplished professionals care deeply for the institutions they lead, volunteer their time, serve on committees, and support the institution financially. Many of them are alumni, and others are parents of current students. More recently I have engaged members of boards on matters of diversity, inclusion, and reconciliation, and we are learning together, searching the Scriptures, seeking to understand the perspective of one another, and supporting each other in the process by listening and through prayer. I am pleased to see more boards willing to engage these important issues.

Chief Academic Officers (CAO)

CAOs also have enormous jobs, as they are expected to lead the faculty, deliver a state-of-the-art curriculum, and meet the standards for regional and national accreditation of the academic programs. In regard to diversity, the CAO is under increasing pressure to diversify the faculty and the curriculum, as well as develop the faculty for culturally responsive teaching and intercultural competencies. In many cases, the CAO is also expected to accomplish such changes despite budget constraints, time constraints, process or procedural constraints, or a resistant faculty culture. And like presidents, the CAO is expected to be personally and professionally committed to racial justice and educational equity, and to personally be on the multicultural journey.

Chief Student Development Officers

Like chief diversity officers, these professionals are entrusted with the responsibility to develop predominantly undergraduate students holistically through creative, engaging, and meaningful programs. These professionals wrestle with how to best care for these complex, yet incredibly talented, millennials who represent the next generation of leaders. In addition, many of these professionals either oversee or work directly with staff in the multi-ethnic programs area; they, too, are asking questions about how best to serve the social, cultural, and religious identity needs of diverse students, while also growing in their own understanding of the issues.

Campus Ministers

Campus ministers play a vital role in caring for the spiritual needs of students attending faith-based schools. In regard to diversity, campus ministers are also mindful that the increase in students from diverse backgrounds has resulted in a diversity of faith traditions and worship expressions beyond that which had been historically valued on many campuses. Denominational institutions are enrolling an increased number of students from outside of the denomination; predominantly Protestant campuses are enrolling Roman Catholic students; and historically non-Pentecostal schools are welcoming an increase in the number of students from Pentecostal backgrounds. As a result of these shifts, some campus ministers are asking how to best care for the souls of their diverse students. At the same time, several campus ministers and members of their staff, sensitive to the need for racial reconciliation on their campuses, are calling their communities to lament, repentance, and confession for falling short in this area.

The White Majority

Recently, I was privileged to attend a student forum on diversity that was hosted by a CCCU member campus. The large room reserved for the gathering was overflowing with students who represented a full breadth of diversity, including a good number of white students. Near the end of the forum, a white female student, speaking respectfully in the context of the Black Lives Matter movement, asked, "How can I use my voice to speak with them [students of color] and not for them?" In my mind, that question summarized much of what I hear from white students, faculty, staff, administrators, and trustees who want to constructively enter into the diversity conversation but do not know how. Certainly there are white allies who are working for equity on their campuses through advocacy, committee service, research and writing, mentoring, and leadership. One of the greater challenges facing predominantly white evangelical colleges is how to engage those in the white majority who see the race problem differently or who remain apathetic.

ENVISIONING THE FUTURE

While progress has been made, the honest portrait of experiences on many Christian college campuses is not always easy to discern or accept. *The Chronicle of Higher Education* article cited earlier reminded us that we have substantive work to do if we are to realize the vision of becoming diverse, inclusive, and reconciled learning communities of faith. One certainty is this: if Christian higher education is to successfully meet the challenges of diversity in the present and future, there must be a resolve to do so. In this final section, I underscore several areas that I believe educational leaders and practitioners at Christian colleges and universities must intentionally address in order to successfully navigate their way forward.

A Guiding Theological Framework

Given the impact of student diversity on our predominantly white evangelical campuses, together with the shifting demographics in the broader evangelical church, there is the chance of the Christian higher education community remaining divided.[12] Given that diversity matters have the potential to polarize our campus communities, Christian educators should strive for consensus and a common understanding. This can be a difficult process, however, as individuals and groups come at these topics from different perspectives and life experiences, often resulting in sharp disagreements. Regardless, we must identify a common theological framework to guide our understanding and approach to diversity and to explore how diversity intersects with faith, beliefs, and institutional practices. My perspective is that the theological framework guiding our diversity efforts should be based upon a robust understanding of the kingdom of God and a vision of shalom.

The Kingdom of God. My own understanding of the intersection between diversity and a theology of the kingdom of God has deepened over the years through personal study, engaging CCCU campuses that hold varying theological positions,[13] and conversations with practitioners and scholars in a wide range of disciplines. An important learning moment for me happened at a CCCU Presidential Symposium for Intercultural Competencies held at Union University in 2004. At that symposium, David P. Gushee (then Union's Graves Professor of Moral Philosophy) cast a biblical vision for intercultural competencies in the CCCU based on a holistic understanding of the kingdom of God.[14] In his presentation, Gushee affirmed the central theme of Jesus's mission and teaching as the kingdom of God; that Jesus taught his followers to seek first his kingdom and his righteousness (Matt. 6:33); and that any Christian multicultural or intercultural effort must be situated in this truth. Additionally, the kingdom of God is defined as "that state of affairs in which God reigns," and the kingdom is something God is doing. It is God that initiates the kingdom, and it is not a human work. The kingdom of God is a divine action in which human beings are called to participate. Finally, Professor Gushee articulated what a kingdom agenda would look like if it were to be applied to Christian colleges and universities seeking to address intercultural competencies. He stated:

> Frankly, a kingdom agenda characterized by such priorities as deliverance, justice, peace, healing, and the full inclusion of the marginalized leads to the conclusion that a vision of "intercultural competency" may be too small. We don't want just to train students for a racially diverse society, internationalize their campus experience, or even "help" our students, staff, and faculty of color succeed. What we should dream of is making our campuses joyful, pioneering communities of interethnic justice and healing, as well as launching pads for social change efforts in the broader local, national, and global communities.[15]

A Vision of Shalom. Similarly, the kingdom of God formed the basis for a vision of shalom as articulated by the philosopher Nicholas Wolterstorff, who spent many years at Calvin College before transitioning to Yale Divinity School.

In *Educating for Shalom: Essays on Christian Higher Education*, Dr. Wolterstorff envisions justice as the ground floor of shalom, and a shalom that incorporates responsible action to God, to nature, to all of humanity, and to ourselves. It incorporates delight—a delight found in right relationships. His thinking about shalom and its relationship to the Christian college was summarized as follows:

> I do not see how the Christian college can do anything else than guide its endeavors by this vision of shalom. If God's call to all humanity is to be liberators and developers, celebrators and mourners, then will not the Christian college also have to find its place within this call? It will keep in mind the uniqueness of its calling. A college is a school, and as such, it places disciplined study at the center of its project. But the lure of shalom will direct and energize it. The goal of the Christian college, so I have begun to think, is to promote that mode of human flourishing which is shalom.[16]

The guiding theological framework of the kingdom and vision of shalom that Gushee[17] and Wolterstorff articulate is profound and ideally suited for the mission of Christian higher education going forward. This framework has practical implications for Christian institutions committed to an agenda characterized by the kingdom priorities of deliverance, justice, peace, healing, and the full inclusion of the marginalized. In this framework, Christian institutions design programs, develop curricula, and implement practices with the objective—as stated previously—of making their campuses joyful, pioneering communities of interethnic justice and healing, as well as launching pads for social change efforts locally, nationally, and globally. A commitment to this framework also has potential to unite Christians who seek to emulate the practices of Jesus and that embody the very kingdom he inaugurated (Matt. 4:17; Luke 4:16–21). Finally, and perhaps most importantly, the priorities of the kingdom and vision of shalom identified here demonstrate God's unconditional love for all people. Therefore, our diversity efforts must be characterized by love of God, love of neighbor, and love for one another as the litmus test for discipleship and to manifest a reconciled and unified people (Mark 12:30, 31; John 13:35, 17:21).

The Student Experience

Racially and ethnically diverse students are choosing to enroll at our colleges and universities in greater numbers, and we should celebrate their arrival. Diverse students are now visibly present on most of our campuses, and they are having an impact on the ethos and culture of our historically white institutions. However, are students of color being fully included in the mainstream of campus life? Are they being retained, succeeding academically, and graduating? Students of color continue to navigate difficult campus climates, and it is uncertain whether they will choose to stay. Therefore, we must examine the effectiveness of our diversity efforts through the lens of the student experience, to ensure that all students succeed and flourish. We must also remain focused on developing *all* students—white, Asian, African American, Latino, Native American, and international—for intercultural living and learning, and to prepare them for the world into which they are graduating. Are we cultivating in *all* students a positive self-identity, cultural humility, respect, and a commitment to going forward together?

A focus on students undoubtedly puts emphasis on student life programming, academic support services, and the cocurricular experience. However, if our institutions are to reach the long-term success that characterizes diverse and inclusive learning communities, there must be synergy between the areas of student life and academics, and the curriculum and cocurriculum. For this to take place, faculty and staff must work cooperatively to engage and educate all students on matters of race and racial justice from a biblical perspective if we are to realize the positive intergroup relations, affirming campus climates, and racial harmony that characterizes shalom. Pastoral care for all students must also be exercised if we seek to build unity in diversity, while also creating the learning environments needed to engage every member of the campus community in substantive conversations on difficult and sensitive topics.

The Importance of Faculty

Faculty are at the center of the teaching and learning experience. The faculty teach, mentor, disciple, and model the ideals of the institution for students. Additionally, faculty share governance, develop curriculum, create academic programs, and serve on committees throughout the institution. Moving forward, the goal to diversify the faculty must remain a high priority for administrators, faculty search committees, and academic departments. Strategies to diversify the faculty must continue to be explored, implemented, and evaluated for their effectiveness. Therefore, we need to remain intentional about diversifying the faculty and equally committed to retaining and developing the diverse talent already within the ranks. We cannot minimize the contributions of diverse faculty.

However, because it is going to take time to diversify the faculty, colleges and universities must continue to invest in their faculty by strengthening the overall academic culture, valuing the work of faculty, and developing robust initiatives to equip them with the intercultural skills and competencies required to teach to a wide range of students. These initiatives should demonstrate sensitivity to faculty at all career stages; solicit faculty input to determine specific needs, content and effective approaches; adapt the content and approaches to the range of academic disciplines; and be applicable to faculty teaching traditional undergraduates, adult learners, and students in professional and graduate degree programs. A variety of methods should be employed, including the use of media, webinars, reading and discussion groups, and experiential learning opportunities. Additionally, faculty development professionals should be adequately resourced and encouraged to explore innovative approaches to cross-cultural development, utilize proven training resources, create new materials, and collaborate with colleagues to identify best practices in faculty development taking place at member institutions and to learn from campus experts engaged in this work, both inside and outside of the CCCU.

Senior Leadership

Christian organizations in North America are operating within the broader national and international religious, political, and economic contexts, and they are becoming increasingly diverse, yet the leadership in these organizations remains predominantly white and monocultural. Given this context, is the leadership of our Christian colleges and universities prepared to provide the kind of bold, yet pastoral, leadership required to address the challenge of racial divisions and the need for interethnic healing so prevalent today? I believe that many leaders are prepared to take on these challenges, and some do so at the risk of being criticized by their constituencies or other leaders. A growing number of presidents are taking an active leadership role on their campuses and within the CCCU to address racial discrimination and inequity, and to advance racial harmony and reconciliation. These compassionate and courageous leaders see the injustices around them, and they are compelled to act, they are emboldened by a moral conviction to do what is right, and they are convinced that this is what God commands them to do. They are committed to doing justice, loving mercy, and walking humbly with God (Mic. 6:8).

There is no doubt that in the higher education environment of today, leaders need to be business smart, fiscally minded, excellent managers, team builders, problem solvers, visionaries, and innovators. The leader of the future will need to build on these skills but also develop capacity in intercultural and social intelligences, and diverse people management. Leaders must also realize the organizational strength that comes from having diverse women and men at the leadership table. Diverse teams see challenges from multiple perspectives and thus contribute an increased number of possible solutions to any given problem. Presidents must also remain intentional about diversifying their cabinets with leaders from many different racial and ethnic backgrounds who contribute manifold gifts and talents, and whose perspectives often reflect the diversity of students enrolled at their institutions. Boards must also see the value of intentionally adding gender, racial, and ethnic diversity at the trustee level. Further, boards, search consultants, and search committees must actively seek diverse candidates for presidential and other senior-level appointments in the CCCU.

Finally, are faith-based schools ready to have the difficult conversations on race, white privilege, the prevalence of white cultural norms, and other systemic barriers that limit the inclusion of diverse leadership and impede genuine progress toward racial solidarity?[18] Regardless of how one answers these questions, the educational institution of the future will be diverse, and we must remain intentional about developing the next generation of leaders who visibly and culturally reflect the depth and breadth of the kingdom of God.

Nurturing the Multicultural Soul

Christ-centeredness, a kingdom focus, faith integration, and a commitment to developing the life of the spirit are distinguishing characteristics that represent the soul of our institutions. But when it comes to faith, what color is the soul? A college or university with the aspiration of becoming a truly inclusive Christian community must be intentional about nurturing its multicultural soul by attending to the spiritual needs of those members who come from diverse racial/ethnic church backgrounds, or who come from outside the faith tradition upon which the school was founded.

The biblical witness is clear: Every human being has been created in the image of God and thus has inherent worth and dignity (Gen. 1:27, Ps. 8:5). Because of the life, death, and resurrection of Jesus Christ, God is reconciling a fallen and rebellious world to himself, and he has given the ministry and message of reconciliation to the church (Rom. 5:6–11; 2 Cor. 5:16–21; Col. 1:15–23). The kingdom of God is inclusive, and people come from the east and west and north and south to participate in it (Luke 13:29). The multinational gathering on the day of Pentecost heard those baptized in the Holy Spirit speaking the wonders of God in their own language; they were converted, baptized, and became part of a unified whole (Acts 2). Jew and Greek have been joined together by the blood of Jesus and are a holy temple to the Lord indwelt by the Spirit (Eph. 2:11–22). The heavenly vision of the redeemed from every people, nation, tribe, and language are united in worship of God (Rev. 7:9). These biblical references are a reminder that the people of God are members of one body, diverse, yet united, and singularly focused on celebrating the Lordship of Jesus Christ, the Lamb of God.

This inclusive model of the kingdom has practical implications for spiritual formation, chapel programming, and leadership. In this inclusive model, we must be cognizant of how we practice faith to guard against religious-ethnocentrism and to ensure that our programming incorporates multicultural and international perspectives, so that the soul of every member of the faith community is nurtured. The chapel program incorporates diverse music and worship styles, regularly invites speakers from diverse backgrounds, and engages in topics that are relevant to the faith communities of all who participate. And campus leaders are guided by a kingdom agenda and are led by the Holy Spirit, demonstrating the spiritual maturity and sensitivity needed to discern the movement of God in the world and its implications for campus life and spiritual formation programming. Finally, these leaders should love always; care deeply about the minority faith experience, including sensitivity to gender; and ensure that the spiritual needs of the weak, vulnerable, and marginalized are addressed.

A Curriculum for Shalom

The prophet Jeremiah wrote to the exiles in Babylon, instructing them to seek the peace and prosperity of the city to which they had been carried and to pray to the Lord for it (Jer. 29:1–14). God intended the exiles to pray for the peace, prosperity, welfare, and shalom of those cities in which they lived, knowing that their welfare was tied directly to the welfare of their surroundings. I think about the implications of these prophetic instructions for the Christian college and university of today, and I am again reminded of the words of Wolterstorff quoted earlier that "A college is a school, and as such, it places disciplined study at the center of its project. But the lure of shalom will direct and energize it. The goal of the Christian college . . . is to promote that mode of flourishing which is shalom."[19] Looking to the future, will the Christian college be directed and energized by the lure of shalom, and will it seek the shalom of the individuals and places it serves?

Pursuant to Wolterstorff, the vision of shalom incorporates responsible action to God, to nature, to our fellow beings, and to ourselves; and it includes delight, a delight that is found in right relationships.[20] I believe Christian higher education is uniquely positioned to educate students for responsible action and right relationships. The Christian mission seeks to educate students in character and intellect, and is intentional in its efforts to graduate students who are virtuous, caring, compassionate, and service oriented. However, will the

Christian college remain equally committed to cultivating in all students a heart toward justice and to equip them with the skills necessary to be peace-makers who contribute to the healing of a fractured society and world? And will a commitment of this kind be reflected in the core curriculum rather than only in the cocurriculum?

Regardless of how institutions choose to engage the curriculum, I am encouraged by the number of colleges and universities forging initiatives to address peacemaking and social justice concerns. Today, several institutions in the CCCU have launched centers that bring together faculty and students, strategic partners, community agencies, and researchers around a significant social concern to find solutions that advance the shalom of the city. Entities like the Global Center for Women and Justice at Vanguard University[21] and the Center for Justice and Reconciliation at Point Loma Nazarene University[22] are educating a new generation of students on substantive social issues like fair trade, immigration, and human trafficking. Another, The John Perkins Center at Seattle Pacific University,[23] is engaging students and faculty in interdisciplinary study in the areas of justice, reconciliation, and community development. I believe these brief examples provide a glimpse of the future and can serve as models of a curriculum for shalom that joins students and faculty on a path toward biblical justice, leading to the peace and prosperity of our cities.

CONCLUSION

We do not know the degree to which diversity will increase on our campuses, just as we cannot calculate the impact it will have in the years to come. Nor do we know how individual institutions will respond to these changes. However, if we believe the present time is a kairos moment, then we need to be completely present in this moment so we do not miss the "new thing" God is doing (Isa. 43:19). We also need to be reminded that the ultimate objective is not the number of diverse people on our campuses or the programs we offer, but rather who we are becoming as the people of God. One leader articulated this well by stating, "We need to move our mission from an emphasis that is driven by numbers and events to being philosophically a core learning value of the university, from 'doing multiculturalism' because it's the right thing to 'doing multiculturalism' because it's who we are."[24] My hope for Christian higher education is to see every college and university adopt diversity as a learning value that is central to the mission of the institution and lived out practically, because this is who we are as representatives of the kingdom of God. Moreover, my hope is for our campuses to embrace diverse people and cultures as full members of the community, to value diverse perspectives and contributions as vital to

higher learning, and to celebrate the kingdom of God in our midst. The CCCU
and its member institutions appear to be uniquely and strategically positioned
to fulfill this vision.

FOR DISCUSSION

1. To what extent is diversity, race, or racial reconciliation discussed on your
   campus? If such discussions are occurring, how and by whom? If not, why
   might this be the case?

2. Do the faculty at your institution meet regularly to discuss substantive
   social issues affecting the church and society such as race, racism, or racial
   reconciliation? If so, what has been the outcome of these conversations,
   and what might future discussions contribute?

3. How does the theological tradition of your institution impact your beliefs
   about diversity and racial reconciliation? How does that theological tradition inform diversity practices on your campus?

4. How would you describe the campus climate for racial and ethnic minority
   students, faculty, or staff at your institution? How would racial and ethnic
   minorities describe the campus climate?

5. Does your college or university have a statement of theology to guide your
   diversity efforts? How is diversity talked about in biblical or theological
   terms on your campus?

6. What would a kingdom agenda look like on your campus if it was based on
   the priorities of deliverance, justice, peace, healing, and the full inclusion of
   the marginalized?

7. Are the scriptures read and studied in cross-cultural context at your institution? To what extent do students and staff have opportunities to come
   together across racial, ethnic, language, and national boundaries to read
   the scriptures, participate in the Lord's table, and worship?

8. How are white students, faculty, and staff being engaged on the issues of
   race and racial reconciliation at your school?

9. To what extent does your institution offer training and development in
   diversity for campus leaders throughout the organization? Are emerging
   leaders of color encouraged to pursue leadership development opportunities on or off campus?

10. In your opinion, is diversity philosophically a core learning value for your
    institution? If not, speculate about what it will take for diversity to be cen-
    tral to the mission of your college or university.

Student Ethnic Diversity in the CCCU - 10 Year Review	2003-04	2013-14	Dif.
Total Enrollment (12 month Headcount/All Education Levels)	**306,034**	**366,039**	**60,005**
American Indian or Alaska Native	0.64%	0.61%	-0.03%
Asian and Native Hawaiian or Other Pacific Islander*	2.27%	3.16%	0.89%
Black or African American	9.45%	11.87%	2.43%
Hispanic or Latino	4.39%	7.97%	3.58%
White (Includes race/ethnicity unknown for 2003-04)	80.94%	71.58%	-9.36%

*IPEDS included both groups into one category in 2003-04. For comparison reasons we have merged the two groups for 2013-14

Table 1.1. Student Ethnic Diversity in the CCCU—10 Year Review

Faculty Ethnic Diversity in the CCCU - 8 Year Review	2007	2014	Dif.
Total Full and Part-time Faculty	**21,356**	**26,106**	**4,750**
American Indian or Alaska Native	0.22%	0.31%	0.10%
Asian and Native Hawaiian or Other Pacific Islander*	2.24%	2.95%	0.70%
Black or African American	4.05%	4.20%	0.15%
Hispanic or Latino	1.79%	2.49%	0.70%
White (Includes race/ethnicity unknown for 2007)	91.10%	88.86%	-2.24%
Full-time	**10,849**	**11,986**	**1,137**
American Indian or Alaska Native	0.25%	0.33%	0.08%
Asian and Native Hawaiian or Other Pacific Islander*	2.70%	3.85%	1.15%
Black or African American	3.00%	3.39%	0.38%
Hispanic or Latino	1.84%	2.25%	0.41%
White (Includes race/ethnicity unknown for 2007)	91.32%	88.94%	-2.38%
Part-time	**10,507**	**14,120**	**3,613**
American Indian or Alaska Native	0.18%	0.30%	0.12%
Asian and Native Hawaiian or Other Pacific Islander*	1.77%	2.17%	0.40%
Black or African American	5.12%	4.89%	-0.23%
Hispanic or Latino	1.74%	2.70%	0.96%
White (Includes race/ethnicity unknown for 2007)	90.87%	88.80%	-2.08%

*IPEDS included both groups into one category in 2007. For comparison reasons we have merged the two groups for 2014

Table 1.2. Faculty Ethnic Diversity in the CCCU—8 Year Review

NOTES

1   Nicholas Wolterstorff, *Educating for Shalom: Essays on Christian Higher Education* (Grand Rapids: Eerdmans, 2004), 171.

2   David P. Gushee, "A Biblical Vision for 'Intercultural Competency'" (paper presented at the Advancing Intercultural Competencies Presidential Symposium, Union University, Jackson, TN, April 23, 2004).

3   Daryl G. Smith, *Diversity's Promise for Higher Education: Making It Work*, 2nd ed. (Baltimore: Johns Hopkins University Press, 2015), *vii.*

4   "Projecting Majority-Minority: Non-Hispanic Whites May No Longer Comprise Over 50 Percent of the U.S. Population by 2044," US Census, accessed May 2, 2017, http://www.census.gov/content /dam/Census/newsroom/releases/2015/cb15-tps16_graphic.pdf.

The Pew Research Center estimates this change to take place closer to the year 2065. "Modern Immigration Wave Brings 59 Million to U.S., Driving Population Growth and Change through 2065," Pew Research Center, accessed May 2, 2017, http://www.pewhispanic.org/2015/09/28/modern-immigration-wave-brings-59-million-to-u-s-driving-population-growth-and-change-through-2065/.

5   Robert P. Jones, *The End of White Christian America* (New York: Simon & Schuster, 2016).

6   "Diversity, Inclusion and the Christian Academy: A Matter of Faith, Excellence and Institutional Survival," *CCCU Advance*, Fall 2015, 19–22.

7   Brenda Salter McNeil and Rick Richardson, *The Heart of Racial Justice: How Soul Change Leads to Social Change* (Downers Grove, IL: InterVarsity Press, 2004), 25.

8   Beth McMurtrie, "Evangelical Colleges' Diversity Problem," *The Chronicle of Higher Education*, January 31, 2016, accessed May 7, 2017, http://www.chronicle.com/article/Evangelical-Colleges-/235112.

9   "Diversity Difference % Report: CCCU Analysis of the 2014 IPEDs" (unpublished report).

10 Karen A. Longman and P. A. Anderson, "Women in Leadership: The Future of Christian Higher Education," *Christian Higher Education: An International Journal of Research, Theory, and Practice* 15.1–2 (2016): 24–37.

11 Ibid., 31.

12 Michael O. Emmerson and Christian Smith, *Divided by Faith: Evangelical Religion and the Problem of Race in America* (New York: Oxford University Press, 2000). This volume remains an important study on white evangelical Protestants and the racial divide.

13 "Protestant Faith Traditions of CCCU Member Institutions," CCCU, accessed May 2, 2017, http://cccu.org/~/media/CCCU_ProtestantFaithTree1.pdf.

14 Gushee, "A Biblical Vision for 'Intercultural Competency.'"

15 Ibid., 6.

16 Wolterstorff, *Educating for Shalom*, 170–71.

17 For a fuller treatment of Gushee on the implications of the kingdom of God applied to race, see Glen H. Stassen and David P. Gushee, *Kingdom Ethics: Following Jesus in Contemporary Context* (Downers Grove, IL: InterVarsity Press, 2003).

18 Anthony B. Bradley, ed., *Aliens in the Promised Land: Why Minority Leadership Is Overlooked in White Churches and Institutions* (Phillipsburg, NJ: P&R Publishing, 2013). Bradley et al. provide an analysis and solutions for the lack of diverse leadership in predominantly white evangelical institutions.

19 Wolterstorff, *Educating for Shalom*, 171.

20 Ibid., 170.

21 "Global Center for Women & Justice," Vanguard University of Southern California, accessed May 17, 2017, http://www.vanguard.edu/gcwj/.

22 "Center for Justice and Reconciliation," Point Loma: Nazarene University, accessed May 2, 2017, http://www.pointloma.edu/experience/academics/centers-institutes/center-justice-reconciliation.

23 "2017 Perkins Lecture Series," Seattle Pacific University, accessed May 2, 2017, http://spu.edu/depts/perkins/.

24 See Chapter Two.

CAMPUS CASE STUDIES

TRANSFORMING INSTITUTIONS WITH A COMMITMENT TO DIVERSITY

Introduction

DIVERSITY, INCLUSION, AND INSTITUTIONAL FAITHFULNESS

PETE C. MENJARES, PhD

CCCU Senior Fellow for Diversity, Vanguard University of Southern California

The Council for Christian Colleges & Universities (CCCU) is a mosaic of faith-based, postsecondary institutions rooted in the liberal arts. These institutions represent thirty-five Protestant denominations, the Catholic Church, and others with no denominational or church affiliation among its 115 members in North America and sixty-three affiliates located in twenty countries. In North America, the membership spans thirty-four states in the continental United States and six Canadian provinces. The member colleges and universities are urban, suburban, and rural. These institutions also vary in enrollment numbers, ranging from several hundred to more than fifteen thousand students in attendance. With respect to academic programs, the CCCU members and affiliates range from traditional undergraduate residential campuses to those that offer numerous undergraduate, graduate, and professional programs at multiple sites and online.

Relative to race and ethnicity, colleges and universities across the council vary in the proportion of diversity for students, staff, faculty, administrators, and trustees. Additionally, institutions are at different levels of understanding and stages of engagement with the principles of diversity, inclusion, and racial reconciliation. A growing number of our colleges and universities have significant numerical diversity in addition to a robust infrastructure to support curricular and cocurricular programs, initiatives, and personnel. Other institutions are beginning to see increasing diversity among their students and for the first time are entering the conversation of what it means to be diverse and inclusive.

UNIQUE STORIES

The colleges and universities that compose the CCCU are diverse in their faith affiliation, theology, geography, programs and initiatives, demographic composition, and levels of understanding and engagement with the issues. In addition, each member institution has a distinctive mission, vision, and set of core values that form its identity. Thus, every institution is unique and has a unique story to tell.

In my various roles within the CCCU, I have had the opportunity to visit many of our member campuses across the United States and to hear their stories. I have been blessed to see firsthand the diversity of students from all races, ethnicities, and nations contributing to the visible and cultural transformation of what were historically white colleges and universities. I have had the joy of interacting with faculty, staff, administrators, and students who enthusiastically embrace the vision of their campuses to reflect the kingdom of God. I have spent time with campus leaders to work through the challenges and difficulties that diversity and cultural change can bring to a faith community, and to pray for a manifestation of God's shalom on these campuses. The stories are not always glamorous, nor are they easy to tell. However, the stories are honest, and they reflect people of faith working through real challenges while trusting that God will help bring about the best of all outcomes.

The section that follows features the stories of four CCCU member institutions at various stages along the journey of becoming more diverse and inclusive. I know these campus leaders and have been privileged to visit each of their campuses, to know of their challenges, and to become familiar with the life-transforming work taking place there. To some extent, the four institutions represent the breadth of diversity that characterizes the CCCU. The authors have written their narratives honestly and faithfully as they recount critical moments in the histories of their institutions when their core commitments or principles were challenged, when strategic decisions and bold actions had to be made on the part of leadership, when students acted courageously to challenge the status quo on campus and in society, and when programs to support increasing diversity and to advance their mission were implemented. These cases demonstrate individual and institutional resiliency in changing times. The authors also write about the importance of campus identity and how there are times in the life of a university when the founding identity needs to be rediscovered or redefined, and the mission recontextualized to meet the needs of a changing environment due to shifts in demographics, economics, or student academic profiles.

THE FOUR CASES

In the first case, the Provost and Vice-President for Academic Affairs of Nyack College, Dr. David F. Turk, tells the story of the single-most diverse American college in the CCCU and one of the most diverse colleges in the United States.

The college was founded by A. B. Simpson and the Christian and Missionary Alliance in the late 1800s in New York City, and now has two campuses: a suburban campus located north of the city, and a lower Manhattan campus located within walking distance of Wall Street and with a view of Ellis Island and the Statue of Liberty. Dr. Turk writes of the college reclaiming its history as an institution that from its founding enrolled African Americans as well as immigrants, and that was intentionally committed to serving the underserved. Since the rediscovery of its history, the college has renewed its mission and has stated its core values as a commitment to be academically excellent, globally engaged, personally transforming, socially relevant, and intentionally diverse.

In the second case, President David L. Parkyn writes of the history and current practice of inclusion at North Park University, located in the city of Chicago and in a neighborhood that boasts the most diverse zip code in the country. As of this writing, when North Park University is celebrating its 125th year, President Parkyn tells the story of the Swedish immigration to America that in time led to settling in cities like Chicago, planting churches, forming the Swedish Evangelical Mission Covenant (today the Evangelical Covenant Church), and founding the school that became North Park University. From the beginning, these immigrants were inclusive and practiced hospitality. The centrality of faith in Christ, inclusivity, hospitality, a global mission, the heavenly vision of the multitude before the throne, and an emphasis on the kingdom of God have characterized North Park's broad, university-wide commitment to diversity and the city since its founding.

In the third case, President Andrea Cook tells the story of Warner Pacific College, a college affiliated with the Church of God (Anderson, Indiana) and located in one of the more socially progressive cities in the country: Portland, Oregon. President Cook is honest about the challenges facing the college in recent years, but in the story, there is also the subtext of God's grace upon the school, its students, the dedicated people who serve there, and the city they have embraced. While the Warner Pacific College story is still being written, due to a renewed commitment to its urban identity, the institution is clearly characterized by a tenacious spirit to serve the historically underserved at a time of enrollment challenges and financial constraints. Institutional integrity and fidelity to the mission are what matter at Warner Pacific College—they are living out a commitment to see lives transformed and the city flourish.

In the final case, the Provost and Chief Operations Officer of Greenville College, Dr. Edwin F. Estevez, tells the story of an institution founded by the Free Methodists in the late 1800s and located in rural southern Illinois. The Greenville College story is the testimony of an institution that has sought to remain faithful over the decades to the theological beliefs of its founders to act justly, love mercy, and walk humbly with God (Mic. 6:8). The interconnectedness of faith, reason, theology, and moral conviction shapes the institutional practices and ethos of Greenville College, as demonstrated through an emphasis on incarnational living, the practice of social justice, and hospitality. The Greenville story also highlights the student experience, with the personal story of Dr. Estevez woven into the larger narrative given that he was a student of the college and, together with his family, a beneficiary of the evangelistic efforts of the church and college to the Dominican Republic in the early 1900s.

CONCLUSION

These four stories reflect a convergence of institutional identity, theological ideation, geographical location, changing demographics, cultural shifts, and living faith. All of these campus leaders are quick to acknowledge the imperfections of their respective schools. They know intuitively that there is more to kingdom living than the number of diverse students or programs offered at their colleges and university. For these leaders, *how* their institutions respond to change is secondary to *why* they should respond to change—and the reason it matters is faith. Ultimately, these stories give testimony to faithfulness, and the campuses featured have been driven by a sincere desire and commitment to be deeply faithful to God and to a mission rooted in faith.

As you read and discuss these chapters, look for themes that each case has in common, as well as ways the cases diverge. But beyond this, look for the ways faith has been practiced, tested, and ultimately rewarded by God. Finally, discover the ways God continues to work amid these learning communities, and the lessons these stories may hold for Christian higher education more broadly.

CHAPTER ONE

Nyack College

David F. Turk, PhD

Nyack College, Provost and Vice-President for Academic Affairs

In May of 2013, I had the privilege of going to India with ten Nyack College nursing students who were doing clinical work in various hospitals throughout the country. Although this first trip to India was an incredible learning experience for me, I still can vividly recall that this land of many peoples and many wonders was hardly as diverse as the nursing students from Nyack. As a group, they were primarily American citizens, but they or their parents had come to the United States from all over the planet: the Philippines, Vietnam, India, Romania, Colombia, and Guyana. Only a few could claim that their families had been in the United States for several generations.

The picture that I keep of this group—taken in front of the Taj Mahal—reminds me that Nyack was once a school that trained missionaries to go forth into all corners of the globe, and now people from all parts of the world come to Nyack. This is never more evident than at commencement ceremonies each May, when names hailing from many lands are called out and faces from countless countries wearing beaming smiles receive their diplomas from Nyack's president. Indeed, because it has become customary to sing *How Great Thou Art* at the close, the commencement bulletin prints the song in the twelve most prominent languages of the largest people groups represented among the graduates.

For the last ten years, *U.S. News & World Report* has listed Nyack College as one of the most diverse colleges in America. The college has marketed this distinction, even claiming that it is one of the most diverse Christian colleges in the country. Nyack has much to be proud of, having transformed itself from a small suburban Christian college with the majority of its six hundred students drawn from suburban and rural white communities in the northeast to a mid-sized college that recruits most of its twenty-seven hundred students from the many ethnic communities of the New York metropolitan area.

As of this writing, Nyack's student body, including approximately twelve hundred graduate students and fifteen hundred undergraduates, has the following ethnic breakdown:

- Asian American   15%
- Black   30%
- Hispanic   30%
- White   20%
- Two or more   5%

Although this level of diversity is common among the colleges and universities that are part of the City University of New York (CUNY), it is quite uncommon among Christian colleges. And while it is often claimed that Nyack's diverse student body might be considered normal for a college that now has, in addition to its suburban campus, a campus in Manhattan where over one thousand of its students are enrolled, the college's diversity is found among its faculty as well. Currently, approximately 45 percent of Nyack's full-time faculty members are Asian American, black, or Latino, a level of diversity that not even CUNY schools can match.

Statistics do not, however, tell the whole story. One of Nyack's core values notes that Nyack is "intentionally diverse," and thereby committed to providing educational access to underserved populations. All of its degree programs have at least one course that focuses on studying the range of issues related to living and working in a diverse society, and the core curriculum required of all undergraduates contains fifteen credits that explore diversity in the liberal arts and sciences. In addition, Nyack's chapel program joyfully embraces black and Latino worship styles.

Nyack's students have been more than enthusiastic in their praise of the diversity at the college and its vibrant spiritual atmosphere. Results of the *National Survey of Student Engagement* show Nyack students to be more confident that they are prepared to work in a diverse world than their peers in all other comparison groups. And, indeed, this confidence is affirmed by employer surveys for accounting, education, nursing, and social work majors that show these graduates as exceptional when it comes to working in teams and working with a variety of people.

By many measures, then, Nyack College's transformation into a diverse college is a success story. Yet Nyack's efforts are not uncommon. Over the last twenty years, many Catholic colleges and smaller liberal arts colleges have taken the same journey. And many member institutions in the CCCU are now beginning this journey. Although the details of these journeys may vary, there is a common set of factors that facilitated the transformations at Nyack and at other colleges.

These principles can be summarized as follows:

- *Leading.* Set goals at all levels to diversify a campus community, including its students, faculty, and programs.
- *Engaging.* Recruit students from one of the urban centers of the United States or establish a learning center or branch in a city.
- *Linking.* Explore the institution's history and theological roots, and relearn the truth that the *missio dei* of the gospel is to reach the poor and underserved.
- *Partnering.* Join hands with urban churches and black and Latino church leaders to educate the emerging demographic—their congregants.
- *Assessing.* Prepare to move far beyond the goals of demographic change, and examine the purpose of higher education, especially Christian higher education.

LEADERSHIP AND CHANGE

When a Latino was hired by Nyack as an admissions counselor in 1989 and began recruiting black and Latino students in New York City, almost no one at Nyack knew how successful he would be. The college president and vice-president for enrollment at that time not only endorsed this recruiter's success, but also ran interference, as many in the faculty, a number of alumni, and even some trustees expressed reservations that Nyack would change too much and thereby lose its identity. Both leaders were strongly committed to pressing ahead and two years later promoted this young man to director of admissions, the first Hispanic to serve in the administration of Nyack College.

A mere three years after Nyack began recruiting heavily in New York City, the face of the campus had changed dramatically. At that point, 40 percent of the student body was people of color, a startling rise from 12 percent a few years before. It is now easy to see how this happened, but from the vantage point of the 1980s, the strong leadership of the president and the vice-president for enrollment was required so that the college could bridge the mere eighteen-mile gap between its campus in suburban Nyack to the George Washington Bridge, the entrance to Manhattan and the communities of Harlem and Spanish Harlem.

Since the college had moved out of Manhattan in 1897, the distance between the suburban college and the city had grown with each decade, so that by the late 1980s, the two seemed to be in separate galaxies. There were even discussions about moving the college to a more rural location, as white students and their parents from the traditional recruiting territories of upstate New York, Western Pennsylvania, and Ohio became fearful of attending a college so close to New

York City. After all, as New York papers noted at the time, the federal government had told New York City to "Drop Dead" rather than providing help for the
city on the point of bankruptcy. Why, then, would the white families who had
sent their sons and daughters to Nyack for so many years want to do so now?

Thus, recruiting in the city and admitting so many students from the broader
urban area was both courageous and revolutionary. But as with any major
change, there was a call for further change from the newly admitted black and
Latino students, followed by a backlash from forces who feared that Nyack was
losing its very heart and soul.

Encouraged by one of the few Latino professors on campus, Latino students
interrupted an early 1990s meeting of Nyack's board of trustees and presented
the trustees with a list of demands for change:

- Hire more professors of color.
- Diversify the curriculum.
- Hire people of color in Student Life.
- Establish scholarships to assist students of color.
- Allow black and Latino students to assist in planning chapel services.
- Make the campus climate amenable to students of color by changing things
  ranging from menus in the cafeteria to student activity programming.

Amazingly, the executive team soon put in place plans to make changes in a
number of these areas; in regard to curriculum, there was real change before a
backlash again slowed the progress to bring true diversity. The vice-president for
academic affairs appointed a faculty committee to revise the core curriculum,
and by 1992, a much more inclusive core that examined world cultures rather
than Western cultures and celebrated diversity in a "multicultural America"
had begun to take shape.

The year 1992 saw the trustees dismiss the president and the vice-president
for academic affairs because of the controversy surrounding a professor who
wore a button that said "Support Gay Rights." There was fear that Nyack was
going too far—a fear that was very much linked to a broader fear that swept
through the white evangelical community when Bill Clinton was elected
president in 1992. However, a new college president, keeping both the vice-
president for enrollment and the director of admissions in their roles, continued
to actively admit students of color and pursue plans to diversify the institution.

In addition, the new president began the process of bringing people of
color onto the leadership team and the board of trustees. He appointed the college's first African American vice-president, and by the time the president had

completed fifteen years in office, people of color represented a quarter of the board members. Most importantly though, the new president launched Nyack's city campus and began the process of reaching out to partner with black and Latino churches in New York City.

ENGAGING URBAN AMERICA

Encouraged by adult students who had studied at one of the college's extensions in the city, the president developed a vision to bring Christian higher education to the residents of the city—to be "in the city for the city." He launched a branch campus in 1997, and within four years (by 9/11), Nyack had over 1,000 students at its city campus, with 750 in its undergraduate program alone. Nyack was also offering a range of graduate programs (counseling, education, MBA, ministry) to almost 250 students as the president began the process of reuniting the college with Alliance Theological Seminary (ATS), which had functioned as separate entities since the late 1980s.

The stunning growth of the city campus by 2001 meant that in terms of the overall student demographics, the minority had become the majority. For the college, this year was a tipping point in terms of diversity. Nyack's student demographics now closely corresponded to ethnic group demographics in New York City. City residents, especially members of black and Latinos churches, increasingly looked to Nyack for graduate education. Soon, 40 percent of the institution's students would be graduate students. ATS's Master of Divinity program became the institution's largest degree program, with more than four hundred students. And the MA degree in Mental Health Counseling became its second largest program. ATS, which had been struggling with declining enrollments, quickly grew to become one of the largest seminaries in the United States. Perhaps more importantly, the face of ATS changed as well, with more than 75 percent of its students being people of color.

The move into New York City and the embrace of an urban student body also reshaped the college's undergraduate programs, as city residents were attracted to professional programs that led to careers readily available to people of color. New undergraduate programs in social work, nursing, and criminal justice were launched and have since become some of the largest undergraduate degree programs. And a number of undergraduate degrees that had once been the central programs of Nyack Missionary College but had dwindled to the point of being moribund were reborn and grew into thriving programs at the city campus: biblical literature, music, and pastoral ministry. The importance of the church in African American and Latino communities throughout the city meant that Nyack rapidly became the school for the training of city ministers.

Interestingly, for both the college and the seminary, enrollments at the suburban campus increased, with many new students coming from the metropolitan New York area. And for both campuses—Nyack and Manhattan—the largest groups of students came from Brooklyn and Queens. What is significant about these two boroughs is that they had become, by 2001, home to very diverse groups of immigrants. So with the launch of the city campus, Nyack became a school in which the majority of its students were first or second generation immigrants. No longer did being black at Nyack mean a student was African American or possibly Afro Caribbean; being black at Nyack now meant that students were just as likely to have come from Trinidad, Guyana, Jamaica, Ghana, Nigeria, or Kenya as they were to have been raised African American. And to be Hispanic at Nyack was no longer synonymous with being Nuyorican (of Puerto Rican birth or descent, living in New York City), given that Hispanic students now hailed from Colombia, Mexico, the Dominican Republic, Brazil, or one of the many countries of Central America. Likewise, to be Asian American at Nyack once meant that a student came from Korea; now students attended from China, the Philippines, Indonesia, and India.

Such a dramatic transformation resulted in a number of major changes. Nyack's admission requirements remained the same—a statement of faith and a pastor's recommendation were still required of all undergraduate and seminary students. And most of the new graduate programs required the same. As with the curricular changes, however, a whole range of student services underwent transformations as the college gradually began the process of hiring faculty and staff in all departments whose faces looked like those of the students. This process was primarily led by the president, academic vice-president, and the chief financial officer.

PARTNERING WITH URBAN CHURCHES

The president also believed that if urban churches saw the evidence that Nyack College seriously intended to be "in the city for the city," then they would send their congregants to Nyack as students. In order to demonstrate Nyack's commitment to the city, he set up regular luncheon meetings with many church leaders and pastors in the city. Speaking to these groups about Nyack's vision for educating the city was central, but the presence of the entire Nyack leadership team at these luncheons spoke volumes to the NYC church community. But probably the greatest indicator of Nyack's sincerity about being willing to partner with NYC churches was that the college hired faculty and staff, for both campuses, from the city church community.

Partnerships with four city churches and their leaders have become extremely important for Nyack: Greater Allen A.M.E. Cathedral, Brooklyn

Tabernacle, the Christian Cultural Center, and Evangel Christian Church. All of these churches are located in Brooklyn or Queens and have played vital roles in helping Nyack be "in the city, for the city."

These churches and others have sent many students from their communities to Nyack, and Nyack has drawn upon their members in order to hire faculty for both campuses. Initially, Nyack reached out to these churches for adjunct professors, and then began hiring as full-time professors those adjuncts who demonstrated a strong calling to teaching in Christian higher education. Often, these professors did not have terminal degrees, so the college began a program to assist new professors to pay for their doctoral programs.

Before this process began, Nyack had bought into the "myth" that there were no qualified faculty members of color who would be willing to work at the college. A new paradigm was born. Rather than advertising nationally for open positions, the college began recruiting its faculty in the city with the help of city churches. No longer would the college have to move a young faculty member and his or her family from the hinterlands of the United States. Faculty hiring now involved, in many cases, identifying seasoned professionals with a history of teaching in city colleges, public schools, or churches—individuals who had established homes in the city and strong ties to local churches. And so, in six short years after launching the city campus in 1997, the college, because of the expansion of its programs, was able to hire an incredibly diverse faculty—45 percent people of color by 2003.

City churches were also a rich mine for helping Nyack fill leadership positions. When the institution fully unified the college and seminary in 2003 and moved to adopt what it called a "university model" by establishing a number of colleges and schools, twelve deans were appointed, half of whom were people of color.

The impact on the curriculum of hiring so many faculty and deans of color has been enormous. Since many had experience in other professional educational settings where issues related to diversity had been embedded into curricula, this process began in earnest in many of the degree programs offered by the institution. This momentum was helped by the move toward specialized accreditation of the professional degree programs like social work and education, as the accreditors required the inclusion of specific courses that examined diversity within particular fields of study.

LINKING PAST AND FUTURE

By 2003, then, Nyack College had made a remarkable transition from a small, majority white, suburban college to a midsized, very diverse college with two campuses—one in the suburbs and one in the heart of the city. Substantial strides had been made in diversifying the faculty, academic administration, and board of trustees, which were then 40 percent, 50 percent, and 25 percent people of color, respectively. And significant programmatic changes had been made to serve the institution's diverse population. Yet this transformation had occurred without the guidance of a new strategic plan or guiding vision.

The launch of the city campus did, however, begin a process whereby the college, in conjunction with archivists from the sponsoring denomination (The Christian and Missionary Alliance), began to explore the college's earliest days in Manhattan from 1882 to 1897. This recovered history told a story that few at the college knew about. A portrait of the founder, A. B. Simpson, emerged that startled yet pleased the community: Simpson was a Canadian who came to the United States in the 1870s to pastor a church in Kentucky and then pastored a church in midtown Manhattan. He was so moved by the racist and anti-immigrant attitudes of "respectable" Christians that he left the pastorate to found a school that would become Nyack College. So from its earliest days, the college had enrolled African Americans as well as recent immigrants from China and Italy. Simpson boldly proclaimed, "Our Master knew no color line except that of the blood red cross"; and thus the diverse college of the twenty-first century had found its roots in the nineteenth century.

Out of the school, a movement developed, an alliance of like-minded Christians motivated by the desire to spread the gospel of Jesus. Yet this was no ordinary missionary movement, as Simpson himself was deeply passionate about confronting the social problems so prevalent in the city around him. He launched numerous parachurch ministries to the homeless, the unemployed, single mothers, the incarcerated, and all others struggling within an urban context. Posters outlining these early aspects of the college, as well as others depicting its early diversity, were created by the denomination and displayed throughout the hallways of the college's Manhattan campus and the college's administration building in the town of Nyack. A history had been reclaimed, and a beginning that had foretold the present was made evident. It became clear that the college's true mission, since Nyack's founding, had been to serve the underserved.

With a new story and renewed mission—one that had been lost and now was recovered—the college, under the leadership of President David Schroeder, laid out five core values in 2005, one of which is "intentional diversity." While the other core values—academic excellence, global engagement, personal transformation, and social relevance—could be found in the aspirational or strategic goals of many colleges and universities, few would, at that time, state that they made diversity a strategic goal. However, Nyack did not develop these as goals that could be measured, so the college could not know whether or not each was being achieved.

ASSESSING THE SUCCESS OF DIVERSITY

Ten years after codifying diversity as an aspirational goal or core value, the need to measure the effectiveness of learning at a diverse Christian college has emerged. A number of areas have been identified for assessment:

1. Nyack now has substantial populations of Asian Americans, blacks, Hispanics, and whites, so members of each group can now find a vibrant collegiate environment solely within their own group. In other words, students are under no compunction to socialize with students from a different group. Is this then really a diverse environment wherein students are learning to work with each other and where students of color are learning to negotiate the still very white world of the careers that they will enter? And will students of color even be able to enter underrepresented fields? And are white students being equipped to be successful in a multicultural world?
2. Nyack's professors now teach a range of courses that explore issues related to diversity, yet do they engage social justice issues, white privilege, institutional racism, and the like? Few graduates, with the exception of those in select majors, seem to be aware of these issues. So what sorts of training should faculty receive to assist them in engaging in the more difficult topics that must be studied at a college as diverse as Nyack?
3. Nyack's retention and graduation rates for black and Latino students lag behind the rates for Asian American and white students. Similarly, these rates at the city campus are far below those at the suburban campus. While many of Nyack's students of color are recipients of Pell grants, and Pell recipients have lower retention and graduation rates than students who don't receive Pell funding, the question must be asked whether the programs that Nyack has in place to assist at-risk students are effective.
4. Furthermore, since a large percentage of the entering class fails out during the first year and the majority of these failing students are students of color, it seems urgent that Nyack redesign the first-year curriculum. The curriculum currently places heavy emphasis on writing, research skills, and study in the liberal arts. Yet most of Nyack's first-year students have been educated in urban high schools that do a dismal job of preparing students to excel in these areas. Nyack needs to develop a curriculum that simultaneously affirms the skills in which they are proficient, such as oral communication and technological literacy, and prepares students to enter the requisite liberal arts courses central to a college education. For instance, should students take statistics before taking college algebra, and should

the first course that develops quantitative analytic skills be a financial literacy course?

5. Finally, and perhaps most importantly for a Christian college, is Nyack actually providing its students with a theological understanding of the Bible that underscores and affirms diversity and speaks to issues of marginalization, sexism, and racism? Nyack's students respond enthusiastically to the worship services and the overall spiritual climate on both campuses, but how many would say they have walked away from Nyack with the knowledge of God's Word as a radical underpinning for their faith?

Assessing these issues will take a good deal of work and involve a tremendous amount of struggle, debate, research, and writing. But the very fact that these questions are asked and these issues are raised is a testimony to the ongoing struggle to make Nyack a diverse Christian college. The easy part of Nyack's journey to become a diverse college is over. Certain demographic percentages have been achieved, certain courses that focus on diversity have been put in place, and the first phase of becoming diverse has been wildly successful. A foundation is finished and is ready to be built upon.

The next phase of becoming truly inclusive lies before us.

FOR DISCUSSION

1. What is the tipping point for your college to become a diverse community?
2. What academic programs best serve students of color at your institution?
3. What changes should your institution make to its admission policies and student services in order to best serve students of color?
4. What strategies can your administration employ to encourage ethnically diverse churches and the broader communities that represent people of color to "buy in" to your institution?
5. What strategies can your college develop to hire people of color as faculty?
6. What goals can your institution set to diversify its faculty, staff, administration, and board?
7. What aspects of your institution's history and early mission provide the foundation for establishing a diverse institution today?
8. Is diversity something that is talked about at your institution, and/or is it emphasized in mission or vision statements, strategic goals, and objectives?
9. What is distinctively Christian about your institution's approach to diversity?
10. What are some of the fears or obstacles standing in the way of your institution becoming more diverse and inclusive?

CHAPTER TWO

North Park University

DAVID L. PARKYN, PhD

North Park University, Retired President

We do not follow the course of other[s] … who simply want to resource their own people.
—Arthur Nelson, *Chicago Tribune*, June 26, 1980

The Homestead Act of 1862, signed into law by President Abraham Lincoln, made 160 acres of federal land available to any individual or family willing to settle and farm the land. During this same period, consecutive years of crop failures, the lack of jobs in cities, and the yearning for independence from a state-church led many Swedes to emigrate to the United States—their relocation and resettlement facilitated by the Homestead Act.

Swedish immigration to America was especially strong between 1870 and 1900. Upon arriving in America, many of these pioneers cleared farmland and cultivated crops in the Great Plains, while others chose to settle in cities, particularly Chicago. Some also started churches. The appeal of a church "free" from state influence led to the birth in 1885 of a new American Pietist church: the Mission Friends, also known in those years as the Swedish Evangelical Mission Covenant (and today as the Evangelical Covenant Church).

Just six years later, this small immigrant church community gathered for an annual meeting at Moses Hill in rural Nebraska. On Saturday afternoon, September 19, 1891, the sixty-one delegates attending the meeting returned to session following lunch to vote on the most pressing item on the meeting agenda. An early record of the meeting describes the action: "By open ballot the sixty-one delegates declared themselves 'as one man' for the establishment of a Covenant educational institution."[1] By unanimous vote, the delegates agreed to establish the school that is today known as North Park University.

Two years later, on September 26, 1893, an event occurred through which we can identify the early philosophy of education and the framework for faith that influenced teaching and learning in this educational institution from its earliest days. To be sure, at the time this was hardly a school—it had not yet been given a formal name—and included only a handful of students, each a recent immigrant to America, speaking little English and huddled in the basement of a Minneapolis church. Still, the school had just concluded its second year.

At that time, twenty-eight-year-old David Nyvall was the school's president. Nyvall visited Chicago early in the fall of 1893 to participate in the Parliament of World Religions, the first ecumenical interfaith gathering of its kind, conceived on the premise that people of different faiths held more in common than they had in difference. The participants came together to learn from each other and, by doing so, to advance the commitment of religious faith around the world.

Nyvall had been invited as one of the speakers at the Parliament to introduce his church and its young school to this interfaith audience. The published record of the Parliament summarizes the descriptive wording used by Nyvall:

> There is no common or fixed creed or special doctrine that binds [the school together]. . . . Differences are permitted to exist as unavoidable in our imperfect knowledge of truth. . . . [That we have] harmony in the midst of this diversity is largely owing to the [fact that] . . . hospitality is especially insisted upon.[2]

Realistically, this was not an accurate description at the time. The school was hardly diverse—it comprised a handful of students, all Swedish immigrants more comfortable speaking and writing in Swedish than English. Rather than describing the school, Nyvall was outlining a vision of educational philosophy and faith orientation in the academy. In his view, a school ought to be a place that acknowledges, in a spirit of intellectual humility, that our understanding of truth is always "imperfect." In this setting, he suggested, there will be differences among us, and because we are the academy, we will own this diversity of thought and language, culture, and faith, and we will embrace these differences through a deep commitment to hospitality.

Could this foundation for learning actually frame a school over succeeding decades? Could people rooted in a Christian faith commitment recognize that one's knowledge of truth is imperfect, that difference should be permitted in the community of faith and its academy? Could this faith community and its school affirm that differences among us are unavoidable yet harmony ought to be—and can be—the norm, even in the midst of difference? Could this learning community, birthed in the immigrant experience of a small band of people from a small country in northern Europe, adopt a culture of hospitality such that over succeeding generations, students from myriad races and ethnicities would study side-by-side on this campus?

HOSPITALITY TAKING ROOT

Fast forward 125 years, when North Park University today enrolls a much larger student body than in its early years, yet there remains a striking continuity from our founding. As in our earliest years, a large portion of students today at North Park—in both undergraduate and graduate programs—reflects the historic and contemporary immigrant demographic trend in the United States. At its founding, students who studied at North Park often came from families who had been welcomed to the United States through the Homestead Act of 1862. Today, students who study at North Park often come from families who have been welcomed here through the Naturalization and Immigration Act of 1965.

Over recent decades, enrollment at North Park has transitioned from a student population drawn from a single national ethnicity and culture (Sweden), speaking primarily the language from home (Swedish) while learning to speak, read, and write another language (English) at school, to a multicultural student demographic comprising an array of cultures, ethnicities, and languages as complex as the United States itself in the twenty-first century.

First-Year Undergraduate Student Enrollment by Ethnicity—1996 and 2016

Student cluster	1996	2016
African American	5%	9%
Asian American	3%	6%
Caucasian	75%	42%
Hispanic/Latino	7%	32%
Pacific Islander	1%	2%
Two or more races	0%	5%
Unreported	6%	1%
International	3%	3%

How did such hospitality take root? How did an institution established by Swedish immigrants become a university that reflects the ethnic and cultural diversity of the United States in the twenty-first century? Central to this evolution of the learning community at North Park has been the adoption, over many years, of three components of institutional culture and identity: *to be Christian, to be urban,* and *to be intercultural.* These three components undergird the institutional history and identity that frames the university today.

Faithful to David Nyvall's description of the early school, where "hospitality is especially insisted upon," North Park's enrollment today is more embracing than ever in the institution's history. The North Park campus community today has no single ethnic or racial majority, a factor that reflects Christ's vision of the kingdom of God recorded in the Gospel of Luke, in which "people will come from east and west, from north and south" (Luke 13:29 NRSV).

In his 2010 study of religious colleges in the twenty-first century, Samuel Schuman applauded the effectiveness with which North Park University has adopted the city as its classroom. He wrote, "North Park work[s] vigorously to push students out into the complexity of a modern urban environment and to pull into the orb of the university the multifaceted neighborhood around it."[3]

Schuman concluded his study by noting that North Park is "quite distinctive and difficult to compare to others."[4] He continued:

[North Park] is, on the one hand, vigorously religious and strongly denominational with a continuing tie to a particular immigrant population, and yet equally strongly and vigorously open to students from the widest diversity of backgrounds. It occupies a pleasant, green, and historical campus, in the very middle of a bustling major American city. Perhaps most impressive and surprising, not only is North Park University Christian, urban, and multicultural, but it has managed to be all those things and also to be coherent.[5]

How this institutional transformation has transpired through the school's 125-year history is a tribute to its integration of the urban social context side-by-side with a commitment to Christian faith in the academy.

FAITH SHAPES LEARNING

North Park claims a core institutional identity illustrated by three central values: the university will be Christian, city-centered, and intercultural. As a Christian university, North Park is dedicated to nurturing faith as part of its educational program, affirming historic Christianity even as students of all faith traditions are welcome to enroll.

Set Free from What Divides

President Nyvall's early conviction that our knowledge of truth is imperfect is rooted in the framework for faith that motivated those sixty-one men to gather at Moses Hill, Nebraska, in 1891 and then decide to start a school. What kind of school? A school formed out of a community of faith (the Evangelical Covenant Church), which today "seek[s] to focus on what unites us as followers of Christ, rather than on what divides us"[6]—a community of faith in which members "offer freedom to one another to differ on issues of belief or practice where the biblical and historical record seems to allow for a variety of interpretations of the will and purposes of God."[7]

Such a framing of faith allows for, and indeed fosters and mandates, a learning community "set free from the power of those things that on their own tend to divide."[8] This is a faith of pilgrims on a life journey, dedicated to truth as it is understood today while open to new understandings of truth as it is experienced tomorrow—and as it is revealed through others fostered by a generous spirit of hospitality. Such freedom of faith and intellectual conviction, such openness to cultural disposition and social practice, such inclusion of multiple perspectives and life experiences is a freedom, openness, and inclusion offered within this community of faith, "to one another . . . not something we claim for ourselves, but offered to the other."[9]

In 1891, this framing of faith was expressed within a small, homogeneous community—a gathering of recent immigrants to America, seeking a new identity while holding on to the "homeland." Nonetheless, an essential commitment was clear: as a community of faith we recognize our "imperfect knowledge of truth," even as "hospitality is especially insisted upon." Throughout the history of North Park, faith has framed the "center" of the university, but it has not sought to identify "boundaries" of thought, or action, or commitment.[10] Faith gives birth to the community of believers, but it does not restrict the limits of study, reflection, institutional mission, or personal identity; indeed, such a community of believers welcomes others (universally, regardless of background) into the community of learners within the academy.

Consequently, today students of many faith backgrounds enroll at North Park. In the early years, students from the school's parent denomination dominated the enrollment pattern. Yet the school historically maintained an active relationship with a neighboring Orthodox Jewish community and welcomed Greek Orthodox students as well. In recent years, evolving demographic patterns have brought increasing numbers of Roman Catholic students, who now represent the largest single Christian denomination in the student body. The Muslim student population has increased modestly in recent years, as has the number of students without a particular faith affiliation or orientation. Student enrollment today reaches across the broad spectrum of Christian church traditions and welcomes students of all expressions of faith.

Learning from Each Other in Faith

Evolving patterns of student enrollment, and a growing awareness across America and in the academy, have prompted more recent attention on campus to interfaith dialogue, understanding, and collaboration. In a recent study (sponsored by the Interfaith Youth Core), responses from first-year students at North Park reflected formation of a "self-authored worldview commitment" at higher levels than students at other evangelical Protestant colleges. At North Park, in the process of developing a worldview, students are more likely to "consider other religious and nonreligious perspectives," "talk with and listen to people with points of view different than [one's] own," and "integrate multiple points of view into [one's] existing worldview." Likewise, students at North Park seem to exhibit a greater propensity than students at other evangelical schools "to serve with those of diverse religious backgrounds," to believe that "we can overcome many of the world's major problems if people of different religious and nonreligious perspectives work together," and to be personally "committed to leading efforts in collaboration with people of other religious and nonreligious perspectives to create positive changes in society."[11]

The physical campus at North Park is marked by two distinct architectural traits. First, there is no identified perimeter to the campus, no fence to inform when one is on or off the campus, no boundary that visitors need to cross in their coming and leaving. Yet, second, there is a clearly identified center, a prominent location established by landscape architects where campus paths intersect. This "center" is where the university seal is laid within the walkway, where students are invited to sit for conversation on a low ledge inscribed with verses from Scripture that are important to the school's heritage. On North Park's campus (and in North Park's culture of learning), boundaries are absent, while the center is always present.

These two images characterize an essential ethos at North Park. The North Park mission, "to prepare students for lives of significance and service," is informed by this center; yet learning is not confined to the center. As an educational community, students are drawn in to be shaped and molded and then released and sent out to serve. The university does so not by defining the edges or saying, "You're welcome to join us if you enter through this gate and then stay within this fence," but rather through a "gravitational pull" that can be likened to "a magnetic field in which particles [i.e., students and student learning] are in motion."[12]

Education for "significance and service" happens as students come to the campus, learn and grow, and some years later leave, all the while remaining connected to the center, drawn inward yet headed outward, receiving nurture and energy from a faith that provides a source of balance, location, and purpose in life, yet always focused on a life of faith that occurs beyond the campus. Faith shapes learning at North Park—faith that is centered without being bounded.

PLACE SHAPES LEARNING

The university's second core value, to be city-centered, illustrates how learning is contextually located. As a community of involved learners, we engage Chicago as our dynamic place of learning.

Becoming Urban

North Park today is an urban university, but it has not always been so. When Old Main was built in 1893, the area was a "sparsely settled community."[13] In his history of the first fifty years of North Park, Leland Carlson described its environs this way:

> Within the North Park community were nine homes established by 1894—less than one house per square block. . . . Old Main stood like a lone sentinel surveying the surrounding territory of onion fields, cabbage patches, and cornfields. . . . Provincial and rustic, lonely and deserted, these were characteristic adjectives applied to the community by the casual observer . . . there were no water mains or sewers, no sidewalks or parking lots, no schools or cafes . . . and hardly any people.[14]

Obviously, this was not a city! But that would change over the ensuing decades. In contrast with Carlson's description, Chicago journalist Alex Kotlowitz, in a recent book, describes the university's contemporary context in the opening sentence of a chapter on the Albany Park neighborhood (home of North Park University): "The world intersects at the corner of Lawrence and Kedzie Avenues,"[15] a street corner within three blocks of the campus.

Over the course of a century, the city and indeed the world has come to the neighborhood and wrapped its arms around the campus. North Park University, once the "lone sentinel surveying the surrounding territory of onion fields, cabbage patches and cornfields"[16] now is at home in one of the most diverse zip codes in the United States.

The phenomenal growth of Chicago during the decades since the founding of North Park has mirrored the growth of cities worldwide. At the beginning of the twenty-first century, specifically in 2008, a monumental turning point and social shift took place: for the first time in history, a majority of the world's people now live in cities. And this trajectory will continue into the foreseeable future: demographers expect that by 2050 more than 80 percent of the world's population will be living in urban settings. Given that this will occur during the working lifetime of today's students, the implications must be reflected in the context within which and for which students are educated.

Remaining Urban

As North Park has grown into an urban university, its students, faculty, alumni, board, and parent church have not always been confident of this trajectory. Twice in the school's history, serious consideration was given to moving the campus out of the city.

In 1950, college and seminary leadership considered the potential for moving the campus to a new, albeit nearby, location: a fifty-acre site just north of the city limits, in Niles, Illinois. School and church leaders determined at that time that the cost of the project was more than could be managed. In addition, student needs for part-time employment could be better serviced in the present location, the proximity to the church offices and the church's hospital added continuing value to the school, and the accessibility of the city's cultural agencies served the educational needs of students in ways that would not be replicated at a distance. These various pragmatic factors, rather than ideals of educational philosophy, played a part in the decision to remain in the school's historic location.

The option to relocate was considered again in 1979–80. On this occasion, land and funding were available to build a new campus far north of the city. The desire to relocate was prompted by a deteriorating city neighborhood, and decreasing enrollment of students from across the country, especially from denominational churches, reflecting a reluctance to leave suburban and small-town communities to study in an urban context.

This time, however, the decision to remain in the historic location was guided by and reflected a burgeoning renewal of educational mission and identity for the college and its seminary. Arthur Nelson, acting president of the college in 1980, explained this reasoning when a reporter with the *Chicago Tribune* covered the decision. Nelson commented:

> The decision is an expression of our faith in Chicago. . . . We are renewing our commitment to the city and to the spiritual values of our founders' sense of mission and education. . . . We do not follow the course of a lot of other denominational colleges who simply want to resource their own people.[17]

As the reporter himself noted in the article, "If the school left the city, it would lose its rich diversity of students."[18]

Being City-Centered

Now thirty-five years later, on the university's 125th anniversary, North Park University recognizes what a critical force—a true tipping point—these two moments of decision in the school's history were for identifying and securing its future trajectory. That commitment is especially significant given that today the population of the world, and of the United States, is majority-urban. North Park remains committed to serving students who live and learn in the city.

The second of the university's seven educational ideals affirms an education that "engages Chicago as a dynamic context for learning and service."[19] When this ideal was introduced by President David Horner near the end of the twentieth century, North Park adopted a commitment in the university's strategic plan for 2000 to embrace the "urban context and culture" as one of three critical rubrics of an "external positioning strategy."[20]

Fifteen years later, in 2016, the board of trustees affirmed a new statement of aspiration, committing to "distinguish" North Park as "the nation's leading city-centered Christian university during the coming decade and beyond."[21] Today, the North Park learning community is differentiated by adopting the city as both subject and place of learning as a foundation for academic excellence.

North Park now stands with the global majority and must assume an enormous responsibility: "to prepare students for lives of significance and service"[22] in tomorrow's cities. In reality, very little happens around the globe that is not shaped, most significantly, by urban systems, whether economic, political, cultural, financial, social, educational, medical, or religious. Today, more than ever, cities shape the world. And so at North Park, educators dedicate their efforts to shaping a generation of young leaders who will link their dedication to justice, their commitment to loving kindness, and their passion for walking with God to the well-being of the city (Jer. 29:7; Mic. 6:8).

With a spirit evident even in its earliest years, affirmed in the extraordinary decision in 1980 to remain in its historic urban location, advanced over the past two decades in steps to adopt Chicago as a classroom, and affirmed as a critical factor in the university's most recent strategic plan, North Park embraces Chicago and "leverages the city as subject and place of learning."[23] This commitment to "Chicago as a classroom" is consistent with the university mission and identity, expands institutional resources for learning far beyond what North Park could otherwise provide, demonstrates that all of God's people have something to teach others (rich and poor, business person and pastor, immigrant and long-time resident), and sets apart the university from most other colleges and universities. It differentiates North Park in the marketplace by showing that learning at this university is especially deep, rich, and engaging, because its home is in Chicago. As cities shape the world, so North Park wants the city to shape learning.

PEOPLE SHAPE LEARNING

We recognize at North Park that learning is a social enterprise—it can happen when a person is alone, but learning is always at its best when it takes place in the company of others. The university thereby seeks to embrace and value all people, welcoming them into the learning community that is North Park.

A Developing American Demographic

Concomitant with the rapid urbanization of the United States and the world during the past fifty years is the lasting effect of the Naturalization and Immigration Act of 1965 that opened the country to a second great wave of immigrants. Many settled in the nation's cities, including Chicago, just as the Swedes in the mid-nineteenth century populated the nation's Great Plains. More than ever before in the country's history, the population is today composed of people representing a broader array of cultures and languages, ethnicities, and races.

In this very context, however, sociologist and journalist Bill Bishop asserts that across the United States the dominant tendency is for communities to be comprised of like-minded people. Bishop argues that while the country has become increasingly diverse, this phenomenon for clustering with the like-minded has radically accentuated the country. Bishop's point is that Americans are increasingly closing in their ideological wagons. He writes:

> We have built a country where everyone can choose the neighbors (and church and news shows) most compatible with his or her lifestyle and beliefs. And we are living with the consequences of this segregation by way of life: pockets of like-minded citizens that have become so ideologically inbred that we don't know, can't understand, and can barely conceive of "those people" who live just a few miles away.[24]

Or even a few blocks away.

American communities, Bishop maintains, are composed of like-minded people. By contrast, North Park University expects just the opposite—the learning community is deliberately composed of different-minded people, people from diverse communities, faith perspectives, ethnicities, and cultures, who learn and live from each other, in conversation with each other.

Learning Together, Insisting on Hospitality

Why is this commitment to a learning community shaped by different-minded people foundational to the identity of North Park? There are several reasons for this—some shaped by educational philosophy and others influenced by the legacy of those godly people who established the institution and those who have since cared for it over the past 125 years. Yet the central reason that drives the university's commitment to diversity in learning is the substance of faith.

Remaining faithful to David Nyvall's description of the early school where "hospitality is especially insisted upon," in recent decades North Park has enrolled a student body that increasingly reflects "the great multitude . . . from every nation" described in John's Revelation 7:9. In this context, an education is offered that "embraces all people and celebrates the richness of cultural difference."[25]

As a result of the Servicemen's Readjustment Act of 1944, soldiers returning from World War II had an impact on enrollment growth at North Park, similar to enrollment change across the nation at that time. Yet those students who enrolled at North Park immediately before this, during the years of the war, reflected on and voiced their perspectives regarding the incongruence of American social norms at the time. This is well illustrated through editorials in *North Park News*, the student newspaper.

In November 1942, for instance, a student editorial noted the important responsibility of America to "give the other people of the world a chance to live in a free . . . country like ours."[26] Yet America was not free of injustice. The editorial continued:

> When I picked up the morning paper about one month ago it was perfectly natural that I should be startled. Two negroes had been taken from the hands of the law by a mob and lynched. In the midst of another great war to free the oppressed people of other lands, we allow two American citizens to be hanged from a tree until dead.[27]

In the spring of that same school year, another student wrote a parallel editorial:

> This is a war about the right of people to live decently and in freedom. We cannot win this war simply by freeing all the people of Europe, Africa, and the Orient. It is harder than that. We must win it also by giving every American the economic and political freedom which is his birthright.

Hundreds of thousands of both Negro and White sharecropper and tenant farmer families live bleak, despairing lives in our own South. . . . Economically pauperized and politically frustrated, they have yet sent their sons to defend our cause throughout the world. Their struggle is the concern of all Americans. . . . We are none of us free while these Americans remain slaves in a vicious economic and political system which crushes their aspirations toward a decent life.[28]

A similar line of editorial comment was directed at the challenges faced by Japanese Americans forcibly removed from their homes and mandated to relocation centers. A year later, student leaders on North Park's campus invited members of the Quaker American Friends Service Committee to campus to help "set up practical work projects in areas of racial tension where people from very different racial and educational backgrounds may work side by side towards a common constructive goal."[29]

Yet the student body remained predominantly Caucasian, with only a small number of people of color, including Japanese American students recently released from wartime centers and African American students from Chicago. Their enrollment was encouraged and supported by a small number of new scholarship programs "awarded to students of different racial, national, or cultural backgrounds."[30]

As enrollment of students of color gradually increased at North Park during the years that followed, the university responded by clustering programs identified for particular audiences. An early example, in 1982, was La Unidad Latina (LUL), organized to "focus on the specific needs of the 90 Latino students at North Park."[31] The organization's purpose also extended to a goal to "break some barriers . . . [and] bring more open-mindedness to people, bring respect for others through learning."[32]

The Center for Scandinavian Studies was established in 1984, and this led during the following decade to the introduction of a number of "cultural centers" linked to individual groups: Korean (1991), African American (1994), Latino (1994), and Middle Eastern (1995).

During these same years, the board of trustees actively engaged topics of diversity for both students and faculty/staff, reflecting "the Board's commitment of North Park becoming a diverse multicultural academic community."[33] One early step was to establish a multicultural committee as part of the board's governance structure, first introduced in 1995. Under the prompting of this committee, in 1996 the board established a mandate for the university administration to (a) consider enrollment by student ethnicity in each academic program, (b) establish "ongoing continuing education regarding multicultur-alism" for faculty and staff, and (c) undertake a "census of ethnic/cultural rep-resentation in all areas (faculty, administration, service, etc.) and determine what are the procedures and processes being developed to culturally inculcate a growing multicultural presence at North Park."[34]

During the next year, the board approved a directive "to give highest prior-ity to adding minority faculty in existing faculty searches . . . and to review the adequacy of the Strategic Plan goals for minority faculty."[35]

In subsequent years, the board's multicultural committee drafted a Multicultural Vision Statement that was adopted in 2002 and revised in 2008. The maturing voice of this institutional commitment is evident in notes from the committee's meeting in October 2007, as a new (and African American) provost was introduced to the campus community. The committee noted that in the near future "we need to move our mission from an emphasis which is driven by numbers and events to being philosophically a core learning value of the university, from 'doing multiculturalism' because it's the right thing to 'doing multiculturalism' because it's who we are."[36] Over subsequent years, as the university's efforts toward inclusion progressed, the campus vocabulary of "multicultural" was replaced with a consistent reference to "intercultural."

In February 2016, *The Chronicle of Higher Education* called attention to the fact that North Park is "one of the few evangelical colleges where the number of minority students now equals white students."[37] In a campus forum later that spring, campus administrators explained the corresponding shift in nomen-clature: "We're trying to make a shift from an objective of becoming multicul-tural—being comprised of people who come from diverse backgrounds, which is about composition as an institution—to being intercultural. How does the crossing of cultures get engrained into the DNA of an institution?"[38]

During the 2016–17 academic year, Provost Michael Emerson introduced a series of campus conversations (with an open invitation to faculty, staff, and students), titled "Many Voices, One Community." He explained:

North Park grows increasingly diverse, which offers our community many advantages. But diversity in and of itself is not the goal. We seek to be a community within our diversity to model how people from many different backgrounds can work together to encourage our faith, our studies, and our impact on the larger world.[39]

Learning to learn together at North Park has taken decades to achieve, and most certainly is still very much a work in progress.

REFLECTIONS ON NORTH PARK'S 125TH ANNIVERSARY

What opportunity, and what challenge, does this context set before North Park University today? What do the school's historic commitments, expressed in the contemporary American context, offer and require of the university—its students and faculty, board and alumni, and parent church—for years to come? As Provost Emerson often asks the campus community: "Can we become the next great urban university, defined by who we include rather than by who we exclude?"

The North Park University community today is characterized by difference and diversity. In fact, throughout the school's history, both educators and trustees have agreed that learning in this academic community is enriched by the inclusion of a wide array of individuals. This commitment is evident, especially in the university's student body.

North Park enrolls students from all walks of life who come from throughout the United States and from around the world, from the Midwest and the South, from cities and small towns. The majority of North Park students are Christians, representing a breadth of denominations and churches from Protestant, Catholic, and Orthodox traditions; other students are Muslim, Jewish, and from other faiths. North Park enrolls students who identify with a variety of sexual orientations and identities. Some North Park students drift to the left politically and others to the right; some are wealthy and others are not; some are first-generation college students and others come from a long line of college graduates. North Park students are African American and Caucasian, Asian and Latino; all North Park students speak English, but many also communicate in other languages.

Such a diverse community requires widespread embrace of a common expectation: that all students who enroll at North Park will be welcomed, accepted, and respected as valued and contributing members of this learning community. Each student brings to North Park an anthology of life experiences that creates a personal narrative. Each student's story is true and to be shared, a story through which others can discover meaning, purpose, and direction for life.

North Park's embrace of difference—of each student's story—makes the university a special place and shapes the learning community. But this medley of personal stories can also be a challenge for living together as a unified community. Disagreement is inevitable in any university community, yet this very difference contributes positively to the learning environment. The assortment of individual student perspectives on any topic fosters, informs, and shapes a dynamic learning community.

The differences between individual members of the campus community—regarding how to express faith; each person's relative position on a political continuum; sexual orientation or identity; ethnic and cultural norms; or a host of other topics, questions, and points of conversation—are real. The question simply is how far apart should these differences keep members from each other? North Park does not seek to eliminate difference or disagreement within the student body; rather, the community aims to draw people closer together through inclusion, civility, dialogue, respect, hospitality, and a mutual love for God and all people.

As was the case 125 years ago, truth is still known imperfectly, and in this imperfection the learning community at North Park must insist on mutual hospitality. And so, we learn. We learn because learning is best done in the company of others, with those who are different from us. It is in and through this process that we learn to love God and each other.

FOR DISCUSSION

1. As reflected in North Park's experience, environmental factors internal to the college or university often shape the broader campus ethos, either in favor of or contrary to a commitment to diversity. What are these factors at institutions you know well? Are some factors common to multiple institutions?

2. Certain decisions in an institution's saga set the course of the school's story toward increased diversity, or they shelter the school against such change. Often these decisions occur at the highest level of governance (i.e., the board of trustees), and their net effect can sometimes take two or more decades to measure. What are the critical points of decision-making, throughout the past decades or century, at the institutions you know well?

3. Faith-based institutions at their very best reflect the social and ethical hermeneutic of their parent church. These legacy lenses of interpretation can focus an institution's attention inward, or they can serve as marking points along the way to becoming a welcoming and embracing community of learning. Again, in the institutions you know well, how has a commitment to diversity been advanced, or hindered, by the school's theological heritage?

4. How can we identify when a university's commitment to diversity has advanced beyond a point of welcome and inclusion, to settle within the institution's very DNA?

5. North Park University and the Evangelical Covenant Church were established by Swedish immigrants who found religious, social, cultural, and

language support from being in community. Yet these Swedish immigrants demonstrated a remarkable openness to diversity in culture, faith, thought, and language. They also valued intellectual humility and an embrace of these differences through a deep commitment to hospitality. Not surprisingly, many of these same core values are characteristic of North Park today. What have been the contributions of immigrants to other Christian institutions over the past century and a half? How do immigrants today contribute to the revitalization of our churches, communities, and practice of hospitality?

6. President Parkyn writes, "Faith shapes learning at North Park—faith that is centered without being bounded." North Park's mission, educational philosophy, and ethos are informed by a clear center and characterized by the absence of boundaries that otherwise might limit their culture of learning by either fencing people in or out. As a result, this core commitment has contributed to North Park being one of the most diverse Christian colleges and universities in the United States today. Is your institution clear on its faith center? Does your institution knowingly or unknowingly, intentionally or unintentionally, erect fences that keep certain people or groups out and others in?

7. The physical campus of North Park does not have an identified perimeter or fences marking a point of entry or exit, yet there is a clearly identified center where the campus paths intersect and visitors are invited to sit. As a result, the physical campus sends the message that all are welcome here. Considering the aesthetics of your campus, is the message being sent one of welcome or exclusion? Do the pictures displayed in prominent spaces, the names on buildings, and campus artwork (or the absence of artwork) communicate a message of inclusion or exclusion? What would an inclusive campus aesthetic look like at your institution?

8. North Park has a long history of diversity leadership on the part of its presidents and boards of trustees. In fact, President Parkyn noted that the board of trustees established a multicultural affairs committee as a part of the board's governing structure as early as 1995. What does diversity leadership look like at your institution? To what degree are your president and board involved in the "multicultural affairs" of the institution? Does your board have a multicultural affairs committee? What do you believe is the optimum administrative structure for your institution to provide diversity leadership throughout the organization?

9. North Park University has fully embraced its theological and urban location, and designates the city of Chicago as their "classroom." As a result, the

curriculum and teaching practices, student learning, and the hiring process and professional development of the faculty reflect this commitment. To what degree has your institution aligned its explicit curriculum (including the core curriculum), teaching and student learning, faculty hiring, and the professional development of faculty with your stated commitment to diversity and inclusion? Is your "classroom" confined to the four walls of the main campus, or does it extend beyond this location to embrace a wider curriculum, and to explore innovative teaching methods and experiential learning?

10. In reference to the university's adopted and revised "Multicultural Vision Statement," President Parkyn writes about the "maturing voice" of the institution, as recorded in the notes of the board's multicultural committee meeting in 2007, that in part stated the university's need to move "from 'doing multiculturalism' because it is the right thing to 'doing multiculturalism' because it's who we are." At what point does your institution's commitment to diversity and inclusion move beyond statements, numbers, events, and programs, "because it is the right thing to do," to become an integral part of your core identity? Where is your institution on this continuum from "doing" to "being"? Do you have a diversity and inclusion vision statement? What is your intercultural vision for the campus community?

NOTES

1 Leland H. Carlson, *A History of North Park College* (Chicago: North Park College and Theological Seminary, 1941), 59.

2 John Henry Barrows, *The World's Parliament of Religions* (Chicago: Parliament Publishing, 1893), 1517.

3 Samuel Shuman, *Seeing the Light: Religious Colleges in Twenty-First-Century America* (Baltimore: Johns Hopkins University Press, 2010), 217.

4 Ibid., 143.

5 Ibid.

6 Evangelical Covenant Church, *What Does the Covenant Church Believe? A Brief Look at Covenant Affirmations* (Chicago: Covenant Publications, n.d.), 2, accessed May 20, 2017, www.covchurch.org/CovenantAffirmations.

7 Ibid.

8 Ibid.

9 *Covenant Affirmations* (Chicago: Covenant Publications, 2005), 20.

10 The concept outlined here reflects the framework of faith formation initially developed by missiologist and anthropologist Paul Hiebert in "Conversion, Culture, and Cognitive Categories," *Gospel in Context,* 11:4 (October 1978): 24–29. Hiebert distinguishes between (a) a "bounded set" in which faith communities (and their academies) create a boundary, a theological border, a doctrinal fence, a lifestyle standard through which the community separates those who are inside the fence from those who are outside the fence, and (b) a "centered set" in which faith communities do not identify boundaries, walls, or fences to keep people out (or keep them in), but in which there is

a "gravitational pull" toward a centering ethos. The Mission Friends, through its historical development as the Evangelical Covenant Church and more specifically North Park University as this denomination's university, reflects the "centered set" typology.

11   Matthew Mayhew and Alyssa Rockenbach, *Interfaith Diversity Experiences and Attitudes Longitudinal Survey* (IDEALS), "Time 1 Report" (Summer/Fall 2015), www.ifyc.org/content/survey-information.

12   Hiebert, "Conversion, Culture, and Cognitive Categories," 28.

13   Carlson, *A History of North Park College,* 179.

14   Ibid., 180.

15   Alex Kotlowitz, *Never a City So Real* (New York: Crown Publishers, 2004), 140.

16   Carlson, *A History of North Park College,* 180.

17   "College Weighs Blight, Stays Put," *Chicago Tribune,* June 26, 1980.

18   Ibid.

19   David L. Parkyn, *Discovering Our Voice: Reflections on Learning at North Park University* (Chicago: North Park University, 2010), 15.

20   "Strategic Plan: A Guide to Growing Excellence" (Chicago: North Park University, August 2000).

21   "Strategic Plan: Essential Elements" (Chicago: North Park University, Summer 2016).

22   Parkyn, *Discovering Our Voice,* 4.

23   "Strategic Plan: A Guide to Growing Excellence" (Summer 2016).

24   Bill Bishop, *The Big Sort: Why the Clustering of Like-Minded America Is Tearing Us Apart* (Boston: Houghton Mifflin Harcourt, 2008), 11.

25   Parkyn, *Discovering Our Voice,* 18.

26   "Editorial," *North Park News,* November 24, 1942, 2.

27   Ibid.

28   "Editorial," *North Park News,* March 3, 1943, 2.

29   "Representative of Quakers' Service Explains Program for Race," *North Park News,* April 12, 1944, 5.

30   "Goodwill Scholarship," *North Park News,* March 21, 1945, 2.

31   *The College News,* March 19, 1982, 10.

32   Ibid.

33   Minutes, North Park University Board of Trustees, February 2–3, 1996, 5.

34   Ibid.

35   Minutes, North Park University Board of Trustees, January 30–February 1, 1997, 3.

36   Minutes, North Park University Board of Trustees, October 25–27, 2007, 3.

37   Beth McMurrie, "Evangelical Colleges' Diversity Problem," *The Chronicle of Higher Education,* January 31, 2016.

38   David L. Parkyn, quoted in "From 'Being Multicultural' to 'Being Intercultural,'" *North Parker,* Summer 2016, 2.

39   Michael Emerson, quoted in "From 'Being Multicultural' to 'Being Intercultural,'" *North Parker,* Summer 2016, 2.

CHAPTER THREE

Warner Pacific College

ANDREA COOK, PhD

Warner Pacific College, President

It was 2005 and I was four weeks on the job in my role as Vice-President for Institutional Advancement at Warner Pacific College. The plague of comparison and lack of city connections became so obvious to me that I sat down and wrote a seven-page letter to the president at the time, Jay Barber. In the letter, I shared with him that I felt we were misplacing our mission emphasis and that we needed to go all-in with our urban identity. While recognizing the risk, this, it seemed to me, was our calling as a Christian college.

After he returned from an extended donor trip, President Barber called me into his office and the letter was facedown on his desk. Concerned that perhaps my letter was a bit too much, too early, I prepared for some pushback. Always pastoral and welcoming, Jay shared in some small talk, and then he turned the letter over on his desk and said, "You nailed us." I'll never forget that moment for the rest of my life, because it was the moment where, for me, everything changed. From that day forward, it was abundantly clear that for Warner Pacific College to survive, let alone thrive, we needed to stop acting like exiles and intentionally live out of our physical and theological location in the city—letting it shape and inform how we prepare students to lead and serve in the world. It was time to be bold, and bold we were.

Warner Pacific College has served students in southeast Portland for more than seventy-five years. Over that period of time, our commitment to deliver an excellent Christ-centered liberal arts education has never wavered. There have been moments when the challenge of limited space in our urban setting and the need to grow enrollment led to talks about leaving the city and moving to a suburban or rural location. Yet only in recent history has it become clear as to why God placed us in the heart of the city.

Over the past twenty-five years, many Christian higher education institutions have experienced dramatic growth. Yet during this period, Warner Pacific has faced a series of financial setbacks that led to a clouded future. Affiliated with the Church of God (Anderson, Indiana), this college has always had smart and passionate staff and faculty, and its distinctive approach to liberal arts education has been deep and intentional. However, growth comes out of coherence. Previously, the institutional identity of Warner Pacific College was disconnected from what we now collectively recognize as God's unique calling for the institution.

Martha Stortz, professor of religion and vocation at Augsburg College, once observed, "Calling is all about location—not just physical location, but also theological location. Calling always comes from and to a particular place." She further developed this thought: "The interplay in vocation between divine address and concrete context creates a lived experience that is thick, messy—and real. That means that whenever calling hits the ground, sparks fly."[1] The Portland metropolitan area is a place of challenge, but also a place of grace. Portland is more than the physical context of our location. Portland is the place we—the staff, faculty, and administration at Warner Pacific College—love. As our love for the city has grown, a new story for our institution has emerged, and I can attest to the fact that sparks are flying at Warner Pacific College in some profound and exciting ways.

When I arrived at Warner Pacific College in 2005, I was struck by the power of the comparison game in the life of the institution. Early on, as I was learning the ethos and environment, I constantly heard "we're like Institution A" and "we're not like Institution B." We didn't really know who we were or who we should be; we were stuck in a spiral of self-doubt. This was a huge liability as the institution worked to increase its enrollment and raise funds to support programs—and both responsibilities were assigned as a part of my role. Chuck Swindoll once wrote,

> Comparisons are odious. Either you are prompted to feel smug and proud because your strengths outweigh his or her weaknesses . . . or, more often, you begin to feel threatened, inferior, and blue because you fail to measure up. Striving to emulate a self-imposed standard, you begin to slide from the pleasant plateau of the real you into the sinking sands of I don't know who. In simpler terms, you've pawned your real personality for a phony disguise. That's odious![2]

The apostle Paul shared a similar sentiment with the Corinthian church that had fallen victim to the game of comparison when he wrote, "We do not dare to classify or compare ourselves with some who commend themselves. When they measure themselves by themselves and compare themselves with themselves, they are not wise" (2 Cor. 10:12 NIV). Upon first reading the Warner Pacific College mission statement, I was struck by the fact that the institution was declared to be "an urban Christian liberal arts college." In spite of scarce institutional evidence and my own minimal experience in the Portland area at the time, it was easy to observe that the word *urban* was meant to highlight the street address of the college rather than a deeply embedded institutional identity and philosophy. We had missed the incarnational premise that to be educating future leaders in the city meant that our daily reality and decision-making would have to collide with the life and environs of the people, quirks, and assets of the city of Portland.

To understand the context of Warner Pacific College and the challenge of leading a Christ-centered college in the city, it is important to consider the two major variables that frame the backdrop of Portland, Oregon. Our city is the twenty-sixth largest in the United States, with 632,309 residents in the city limits and a total of 2.35 million in the Portland metro area. Home to *Portlandia*, food carts, and legalized marijuana, Portland and Oregon are respectively ranked among the least religious cities and states in the nation. A recent Gallup analysis of its polling data from 2012 found that, no surprise, Oregon has the lowest percentage of respondents in the West who could be described as "very religious."[3] Only a handful of states from the Northeast have a lower number of respondents who fit the category of very religious, which Gallup says is based on responses to questions about the importance of religion in daily life and frequency of church attendance.

To compound complexity, Portland, ironically known for its "progressivism," was also recently dubbed "the Whitest City in America" by *The Atlantic* magazine. Portland has earned that title among the nation's big cities because of its history of racialization and the fact that 72.2 percent of residents are white, while only 6.3 percent are African American.[4] Portland is whiter than Omaha and Salt Lake City,[5] and no matter how much the city celebrates its liberal commitments, a deep pain is present on the streets of historically marginalized communities. More than 40 percent of African American residents of north and northeast Portland have been priced out of their neighborhood of origin as a result of gentrification. Portland has been named the most gentrified city of the century,[6] and home prices are only on the rise. At Warner Pacific, we are watching the city change and framing our Christ-centeredness and commitment to serving diverse students around the trends that are affecting historically underrepresented students. While some might consider Portland to be hostile territory (and rightfully so, in many cases), we believe it is a place where God and his grace are evident in real and beautiful ways.

By 2008, the new framework of our identity was clear, and we were in the midst of making some decisive commitments. Recognizing that we were not attracting the upper-middle-class white students private colleges have historically served, it was clear we were no longer in a position to offer discount rates on par with other private colleges. With the goal of making the cost of education more tenable for underrepresented students, we lowered tuition by 23 percent. And as part of our intentional investment to build relationships with historically marginalized communities in the city, we partnered with Portland Leadership Foundation to start the Act Six Leadership and Scholarship Initiative.[7] At that time, 11.9 percent of the students at Warner Pacific were students of color. While the changes were slow at first, as staff and faculty began to see a shift in student demographics, they harnessed the power of the relational hallmark of Warner Pacific instruction and focused on encouraging students, particularly those who might never have imagined the possibility of enrolling at a Christian college, to engage and persist as they discovered their purpose and calling. Within the year, the Adult Degree Program (ADP)—the robust delivery model we developed to serve evening adult learners—began to grow. In 2005, we had 191 students enrolled in ADP, and by 2008 we were serving 568 students. This development led us to a place where regularly operating from a positive variance would be possible, but we knew we had to keep pushing. Over time, the ADP student population has become gender balanced, changing from 60 percent female/40 percent male to now a 50/50 gender mix. And the racial and ethnic diversity of the ADP program has increased from less than 15 percent students of color to nearly 30 percent.

We were making strides, and the hope was palpable, with leaders internally beginning to believe that we would live on. I could never have prepared for what happened next; my colleague and mentor, Jay Barber, announced his retirement, and I was immediately appointed to be the interim president while the college did a national search. After applying for the position and walking through a comprehensive selection process, I was selected to be the seventh president of Warner Pacific College. I was honored to accept the position, and after working for twelve presidents over my prior thirty-three years in higher education, I was now thrust into the position of discerning what it meant to be one. We had made some great strides, but we were still in the infancy stage of a deep change. I knew that the new president needed to declare a bold clear vision and dig in for the long haul, but I was still shocked when it became clear that the person to declare such a vision was me! Being a college president was never my vocational goal, yet a calling like that can only be birthed by the Holy Spirit. Deep in my soul I knew that my personal calling and the calling of Warner Pacific College were converging.

It took me six months to write my inauguration speech, because along the way, I had to do some gut checks. Could we really pull this off? *I had to pray.* Was the Lord truly calling us to such a dramatic shift of mission and vision? *I had to dream.* What would the preferred future of Warner Pacific College actually look like? *I had to take inventory.* Did we have the intuition and assets to pivot in such a massive way?

On September 20, 2009, in front of a filled auditorium, I gave my inauguration speech and declared:

> Warner Pacific College will be a Christ-centered, liberal arts college that makes our urban identity an institutional priority. We will serve diverse students in radical ways, and every decision we make will be run through the lens of what it means to provide a private education for students who historically have been on the margin of Christian higher education.

WARP AND WOOF: THE FABRIC OF CHANGE

Martin Luther King Jr., in his *Letter from Birmingham Jail*, wrote, "We are caught in an inescapable network of mutuality, tied in a single garment of destiny. Whatever affects one directly, affects all indirectly."[8] King's message called Warner Pacific College to recognize that to be urban is to embrace the idea that we are not only a city institution but one piece of an interrelated community—both in Portland and in the Council for Christian Colleges & Universities. I am convinced that we cannot answer our world's "big questions" as a mere intellectual exercise; rather, as followers of Christ, we must consider how the answers immediately impact the lives of those most vulnerable across the globe—most of whom live in urban environments. Therefore we ought to be held accountable to ask questions such as the following: How do cities function, and what is our response to Portland? How does our academic vision create citizen-servants who are embedded in and influence urban Portland? How are we, as a Christian college, committed to making education available to *all* students?

In higher education, great questions are common. What's difficult is to find strategies that parlay those questions into quick and aggressive "hit-the-street" answers. Early on in my presidency, it became clear to me that we would never fully vest our institutional resources until we were able to write a strategic plan that captured our commitment to urban education. Structurally, we were smack dab in the middle of a previous strategic plan, with three years left until it culminated in 2012.

Inspired by Kotter's eight-step process for organizational transformation, we had successfully established a sense of urgency. The next step, it became clear, was to form a powerful coalition.[9] I appointed a group of thirteen influential members of the college's staff, faculty, and administration to form the President's Urban Commission. With the goal of thinking outside of ourselves and our experience, we invited the Portland Leadership Foundation to facilitate this commission, which resulted in a dynamic two-year culture shift for the entire institution. At first, it seemed counterintuitive to bring in an outside organization to help Warner Pacific plan for the future, but it was important for the institution to recognize that it had been insular for so long that we had not earned the right to be heard in underrepresented communities in the city of Portland. Portland Leadership Foundation's executive team embedded itself within the institution, testified on our behalf to city leaders, and introduced us to a new set of relationships in the region; this relationship proved to be invaluable. God has been at work in underrepresented communities long before Warner Pacific got involved, and we have reoriented our posture to show deference to those street-level experts who have much to teach those of us with discipline-specific doctoral degrees.

The Urban Commission developed a fifty-page "bridge plan" that clearly propelled the new vision forward. Once the document was published, it became a statement to the world that said, "Warner Pacific College has a plan—what was dubbed the 'Call to Action'—that ensures from this point forward that our curriculum, student recruitment, services priorities, internship opportunities, student-teacher placements, adult education offerings, and church relations will all be run through the organizing principle of our urban identity." We launched new initiatives and academic programs, successfully raised our first $1 million toward this initiative, and recalibrated our mission statement to read, "Warner Pacific College is a Christ-centered, urban, liberal arts college dedicated to providing students from diverse backgrounds an education that prepares them to engage actively in a constantly changing world."

The future is percolating in urban America, yet cities are also the center of our country's most vexing problems. We decided that if Christian colleges are going to seriously pursue the calling to seek peace, prosperity, and shalom for our cities (Jer. 29:4–7), Warner Pacific needed to assume a leadership role and get involved in finding solutions rather than hedging against the impact of the problem. We could no longer idly sit by. With the launch of the new strategic plan in 2012 (which culminates in 2019), we felt, perhaps for the first time in decades, that we were on the edge of innovation.

In the case for Warner Pacific College, our design for urban higher education also codified the new institutional reality that short of a large unexpected gift, Warner Pacific would have to grow comfortable working within a financial model with a very, very thin cash margin. We have stopped comparing ourselves to other Christian colleges, and we have developed new systems to ensure we are very careful to minimize any expense that could potentially increase the cost of education for the students we serve. Warner Pacific's Mt. Tabor site—where we host traditional students (generally, eighteen- to twenty-two-year-olds)—has not been independently financially self-sustaining from the day I arrived at Warner Pacific. Our four satellite sites (East Portland; Southwest Portland; Vancouver, Washington; and Longview, Washington), which offer the Warner Pacific Adult Degree Program (ADP), supply the revenue to keep our Mt. Tabor site financially viable. Simply put, the tapestry we are weaving at Warner Pacific College is heavily dependent on the warp and woof of the ADP and the revenue it provides.

In the Portland region, there are thousands and thousands of adults who are unable to land the job they desire, receive the promotion they deserve, or fulfill the dream of setting an example for their children because they do not yet have a college degree. Warner Pacific is the place where Oregonians looking for a second chance or a vocational advancement go to college at night, after work, or after the kids have been picked up from school and dinner has been served. ADP is critical to our mission, and you'll find no college president with more appreciation for the critical work being done by the talented professionals serving evening learners. Adult degree programs throughout Christian higher education are often misunderstood, and my desire for sustained enrollment in our Adult Degree Program is first and foremost driven by the fact that we are providing a much-needed service to Portland's families. The financial realities, while prescient in budget discussions, are not the sole driver for my hope to grow ADP enrollment.

At our enrollment height in 2011, Warner Pacific's enrollment was 1,679. As of August 2016, our enrollment was 1,132. Because of this fluctuation, on more than one occasion, we have had to make incredibly difficult decisions and required a reduction in force. Any time employees transition because of financial realities, it is a challenge to all involved, and while I would never want to gloss over the weight of these experiences we have faced together, I have been proud of the fact that the women and men of Warner Pacific College have not once wavered in the mission God has set before us. The number of students enrolled is an obvious indicator all higher education institutions watch; however, we must not make the mistake of assuming that bigger is always better. Sure, we want to grow, but not at the expense of our most important enrollment statistic: as of fall 2016, 57 percent of the students at Warner Pacific College are students of color. This is more than a 400 percent increase from when I arrived in 2005!

This shift in diversity in the student population did not happen by accident, particularly in a city that is predominantly white. We have changed our approach to recruiting students, staffing the admission and financial aid offices, and are aggressive in addressing the obstacles often faced by diverse student populations at private Christian colleges. We have worked creatively to address language barriers, provide professional development for staff as they seek to understand the cultural identity and needs of students and their families, and have embraced the importance of building external partnerships with programs specifically focused on serving first-generation, low-income, and diverse high school students (e.g., Latino Network, Adelante Mujeres, Self Enhancement Inc. [SEI], College Possible, Future Connect, Gear-Up, and Advancement Via Individual Determination (AVID).

We have found that an educational environment that is both demanding and relationally supportive builds grit and aids students in their development of competence and resolve to persist and complete their college degree. In order to appropriately support students as they enroll and persist, the college has invested significantly in an expanded First Year Learning Community (FYLC) program. Each student is enrolled with fourteen other students in an FYLC that is supported for their first full academic year by two faculty members and two student mentors. Students engage in a three-course, freshman-year series that includes an urban topical course and two sequenced general education courses. The FYLC takes all three courses together and is supported throughout in regular meetings with faculty and mentors. Through the FYLC, students learn to navigate the systems of higher education, work through the stress of college life, and find support for academic achievement. With 59 percent of our students being first-generation college students, most do not have family members able to provide counsel about the realities of the college experience. In addition to the FYLCs, the college has built a strong Academic Success program and a network for Student Success that engages athletic coaches, counseling staff, and a staff volunteer mentoring program. Student Affairs has developed a strong support network and programming through the Student Diversity Council and Multicultural Student programming office. Students are encouraged to both lead and serve in organizations that address issues of justice and equity, as well as serve in organizations across the city of Portland that relate to their interests and address the significant issues of economic equity, gender equity, racial/ethnic equity, support for youth and children, support for the elderly and disabled, interfaith relationships, and ecological justice.

As more and more diverse students enroll at Warner Pacific, another significant challenge we face is the recruitment and retention of diverse staff and faculty. At present, the diversity among our employees and board is increasing, but not nearly as quickly as that of our students (with faculty of color at 15 percent, staff of color at 22 percent, and board members of color at 29 percent). We have an incredible opportunity and responsibility to invest in the next generation of diverse leadership, and who we hire is at the crux of our mission. It has never been truer that the "who" is more important than the "what." In the years ahead, our ability to grow and continually innovate will be predicated upon our ability to recruit Christ-centered leaders to serve at Warner Pacific who have experience working within historically marginalized communities. Our hiring, I am convinced, is what will propel us to the next level. We have intentionally implemented a diversity hiring plan that will provide a new level of accountability and intentionality to the hiring process. There are simply no shortcuts for what happens when the right people are in the right place at the right time. While progress has been made, our efforts over the last seven years have not yielded the results I desire, and this is an area of focused improvement for our leadership team—myself included.

Finally, and perhaps most challenging, is the fact that the resurgence of Warner Pacific College over the last seven years—no matter how forward thinking—has tactically, at times, felt a day late and a dollar short. The college is in great need to develop new academic programs, yet much of the market is currently saturated by other institutions that grew ahead of Warner Pacific. Many of the new programs we need to build require start-up capital, and our lack of historic fundraising success requires moment-by-moment donations to spur start-up projects.

Our donor base isn't nearly as broad and sophisticated as we need it to be in order to fully invest in the buildings and innovative projects we hold in the queue in our strategic plan. Warner Pacific needs to grow programs that fit the convergence of the needs of our students and the needs of the city of Portland. We are now listening well to the city, and we are at the table. It is clear that our commitment to serving diverse students puts us in an advantageous position. As a result, we will grow differently, and it is important for the city that we become more aggressive than we have been in previous decades. We see a distinct advantage to our urban location. When living in a city committed to innovative space and a green footprint, it's more responsible for us to *not* build sports facilities or additional buildings for evening learners. We are partnering with other organizations to fulfill our needs, which rings true in Portland and counteracts the mind-set that to flourish in private education, new buildings are required. Enrollment goals notwithstanding, for Warner Pacific to serve the city, it is our responsibility to consider how we commit to being a good neighbor, partner with other city organizations, and make investments to develop programs that reflect our city's needs for more students to graduate with applied liberal arts and more technical degrees.

No matter how frustrating these realities can be at times, I am encouraged and emboldened by the faithfulness God has displayed toward our work. The story of Warner Pacific College is a story of the loaves and fishes (Matt. 14:13–21). We bring what we have to Jesus, and he is the one responsible for feeding his people and taking care of the details. I trust God with Warner Pacific because I know he cares deeply about the students we serve. Too much is at stake for us to allow discouragement to derail our momentum now. We are following Jesus in the city. The call is clear. There is a powerful relationship between the students we serve, the education we provide, and the flourishing of the city.

HUMAN FLOURISHING

Jesus said the kingdom of God is "like a mustard seed, which is the smallest of all seeds on earth. Yet when planted, it grows and becomes the largest of all garden plants, with such big branches that the birds can perch in its shade" (Mark 4:31–32 NIV). I've been struck that the most common images Jesus used to describe life in the kingdom of God were things that grow. When you drop a mustard seed into the ground, it is nearly impossible to see. If it is in your pocket, it may be impossible to find. How could something so small become so impactful? Jesus is challenging his followers to remember that the kingdom of God requires initiative and time. In due time, all will see the seemingly insignificant flourish!

As an urban higher education institution designed to serve students from diverse backgrounds, Warner Pacific College knows that for Portland to flourish, its leaders of the future must reflect its demographics and be prepared to engage actively in a constantly changing world. Our Christ-centered, liberal arts approach challenges students to see the interrelatedness of all things. We believe that both learning and faith development happens best in the context of an authentic and supportive community. To flourish is to seek the answer to the question, who did God make us to be? Whether online or on campus, you can't spend much time at Warner Pacific without recognizing our declaration: We are Christ-centered! We are urban! We are diverse! We practice inclusive excellence and the liberal arts! We are preparing the leaders of the future!

Consider the story of Adam, a 2013 Warner Pacific College alumnus. Having lived his entire life in the often-tumultuous streets of inner Southeast Portland, Adam Ristick has had to overcome adversity since he was a small child. Raised in the chaos of situational poverty and addiction, a Young Life leader stepped into Adam's life and began to mentor him—pushing him to break through. (Young Life is a group of caring adults who go where kids are, win the right to be heard, and share the Gospel of Jesus Christ with them.) Adam was the first in his family to graduate from high school. With an insatiable desire to learn and a natural gift for loving others, Adam cultivated a deep connection to his community, which ignited a dream that seemed impossible to others in his situation. Adam wanted to go to college. Through hard work and determination, he was awarded a spot in the inaugural Act Six Scholarship cadre at Warner Pacific. Adam struggled early on in the classroom—even failing Math 101 twice. A community of believers came alongside Adam in his adversity, and Adam showed the world he had grit. By his junior year, Adam was involved in tutoring middle-school students from his neighborhood as he flourished in his Human Development major. On campus, Adam eventually ran for office and became the student body president at Warner Pacific.

Today, Adam's passion for the transformative work of Christ has developed a longing within him to see his city flourish. As the Director for Scholarships and Internships at Portland Leadership Foundation, Adam is now responsible for annually recruiting and selecting five diverse, multicultural cadres of Oregon's most promising emerging leaders (forty-nine per year). Adam also leads Portland's largest internship program, designed for diverse college students.

Jesus suggests that if you want to know if a tree is healthy, look at its fruit (Matt. 7:17–18). During his time at Warner Pacific College, Adam was able to find a unique balance between academic striving and community service, all while honoring his Roma Gypsy heritage and family. Through academic achievement, leadership development, and personal introspection, Adam has discovered that he can be of two cultures and still follow one Christ. With his strong mind and humble heart, Adam is able to function within the many subcultures of Portland, blending his wide variety of coursework and his diverse cultural experience into a single voice for the Christ he follows.

Adam is the prime example of how equitable access to Christ-centered, liberal arts higher education can change the trajectory of an entire community. Warner Pacific exists for the flourishing of our students and our city. Adam Ristick is the embodiment of how this commitment hits the street. His vocation is directed and guided by the Christ-centered calling to love our neighbors as ourselves. He has embraced his urban roots and is working to see Portland flourish. He faces obstacles armed with the critical thinking and collaborative problem solving learned in his liberal arts training, and since his graduation in 2013, Adam has already empowered hundreds of diverse students to successfully pursue their dreams of higher education. Adam's is one among the many stories of transformation of Warner Pacific College students and graduates who are now helping the city flourish through the investment of their talent and leadership.

CONCLUSION

I grew up the daughter of a cattle rancher in a small rural town in eastern Oregon. Many of my intuitive leadership skills come from the ranch and the experiences I was privy to, working with my dad. My father, Wayne Cook, is eighty-eight years old, and to this day, he still works twelve-hour days caring for those in his herd. Over the years, I've tried to figure out ways to share my concern for his safety and his health. We've talked on multiple occasions about transitioning into a more relaxed lifestyle. The truth is, there is just no quit in Wayne Cook. No matter how he feels or what the weather holds, he will be out working the sprinkler pipe tomorrow morning.

Over the years, I have often been misunderstood because of the number of hours I put in at work. I inherited my dad's "no quit" attitude. I am certain that although I never sought to be a college president, God has been preparing me for this work. Serving as the president at Warner Pacific College has challenged me to give my very best, and in the face of adversity, I am often aware that no matter how hard I work, there is nothing I can personally do to take Warner Pacific to the next level. God loves the city, and he loves the students we serve. This is his work. If we are available and willing to take the risks as he beckons, I believe the days ahead for Warner Pacific and for Christian colleges and universities across the world are very bright.

I cannot predict what is ahead, but I can promise this: we are holding tight to God's leadership at Warner Pacific, and we will not quit.

FOR DISCUSSION

1. President Cook stated that in order for Warner Pacific College to move from a position of surviving to one of thriving, the institution would have to be bold and "all-in" with regard to its urban identity. What would an "all-in" commitment to diversity and inclusion look like for your institution? What does it mean to "be bold," and what bold steps would need to be taken on your campus to realize cultural and systemic change?

2. What is your institution's "identity"? How is your current institutional identity helping or hindering your efforts to become a diverse and inclusive campus? At what point does an institution alter its identity in order to become diverse and inclusive? To what extent, if any, is this conversation taking place on your campus?

3. The leadership of Warner Pacific made numerous strategic decisions and developed a plan to position the college for effective service in the rapidly changing greater Portland area. What are your institution's strategic

priorities? Does your institution have a strategic plan for diversity and inclusion? If so, is it being implemented and assessed for effectiveness? If not, what will it take for your institution to develop one?

4. As Warner Pacific College more boldly embraced its urban Christian liberal arts identity, President Cook appointed thirteen leaders from the college to form the President's Urban Commission. Warner Pacific then invited the Portland Leadership Foundation to facilitate the commission to help with planning the future. This strategic partnership led to the formulation of a bridge plan, new initiatives and academic programs, and a recalibrated mission statement. In what ways is your institution forming strategic partnerships with key constituents and stakeholders to help plan your future and to develop new initiatives and programs? Why are these partnerships important?

5. In the process of becoming an intentional urban Christian institution, those representing Warner Pacific College maintained a posture of humility and learning. They did not claim to have the answers to the needs of the city, nor did they presume to know what academic programs they should offer; rather, they sought out and learned from key constituents and stakeholders in the city, as well as from "street-level experts" already doing the work. How is your institution learning from experts in diversity and inclusion, urban ministry, and education? Why is it important to listen to those communities we seek to serve? How can we guard against presuming to know what diverse communities need from our colleges and universities without first asking?

6. In 2008, Warner Pacific recognized that it was no longer attracting the upper-middle-class white students that private Christian colleges had historically served. The college did not panic at this realization; rather, the leadership embraced a "decisive commitment" to serve the historically underserved by lowering tuition and adjusting the discount rates to make their education more accessible to these students. What are some of the concrete steps your institution is taking to make education more accessible to diverse students, including underserved, first-generation, low-income students?

7. In addition to modifying the historic approach to enrollment and financial aid, the college also provided professional development for faculty and staff, while also adding cocurricular programs to support these students once they arrived. What programs and personnel need to be added at your institution in order to support your students sufficiently? As a result of an increase in student diversity at your college or university, what are the professional development needs of faculty and staff? Do you have a plan for hiring diverse faculty and staff?

8. Further evidence of Warner Pacific College's commitment to the city and its people was the adoption of new initiatives and the launch of new academic programs such as the Adult Degree Program. How do the changing demographics or economic conditions of your community, sponsoring church, or denomination inform the planning of new initiatives and academic programs? Are there specific academic programs, majors, minors, certificates, locations, or delivery systems that should be considered in view of these ongoing changes?

9. President Cook wrote, "No matter how frustrating these realities can be at times, I am encouraged and emboldened by the faithfulness God has displayed toward our work." The work of diversity and inclusion is difficult and can be frustrating. Regardless, we believe this work is the will of God. Do you and your institution have a sense that God is in this work? How is God manifesting his presence and faithfulness toward your work? Are students' lives being transformed as a result? How are you being changed in the process?

NOTES

1   Martha E. Stortz, "Deepening the Theological Exploration of Vocation" (presented at the 2011 NetVUE Conference, Augsburg College, Concurrent Sessions, Indianapolis, IN, March 12, 2011).

2   Charles R. Swindoll, *Growing Strong in the Seasons of Life* (Grand Rapids: Zondervan, 1994), 322.

3   Jeff Mapes, "Oregon Not Quite Most 'Unchurched' State—But Close, New Survey Finds," The Oregonian/OregonLive, February 13, 2013.

4   Aimee Green, "*The Atlantic* Magazine Dubs Portland 'The Whitest City in America,'" The Oregonian/OregonLive, July 24, 2016.

5   Casey Parks, "After Gentrification," Oregonian/OregonLive, August 19, 2016.

6   Rob Wile, "Portland Is the Most Gentrified City of the Century," Fusion, February 4, 2105. *Priced Out: Gentrification beyond Black and White* (2015), documentary trailer. (Full documentary to be released in winter 2017.) A nonprofit project in partnership with Northwest Documentary Arts & Media, Production of SYDHONDA MEDIA, LLC.

7   See http://www.actsix.org.

8   Martin Luther King Jr., *I Have a Dream: Writings and Speeches that Changed the World*, ed. James M. Washington (San Francisco: Harper Collins, 1992), 85–86.

9   "Kotter's 8 Step Process: Identifying Important Elements to Successful Organisational Change," EBA, accessed May 3, 2017, http://www.educational-business-articles.com/8-step-process/.

CHAPTER FOUR

Greenville University

EDWIN F. ESTEVEZ, PhD

Greenville University, Senior Vice-President and Chief Operations Officer

After countless hours of practice, many innings played, and the ecstasy of achieving yet another win, Julio soaks in one last moment of glory. He had just hit the winning home run at his last high school baseball game. "You're the man!" friends and family shout, crowding around him. Julio feels capable, strong, and confident; he is a winner. *There is nothing that I can't do*, he thinks.

Meet Julio Gonzalez, eighteen years old and soon to be a first-year student at Greenville College in Illinois. (Note to readers: the institution officially became Greenville University on June 1, 2017.) Julio's family migrated from the Dominican Republic twelve years ago. His parents struggle economically and socially. They may not fully understand the systems that surround them and the opportunities available to them, but they still live the "American Dream" through their son. Julio stands on the threshold of an opportunity they have never known: attending college. The prospect excites them, yet also confuses them. With a deep understanding of their realities as Latinos in the United States, they made sure that Julio knew from a very young age that he must achieve good grades, graduate from high school, and go to college; they made sure he understood college was the key to his success.

Julio does his best to live up to the expectations of his family. Yet when he arrives at Greenville College, he carries with him some invisible "baggage":

- He arrives with a good but not fluent command of the English language.
- He expects that the degree he receives will serve as his ticket to greater freedom and economic security.
- He is excited about developing the independence and socialization required for adulthood, something he learned from peers who preceded him in leaving home and "going away" to college.

- If a baseball scholarship figures into the mix, Julio expects his athletic skills to be further developed under the leadership of a college coach.
- If he does not seek advice about how to prepare for the rigors and realities of college, he may enter with a measure of naiveté about the kinds of personal adjustments that will be required in the days to come.

As a first-year college student, and despite the baggage, Julio is full of excitement. He makes friends, attends classes, and gets to know his teammates. He recalls his grandmother's parting words of encouragement: "*Se un hombre de bien, mi hijo*" (be a good man, my son). He knows that the money she has been saving will contribute to helping him accomplish his goal—earning a degree in biology.

As the first weeks unfold, Julio sometimes feels encouraged in his classes, but often struggles to make sense of all the terms and concepts that are new to him. He wants to be a doctor; his family wants that for him, too. But his family isn't here. He feels isolated in this strange environment, limited by his less-than-native proficiency in the English language, and disconnected from his familiar sociocultural supports. He has not received even a single "A" on his papers, a grade his parents expect. Red marks fill the margins of his essays, along with comments like "needs further analysis," "weak sentence structure," and "improper use of pronoun." At midyear, he receives notification of low grades in two of his classes, one of them biology.

Julio is the backup shortstop on the baseball team, but he has also found collegiate ball to be more challenging than he had expected. Although he loves the team and the sport, here too he feels unplugged. He is one of two Latinos on the team, and, thus far in his college experience, he has not met any Latinos aside from his teammate. Adding to his sense of disconnectedness, there are few racial and ethnic minorities represented among the coaches, faculty, or staff.

Julio is unsure of what to do and where to go for help. He sometimes questions his decision to come to Greenville College and wonders if he can survive. His confidence fades. Anxieties and fears overwhelm him. He no longer feels prepared or well equipped; instead, he feels like he doesn't belong. *Why am I not with my family? How much will I have to give up to succeed? I feel like I have nothing left to give. What do I want in life? How will I get there? Will anyone help me? Is this place designed to help me thrive, or will I simply get lost in the crowd?*

As a student-athlete for whom Christian faith matters, Julio chose Greenville College. Although he feels capable and ready, is Greenville College ready for Julio? Does Greenville College have the support structures in place to help Julio succeed academically, spiritually, socially, and culturally? Julio will need help on several fronts.

A TRUE STORY: THEOLOGICAL ASSUMPTIONS, PRACTICAL THEOLOGY, GOSPEL-CENTRIC HOSPITALITY

Much of Julio's story is my story, just as his journey reflects my journey. Today, I serve as one of the few ethnic minority cabinet-level leaders in the membership of the Council for Christian Colleges & Universities. Like Julio, I emigrated from the Dominican Republic to the United States to complete my high school education. Like Julio's parents, my parents were motivated by the dream of seeing me pursue a better and more fulfilling life. However, unlike Julio's journey, our family's odyssey was intricately connected to the work of Greenville College long before I enrolled as a student—a connection that made all the difference in my journey to success.

Greenville College is rooted in the Free Methodist Church, a church that placed missionaries in the Caribbean island-nation of the Dominican Republic long before I was born. In 1918, about twenty-six years after the founding of Greenville College, these missionary-graduates of the college began the work of building relationships that would impact generations of persons in the Dominican Republic, including me. As a result, my family found Jesus Christ in the Free Methodist Church, and that link eventually led me from the Dominican Republic to Greenville College as an undergraduate student.

And while it is important to recognize that my story does not necessarily reflect the experience of every student of color at Greenville College, my experience can inform the decisions that lead to the intentional formation of a culturally sensitive and supportive campus.

At Greenville College, this level of intentionality can be categorized into three functional areas: a commitment to key theological assumptions, a strategy to develop bridge programs and activities, and a climate characterized by gospel-centered hospitality. I would not be a senior vice-president and chief operating officer at Greenville College today if it were not for the dedication of a few courageous leaders who were committed to the principles of diversity and inclusion stated in the three-pronged model shown in Figure 1.

Figure 1. Intentionality matrix at Greenville University

THEOLOGICAL ASSUMPTIONS AND INCLUSION

Picturesque Greenville (population 7,000) is nestled in the farm-rich region of south-central Illinois. Bordered by fertile corn and soybean fields, the campus is situated just off the interstate highway that neatly divides Bond County. St. Louis (population 317,000), a city that spans the Mississippi River, with "East" Saint Louis located in Illinois, is situated forty-five minutes to the west.

Seventeen structures on fifty acres within the Greenville city limits compose the mainly "red brick" campus of Greenville University. For nearly 125 years, this campus has served as a home to generations of eighteen- to twenty-two-year-old students from across the United States and around the world. The institution's rich history in the landscape of Christian higher education is marked by an institutional commitment to serve diverse populations. This historic commitment to inclusion purposefully reflects the kingdom of God and is rooted in the biblical teaching of Micah 6:8: "to act justly and to love mercy and to walk humbly with your God" (NIV).

This is the campus and ethos that I entered in 1990 as a sixteen-year-old from the Dominican Republic. That year I was one of fifty-seven new arrivals from ethnic and racially diverse backgrounds. We joined a student body already on campus that included 115 students of color. We settled into residence halls and attended classes. In my comings and goings, I often passed Almira House, a humble two-story frame building that comprised the entirety of the original college 135 years before my arrival.

Almira: Identity Rooted in Social Justice

In the mid-nineteenth century, Stephen Morse moved from New Hampshire to Greenville, where he met and married Almira Blanchard in 1844. The pair shared an interest in education, and specifically in educating young women in the way that Almira had been educated. More than a decade later, in 1855, Morse established a college for young women, supported in part by Almira's inheritance. He named the college in her honor.

A college for women was countercultural to the prevailing educational norms of the time and, more specifically, to the male-dominated culture. The choice demonstrated a level of thought and commitment on the part of Stephen and Almira Morse that would later pave the way for the institution's inclusion of other underserved groups and persons on society's margins.

Stephen Morse called on John White, his former classmate at Brown University, to lead the school, and White agreed. He journeyed from Tennessee up the Mississippi River by boat to St. Louis, with plans to make his way by stagecoach to Greenville. However, something on the trip stirred him to action on another matter of great social and moral significance. History tells us that by the time White reached St. Louis, he—a slave owner—had decided to free his slaves.

The story also goes that once in Greenville, White found himself standing on the footsteps of the local municipal building publically supporting the vision of presidential candidate Abraham Lincoln, who campaigned in the area sometime in 1858.[1] The prevailing themes of liberation and integration that fueled public debate during that presidential campaign influenced Almira College's unfolding identity.

The social and spiritual reform of the mid-nineteenth century also had an effect on the college. The demonstrated commitment of the founders of Almira College to a Christ-centered enterprise provided a fresh perspective on the importance of faith in action and a platform on which to develop and deliver an education in the Christian liberal arts.

Over time, such themes defined the work of the college and began to give it shape:

- A Christian liberal arts institution that served persons from all stations in life, including the marginalized and disenfranchised
- An educational mission fueled by the dedicated pursuit of justice and love of mercy
- A strong commitment to ideals that welcomed innovation

Enter the Free Methodists

After twenty-three years, ownership of Almira College passed to James Park Slade, who expanded it into a coeducational institution. In 1891, however, significant financial struggles prompted the sale of Almira College once again. This time, the prospect of new owners raised questions:

- Would the new owners continue the legacy of inclusion and diversity?
- Would they abandon the dedication to a Christian liberal arts education rooted in the pursuit of justice and love for mercy?
- Had the vision for social reform faded?

In 1892, ministerial and lay leaders of the Central Illinois Conference of the Free Methodist Church purchased the one-time lighthouse of education for women in south-central Illinois. They paid $12,200 for the college, which consisted of "Old Main" and several acres of land.[2] The new owners intended to

provide higher education for both men and women, with a commitment to
distinctive Christian influences. Reincorporated as an independent institution
under the name of Greenville College Corporation, authorization was granted
to confer the standard academic degrees.

Since reincorporating in 1893, the college and the Free Methodist Church
have shared a commitment to the Wesleyan theological tradition and have
maintained a rich legacy of mutual support in a voluntary relationship.[3]

While the sale of Almira College marked the end of an influential era, a
vibrant new vision began to take shape. A set of theological and philosophical
principles that also flowed from justice and mercy guided these new owners:

- Humility permeated their teaching and learning philosophies.
- They valued the liberal arts.
- Their mission to educate was Christ-centered.
- They believed that higher education must be made available to the poor and
  societal groups marginalized by systemic oppression.

The Methodist movement that began in England during this period "was
rooted among the industrial workers and miners and was finding its way to the
industrial laborers, coal miners, farmers, and slaves of Illinois."[4]

Free Methodists were catalysts in ensuring that this revolution within the
Christian church included a commitment to those in the population who had
been enslaved. Founded by Benjamin Titus Roberts in 1860, this Methodist
subgroup held to a theology that was socially conscious. Its members engaged
the systemic transformation of societal structures that prevented freedom for
all: they rejected class structures and segregated systems, and their outright
rejection of slavery and relentless commitment to the ordination of women set
them apart from others.

W. Richard Stephens, who was the eighth president of Greenville College
and a significant contributor to the diversification of the college, put it this way:

To us (Free Methodists), the gospel of Christ, which offers to set people
free, caused us early in our history to stand on the side of personal freedom from sin in all of its debilitating forms, both external and internal.
It caused us to stand for those key freedoms characteristic of historic
Protestantism. Our experience of Christ also caused us to stand for:

- Freedom of slaves,
- Freedom of women to be ordained as ministers,

- Freedom of farmers to pay fair railroad rates to ship their products to market,
- Freedom to sit in any pew in the church without regard for one's social class or ability to pay,
- Freedom [of] businessmen to take their place in the free enterprise market,
- Freedom of craftsmen/women to organize in unions,
- Freedom of conscience to refrain from or to participate in national wars,
- Freedom of members to participate in church government,
- Freedom for anyone—member or not—to worship in our churches and to receive the sacrament of communion upon confession of faith.[5]

In 1892, through the leadership Wilson T. Hogue, the young and vibrant scholar who served as its first president, Greenville College lifted it sails in the world of Christian higher education. A socially conscious intellectual and educator, Hogue placed effort in resuscitating the centrality of Wesleyan theology that focused on elevating the conditions of "the least of these." In turn, two social reformers, B. T. Roberts and Wilson T. Hogue, who strongly believed that character education through the liberating arts should be offered comprehensively to all, envisioned the development of an institution committed to seeking justice and loving mercy. Over many decades, this lighthouse in the most unlikely of geographical locations has served as an extension of a healthy interdependent partnership with the Free Methodist Church.

BRIDGE-BUILDING PROGRAMS: AN INSTITUTIONAL MODEL

While the story of Free Methodism and Greenville College (now Greenville University) is ongoing and the challenges continue 150 years later, an intentional dedication to hospitality drives the church and the college up to the present day. This "spirit" and desire to invite those on the margins has reached all over the world. Today, the number of those who identify as Free Methodists internationally is five times larger than the North American representation, yet the same commitments distinguish the denomination worldwide. As an institution of higher learning committed to freedoms that should produce access, Greenville University continues a journey that has yet to be completed. Recognizing that fact, the institution continues its intentional commitment to theological interpretations that promote access, persistence, and success for its students of color.

Bridging Theology and Mission

The relentless dedication of Free Methodists to the development of all people during the early part of the twentieth century triggered a number of missionary trips to the Dominican Republic. Through the early 1900s, young graduates from Greenville College and other Free Methodist institutions participated in trips to the island, then called Hispaniola, that planted seeds in a number of young minds interested in being light and salt around the world. While the struggles of the mid- to late 1800s in the United States affected the poor, the enslaved, women, and other minority groups, these struggles were no different in the developing world. Motivated by a theology of liberation, freedom, inclusivity, and hospitality, Free Methodists reached out to Santiago in the Dominican Republic. There, in this small town in the northwest part of the island, surrounded by beautiful mountain ranges, Free Methodists applied Wesleyan principles and put feet on their faith through social action. Also grounded in the Free Methodist movement was a dedication to education, and as a result of the missionary and seed-planting efforts, a bridge was built for students like Julio and me, leading to our subsequent enrollment at Greenville College.

Bridging Faith and Learning

The value of integrating faith and learning were evident in the early stages of Greenville College. B. T. Roberts, founding parent of Free Methodism, was convinced that

> education and religion should by no means be separated. Indeed, to divorce them is dangerous, as is proved by the history of the past. Ignorance is the mother of superstition and religious error, and a system of education that does not comprehend the great truths of revelation, fosters skepticism and infidelity in the youthful mind.[6]

This educational philosophy was a direct response to the practical theology that permeated the college's curriculum and practice. An active relationship between reason and faith, in addition to Scripture and experience, instilled character and service into the lives of Greenville College students. As Stephens (1991) noted:

> Some of the key factors which had contributed to success, and which remain to this very day, had been built in earlier years, and these include: (1) a clear and compelling mission that focuses on the educational imperative in the Christian faith, and the discipline motive to serve the present age which is provided through the prism of Wesleyanism and Free Methodist heritage; (2) a curriculum that is academically sound but always focused on the individual student (especially those from homes

of modest means) and his/her unique needs, talents and circumstances; (3) a most competent and spiritually committed faculty who have a missionary call to teach excellently, counsel caringly, and pray without ceasing in order to see Christ formed in each precious student, (4) a community of students who come to believe in themselves because they come to know the God and Father of our Lord Jesus Christ; and (5) a loyal, wide-ranging community of alumni and other friends, and trustees who give selflessly of their work, wisdom, and wealth.[7]

GOSPEL-CENTRIC HOSPITALITY

The commitment of Greenville College to offering an education based on character and service is reflected in its history of inclusion, rooted in a vision of the kingdom of God and the practice of justice and mercy. This commitment has not always been perfectly lived out at the college, and there is still much to accomplish in these areas and beyond. Nevertheless, the unshakeable dedication to a spirit of hospitality provides a degree of institutional success by welcoming and serving students of racial and ethnic diversity. The spirit of hospitality is central to the gospel of Jesus Christ. Otherwise, how would it be possible for students from Latin America, Asia, Africa, East St. Louis, South Side Chicago, California, and Miami to find themselves thriving in a completely foreign environment in the midst of cornfields and bean farms? Over the decades, "making room" and receiving diverse groups as gifts to the community serve as examples of the theological and philosophical DNA of the college. International student housing, student orientation programs to diverse populations, multicultural festivals, dinners at faculty homes, and transportation to urban amenities constitute a few examples of how Greenville College over the years welcomed students from diverse backgrounds.

My maternal grandfather Pedro would often say, "When I visit friends, I'd like to be treated as a guest, not as family." He would declare: "When you are treated as 'family' in a guest's house, they ask you to serve yourself. When you are treated as guests, they serve you." His attempt at ensuring that a spirit of hospitality would never die has stayed with me until today, and it is reflected in the Free Methodist approach to hospitality evident on the Greenville campus.

HONEST REFLECTION: LINKING THE PAST WITH THE PRESENT

Forthrightness in the intentional interdependent relationship between the Free Methodist denomination and its churches, its theology, and its history undergirds the commitment of our campus to educate students in an inclusive environment. From the planting of the first Free Methodist church to the establishment of its colleges, from the first president to today's leadership, Greenville was, and still is, fully committed to a theology of integration and a gospel of hospitality.

Greenville University's journey from the past to the present has not been perfect, nor have the ideals of our founders been fully realized. I am not blinded by idealism or sensationalism regarding the early stages of our history—for as good and effective as the theological implementation was, shortcomings persisted. Over the course of the 1990s and 2000s, while international students of color enrolled frequently, African American students still struggled to be accepted at the college. Regarding faculty diversity, despite the significant efforts to attract faculty of color by chief academic officers like Dr. Karen Longman, such faculty found it hard to thrive in what at times seemed like a non-inclusive rural campus environment.

Further, it was not until the 2015–16 academic year that a program to attract high achieving students of color was instated. During a time of financial constraints in higher education and at the college in particular, the board of trustees authorized the creation of the "Mosaic Scholars Program" to provide a solid platform that intentionally and strategically carried out Greenville's historic commitment to gospel-centric hospitality. Now in its second year of operation, the Mosaic Scholars Program has resulted in more than thirty students of color being recruited to the college, and this effort has strengthened our connection to our theological roots. Further, the growing number of diverse students on our campus benefits the entire campus community and enriches the learning environment in new and profound ways.

In an address to the faculty during the 1989 Faculty Fall Fellowship, President W. Richard Stephens described a distinctive dimension of the Greenville student body as follows:

> Students will bring those Christian ideals of stewardship of one's time and talent, which often helps them achieve far beyond what one may expect, and even excel over many other students with richer intellectual and cultural backgrounds. Socially, culturally, and racially, our students very likely will not be representative of the larger population. . . . It is clear that the lion's share of our students are not spoiled children from affluent families. . . . Culturally and racially, the student body will be comprised of 10–15 percent minorities. These minorities will be the rare ones who make it to college, and they will bring much potential and, as well, the needs which characterize most minorities in higher education today.

These students are precious resources and we have learned much as a faculty about how to teach and work with them to [ensure their success]. Beyond what the college can do for them, the presence of our minority students helps us enrich the Christian liberal arts education of all of us.[8]

In reading these words, I sense how students like Julio and I were able to benefit from the institutional support that enhanced our growth. This practical implementation of theological convictions has been present at Greenville College through the generations and triggered the implementation of programming to achieve deeply held commitments. The benefits of such commitments and programming not only reach the students, they also grow and develop the institution as a whole. The spirit of Free Methodism, rather than an isolated effort of compliance, in turn, shapes institutional structures, programs, services, and leadership. This spirit creates opportunities to develop "homegrown talent." History shows that when this sprit is absent, the challenges are real and the lack of progress is evident.

Small institutions like Greenville University cannot afford to miss the opportunities of developing intentional mechanisms that maximize the power of a diverse community. Geographical location cannot be used as an excuse to not attract and develop the critical mass of diverse students necessary to enrich the campus. Over the last decade, Greenville averaged a 14 percent minority student population. Today, the university serves a student body that is 22 percent people of color, with a goal to reach 30 percent by the year 2020. These goals are possible because the legacy of intentionality continues, as does the courage to live out the institution's theological convictions, building supportive bridges and extending hospitality to promote a Christ-centered environment for all students.

WHAT WE CONTINUE TO LEARN

Our best intentions must generate positive impact and progress, as well as create a climate for ongoing learning and conversation. The Greenville community continues to engage in substantive reflection, analysis, and conversation around diversity that characterizes our commitment to better reflect the kingdom of God. The following points represent a few of the conversations that continue to take place among the leadership and broader campus community.

Student Engagement, Support, and Success

The Greenville University of today remains a work in progress when it comes to the design and implementation of appropriate support systems for students of ethnic and racial minority groups. At present, many students like Julio arrive at the college's doorstep and fail to find the support they need for success. In reality, the college falls short in the delivery of intentional efforts that support the holistic growth of minority students. Yet we are honest about our shortcomings, and we continuously work to serve our students with excellence, while also living out the ideals of our founders.

Nevertheless, students like Julio and I received a direct benefit from the theological practices that involve the inclusion of "the other." Institutions like Greenville that firmly believe in an applied faith, whereby works give testimony to the beliefs, are positioned to nurture campus environments that promote diversity and inclusion. Within the parameters of a liberating education, early Free Methodists were committed to promoting and advancing the kingdom of God on earth in creative ways. This early movement didn't have boundaries or borders. In fact, Free Methodist institutions facilitated creative endeavors and pushed for the elimination of all systemic boundaries that excluded those most oppressed by our systems.

While some systems of higher education around the world seek to model aspects of what US colleges and universities offer, higher learning in the United States continues to be respected and even ranked at the top in the eyes of many. Applications for the I-20 visa—the permit required for international students to study in the United States—had increased dramatically over recent years, although the situation has become more challenging due to changing federal guidelines. According to the US Department of Commerce, in 2015 international students contributed approximately $30.5 billion a year to the US economy.[9]

When it comes to serving diverse high school graduates like Julio, however, the US system falters. Despite billions of dollars invested in remedial education, academic support services, and special ethnic-centric programs designed to help them succeed, students of color and low-income students from all ethnic and cultural groups graduate at much lower rates than high-income and majority group students.[10] This shortcoming could easily negatively influence the outcome of the stories of students like Julio.

Effectively engaging students in the learning process affects college completion rates. Research indicates that a lack of academic engagement contributes to early departure for many students. And while academic engagement is critical, so is the need for strong sociocultural engagement.

Access and Affordability

Degree completion is important at Greenville University, and the institution's response to key questions may determine what transpires next: Can Greenville help students like Julio acquire the skills needed to adapt to this strange and new landscape? Is Greenville equipped with the necessary infrastructure to support diverse students? Are its leaders equipped with the emotional intelligence that will provide the needed support? What theological convictions will continue to motivate the policies and practices of Greenville University, particularly in terms of determining the appropriate level of support, including financial aid?

Interested stakeholders from academia have called for a recommitment to student learning and personal development as the primary focus for higher education. Over the past thirty years, increased attention has been paid to the "preparation of graduates."[11] Such attention has been coupled with incremental concerns about the overall behavior of students and a general institutional responsibility for the outcomes of a college education.[12] Student retention and graduation rates that are lower than desired have created alarms throughout higher education given increased awareness of the importance of having a well-prepared citizenry. When race and economic background are determinant demographical factors, the importance of this issue is even more pronounced.

Concerns have intensified as higher numbers of minority students are attending postsecondary institutions all over the country. In addition, various factors have triggered higher tuition rates among US colleges and universities, making it harder for institutions to attract, retain, and issue degrees to students like Julio. In addition, because of the complex problems eroding US elementary and secondary school systems, the new pool of high school students is significantly underprepared for a college education. Institutions like Greenville must subsequently wrestle with how to address the challenges related to accessibility and the affordability of a college education.

Beyond Hospitality: Emotionally Intelligent Programming

The shortcomings of Greenville College over the years have led to honest introspection and institutional learning. As a result, the institution was motivated to integrate ongoing organizational change in an emotional intelligence framework. According to noted psychologist Daniel Goleman, to be emotionally intelligent involves the ability to integrate intelligence, empathy, and emotions in order to enhance thought and understanding.[13] While the research on this model can be categorized as incomplete, for our purposes, the five key elements proposed by Goleman become the central focus in understanding how individuals demonstrate emotional intelligence. I believe that Christian colleges, like individuals, have the capacity to develop and demonstrate these same key elements. In addition, as history shows us, the Wesleyan roots of the Free Methodist movement are centered on a unique balance between reason, tradition, experiences, and Scripture.

According to Goleman, 67 percent of the high-performance abilities in leadership can be attributed to emotional intelligence. How then can emotional intelligence be incorporated into the organizational culture of a Christian college in which the gospel of hospitality, merged with key theological assumptions, creates a campus environment where students from diverse backgrounds thrive? Goleman describes the five characteristics of emotional intelligence in the following ways.[14] In response, I offer comments and ask questions from the perspective of diversity within the context of Christian higher education.

- *Self-awareness.* The ability to recognize and understand the emotional/ affective response as well as the effect on others. It is critical that institutions expand their understanding of the narrative that feeds diversity and inclusion stories. Singular narration by those in power is dangerous. In turn, self-awareness of how all stories unfold is necessary.

    > *Theological awareness.* Are institutional leaders and educational practitioners familiar with the historical and current issues that influence students, faculty, and staff from ethnic and racial minority groups? How can Christian colleges and universities expand an understanding of their theological assumptions and how those assumptions either support or hinder the development of members from ethnic/ racial minority groups?

    > *Policy.* Is the campus leadership aware of the policies and procedures that may perpetuate an unwelcoming environment for people from ethnic/racial minority backgrounds?

    > *Programs.* To what extent has the institution designed appropriate programming to promote and enhance the growth of its ethnic/ racial minority students?

- *Self-regulation.* The ability to control or redirect disruptive impulses and moods. In other words, thinking before acting. Organizational responses often lack appropriate thought about issues that directly affect students from ethnically and racially diverse backgrounds. Appropriate institutional self-regulation invites the difficult conversations, does not pretend that racially charged problems are nonexistent, and seeks to provide safe spaces for students who otherwise find themselves threatened or in an isolated environment.

- *Motivation.* A passion to work toward a gospel-centric approach to diversity. The goal is for institutions to move from "doing diversity programs" to "being diverse." This movement is fueled by an intrinsic motivation that intelligently places matters of diversity at the forefront of institutional planning, leadership, and student body representation, with a faculty and staff composition that is at least representative of the student body.

- *Empathy.* The ability to understand the challenges and difficulties of those in the minority. The attempt to understand how these experiences impact students from underrepresented groups and to promote empathic responses that connect the institution to the depth of these experiences. Can colleges and universities feel the totality of the challenges that students from ethnic/racial minority groups experience?
- *Social skill.* The ability to build rapport, common ground, and support. From residential life to the classroom experience, the capacity of a college or university to skillfully build rapport, create common understanding, and promote relational dialogue. Does the institution know how to relate socially to its diverse student population?

CONCLUSION

The story of Julio Gonzalez is representative of the stories of thousands of ethnic and racially diverse students throughout the United States who are considering enrollment, or are currently enrolled, at one of our many Christian colleges and universities—stories of students who find themselves in need of a supportive educational environment that can assist them holistically in the fulfillment of their dreams to achieve a college degree and who hope for a better life for themselves and their families. But perhaps the greater story is found in the valiant efforts of small rural colleges and universities like Greenville. Despite facing numerous challenges including declining populations in the Midwest region, fewer numbers of diverse students in the region, and significant fiscal constraints, kingdom priorities are honored as the campus community continues to persevere toward the vision of being a diverse and inclusive campus community.

FOR DISCUSSION

1. Compare the journeys of Julio and the author, Edwin. Can you speculate about what factors may have contributed to Edwin's success at Greenville College and those that may have contributed to Julio's struggles?

2. In telling the story of Julio, Dr. Estevez writes, "Julio will need help on several fronts." Given Julio's story, in what specific ways does Julio need help and support? Why?

3. What is the responsibility of ethnic/racial minority students to adjust to the demands of college? What is the responsibility of the college to help its ethnic/racial minority students succeed?

4. What theological convictions motivated the faculty, staff, and administration of Greenville College to provide the necessary and appropriate support systems to help students like Julio succeed?

5. In what ways can collegiate athletics provide access, meaning, purpose, sociocultural support, and mentoring to ethnic/racial minority student-athletes? What are some of the benefits and limitations of the cocurricular experience for ethnic/racial minorities?

6. The lesson from Grandpa Pedro offered a unique perspective on the concept of hospitality. Grandpa Pedro believes that one is treated better as a guest than as a member of the family. Do you agree or disagree with Grandpa Pedro?

7. The Free Methodists and Greenville College adopted both long-term strategies (mission trips to the Dominican Republic beginning in the early 1900s) and much more recent enrollment strategies (the Mosaic Scholars Program). Has your institution made a commitment to having a variety of enrollment strategies to reach and then serve diverse students, both in terms of US ethnic/racial minorities and international students?

8. Edwin benefited from being mentored and encouraged to pursue his doctoral studies, professorship, and administrative roles by caring professors, administrators, and other key leaders at the school. In what ways is your institution intentionally identifying and mentoring emerging leaders of color or potential members of the faculty?

9. Does your institution regularly engage in a process of self-study, introspection, and assessment of its diversity programming? Can you think of forums, formal or informal, in which your institution openly talks about its shortcomings and how they can be addressed? How does your institution learn from failure or setbacks?

10. One of the testimonies of the Free Methodist Church is the commitment over a long period of time to specific core values, key theological assumptions, and faith in action. How does a faith-based institution sustain a long-term commitment to doing justice, loving mercy, and walking humbly with God, despite the challenges, trials, and setbacks?

NOTES

1   W. Richard Stephens, *A River of Streams: Writings* (Greenville, IL: Tower Press of Greenville College, 1991). Mary A. Tenney, *Still Abides the Memory* (Greenville, IL: Tower Press of Greenville College, 1942).

2   Tenney, *Still Abides the Memory,* 48.

3   Ibid., 49.

4   Stephens, *A River of Streams*, 4.

5   Ibid., 30.

6   Ibid., 4.

7   Ibid., 12.

8   Ibid., 109.

9   Institute for International Education, "Open Doors Data Report 2016," accessed May 6, 2017, https://www.iie.org/en/Research-and-Insights/Open-Doors/Data.

10 National Center for Education Statistics, "Degrees Conferred by Race and Sex," accessed May 15, 2017, https://nces.ed.gov/fastfacts/display.asp?id=72.

11 Wingspread Group on Higher Education, *An Imperative: Higher Expectations for Higher Education* (Racine, WI: Johnson Foundation, 1993).

12 Ernest T. Pascarella and Patrick T. Terenzini, *How Colleges Affect Students* (San Francisco: Jossey-Bass, 1991). Alexander W. Astin, "The Cause of Citizenship," *The Chronicle of Higher Education*, 35 (1995): B1–2.

13 Daniel Goleman, *Emotional Intelligence* (New York: Bantam, 1995).

14 Daniel Goleman, *Working with Emotional Intelligence* (New York: Bantam, 1998).

WHY WE STAYED

LESSONS IN RESILIENCY AND LEADERSHIP FROM LONG-TERM CCCU DIVERSITY PROFESSIONALS

Introduction

SPEAKING UP FOR SUCH A TIME AS THIS

Michelle R. Loyd-Paige, PhD

Calvin College, Executive Associate to the President for
Diversity and Inclusion, Professor of Sociology

> For if you remain silent at this time, relief and deliverance for the Jews will arise from another place, but you and your father's family will perish. And who knows but that you have come to your royal position for such a time as this?
> —Esther 4:14 (NIV)

For such a time as this. This, a time when colleges and universities across the United States and around the world are experiencing an increase in the number of underrepresented students and yet have not experienced a similar increase in underrepresented faculty and staff. This, a time when the ugly truth of unresolved racial tensions have rocked college and university campuses. This, a time when underrepresented students are demanding a more diverse faculty and administration. And this, a time when Christian colleges and universities are looking for ways to grow and retain diverse leadership. Five long-term CCCU member institution diversity professionals have come forward to share their experiences as leaders who have shaped and continue to shape the conversation around how diversity matters on their campuses.

The contributors to this section—Glen Kinoshita, Jeanette Hsieh, Kimberly Battle-Walters Denu, Michelle Loyd-Paige, and Rodney Sisco—were specifically invited to reflect and write about their experiences at Christian colleges and universities. Their selection was based on several criteria: a person of deep Christian conviction who speaks openly about their faith in connection with their work; self-identifies as a person of color; employed at a Christian college or university for twenty or more years; holds a reputation for implementing positive diversity change at their respective institution; and a person who has been sought by those within the CCCU and outside the CCCU for their expertise as a diversity professional. Collectively, these five represent more than

140 years of experience in the CCCU. Individually, they average more than twenty-five years of leadership and service at a single institution. Over the years, they have experienced obstacles and disappointments, grace and triumph, and weariness and joy on both a personal and institutional level. Their stories are stories of resiliency.

Each contributor was invited to respond to a question often posed to each them, "Why have you stayed?," and to share the lessons they have learned along the way about resiliency, leadership, diversity, and "moving the needle" on diversity efforts. Each was eager to speak up for such a time as this. The authors not only addressed the question of "why" they have remained in Christian higher education for so long, but also the questions of "how?" and "at what cost?" Each person easily identified the lessons that had been learned on the higher education journey, which have been many and varied. As an example, Glen Kinoshita writes about connecting vocation and intrinsic values, encouraging readers to be self-aware in doing diversity work. Rodney Sisco reflects the goal and challenge to "finding the win" in his diversity work. Kimberly Battle-Walters Denu articulates a set of spiritual strategies that have defined her work, reminding us all that this work is kingdom work. Michelle Loyd-Paige writes about being surprised at her own longevity, and Jeanette Hsieh reflects on the importance of developing and utilizing a cultural lens to usher in institutional change. The content of these lessons and many more await the reader.

Each chapter is a personal narrative containing an individual story. Each chapter begins with an intimate story that is usually reserved for sharing only with close friends and known allies; these are not the stories shared with strangers, because of the vulnerability required of each author. Longevity, earned competence, and self-awareness have empowered each essayist to be courageously vulnerable. In addition, there is strength in numbers. These contributors were able to share their personal stories because they are not stories being told as isolated expressions of experience. When people of color share their experiences, their statements are often questioned, dismissed, or met with stories from members of the majority about how they have also faced microaggressions or felt alone. But in this section, people of color are sharing their experiences without having to worry about not being believed or having to think about how to manage the feelings of the person they are addressing.

These stories, their stories, provide a window into the calling and challenges the authors have experienced while leading diversity efforts on their campuses. As one can imagine, the road has not been easy, and each author bears battle scars. Yet these chapters are not solely about challenges and hardship. On the contrary, within these pages, the reader will find hope, commitment, resolve, and resiliency. Each chapter can, and does, stand on its own; however, collectively these stories strengthen a threefold cord that is present in each story: faith that is personal, connections that are supportive, and convictions that are bigger than the individual. The next five chapters contain the wisdom of "tall oaks." There are lessons that have been learned the hard way. Lessons that are freely and honestly shared in hopes that others will benefit and that the future of diversity at our Christian colleges and universities will be brighter.

Chapter Five

GOING DEEP: CONNECTING VOCATION, CONVICTION, AND HUMAN THRIVING

GLEN K. KINOSHITA, MDIV

Biola University, Director of Imago Dei Initiatives

The place God calls you to is the place where your deep gladness and the world's deep hunger meet.
—Frederick Buechner[1]

"I have nothing left to give!" These were the words of a diversity professional who had just attended a workshop on diversity I conducted at a national conference a few years ago. The feelings of exhaustion overwhelmed her as she connected with me after the session. Through my years of doing diversity work in Christian higher education, I also have experienced the painful challenge of navigating resistance and being frustrated at the slow pace of change. All too often, I have had conversations with colleagues from across the country as they were processing the decision of whether or not to leave their institution. Many enter the work with high hopes that change will come, but in the end, the vast majority leave after a few years, feeling dejected and defeated. A term that describes this reality is "racial battle fatigue," which is "the anxiety experienced by racially underrepresented groups as well as those engaged in race work with a focus on the physical and psychological toll taken due to constant and unceasing discrimination, microaggressions and stereotype threat."[2] We experience racial battle fatigue because the dominant culture pushes back to maintain its status quo while we are seeking to promote inclusion and equity on our campuses. The resistance to institutional change is thus systemic in nature. Given this reality, I have often been asked: "Why do you stay?" In order to answer, I have had to search deep within.

SOWING SEEDS IN FALLOW GROUND

My career in Christian higher education started more than twenty-five years ago. I originally aspired to serve in ministry as either a pastor or missionary, so to equip myself I enrolled at Biola University and then Talbot School of Theology. Upon completion of my master's of divinity degree, the door that opened to me was not in ministry but in student development. Apart from a few student clubs, programs to promote diversity or to support students from diverse backgrounds did not exist on my campus. As a result, I began attending workshops and conferences on secular campuses to learn how programming was done and how discussions were facilitated. These opportunities represented rich learning experiences, as I found the interaction about diversity and social issues to be energetic and insightful.

As a result of the exposure I received from secular campuses, I sought to implement similar programming and discussions on my campus. I would advertise various program opportunities to the general campus community, as well as introduce topics of diversity to the students in the classes I was teaching. The campus reaction, however, was rarely receptive and even at times hostile. Common complaints were that diversity was a political agenda and not central or relevant to a biblical worldview. My use of the term "reconciliation" to describe our work in a Christian context was also met with significant pushback. Many people took exception to the term because they felt it inferred the reality of problems or conflicts with diverse others on our campus. Some who pushed back insisted they had no need to be reconciled with anyone. In one instance, a faculty member sent me an email protesting my use of the word *reconciliation* because he felt that the biblical usage was strictly vertical and not horizontal.

Generally speaking, students of color were more prone to embrace the conversations on diversity than were the white members of our campus community. Yet walking with them to process their pain of marginalization was also a challenge. The constant pressure for students of color to adapt to the dominant culture in order to survive necessitated the creation of safe spaces for them to breathe, to be their authentic selves. Much of my time was devoted to providing a listening ear and emotional support for students as they worked through racial battle fatigue. I learned early on that I would daily have to navigate working in disparate social contexts throughout my campus.

The resistance I encountered through the years related to the belief of many in our society that engaging in conversations about diversity is only necessary for people who display explicit attitudes of bias and intolerance. Because most people on Christian college campuses consider themselves "good people," they conclude that such discussions are not relevant to them. The varied responses to the conversation on diversity made it apparent that our society is divided along lines of race and class, with many of us living socially separate lives, which results in a lack of intercultural awareness and competence. These reactions are often indicative of thought patterns that shape the culture of many institutions, thus making progress difficult.

The longer I stay in this work, the more I am asked how have I persevered. In thinking about how to respond, the key question for me became not so much "Why continue?" but rather "Who am I?" In his book *Let Your Life Speak: Listening for the Voice of Vocation*, Parker Palmer offered this response to a similar question: "I must listen to my life telling me who I am. I must listen for the truths and values at the heart of my own identity, not the standards by which I must live—but the standards by which I cannot help but live if I am living my own life."[3] Reflecting back, I can see many signposts along the way that aided me in hearing what my life was saying. The result is a connection between vocation and my intrinsic values that keeps me grounded to this day.

CALLING: BRIDGING CULTURAL CHASMS

My great-grandparents were among the thousands that emigrated from Japan to Hawaii to work in the sugarcane industry in the late 1800s. Our family tree grew from there for three generations on the island of Oahu. I was the first to be born on the West Coast when my parents moved to Los Angeles to find employment. When I was about seven years old, my grandmother moved from Hawaii to live with our family. My grandmother was what we refer to as "Kibei"—she was a Japanese American who was born in Hawaii but socialized as a child in Japan with her grandparents. As a result, though she was a second generation Japanese American (Nisei), the language and culture most comfortable to her reflected that of her grandparents in Japan. My parents were third generation Japanese American (Sansei) and grew up in Hawaii, and my siblings and I are fourth generation (Yonsei), born and raised in Southern California.

The home I grew up in consisted of three generations of Japanese Americans—three distinct cultures that resulted in culture clashes on a daily basis. Growing up in Southern California also provided a rich socialization process outside our home, as I was exposed to a wide variety of people and cultures on a daily basis. This cultural context also created many challenges, as I was growing up to be a person who embodied worldviews that were unfamiliar to my parents and grandmother; thus, the generation gap between us was also a cultural chasm. The middle school I attended was urban and predominately African American. As time passed and I acclimated into this culture, my family moved and, as a result, I was thrust into a predominately white, suburban middle school. Again, I had to acclimate to an entirely new environment, culturally and socioeconomically.

My college and graduate school years were spent on a predominately white campus. Although I sought to adjust to the campus environment, I kept coming up against what seemed to be an invisible wall of exclusion. Eventually I found a circle of friends that was primarily a global community, consisting of third culture and international students; that network of support continued throughout graduate school. My church affiliation through the years consisted of white, Asian American, African American, Filipino immigrant, and multiethnic congregations. International travel to seventeen different countries provided me with rich learning opportunities as well as milestones in my identity formation.

Culture shock, adaptation, and paradigm shifts have been a regular part of my life since my formative years. Ethnic identity development would be a long, arduous process that was a struggle throughout most of my youth. Not until I entered my young adult years did I embrace these complexities as a gift. Wrestling with issues of marginalization, navigating differences, and unpacking the layers and nuances of my personhood all helped form the context in which I determined my calling and became the person I was born to be. I heard my life speaking, moving me to explore deeper intrinsic values of being a Christ follower.

SHALOM: A VISION OF HUMAN FLOURISHING

> ...the Lord lift up his countenance upon you and give you peace.
> —Numbers 6:26 ESV

> ...and you shall be like a watered garden...
> —Isaiah 58:11 ESV

Through the years, I have made connections with individuals who are deep in the trenches of challenging work such as immigration, serving the urban poor, and racial reconciliation. I would often hear them talk and write about a life-giving concept called *shalom*. Because I could relate to many of the same challenges, I committed to learn about shalom and how it could apply to my vocation. Through my studies, I discovered that shalom permeates the pages of Scripture. Author Lisa Sharon Harper offers this framework in describing shalom:

This good news inspires work toward a world where justice and mercy roll down together into a mighty stream. It guides the journey toward a world where all the relationships in creation are brought back into right relationship with each other. A vibrant peace will prevail between people and God, men and women, families, ethnic groups, nations, and humans and the rest of creation, and oppressive systems and structures will be transformed to serve humanity and help each person thrive. The bible captures this kind of world in the word *shalom* (holistic peace). *Shalom* is what the kingdom of God smells, tastes, feels, and looks like. It is justice, peace, mercy, reciprocity, harmony, integrity, beauty, truth telling, restoration, and reparation, just for starters.[4]

Shalom is the vision of wholeness for the people of God, where flourishing occurs within a faith community. Shalom gave depth and meaning to my work in higher education, as I would frame the overarching vision and goals back to the concepts of thriving and wholeness for the people of God. Theologian Cornelius Plantinga has summarized this key biblical concept: "Shalom, in other words, is the way things ought to be."[5] Shalom gave direction in the midst of confusion, it gave comfort in the midst of pain, it grounded me in the midst of feeling isolated. I began to make the connection that shalom is not only God's will for each of us, but for our institutions as a whole. As the psalmist declares, ". . . seek peace (shalom) and pursue it" (Ps. 34:14 NIV). Understanding the concept of shalom provided depth and meaning to every aspect of our diversity initiatives.

SEARCHING THE SCRIPTURES: A CROSS-CULTURAL EXPERIENCE

As my biblical paradigm continued to expand, I began to wonder about the composition of "ethnic diversity" during biblical times. A word study of the Greek word *ethnos* proved to be pivotal. *Ethnicity* and *ethnic groups* are derivatives of *ethnos* and its plural *ethne*. In our English Bibles, *ethnos/ethne* is translated as either "nations" or "gentiles." Understanding this term helped me form a common practice in my reading of Scripture: each time I saw "nations" or "gentiles," I would replace it with "ethnicity" or "ethnic groups" in the context of the passage. For example, when reading a passage like Mark 11:17 ESV, in which Jesus said, "My house shall be called a house of prayer for all the *nations*," I would take note and insert "ethnic groups," in place of "nations." Hence, "My house shall be called a house of prayer for all the *ethnic groups (ethne)*."

I also began to take note of the many people groups acknowledged by ethnicity in Scripture. Acts 2:7–11, for example, provides a list of *ethne* in describing those present on the day of Pentecost: Galileans, Parthians, Medes, Elamites, Mesopotamians, Judeans, Cappadocians, Pontusians, Egyptians, Libyans, Cyreneans, Cretans, Arabs, and Romans. The Mediterranean world of New Testament times also provides a very diverse context for the narratives we read in Scripture. Jesus spent much of his life and ministry in the region of Galilee, or as Matthew describes, "Galilee of the Gentiles" (Matt. 4:15 NIV). In their book *United by Faith: The Multiracial Congregation as an Answer to the Problem of Race*, authors DeYoung, Emerson, Yancey, and Kim describe the world in which Jesus grew up and ministered:

> The diverse mix of people in Galilee reflected the demographics of much of the Roman Empire. The Galilee in which Jesus grew up included Assyrians, Babylonians, Egyptians, Macedonians, Persians, Romans, Syrians, and indigenous Canaanites. In the mind-set of first-century Jews, all these groups were Gentiles. Also, Greek cultural influences and Roman economic and administrative functions shaped Galilean society. Jesus was raised in Galilee and influenced by this milieu.[6]

As I applied this lens throughout the reading of Scripture, the Bible became, and continues to be, a very colorful book. Not only did I ponder diversity in the Bible; I also explored the social dynamics between people groups. Tension through biblical times between people groups was common, as illustrated by the relationship between Jews and Gentiles. The inauguration of the new covenant meant that Jews and Gentiles were now "one new humanity," and as a result, "thus making peace (shalom)" (Eph. 2:14–15 NIV). (The Greek word for peace, *eirene*, is a cognate of the Hebrew word *shalom*.[7]) Reading through the lens of *ethnos*, Jews and Gentiles as ethnically diverse people with a mandate to engage in reconciliation, and thus shalom, created a whole new context and meaning for me. In my "re-reading" of Scripture, I would study how several epistles written to churches in the New Testament would exhort Jews and Gentiles to be a unified body, with shalom as the result of that unity (Rom. 15:8–13; Eph. 3:6–17; Col. 3:10–17). This search through the Scriptures informed me that the basis for doing diversity work connects us to a rich tradition—a ministry of inclusiveness and equity that pervades the biblical text. Enhancing the thriving of all humanity in covenant community is the embodiment of shalom. In the words of the noted Old Testament scholar, Walter Brueggeman, "The consequence of justice and righteousness is *shalom*, an enduring Sabbath of joy and well-being."[8] The vision for shalom and my passion for crossing cultures would inevitably connect with another deep gladness—working with college students.

CULTIVATING YOUNG MINDS AND HEARTS

For a seed to achieve its greatest expression, it must come completely undone. The shell cracks, its insides come out and everything changes. To someone who doesn't understand growth, it looks like complete destruction.
—Cynthia Occelli[9]

Just as my great-grandparents in Hawaii planted and harvested sugarcane, my vocation led me to sowing and watering in students' lives and in my institution. Professor Sherry Watt has likened educators to gardeners: "These professionals view their work as if they are tending to a garden where they plant seeds, fertilize the soil, and facilitate the growth of the people and the organization."[10] Whether I'm in a classroom teaching or in a cocurricular program setting, the world of undergraduate students is always a place where transformative growth occurs. I am energized by the boundless potential all around me. The tilling, sowing of seeds, and watering in students' lives always make me feel a deep sense of satisfaction, purpose, and gladness.

The socialization process in our society often results in damaged self-esteem for young people. This is the result of systemic racism, sexism, and classism. Facilitating the process of ethnic identity development can be likened to sowing seeds, pruning, and watering so growth can occur. To accomplish this, I create spaces for students to engage in a facilitated process in what many would call *learning communities*. Students are often exposed to harmful stereotypes, and they may internalize projections of inferiority; from this point, a reconstruction process can follow. Similar to gardening, the process of growth requires patience and a clear vision of the harvest. Consider the following story from my classroom years ago, when I became acquainted with a student named William. He was a participant both in a class I taught as well as many events on campus that fostered multiethnic awareness. In a letter written to the dean of students, William described his experience with internalized racism as it related to academics:

> In the fourth grade I was administered an IQ test. It was determined that I had an intelligence quotient of 184. This assessment, considered very good according to our society, profited me little because I had already accepted the label of being an intellectually inferior being—a label commonly ascribed to African Americans, a label that has negatively impacted my life in all aspects, including my academic performance. This label instilled in me such a tremendous expectation of failure in the world of academia that I fearfully avoided college for eight years and a fear that caused me to attempt to find contentment working in positions far beneath my ability.

William's self-awareness of the influences that had shaped his life came as a result of engaging in dialogue on topics such as internalized inferiority attributed to people of color in our society. In the midst of a diverse student community, a transformational process began to occur. William then described how his college experience contributed to his transformation:

> I learned that there are definite psychological effects that stem from the wounds of racism. This has permitted me to understand the source of my fears and my feelings of inferiority and inadequacy. Because of this, I am eagerly awaiting this semester. My insecurities in the world of academia have been replaced with the excitement of actually tapping my potential, no longer to be ruled by imagined mental limitations and fear. My academic performance will no longer be the result of psychological scars but a true assessment of my ability or effort.[11]

Even as many students of color wrestle with the scars of societal and internalized racism, William was able to gradually find healing. In learning communities, students engage in dialogue, think critically, listen deeply, and affirm one another. They acquire life skills such as intercultural competency and a capacity to engage complexity in the world. Today William is a principal of an urban middle school in Los Angeles, making a difference in the lives of hundreds of young people each year. As I have done this work over the past twenty-five years, stories have mounted of students who became pastors, school teachers, social workers, elected government officials, college professors, deans and vice-presidents in academia, and the list goes on. This growth process can be messy and confusing, but ultimately results in shalom increasing in the lives of students, the institution, and in my life as well. Just as in a garden, growth is beautiful to behold.

"WHERE DEEP GLADNESS MEETS THE WORLD'S DEEP NEED"[12]

Reflecting on the life path God has orchestrated for me, it's clear how my vocation would inevitably connect with cross-cultural adaptation, addressing marginalization and seeking to promote an inclusive environment. In summary, I visit the words of Parker Palmer once more:

> Our deepest calling is to grow into our own authentic selfhood. . . . As we do so, we will not only find the joy that every human being seeks—we will also find our path of authentic service to the world. True vocation joins self and service, as Fredrick Buechner asserts when he defines vocation as "the place where your deep gladness meets the world's deep need."[13]

Facilitating growth in young peoples' lives, as well as enhancing the organizational culture for all students at my institution, connects me to the "authentic service" that Palmer describes. The current reality is that many Christian colleges and universities continue to be, in Buechner's words, places of "deep need."[14] Much progress has occurred at my institution and others, but we still have a long way to go. Systemic change is a process, and deep change does not happen quickly. Shalom takes time. I am reminded of a Greek proverb, "Society grows great when old men plant trees whose shade they know they shall never sit in."[15] Regardless of age or gender, this proverb applies to all of us. There were those who went before us; there will be others to succeed us. I believe my task is to be faithful in the moment as part of God's grand scheme of building his kingdom on earth as it is in heaven. This is why I stay.

FOR DISCUSSION

1. What has been your experience with racial battle fatigue? How have you seen this evidenced in yourself or colleagues doing diversity work in your institution? What are some aspects of your institution's culture that contribute to racial battle fatigue? In what ways might the content in this chapter help individuals "in the trenches" to cope with racial battle fatigue? Who are potential colleagues you can identify that can assist your efforts in moving forward?

2. How is resistance to diversity manifested on your campus? What strategies are being developed to engage resistance when it occurs? How are those who provide diversity leadership on your campus supported as they face resistance to their services?

3. Incidents of resistance to diversity can also be teachable moments or opportunities. How might you respond in ways that leads to growth and transformation when such resistance occurs? Can you respond with principles that connect diversity to biblical and institutional priorities? If not, what steps can you take to further your understanding and skills in this regard?

4. How is dialogue fostered on your campus? Are there spaces cultivated for diverse communities to meet and engage the crucial issues occurring across the nation and on your campus? Are there skilled facilitators available to lead and cultivate such spaces? If not, what is needed to develop facilitators skilled at cultivating these kinds of spaces?

5. How might the concept of shalom influence your understanding of diversity as a spiritual value in your life and institution?

6. Have you explored *ethnos* throughout scripture in your devotions or study? Take some time and examine the passages where the word *nations* appears in our English translations and read the text considering the concept of *ethnos* (Matt. 28:19–20; Acts 10:34–35; Gal. 3:8; Rev. 7:9). How does this influence your understanding of diversity in a biblical context?

7. Self-care is one key to longevity in the work of diversity, whatever the setting. What coping strategies do you cultivate in your life as you engage in

diversity work on your campus? To what extent are you in community with those who share your passion for diversity? How is your balance with life and work? How do you manage stress on a regular basis? Who is the voice of wisdom in your life?

8. It is important to acknowledge progress (be it large or small) along the way. Reflect on the growth you have seen in colleagues and your institution. How has the Lord used you to cultivate awareness, knowledge, and insight? Where are you making a difference? How has your work transformed others? How has this work transformed you?

9. What is your deep gladness? How might your "deep gladness" be instrumental in addressing the "deep needs" of your institution regarding diversity and reconciliation?

NOTES

1 Frederick Buechner, *Wishful Thinking: A Theological ABC* (New York: Harper & Row: 1973), 95.

2 Roland W. Mitchell, Kenneth J. Fasching-Varner, Katrice A. Albert, and Chaunda M. Allen, *Introduction in Racial Battle Fatigue in Higher Education: Exposing the Myth of Post-racial America*, ed. Kenneth J. Fasching-Varner et al. (Baltimore: Rowman & Littlefield, 2015), xvii.

3 Parker J. Palmer, *Let Your Life Speak: Listening for the Voice of Vocation* (San Francisco: Jossey-Bass, 2000), 4–5.

4 Lisa Sharon Harper, *Evangelical Does Not Equal Republican or Democrat* (New York: The New Press, 2008), 10–11.

5 Cornelius Plantinga, *Not the Way It's Supposed to Be: A Breviary of Sin* (Grand Rapids: Eerdmans, 1995), 10.

6 Curtis Paul DeYoung, Michael O. Emerson, George Yancey, and Karen Chai Kim, *United by Faith: The Multiracial Congregation as an Answer to the Problem of Race* (New York: Oxford University Press, 2003), 15.

7 Terry McGonigal, "'If You Only Knew What Would Bring Peace': Shalom Theology as the Biblical Foundation for Diversity," accessed August 16, 2016, http://citeseerx.ist.psu.edu/viewdoc/download?doi=10.1.1.486.658&rep=rep1&type=pdf.

8 Walter Brueggeman, *Peace* (St. Louis, MO: Chalice Press, 2001), 18.

9 "Cynthia Occelli Quotes," Goodreads, accessed July 17, 2016, https://www.goodreads.com/quotes/1013836-for-a-seed-to-achieve-its-greatest-expression-it-must.

10 Sherry K. Watt, "Designing and Implementing Multicultural Initiatives: Guiding Principles," in *Creating Successful Multicultural Initiatives in Higher Education and Student Affairs,* eds. Sherry K. Watt and Jodi L. Lindley (San Francisco: Jossey-Bass, 2013), 5.

11 William Brown, personal communication, July 27, 1995 (used with permission).

12 "Frederick Buechner Quotes," Goodreads, accessed July 17, 2016, https://www.goodreads.com/author/quotes/19982.Frederick_Buechner.

13 Palmer, *Let Your Life Speak*, 16.

14 "Frederick Buechner Quotes," Goodreads, accessed September 13, 2016, https://www.goodreads.com/quotes/496215-vocation-is-the-place-where-our-deep-gladness-meets-the.

15 "Anonymous Greek Proverb," Goodreads, accessed July 20, 2016, https://www.goodreads.com/quotes/666987-society-grows-great-when-old-men-plant-trees-whose-shade.

Chapter Six

RESILIENT LEADERSHIP THROUGH A CULTURAL LENS

JEANETTE L. HSIEH, EdD

Trinity International University, Special Assistant to the President
for Academic Administration, Provost Emerita

If you want to go fast, go alone. But if you want to go far, go together.
—African proverb

It was a typical day when I received an urgent phone call informing me that we had a crisis on campus. Over a two-week period, three female students of color at our Midwestern university had received "hate letters." The handwritten notes sent to two African American and one Latina coeds had a clear message: students of color were not welcome in our community. The third message warned that the author had a concealed gun in chapel and wanted to shoot all the "niggers."

The news of the third letter flooded the campus, and a large group of angry, fearful students gathered in our student center threatening to "take matters into their own hands." Anglo football players vowed to find the person who sent these detestable messages.

We quickly implemented our "Crisis Management Plan," which gathered a group of university leaders who could communicate updates from a centralized location. Our goal was to keep our students safe both emotionally and physically. To complicate matters, we discovered the master key to the residence halls had been stolen, making it impossible to secure the campus. After deliberation, the decision was made to evacuate students of color to undisclosed off-campus locations until their safety could be ensured. Close to two hundred students were relocated. Our campus hotline was besieged with calls from parents and stakeholders. After three days, the FBI and local police identified the author of the "hate mail," and our students returned to campus. The events on our campus received news coverage in the *Chicago Tribune* for six consecutive days.

Some constituents called our decision to relocate students an "overreaction." A few labeled it discriminatory. When the Reverend Jesse Jackson called to tell us he was coming to campus, our president, a strong advocate for "kingdom diversity," wanted to make sure Jackson interacted with our senior leadership team, which was known as the Executive Council (EC). Of the seven-person EC, three were people of color: the Senior Vice-President for Education (an African Burkina Faso male), the Senior Vice-President for Student Affairs (an African American male), and the Executive Vice-President/Provost (an Asian American female).

During his visit, Jackson offered to join our president at a press conference. When a reporter asked if the university had overreacted, Jackson took the microphone and "praised Trinity's leaders for the precautions they took in keeping students safe."[1] He defended the evacuation as "taking the high road" that resulted in a press conference instead of a memorial service.

Serving together for several years, the EC had developed into a team based on mutual trust, shared commitment to mission, and frank conversations. Together, we made collaborative recommendations to our president. In this crisis, our attention to building that "first team" of leaders paid off.[2]

Each EC member had a legitimate and influential voice at the table. My colleagues of color and I, as an Asian American woman, were not "window-dressing" in our deliberations. At a university where 25 percent of our students were of color, we looked at the situation through the eyes of our minority population, particularly the women who were the recipients of the hate mail. The anxiety on our campus was palpable. Students feared for their safety. When determining which course of action should be taken, our president modeled for us how to listen carefully to multiple perspectives around the table. He trusted his leaders and did not question our recommendations, even though they had implications for our annual budget and institutional reputation.

Tough times like this incident point to some factors that have led me to persist in Christian higher education for more than four decades. In that span of time, I served at three faith-based institutions, worked for seven presidents, and functioned in positional leadership roles ranging from department chair, dean, executive vice-president/provost, interim president, and a trustee at a sister institution.

In my forty-plus years in Christian higher education, I experienced a mixture of reassuring accomplishments and discouraging setbacks. Any one of those stressful challenges could have prompted me to succumb to my natural inclination to flounder, withdraw, and doubt whether I was capable of accomplishing the task. But I was certain that God had called me to leadership in

Christian higher education. My work was meaningful and contributed to the mission of our university. I made purposeful choices to capitalize on my personal strengths and employ appropriate coping skills to recover from the adverse events that face every leader.[3] I looked for a path where I could flourish and serve long-term.

To understand how circumstances in my life shaped my perspective and facilitated my resilience as a leader, it may be helpful to know that as a third-generation, Asian American woman, I was a late bloomer. Many people talk about midlife crisis, but it was not until my twentieth year in higher education that I experienced a midcareer identity transformation, a defining moment that changed my viewpoint about leadership and my role.

As I led an ethnicity breakout group at a conference, I experienced an overwhelming sense of comfort and healing that comes from transparent, frank, intercultural conversations with sisters and brothers in Christ. Until that time, I believed that professional success in leadership required me to be as Anglo and masculine as possible in my interactions. I suppressed any evidence of my roots as an Asian woman; however, I was weary of negotiating everything from the perspective of the majority culture. It was at that conference that I realized how important it was for me to recognize who I was as an Asian female and to celebrate the impact, joys, advantages, hurts, pain, slights, and humorous encounters I experienced as a Chinese American woman.

My father emigrated from China to America when he was fourteen, knowing very little English. In those days there were no English as a second language (ESL) classes, and he told us that learning English was like "pulling a cow up a tree by its tail." It was so difficult for him that he gave up and dropped out of high school. When my mother started school in Northern California, she too knew no English. My grandparents only spoke Cantonese at home. She attended a segregated primary school where Asians were separated by a playground from the Anglo students.

Even though I am third-generation Chinese and English is my first language, I am regarded by many as a perpetual foreigner because of my physical features. I am a visible minority. In my first job as a sixth grade teacher, I was the first Asian that my students had seen other than on television. Initially, I thought I was a tremendous disciplinarian because everything I asked of those twelve-year-olds they did promptly and respectfully. Later, I learned that because I was Chinese, they expected me to know karate like all the other Asians they had seen on television. I never told them that karate was not in my genes. In my initial years in higher education, I served as a faculty member and resident hall director at a faith-based institution. One fall, as the men moved into the residence hall, a mother inquired how often I would strip the beds and wash her son's laundry. She must have assumed that all Chinese people ran laundries, even in men's residence halls.

These types of experiences made me want to be as Anglo as possible to fit in with the majority culture, so that people wouldn't assume that I knew karate or was especially gifted at doing laundry. My parents reinforced the idea that if my siblings and I were to achieve the American dream, we needed to speak English well and become part of the "melting pot" mentality. We did not learn to speak Cantonese, and when we were with our Anglo friends, we suppressed our differences. I lived in a "liminal world." Paul Tokunaga, author of *Invitation to Lead: Guidance for Emerging Asian American Leaders*, described this as having one foot in each culture and not feeling entirely "at home" in either American or Asian culture.[4] Matsuoka Fumitaka said it this way:

> The liminal person is one who has internalized the norms of a particular group but is not completely recognized by the members of that group as being a legitimate member. As long as this relationship prevails, one's role in countless situations will be ill defined, or defined in different ways by the individual and the group as a whole. Such liminality leads to uncertainty, ambivalence, and the fear of rejection and failure.[5]

As an Asian American Christ-follower, the impact of a Confucian-based mindset, consistent with biblical values, is woven into the fabric of how I see life and how I lead others. For example, I place high importance on respecting authority, working in community, and seeking social harmony in my relationships.[6]

Emerging out of my cultural and biblical lens as a countercultural Christian, an Asian American, and a woman in leadership in evangelical Christian higher education, there are three principal factors that contributed to my resilience for over four decades:

- The importance of working for top leaders who shared the same commitments
- The importance of building a community of trusted advisors and faculty partners
- The importance of maintaining a hopeful outlook for the future

WORKING FOR TOP LEADERS WHO SHARED THE SAME COMMITMENTS

Before arriving on campus for my first cabinet-level position, I faced an unexpected challenge. I was informed that my immediate supervisor who recruited me had been reassigned to another position in the university. I had a choice to either be defeated by this disappointment or to look for ways to thrive and rise to the challenge. I worked to reframe this unforeseen event by viewing it as an opportunity for my professional growth. For resilience, a positive perspective is foundational for a leader to come to terms with a negative event.[7]

From earlier experiences, I knew that I could thrive as a leader when I worked for supervisors who shared my same commitments. Our president's vision was for our university's DNA to be a "welcoming community." He envisioned a place where, as author Brenda Salter McNeil stated, "People of every tribe and nation can flourish and reach their full God-given potential."[8] I resonated with our president's commitment for kingdom diversity, recognizing that on his leadership team, I would no longer need to live in a liminal world with fear of rejection and failure. He would encourage me to express my perspective in light of my background and experience. Effective leaders make wise decisions by surrounding themselves with people who hold alternative perceptions about issues and consider various options.[9] In my attempt to cope by reframing a negative event into a learning opportunity, I discovered the significance of working for top leadership who held the same vision and could set the tone for the university.

BUILDING A COMMUNITY OF TRUSTED ADVISORS AND FACULTY PARTNERS

Building a Christian community involves a deep commitment to working and learning together as Christ-followers. The relationships nurtured in community provide opportunities to serve others by teaching, supporting, encouraging, admonishing, and correcting each other. When we face adversity and failure, a caring community can be a source of strength to deepen our resolve and provide the courage to continue.[10]

Building a Community of Trusted Advisors

As an Asian American woman, I value the importance of relationships developed in community. A critical support for me came from two trusted colleagues of color who were members of our senior leadership team. I shared the complexities of leadership with these two men who served at our institution for a combination of more than forty-two years. As EC members we were kindred spirits, wholeheartedly committed to our university's Statement of Faith but who had faced similar hurdles as leaders in Christian higher education.

Our inner circle of three was a safe haven for me to test ideas with my two colleagues. My colleagues provided frank feedback, encouragement, reassurance, and correction. They were my safety net. Conversations in this inner circle helped guide me through the complexity of our male-dominated institutional structure. For females, the "route to leadership winds through a labyrinth, where they find themselves diverted—sometimes by doubts about their competence, sometimes by doubts about their worth and sometimes by resentment of their very presence."[11]

I also met regularly with female leaders at sister faith-based schools. These peers served in comparable positions and understood the twists and turns of leadership in higher education. They comprehended the emotional, intellectual, and spiritual challenges in our places of service. We celebrated each other's successes, and we grieved together in our disappointments. Their backing strengthened my resolve and helped me when necessary to reframe my perspective. Developing trusting relationships both with institutional colleagues and with peers from other campuses is critical in developing resilience.[12] In the book *Thriving in Leadership*, Schreiner writes, "both psychologists and leadership researchers agree that the emphasis leaders place on personal relationships is often an indicator of leaders' success. . . . Those who find the most meaning in their role as leaders also report the strongest relationships with others at work."[13]

Building a Community of Faculty Partners

Another group that enhanced my resilience was the faculty. As the chief academic officer, I learned the importance of "shared governance," where faculty has primary responsibility for formulating and implementing the educational work of the university. This concept may be alien to many board members and some nonacademic administrators who come from the corporate world with well-defined hierarchal lines of authority.

In the academy, much of what a leader is able to accomplish is built on trust and influence, not positional authority. Leaders who are effective in higher education foster a climate of trust and a culture of collegiality with the faculty. Some faculty colleagues once told me a story about a new president who believed he had a mandate from his board to implement drastic changes. At his first faculty meeting, he proclaimed, "There is a new sheriff in town." After the meeting, he reported to trustees there was a "culture of resistance" at his institution. His board and his faculty had conflicting expectations about how change was to take place. Change can't be forced. For genuine change to take place, the time, issues, and conditions must be considered.

For faculty, almost as critical as establishing a climate of trust is the importance of a transparent process for making decisions. An early mistake I made was to announce to the faculty that we needed to strengthen our brand by identifying and publicizing "signature" academic programs. Several faculty members questioned what process I would use to determine these signature programs. The furor surprised me, given that I thought my announcement was insignificant. In retrospect, I realized I made at least three errors. I did not attend to process. I underestimated the threat to undersubscribed academic programs. And I framed the initiative in corporate, rather than mission-driven, language. In private conversations, I was told the faculty extended grace to me, as this was a rookie mistake. I began to blossom as a leader under their loving care.

Over the span of my service, I discovered that my preferred style of leadership was to partner with faculty and lead by influence, not hierarchal authority. As I observed and listened carefully, I began to ascertain the tone of the faculty to better understand their perspective. I found that questions posed by faculty did not necessarily mean opposition or disloyalty. Many just wanted to know the context so they could understand the process and support decisions.

Another vehicle for me to develop a relationship with faculty was at our weekly faculty prayer gathering. This prayer time helped strengthen our shared commitment to our mission as we prayed for students, faculty, families, the university, the nation, and the world. As we shared soup and a hunk of bread over lunch, that hour became a vulnerable space in our lives where we could frankly and openly share and pray about mutual concerns that touched our minds and hearts. When members in a community feel heard, validated, and cared for by others, they are much more willing to be active partners in a shared mission.

In developing partnerships with the faculty, the concept of "relational capital" was productive in framing my interactions. Relational capital is the notion that relationships are like a bank account and begin with a zero balance.[14] Each positive interaction deposits capital, and each negative interaction represents a withdrawal from the account. Trustworthy transactions are investments in the future and contribute to a positive balance. In a climate of goodwill, the positive balance in the account has enough surplus capital to search for win-win solutions.[15]

When inevitable disagreements surfaced, as they did in the 2008 economic downturn, the goodwill that had been earned by a history of trustworthy interactions provided space for fruitful conversations. In conflict, it was helpful to elevate the conversation into a broader perspective, consistent with the mission of the university.[16] One day a professor asked for my rationale about a personnel decision. Without violating confidentiality, I framed the decision in the context of mission, and he responded, "I knew it had to be something like that." As a colleague in partnership, he gave me the benefit of the doubt because of our shared history.

In contrast, a bankrupt account has no reserves to find common ground or the will to collaboratively address concerns. When a climate of suspicion prevails, disputes are viewed as adversarial, resulting in winners and losers. In a profile developed by many presentations and discussions at the Association of Theological Schools (ATS), several Asian theologians felt that scholarly work at their institutions was defined as "white theology." They reported that the tenure process had "unspoken rules that trumped faculty handbooks. Without competent and transparent mentors, many have to come—on their own—to discover what is trustworthy in this process."[17] A sense of mistrust and the lack of experienced mentors who "show them the ropes" exposed a bankrupt account in which genuine conversation for the common good was extremely challenging.

Strong relationships at work create a climate of trust and provide the care, support, and encouragement critical to developing resilience for all partners. As trusted partners in a vibrant intellectual and spiritual community, faculty and leadership worked together to "mind the mission" of the university. A. Bartlett Giamatti, the former president of Yale University, described this process within the academic arena:

> It is that civil conversation—tough, open, principled—between and among all members and parts of an institution that must be preserved. If it is, a community is patiently built. If it is not, the place degenerates into a center of crisis management and competing special interests. What must be open and free is the conversation between young and young, young and old, scholar and scholar, present and past—the sound of voices straining out the truth.[18]

MAINTAINING A HOPEFUL OUTLOOK FOR THE FUTURE

My natural inclination is to see the world as a "glass half empty." To overcome that tendency, each day I intentionally looked for "God sightings." How and where did I see God working in my life and in the life of my institution? I worked to develop an optimistic outlook for the future based on God's faithfulness in the present. Developing and maintaining a hopeful outlook for the future enhanced my road to resilience.

Again referencing *Thriving in Leadership*, Laurie Schreiner has emphasized, "The single most powerful predicator of employee engagement in their work was whether their leaders made them feel enthusiastic about the future."[19] Fortunately, I served a president who was masterful in helping our community develop a sense of hope as we monitored tangible progress in achieving our strategic plan. Several months after his appointment as our chief executive officer, our president gathered the leadership team together and he asked us to develop "a shared vision and common goals for a unified future."[20] As we hammered out the components of that strategic plan, we gradually developed shared ownership for envisioning our future. The strategic plan set as a goal twelve priorities to be accomplished by our 125th anniversary in 2023. I flourished when I recognized that we as a community were effectively engaged in mission together.

In our president's biweekly communication to stakeholders in our community, he religiously updated what was accomplished in progressing toward various initiatives, which he called "markers of hope." He framed our efforts as "hope-filled" and a "hope-inspired" plan, as he articulated how each of us contributed to that common vision.

A central factor contributing to my resilience was realistic hope. It was important for me to see real progress, no matter how small or slow, and it was in that progress that I found meaning in my work. Our president's regular reminders helped me acknowledge the markers of hope at our university and encouraged me to persist in my calling. I needed to focus on the big picture to be hopeful, flourish, and remain engaged.

CONCLUSION

In this chapter, I attempted to answer the question of why I persisted in Christian higher education for more than four decades. I stayed because I had an undeniable sense that God called me to do kingdom work in faith-based institutions. But more than that, I felt God's continuing presence on earth through our rich life together as a part of a vibrant intellectual, spiritual, and relational community.

I was surrounded 360 degrees by community from every direction. I reported to presidents and supervisors who shared my commitments, offered me hope for the future, and invested in developing my leadership skills. My responsibility was to lead by influence and offer fresh perspectives to those who had authority over me.

I served with trusted colleagues who became part of my inner circle and my safety net. I had no doubt they had my best interest at heart as they helped me reframe perspectives and navigate the occasional turbulent waters in evangelical higher education. Peers at sister institutions understood, without much explanation, the intellectual, spiritual, and relational challenges of my calling.

Faculty and staff who were under my care were true partners in community. We trusted, prayed, supported, encouraged, admonished, forgave one another, and worked to hammer out acceptable solutions when we disagreed. We were sisters and brothers in Christ, working together "to mind the mission" of our university. We blossomed under each other's loving care. I persisted, thrived, and flourished because I was an integral part of a 360-degree community. My wish is that my story may be an encouragement to others on a similar journey by nurturing hope instead of dread, confidence instead of apprehension, and optimism instead of pessimism as they follow God's path for their lives.

As I write this conclusion, I realize afresh how being a Christian, Asian American woman has played and continues to play a significant role in how I serve the living God. Celebrating and cherishing who I am as a countercultural Christian, as an ethnic minority, and as a woman in leadership honors God's creation and Christ's redemption. Hiding, suppressing, or ignoring my uniqueness dishonors our Creator's work and our Savior's sacrifice. Scripture calls for men and women from every tribe, language, people, and nation to serve our God in leadership roles as we do kingdom work.

FOR DISCUSSION

1. What kinds of professional setbacks have you encountered in the last several years? In what ways did you cope with those disappointments? What other coping mechanisms do you wish to develop?

2. In what ways do relationships in your life encourage you to persist and flourish in your position? What are some new relationships you wish to develop?

3. How are you enhancing a sense of community and trust in your sphere of influence?

4. What personal strengths do you bring to your position? How do you capitalize on those strengths as you lead others? How do others in your community help offset areas in which you require growth and development?

5. How did your experience and background help you develop the skills necessary for resilience? In what ways has your life journey caused you to withdraw and doubt your abilities to accomplish the tasks before you?

6. In what ways do you lead by influence? In what ways do you lead from positional authority? How have these two approaches to leadership enhanced or detracted from your resilience as a leader?

7. What are some defining moments in your leadership journey that have altered your perspective on how you lead others and enhanced or detracted from resilience?

8. What kind of power dynamics have you had to navigate in your role as a leader? Can you offer a few examples of successful navigation of difficult situations, and articulate what you learned in that process?

NOTES

1   Courtney Flynn and Barbara Bell, "Racial Threat Called Hoax of Unhappy Black Student," *Chicago Tribune*, April 27, 2005, 1 and 28.

2   Patrick Lencioni, *The Five Dysfunctions of a Team* (San Francisco: Jossey-Bass, 2002).

3   Laurie Schreiner, "Thriving as a Leader: The Role of Resilience and Relationships," in *Thriving in Leadership: Strategies for Making a Difference in Christian Higher Education*, ed. Karen A. Longman (Abilene, TX: Abilene Christian University Press, 2012), 44–47.

4   Paul Tokunaga, *Invitation to Lead: Guidance for Emerging Asian American Leaders* (Downers Grove, IL: InterVarsity Press, 2003), 50.

5   Matsuoka Fumitaka, *Out of the Silence: Emerging Themes in Asian American Churches* (Cleveland: United Church Press, 1995), 61.

6   Tokunaga, *Invitation to Lead,* 15.

7   Schreiner, "Thriving as a Leader," 40–41.

8   Brenda Salter McNeil's review of Andy Crouch's *Strong and Weak: Embracing a Life of Love, Risk and True Flourishing* (Downers Grove, IL: InterVarsity Press, 2016).

9   Doris Kearns Goodwin, "The Secrets of America's Great Presidents," *Parade Magazine,* September 14, 2008, 4–5.

10 Dietrich Bonhoeffer, *Life Together: The Classic Exploration of Faith in Community* (New York: Harper One, 2009).

11 Alice Eagly and Linda Carli, *Through the Labyrinth: The Truth about How Women Become Leaders* (Boston: Harvard Business School Press, 2007), 117.

12 Harry Reis and Shelly L. Gable, "Toward a Positive Psychology of Relationships," in *Flourishing: Positive Psychology and the Life Well-Lived*, eds. C. L. M. Keys and J. Haidt (Washington, DC: American Psychological Association, 2003) 129–59.

13 Schreiner, "Thriving as a Leader," 47.

14 Stephen M. R. Covey and Rebecca R. Merrill, *The Speed of Trust: The One Thing That Changes Everything* (New York: Free Press, 2006).

15 Stephen R. Covey, *The Seven Habits of Highly Effective People: Restoring the Character Ethic* (New York: Free Press, 1989).

16 Harry L. Peterson, *Leading a Small College or University: A Conversation That Never Ends* (Madison, WI: Atwood, 2008).

17 "Profile: Asian Faculty Member." This profile is drawn, in part, from presentations and discussions held at the Association of Theological Schools' Seminar for Racial/Ethnic Faculty Members at Predominantly White ATS Institutions, Pittsburgh, PA, October 5–7, 2001.

18 A. Bartlett Giamatti, *A Free and Ordered Space* (New York: W. W. Norton & Company, 1989), 45.

19 Schreiner, "Thriving as a Leader," 53.

20 "Trinity 2013: Heritage and Hope," *Trinity Magazine*, Autumn 2015, 21.

Chapter Seven

GOD'S BATTLE: USING SPIRITUAL STRATEGIES IN DIVERSITY WORK

KIMBERLY BATTLE-WALTERS DENU, PhD

Azusa Pacific, Vice-President and Chief Diversity Officer,
Professor of Sociology and Social Work

Finally, my brethren, be strong in the Lord, and in the power of his might.
Put on the whole armour of God, that ye may be able to stand . . .
—Ephesians 6:10–11 (KJV)

"People like *you* don't normally make it here." These were the first *welcoming* words that I received from the coordinator of my doctoral program just prior to my first week of classes. Caught off guard by his statement, my previously cheerful and excited anticipation of starting a rigorous doctoral program quickly dissipated as I stood alone in the middle of a massive concrete-grey academic hallway. This was a "research one" university. I suddenly found myself trying to discern what he meant. Was my status as an African American, a female, a Christian, a person from a lower middle-class background, or the intersectionality of all of these factors potentially problematic? Quickly deducing that others in my program represented some of the previously mentioned social identities minus one, I was left to grapple with one aspect of my identity, to which he was likely referring—race. I was now in the Deep South and suddenly second guessing if I truly belonged.

Only a year prior this had all been a dream. As a first-generation college student, neither my family nor I would have ever guessed that I would one day receive a fully funded fellowship to attend a research-intensive university of my choice and study under an internationally recognized Harvard-trained sociologist.

Although I had always been a good student, my decision to attend college came late, but once I started, I flourished. I graduated from high school and college with honors, received full scholarships and fellowships to complete both my master's and doctoral degrees, lived abroad as an exchange student, and was awarded a Fulbright grant to conduct research in South Africa. It felt like the world was at my fingertips. But following that doctoral hallway incident, I had to determine if the university administrator's words would be prophetic, or if I would rewrite the script. By the grace of God, I not only rewrote the script, but I excelled in the arduous program, drawing from my heritage of overcomers. I was only one of two, out of several who started, who would complete the program in three years.

OVERCOMERS

Although momentary setbacks are inevitable, overcoming the odds is part of my narrative. As the daughter of a teenage mother and a descendant of slaves, I come from a proud line of people who are resilient, resourceful, and deeply religious. Under the protracted legacy of systemic racism, sexism, and classism, I have had to determine what my story would be numerous times, and write it or risk society writing it for me. To assist me with my journey, early on my grandparents deposited into me a deep Christian faith that would guide and sustain me throughout my life. But my story would be myopic if I did not pause to recognize the strength, sacrifices, and legacy of generations of African Americans who paid a price before me. Their stories, and our collective story, are those of triumph out of tragedy, hope in the midst of hopelessness, and songs out of sorrow. In her poem "Our Grandmothers," Maya Angelou said, "I go forth along, and stand as ten thousand."[1] In other words, others may see me as one person, but I move forward with the strength and from the sacrifices of many!

While social scientists are quick to cite pathological data about the African American community, very few capture the "racial and gender victorization"[2] narrative that exists today despite slavery and its rippling effects—the dismantling of black families, the raping of black women, and the financial hegemony of blacks, just to name a few. Trained to diagnose the social ills and dysfunctions, social scientists often view social patterns in the African American community from a deficit model as opposed to a strengths lens. The *Strengths Perspective*,[3] coined by Dennis Saleebey, takes a different approach. It highlights the resilience, tenacity, and resourcefulness of marginalized groups and sees the assets versus the deficits. To do diversity work justice, one has to acknowledge the strength and resilience of oppressed, marginalized, and stereotyped people. Despite unspeakable hardships and inequities, they have garnered the courage to survive and thrive in the midst of life's battles.

GOD'S BATTLE

Pulling from my heritage and history, I have the privilege of serving my institution in the area of diversity. In this role, I often find it ironic and a bit humorous that part of my last name is Battle, in light of the battles that come with diversity work. Perhaps by default of my name and job, I am fascinated with stories about battles and warfare in the Bible. While the Old Testament is full of vivid battle stories, the New Testament is also rich with applications for Christians today and warnings not to lose sight of battles that take place in the spirit.

In the current social and political climate, as the vice-president and chief diversity officer at my campus, I would be naive if I did not consider the spiritual factors and ramifications of the diversity work that my team and I do. Demolishing paradigms of "isms"—racism, classism, and sexism, to name a few—requires boldly recognizing the systemic and spiritual roots that are not easily broken. I have seen many people become disillusioned with the arduous work of diversity and wonder why change does not manifest more quickly. It is easy to become discouraged in the face of systemic injustices that are as old as the institution itself. Yet I think it is important to remember that hegemonic roots go deep, and that systematic and long-lasting change takes time. In the midst of slow change, our sustaining hope is remembering that the battle is not ours alone, but it belongs to God.

In one passage of Scripture, King Jehoshaphat, who is facing multiple enemies, is reminded of this very point; despite the opposition that is coming against him, the battle is not his but God's. ". . . Hearken, all Judah, you inhabitants of Jerusalem, and you King Jehoshaphat. The Lord says this to you: Be not afraid or dismayed at this great multitude; for the battle is not yours, but God's" (2 Chron. 20:15 KJV). Although this passage is referencing a specific part of Judah's history, I believe there are many implications for those serving in the area of diversity today. We will face many battles, but we must remember that ultimately the fight for justice, reconciliation, racial healing, and love is not just our battle but it belongs to the Lord. When we remember this, the burden and weight shifts from our shoulders to the one who is all-powerful.

If the battle belongs to the Lord, does it presuppose that we get to take a passive stance and wait for God to change the hearts of the people? The answer is no. The strategy that we see with King Jehoshaphat and the people of Judah is to go before God in prayer and with fasting, wait and listen for God's guidance, and execute the strategy to address the enemies of their day. I believe this same approach works today in leadership, in diversity, and in life. As a West African proverb says, "When you pray, move your feet."[4] In other words, God will act, but we must too.

THE ARMOR: SUIT UP!

Put on the full armor of God so that you can take your stand against the devil's schemes.
For your struggle is not against flesh and blood … (Eph. 6:11–12a NIV)

A strategy that has sustained and renewed me as a diversity officer and leader has been to apply Ephesians 6:10–18 to the work that I do. This passage of Scripture addresses the importance of putting on the full armor of God so that we will be able to stand against evil in its many forms. In this section, I describe and connect the armor from these verses to diversity work.

The Belt of Truth

Stand firm then, with the belt of truth buckled around your waist … (Eph. 6:14 NIV)

Truth is the foundation for the other parts of the armor.[5] It is an anchor or holder for other weapons in a battle. Truth is also an anchor in diversity work. Speaking truth in love on our campuses is paramount to carrying out the work of reconciliation. After the first democratic election in South Africa's process of building a democratic country, the new leadership embarked upon a process known as the Truth and Reconciliation Commission. Through this commission, people shared horrific truths about atrocities that had happened to marginalized citizens during apartheid, so that they could address the ugly past and begin to move forward and start healing as a country. Although many South Africans would note that the process was not perfect, it did open a door in which acknowledgement, ownership, and forgiveness could take place. Within Christian higher education, truth is critical for progress, reconciliation, and transformation to take place. It is important to speak truth as it relates to the paucity of diverse presidents and leaders within Christian colleges, hegemonic social practices that lead to the systematic killing of African American men in US cities, and health disparities within Latino and African American communities. Without truth, we remain comfortable with the status quo.

The Breastplate of Righteousness

… with the breastplate of righteousness in place … (Eph. 6:14b NIV)

During battles, the chest was a central area that needed protection to guard the heart and other vital organs. The breastplate protected these key areas. When it comes to diversity work, protecting our hearts from bitterness, hatred, or constant rage is important. It is easy to become bitter, habitually angry, and disillusioned as we address many of the ills of society that are often reinforced through the Church and within Christian communities. Regularly checking our hearts and motives are central components of this work, so that we can fully serve others from a place of justice, mercy, and humility, as noted by the prophet Micah (6:8 NIV). Philosopher Nicholas Wolterstorff talks about this perspective as being related to *shalom*.[6] According to Wolterstorff, practicing shalom should result in right, reconciled, and flourishing relationships with God, others, and ourselves.

The Gospel of Peace

… and with your feet fitted with the readiness that comes from the gospel of peace. (Eph. 6:15 NIV)

Between the fall of 2015 and the summer of 2016, domestic and international terrorist attacks were numerous. People throughout the world are in search of peace. Peace of mind is a luxury that many can't afford, yet for Christian educators and diversity advocates, we must lead and act from a place of peace. Peace should not be equated with comfort. Social work educator Brené Brown makes the point, "You can't be comfortable and courageous at the same time."[7] Advocacy and justice work is frankly scary most days. In contrast, peace is that quiet centeredness that comes when we know we are doing what is right and just and are walking within our calling and purpose. It is then that we can be confident that we are wearing our shoes of peace and bringing good news to those who are oppressed.

Shield of Faith

In addition to all of this, take up the shield of faith … (Eph. 6:16a NIV)

I am struck by this piece of armor, as the preface in the King James Version reads, "above all, taking the shield of faith … ." Here the writer Paul wants to ensure that we understand the importance of this protective gear. Diversity workers and leaders are often bombarded by *issues*. Some issues are dumped on us, hurled at us, or simply transferred to us. If we don't have a shield protecting us from the issues, it is easy to become overwhelmed and anxious. As a supervisor once told me, "Just because someone throws you a ball doesn't mean you have to catch it." Instead of "catching" everything, we need to deflect some things, step away from some things, or partner with others on some things, lest we become loaded down and overwhelmed with the cares and *toxicity* of others. What does this mean in practical terms? Don't read every negative email; don't let people tell you all the ills of the institution without input about how to make it better; don't listen to feedback that attacks you personally as opposed to suggestions about behavioral changes that can be made. While we all need to be open to hearing hard feedback, each of us has to discern what is necessary and helpful, versus being pierced by various kinds of destructive "fiery darts," in order to preserve our spirits and minds.

Helmet of Salvation

Take the helmet of salvation … (Eph. 6:17a NIV)

Today in our ultraprotective society, helmets are an important piece of equipment. In battle, helmets are essential. We know from research that head trauma and serious concussions can cause permanent damage. If the head is damaged, there goes the warrior. Doubt and discouragement are two real enemies for diversity leaders. In fact, many battles start in our minds.[8] Did we respond quickly enough to a particular situation? Did we say the right thing to a troubled student? Are we the right person for the job? A litany of doubt can flood us at any given time. The assurance that we gain in our relationship with Christ can help buffer us from the barrage of negative thoughts that can overtake us when we don't rest in Christ's sufficiency despite our own limitations. We can rest in the fact that in our weakness, God is strong and will use us despite our limitations and imperfections. Some things that diversity workers use to protect their thoughts are meditation, music, Scripture memorization, counseling, regular meetings with mentors or spiritual advisers, art, exercise, and the list goes on.

Sword of the Spirit

… and the sword of the Spirit, which is the word of God. (Eph. 6:17b NIV)

As an ordained minister, I am in love with the Word of God. It is life and health for me. What and how will God speak to me today? I look forward to the answer of that question each day as I read my Bible. In battles, swords can be used offensively and defensively. They can hurt or help. When it comes to diversity work, when we know and speak the Word of God, it can comfort and encourage us, as well as aid us in fighting spiritual battles. I recite specific Scripture verses for specific situations, as affirmations, or as prayers for identified problems. In speaking the Word of God, I have witnessed situations and the hearts of people changing, including that of my own.

Pray at All Times

And pray in the Spirit on all occasions with all kinds of prayers and requests. (Eph. 6:18a NIV)

While most people stop at the reference to the sword, the latter part of this passage highlights the importance of always praying and being conscious of spiritual matters, which includes matters of diversity—justice, love, reconciliation, truth, advocacy, and grace. Prayer is one of our most powerful weapons. What would happen if leaders bathed each day in prayer, prayed for their enemies, prayed for members of their leadership teams, prayed for their university presidents, prayed for students and employees, and prayed for their local community and nation? I dare to think that we could be used by God to make an eternal impact that ripples beyond the here and now, in ways we never anticipated. It's time to suit up and join this revolution.

MEDIATING THE MESSY

My university president and boss once told me, "We don't always get to choose our battles. Sometimes our battles choose us." At the time, I remember contemplating his words and the implications of facing battles that we would have preferred to avoid yet were forced to adjust to and address. Little did I know that one spring semester, after my fresh return from Christmas break, I would need to quickly adjust to, help address, and mediate a difficult yet important campus situation. Known as "Activate," a student group began to protest on campus, communicating their concerns with aspects of the campus climate and practices on campus. At the time I was not the chief diversity officer, but I was serving in a dual role as both a faculty member and special advisor to the president and provost on diversity matters. As a person who has "harmony" as one of my strengths on the Clifton StrengthsFinder test,[9] disharmony among our students and administration left me more than a little out of tune! I wish I could say there was a quick fix and that our Christian love magically made all things better. It didn't. After months of listening to students, *really* listening, we were finally able to hear, understand, and begin to address some critical concerns on campus. Are we done addressing issues as of today? No, but out of what seemed like a stressful and messy situation at the time came a host of listening sessions and collaborative efforts that involved both students and administrators, some of which have become a model for other institutions.

What did I learn from this? Diversity work and leadership is about relationship, relationship, relationship. We cannot do this work if we don't *like*, *respect*, and *listen* to people—*all people*, including people whose voices are often marginalized or unsolicited.

CHOOSING YOUR BATTLES

While it's true that we don't always get to choose our battles, sometimes we do, and we must choose those battles carefully. Skilled fighters know when to fight and when to refrain from fighting. Although many of my family and friends would find this hard to believe, when I was a child, I was a fighter. Truth be told, I still am. I just fight differently. I have always been a person who has supported the underdog and who would sometimes fight for those who seemed unable to fight themselves. On one such occasion, when I was in elementary school, a person was aggravating a friend of mine. It wasn't anything serious or even worthy of addressing, other than to walk away. However, feeling a little overly confident with my fighting skills, I jumped in the middle of a situation that had nothing to do with me, and ended up getting beat up! Surprised by this embarrassing turn of events, that day I learned some important life lessons. When the fight was all over and I had a chance to dust myself off, I realized three significant things: don't let pride get you involved in things that are not your business; fight *your* battle, not someone else's; and choose your battles wisely so that regardless of whether you lose or win, it will have been worth it.

Don't Let Pride Derail You

In his book *In the Name of Jesus,*[10] Henri Nouwen warns Christians about various temptations: the desire to be relevant, the desire to be spectacular, and the ambition of power. Drawn from the passage of Scripture in which Jesus is tempted (Matt. 4:1–11), Nouwen links these temptations with selfish pride and insecurity. The end result of selfish pride is always death and destruction. Most leaders want to leave a legacy, but when the legacy is more about us and our accomplishments than about God and others, the fruit is usually pretty rotten. While I believe we should all want to do our best, we should avoid allowing pride to take us on detours that hurt us, our institutions, and others.

Fight Your Battle

I strongly believe that we each are given assignments in life. I believe God directs our steps and gives us each a passion and conviction for certain things. Sometimes these assignments are for a brief season. Other times the assignment is a lifelong journey. Part of life is just trying to discern what our assignment is, separate from someone else's agenda or assignment for us. Using the battle metaphor, when we fight someone else's battle that we were not meant to fight, we are neglecting the real battle in which we were assigned to engage. This is not to suggest that we seek to serve our own interests, but rather that we be clear on who and what we are there to serve. When it comes to diversity work, a thousand people will tell us what the problem is and what we should be doing. If we are not careful, we can invest a lot of time, attention, and resources on rabbit trails or dead ends. Instead, we need to listen carefully and respectfully, but not act unless we are clear that our purpose and their passion, on *that* day, are congruent. We want to avoid investing a lot of time and attention on too many competing issues or problems that distract us from our true purpose, which is to serve God and the entire community.

Choose Carefully

It has been said, "You win some, you lose some." It has also been said, "It matters not whether you win or lose, but how you play the game." We all want to win, but the truth of the matter is sometimes we lose. Sometimes the outcomes that we are seeking don't come to pass and, in fact, some negative outcomes may be the end result. While we can't always predict or control the outcomes, we can *choose* our priorities and check our motives. But when our priorities have been carefully chosen and our motives are right, we can commit to doing our best and leave the results to God.

> The world is full of cactus, but we don't have to sit on it.
> —Will Foley[11]

WHY I STAYED

Reflecting on a career of twenty years at one institution, I am amazed at both my longevity and commitment to the university, and the university's commitment to me. With the support of my university I have developed personally, professionally, and spiritually. And to boot, the university played a part in helping me meet my husband, for which I am extremely grateful, but that's another story!

Aside from such personal perks, why have I stayed this long? In answering this question, many things stand out, but I want to highlight four in particular. First, I believe God opened the door for me to serve at my institution and granted me favor. When I first interviewed for a faculty position twenty years ago, I intended to stay for a maximum of five years. Prior to that time, I hadn't lived or worked in a place for more than four years. In academia, the unspoken rule is that you move to multiple institutions to increase both your salary and professional opportunities. Graduating from a "research one" university, I came to a primarily teaching institution (against the wishes of my dissertation chair), but I can honestly say I have had no regrets.

Second, by working at my institution, and in Christian higher education, I have been able to bring my two great loves together—my love of God and love of education. The fact that I *get* to do kingdom work—educating, equipping, and empowering lives—is priceless. In my everyday work, I'm not just living for today, but building for eternity. I have had the opportunity to mentor and support students both academically and spiritually. One highlight that I'll mention has been serving at my institution long enough to see three African American females that I mentored on campus graduate and go on to do great things. One became a successful social worker, one started her own school in the inner city, and the third is now a professor here on campus—not a bad return on my investment!

Third, as I mentioned earlier, my institution has invested in me and allowed me to grow. I started off as a full-time faculty member, later earned the rank of full professor and served as moderator of the faculty senate, became an associate provost, served as vice-provost, then served as a special advisor to the president and provost, and I now serve as the vice-president and chief diversity officer. Although I've been at one institution, I've experienced a plethora of jobs—and still have the nameplates to prove it! My long-term relationship with my institution has fortunately afforded me earned trust and a variety of opportunities that impacted me overall for the good. This institutional investment I will not take for granted. I am deeply grateful for my institutional support and each of my boss-mentors, all of whom just so happened to be white males.

Finally, I've stayed because despite episodic battles, I've been able to be a bridge builder between very different types of people, which I believe is part of my purpose. At times these bridges have been between faculty and administration, students and staff, traditionalists and progressives, Christians and non-Christians, people of color and whites, affluent and the poor, and the list goes on. In a world that often lacks civility and is full of conflict, I value this bridge-builder role the most. Although not always smooth, it is a high calling.

LESSONS LEARNED

What advice can I offer on both institutional longevity and serving in difficult or demanding roles, including that of a diversity officer? My advice would be simple: honor God, honor yourself, and honor others.

Honor God through Your Institution

No institution is perfect, and when we become aware that we are at imperfect places, the temptation may be to treat our institutions the way they treat us. Instead, if we follow Colossians 3:23, we will do all of our work as if God is our boss, not people, departments, or offices. When we honor God by serving our institutions well, despite their imperfections, God will honor us.

Honor Yourself

Take care of yourself. People in the helping professions—social work, nursing, ministry, counseling, and diversity officers—can get so caught up in caring for others that we can lose sight of caring for ourselves. Professionals in these jobs are also at risk of "compassion fatigue,"[12] burnout, and a myriad of health problems. These kinds of high-stress jobs require intentional and routine self-care to refresh, renew, and replenish one's body, mind, and soul. Some have found mindfulness techniques, meditation, and art as ways to care for themselves. Others use vigorous exercise and sports as a way to stay fit and emotionally healthy. As an introvert, I have found fitness and family, coupled with space— working from home one day a week—to be an effective way for me to clear my focus, renew my mind, and revamp my energy.

Honor Others

Just as we impart on our students, we must continue to be lifelong learners and must continue to learn as a way to honor others. To stay on the cutting edge, we must be aware of current literature in our fields, use technology, and engage in conversations with others that help sharpen our ideas, broaden our perspectives, and abide in cultural humility. In order to speak, we have to first listen. It is only through listening that we gain the right to speak. If we want others to listen to us when we speak truth, we must be willing to listen to them, including people who think very differently than we do. When we listen to diverse perspectives, without jumping to quick solutions, it enables us to think generously and creatively in order to effectively problem solve and serve our entire campus community.

CONCLUSION

Battles in life and work are inevitable, but how we choose to engage them is important. For Christian leaders, the utilization of a spiritual strategy is critical in helping us serve the institution, serve the community, and serve God. Acknowledging that the battle is not ours alone frees us up to collaborate with others and to incorporate our faith in ways that provide better systematic and long-term solutions, while preserving our souls.

FOR DISCUSSION

1. How have you applied Ephesians 6:10–18 to the responsibilities of your current position?
2. In what ways does acknowledging the spiritual aspects of your work/ministry help you lead more effectively?
3. Which battles are you fighting that are not yours to fight? What are the short- and long-term effects of fighting battles that are not yours?
4. Why have you stayed in your position so far, and how will you discern when it is time to go?
5. How will you incorporate a strengths perspective or "victorization" narrative into your diversity work, as opposed to victimization?
6. What strategies will you enact to honor God, yourself, and others?

NOTES

1   Maya Angelou, "Our Grandmothers," in *The Complete Collected Poems of Maya Angelou* (New York: Random House, 1994).

2   Kimberly Battle-Walters, *Shiela's Shop: Working-Class African American Women Talk about Life, Love, Race, and Hair* (Lanham, MD: Rowman & Littlefield, 2004).

3   Dennis Saleebey, ed. *The Strengths Perspective in Social Work Practice*, 2nd ed. (White Plains, NY: Longman, 1997).

4   As quoted by Paula Gordon in "When You Pray, Move Your Feet," The Blog, *Huffington Post*, May 25, 2011.

5   Priscilla Shirer, *The Armor of God* (Nashville: LifeWay Press, 2015).

6   Nicholas Wolterstorff, "It's Tied Together by Shalom." Faith and Leadership, accessed March 3, 2016, https://www.faithandleadership.com/qa/nicholas-wolterstorff-its-tied-together-shalom.

7   Brené Brown, *Super Soul Sunday*, OWN Network, March 17, 2013.

8   Joyce Meyer, *Battlefield of the Mind* (New York: Warner Books, 1995).

9   The Clifton StrengthsFinder instrument developed by the Gallup Organization, http://www.strengthsfinder.com/home.aspx.

10 Henri Nouwen, *In the Name of Jesus* (New York: Crossroad, 1989).

11 Will Foley, "Forbes Quotes," *Quotations Book*, Open Commerce, Ltd., August 19, 2010, accessed August 28, 2016, http://www.forbes.com.

12 Dr. Charles Figley, Compassion Fatigue Awareness Project, accessed May 7, 2017, http://compassionfatigue.org.

Chapter Eight

UNINTENTIONAL LONGEVITY: THE ROLE OF RESPONSIVITY AND RESILIENCY

MICHELLE R. LOYD-PAIGE, PHD

Calvin College, Executive Associate to the President for Diversity and Inclusion, Professor of Sociology

It's not the load that breaks you down, it's the way you carry it.

—Lena Horne[1]

I wasn't supposed to be at Calvin College this long. In December of 1984, having completed all but my dissertation for my PhD program at Purdue University, I was asked to teach a three-week class on my dissertation topic at my undergraduate alma mater, Calvin College. I agreed to do so with no thought of working there any longer than those three weeks. My plans were to teach the course, collect a paycheck, and have some limited conversations with a few of my former professors about my dissertation topic. But, as I write this chapter, I have been working at Calvin College since January 1985. For the first twenty-five years, I was a faculty member in the department of sociology and social work. During those twenty-five years I would obtain tenure, serve two years as the department chair, serve on key faculty governance committees, and produce several scholarly works. After twenty-five years as a teaching faculty member, I moved into administrative roles. First, I became the second Dean for Multicultural Affairs—a position reporting to the provost and working primarily within the academic division. After nine years as dean and after a national search, I became the first Executive Associate to the President for Diversity and Inclusion—a position reporting to the president and a member of the president's cabinet responsible for leading deep, pervasive, meaningful change in the college's understanding and practice of diversity and inclusion. But, I never intended to remain at Calvin so long.

While I would not say that my being an employee of Calvin College for over thirty-plus years is a miracle, I would say that my longevity is surprising to many—including myself. As an African American woman who did not grow up in the Christian Reformed Church (Calvin College being the college of the Christian Reformed Church), people are surprised that I attended Calvin and graduated from Calvin College in the early eighties, when 85 percent of the student body and all of the faculty were Christian Reformed. I would be a rich person if I had a dollar for every time I told someone that I have been working at Calvin since 1985 and their response was either "Really, how can you stand it?" or "Why have you stayed so long?" Yes, remaining at Calvin has been lonely and a struggle at times. There was a point in my career when I was the only faculty member of color on campus. I have experienced many of the challenges identified by Christine Stanley in *Coloring the Academic Landscape*,[2] JoAnn Moody in *Faculty Diversity*,[3] Anthony Bradley in *Black Scholars in Whites Space*,[4] and Leonard Valverde in *Leaders of Color in Higher Education*.[5] And given the fact that the number of people of color working in Christian higher education are few and far between, it is not unanticipated that people, both inside and outside the college, are surprised by my longevity at Calvin College.

However, *my* surprise at my longevity is more closely tied to how I began my career at Calvin than to the challenges I have had to overcome. In particular, three things led me to believe that my time at Calvin would be short-lived. The first was the fact that initially I was only asked to teach as an adjunct and only for three weeks. I was working on my dissertation and saw teaching as a welcome diversion. I had planned that after the interim class, I would push through completing my dissertation, and once the dissertation was complete, or near completion, I would seek employment at another college or university. Unlike some of my colleagues, I did not see a teaching job at Calvin as winning the brass ring. At the time, I simply could not picture myself as a Calvin faculty member—neither short- nor long-term.

Not being able to see myself as Calvin faculty member is directly related to the second reason that my longevity surprises me—I was not a member of the Christian Reformed Church, nor had I enrolled my children into Christian day school. The faculty handbook specifically states,

> Calvin College faculty members on regular appointments are required to be professing members in good standing and active participants in the life, worship, and activities of a Christian Reformed Church (CRC) or of any church which is a member of a denomination in ecclesiastical fellowship with the CRC as defined by its Synod.[6]

In addition,

> Calvin College faculty members on regular appointments are normally required to provide their children with Christian schooling. The requirement is applicable to grades K through 12. Christian schools that are members of Christian Schools International are expected to be the primary schools of choice for faculty.[7]

In 1985, the year I began teaching at Calvin, I was a member of the Church of the Living God—a historic African American denomination. But since I was not on regular appointment, the church membership requirements did not apply to me. In 1986, I began the process of becoming a licensed minister within the Church of the Living God, with the intention of becoming fully ordained. In 1987, I was invited to become a regular member of the faculty. My church membership status was an issue. Eventually, I would be granted an exception to both the church membership and the Christian schooling requirements on the grounds that (a) the Christian Reformed Church (at the time) did not ordain women and, as such, there was no place within the church for me to fulfill the call on my life to preach, and (b) my husband was an administrator in a public school system, and removing "his" kids from the public schools where he worked to place them in a private school was not a discussion point for him. I was the first faculty member in the college's 100+ year history to be granted a double exception. The exception process took years, testing my faith and my resolve.

The third reason for my own surprise at my longevity stems from a conversation I had with a senior member of my academic department very early in my teaching career. I had made an appointment to talk with him about my future in the department. When we met I asked him, "Where do you see me in ten years?" His response, "Not here." His response hurt. I interpreted his response as him saying that there is no place for me at the college. (Note: I was only one of two African American faculty members at the time and the other one had just accepted a position at another institution.) In my mind, I thought that if he could not see me still working at the college in ten years, I probably would not be teaching at the college in ten years. However, thirty-plus years after teaching that initial January interim class, I am not only still at the college, but I have flourished. I have outlasted the colleague who said that he could not see me still at the college in ten years. Staying so long at Calvin was unexpected and unintentional and it has not been without struggles. Yet I have stayed. Although my longevity was unintentional, "why I stayed so long" has been very intentional.

RESPONSIVITY: WHY I STAYED SO LONG

The answer to the question of why I stayed so long at Calvin College can be found in the unpacking of three words: mission, obligation, and belief. I'm not sure that I have always been aware of the impact and import of these three words on my reasoning for remaining at Calvin when it would, seemingly, have been so much easier to have just left rather than to fight policy and to endure the indignities and high levels of scrutiny that often challenge faculty of color. While I am fond of telling people that the reason I am still at Calvin is that "God hasn't released me to leave yet" (and there is a measure of truth to that statement), a more nuanced response would be that the intersection of the college's mission and my personal mission has kept me. My understanding that "from everyone who has been given much, much will be demanded" (Luke 12:48 NIV) obligates me to press on. My belief that God has not finished shaping the college and my belief that the college wants to change requires me to embrace God's timetable for transformation.

MISSION: THE INTERSECTION OF PERSONAL AND INSTITUTIONAL COMMITMENTS

My personal mission statement reads: *I am a Christ-centered transformational leader in the academy and the church.* It is a statement that has taken years to develop and is one that reminds me that I am called to be a change agent. "Leading deep, pervasive, meaningful change in the college's understanding and practice of diversity and inclusion" is the big-picture focus for my work as the Executive Associate to the President for Diversity and Inclusion. This focus or vocational mission, if you will, was assigned to me by the college president and aligns with the college's commitment to antiracism, not just to diversity. The college's commitment to antiracism was formally articulated in 2004 with the adoption of the "From Every Nation: The Revised Comprehensive Plan for Racial Justice, Reconciliation and Cross-Cultural Engagement at Calvin College"[8] document—a key institutional identity document for the college. Antiracism work is the one of the three pillars of my work as a transformational leader. The other two pillars are gender equity and the promotion of a plant-based diet. I have stayed at the college because both the college and I are committed to antiracism as a tool for organizational transformation.

OBLIGATION: THE SENSE OF INDEBTEDNESS

I have a mouse pad beside my computer keyboard in my office at Calvin with a black-and-white image of African American cotton separators working around

1885. Above the image in large letters is the word *Obligation.* Below the image are the words "We owe it to our ancestors and to the sacrifices they made, to continue to achieve higher goals, while maintaining our identity."[9] The image is a daily reminder that I have been able to work at a place like Calvin College because of the hardships that those who have gone before me have had to endure. I am who I am because of the courage and perseverance of my ancestors. I carry with me a sense of indebtedness to those known and unknown people who sacrificed so much, some even their lives, in hopes that the lives of their descendants may be easier and free of oppression. Because others have labored and endured much so that I could have access to an education and equity in the workplace, I feel an obligation to do what I can to help the college become an even more welcoming and equitable place for those who will come after me—those students who will make up the class of 2030, the faculty and staff who will be hired in the twenty-second century, and that administrator who will one day succeed me.

I also carry on my shoulders the mantle of being a symbol of what is possible. In all my years in higher education, I have never compromised nor apologized for my blackness. My ethnic identity—my blackness—shows up in the way I wear my hair, the art on the wall in my office, my style of communication, and the way that I worship God in community with other believers. I hold on to my blackness, not only because it is a part of who I am, but also to demonstrate that blackness is not antithetical to being a professional. I hold on to my blackness to remind people that whiteness is not normative for everyone. I hold on to my blackness as a reminder that I am more than a brown face that adds a little color at committee meetings. Racial diversity is more than color; it is also culture and ethnicity. My remaining in Christian higher education demonstrates that it is possible for African Americans to retain their ethnic identity and thrive.

Additionally, in the same way that the legacy and work of people like Ida Bell Wells-Barnett[10] have inspired me to see myself as an advocate for justice and equity, my remaining in Christian higher education has allowed students, young academics, and emerging administrators to see themselves as being able to flourish in Christian higher education, to be a change agent, and to maintain their identity while doing so. (I have a picture of Ida Bell Wells-Barnett on my office wall, along with several other women with a plaque that reads "Well-behaved women seldom make history.") I have stayed at the college for over thirty-one years because my grandparents (all self-identified African Americans) could not go to college as young adults in the Deep South. I have stayed at Calvin College because I did not have professors of color when I attended Calvin as an undergraduate, nor as a grad student at Purdue

University, and it is important for students—and students of color especially—to see, interact with, and be led by professors, staff, and administrators of color. I have stayed at the college so as to be "evidence" that there is a place at the college for people of color.

BELIEF: BEING CERTAIN THAT THE COLLEGE WANTS TO CHANGE

My top signature strength on the Clifton StrengthsFinder assessment is *belief*, which is described by the Gallup Organization, "People strong in in the Belief theme have certain core values that are unchanging. Out of these values emerges a defined purpose for their life."[11] This description resonates with my understanding of myself and of what drives me. Additional insight about the connection between the signature strength *belief* and vocation was provided from the *Gallup Business Journal*: "Your Belief makes you easy to trust. It also demands that you find work that meshes with your values. Your work must be meaningful; it must matter to you."[12] This linkage between belief and values gets to the heart of why I stayed so long in Christian higher education in general and at Calvin College specifically.

I have stayed at Calvin College because my work as a faculty member, dean, and an executive associate to the president has been meaningful. I have had multiple opportunities to develop courses for students and to design professional development trainings for faculty, staff, and board members. I have served as a peer mentor and cultural competency coach to every member of the president's cabinet. I have helped design climate surveys for the college and have led cultural assessments. My work, on most days, energizes me and reflects my commitment to an antiracism approach to organizational change.

On most days my work energizes me, but there are other days where the work is hard and challenging. It is a hard day when I am met with resistance to the idea that racism is still an issue in the United States. It is an emotionally draining day when I am brought in as an investigator to respond to a complaint of racial intimidation. It is a crushing day when the college is in the news for a racialized incident. It is a defeating day when one more faculty or staff of color decides to leave the college for work at another institution. And it is an overwhelming day when I am painfully reminded that there is much work to be done as the college strives to strengthen its diversity and inclusion efforts as identified in our current strategic plan.[13]

Yet in spite of the hard, draining, crushing, defeating, and overwhelming days, I remained at the college. I have remained because I have been unwilling to surrender my hope and belief that the college wants to do the right thing. Yes, there are times when the college's efforts to become a more welcoming and inclusive campus are awkward, halting, and counterproductive. But at the end of the day, I am convinced that the college's heart is in the right place and that, in God's timing, the college will be fully exhibiting all the hallmarks of a campus that is inclusively excellent.

I used to want the words "She tried" on my tombstone. Now I want "She did it."
—Katherine Dunham[14]

RESILIENCY: HOW I STAYED SO LONG

In his book, *The Resiliency Advantage*, Al Siebert describes resiliency as "being able to bounce back from life developments that may feel totally overwhelming at first . . . the ability to sustain good health and energy when under constant pressures."[15] When answering the question of *how* I have been able to stay at Calvin for more than thirty-one years, the word *resiliency* is the first thing that comes to mind. As one might imagine, I have utilized a number of practices to both develop and maintain a level of resiliency that has sustained me over time. Most of these practices fall into three categories: empowering affirmations, therapeutic spaces, and centering indebtedness.

EMPOWERING AFFIRMATIONS

Words are powerful. They have the ability to build confidence or to destroy confidence in one's self or in others. Affirming words are sometimes all that I need to get through a particularly challenging experience or a bad day. For example, on those days when I wonder whether I am making any progress, I will read the words written by my supervisor—the president—from my latest performance review that celebrate my achievements and note the positive impact of my work on the college, or I will re-read a handwritten thank-you card from a colleague that expresses appreciation for the time I took to respond to a concern.

Several times a week, as part of my morning devotions, I incorporate a series of affirmations that I wrote to remind me of who I am in Christ and of the promises of God to sustain me in every season. Countering the negative experiences and wounding voices with empowering affirmations is an important aspect of my being able to stay so long at Calvin.

THERAPEUTIC SPACES

Words are powerful for developing resiliency, but words are not enough. I have learned the hard way that if I do not take care of myself physically, emotionally, spiritually, and culturally, if I do not make room for therapeutic spaces in my life, then I will not have the reservoirs necessary to draw from to do my work—even on the good days. Physically, I work out with a personal trainer twice a week. Emotionally, I no longer take the seemingly slow process of the college's transformation personally. I also seek opportunities for creative expression by dancing regularly with my church's liturgical dance team. Spiritually, I practice several spiritual disciplines. I have found personal retreat days to be particularly restoring. Culturally, I live in a black neighborhood and I attend a black Christian Reformed church—a church where the worship style is expressive, the songs are soulful, the prayers directly connect to the issues of black life, and the sermons expound the Word of God and draw congregants closer to God.

CENTERING INDEBTEDNESS

Centering is a tool used to sharpen or maintain focus. As described earlier in this chapter, I carry with me a sense of obligation and indebtedness as to the *why* I remain in Christian higher education in general and specifically at Calvin College. *Centering indebtedness* is a concept that I have coined to describe being other-focused in a particular way; the other being identified as those with which there is a sense of indebtedness. Centering indebtedness keeps me from getting stuck in the pain, disappointments, and challenges that often accompany diversity work in diversity in higher education. By focusing my thoughts—centering—on those who have struggled in this cause before me and on those who will be following after me, I am able to redirect negative thoughts and remind myself that this work that I have been called to is bigger than I am. Centering indebtedness reminds me of the greater purpose of diversity work in Christian higher education: this work is not about my comfort, my agenda, or my timetable; this work is kingdom work. A work that began on the cross so that all might be reconciled to God, a work that has continued through the ages by the efforts of faithful men and women, and a work to which I, too, am called.

CONCLUSION

All of this requires that I take up my cross daily and become a witness, agent, and evidence of God's love, grace, and reconciliation of all things. And I will do all of this while building a reputation of integrity, authenticity, and joy in my spiritual, personal, and professional life.
—Michelle Loyd-Paige[16]

I had no intentions of being at Calvin College for more than thirty-one years. When I think about this fact, I am reminded of a passage of Scripture that reads "'For my thoughts are not your thoughts, neither are your ways my ways,' declares the Lord" (Isa. 55:8 NIV). I may not have had plans to be at Calvin for so long, but clearly God did. As the years passed, I became more and more aware that I stayed as a response to a sense of mission, obligation, and belief. Yes, along the way, I have seriously considered washing my hands of this challenging diversity work and moving on. But when I inquired of the Lord about leaving, his response was always "Not now, not yet; my grace is sufficient." And so I have stayed. Staying has taught me how to cultivate resiliency through receiving empowering affirmations, resting in therapeutic spaces, and nurturing centering indebtedness. It has been good to stay.

FOR DISCUSSION

1. Do you have an idea for how long you plan to be employed at your institution? What factors would lead you to shorten your time or to extend your time? Are these factors primarily internal to yourself, primarily external to yourself, or a combination of both?

2. Think back to the first months or years of employment at your current institution. What experiences or words directed to you helped you feel a connection to the institution? What experiences or words created a disconnection between you and the institution?

3. Have you ever experienced a microaggression or some type of discrimination? How did you respond? Was that response helpful? What would you now do differently?

4. What advice would you have given the young faculty member Michelle if she had come to you to tell you that she wasn't sure if she belonged in Christian higher education? What would inform your response to her?

5. Do you have *therapeutic spaces*? What are they? How often do you utilize them? If you had to give up one, which one would it be and why?

6. In what arenas other than employment might the idea of *centering indebtedness* be useful? How so?

7. If you had the power to immediately implement one new program or policy or to change an existing policy to improve the retention of faculty and staff of color at your institution, what would it be and why? What would it take to make this policy or program a reality?

NOTES

1   "85 Quotes from Black Women to Inspire You," ForHarriet.com, accessed June 23, 2016, http://www.forharriet.com/2012/03/85-quotes-from-black-women-to-inspire.html#axzz4CQTfKool.

2   Christine A. Stanley, "Coloring the Academic Landscape: Faculty of Color Breaking the Silence in Predominantly White Colleges and Universities," *American Educational Research Journal* 43 (4; Winter 2006): 701–36.

3   JoAnn Moody, *Faculty Diversity: Problems and Solutions* (New York: Routledge, 2004).

4   Anthony B. Bradley, *Black Scholars in White Space: New Vistas in African American Studies from the Christian Academy* (Eugene, OR: Wipf and Stock, 2015).

5   Leonard A. Valverde, *Leaders of Color in Higher Education: Unrecognized Triumphs in Harsh Institutions* (Walnut Creek, CA: Alta Maria Press, 2003).

6   *Calvin College Faculty Handbook*, May 2016, 67, https://calvin.edu/contentAsset/raw-data /225e6a56-bd6a-49a6-b7c9-a0992dc57399/fullTextPdf.

7   Ibid.

8   "From Every Nation: The Revised Comprehensive Plan for Racial Justice, Reconciliation and Cross-cultural Engagement at Calvin College," Calvin College, accessed May 7, 2017, http://calvin.edu /about/diversity-inclusion/commitment/from-every-nation.html.

9   "Obligation," D'azi Productions, accessed June 24, 2016, http://www.blackartdepot.com/products /obligation-by-dazi-production.

10   Suffragist, sociologist, and feminist who led antilynching crusades in the 1890s. See "Ida B. Wells," Biography.com, accessed May 7, 2017, http://www.biography.com/people/ida-b-wells-9527635.

11   "Strengths Test," accessed May 7, 2017, http://www.strengthstest.com/theme_summary.php.

12   "Belief: Clifton StrengthsFinder Theme," Gallup, accessed May 7, 2017, http://www.gallup.com /businessjournal/637/belief.aspx.

13   "Calvin College Strategic Plan 2019," Calvin College, accessed May 7, 2017, https://calvin.edu /about/strategic-plan/.

14   85 Quotes from Black Women to Inspire You," ForHarriet.com, accessed June 23, 2016, http://www .forharriet.com/2012/03/85-quotes-from-black-women-to-inspire.html#axzz4CQTfKool.

15   Al Siebert, *The Resiliency Advantage: Master Change, Thrive under Pressure, and Bounce Back from Setbacks* (San Francisco: Berrett-Koehler, 2005), 5.

16   Michelle Loyd-Paige, personal communication.

Chapter Nine

THE MUSIC GOD PUTS IN YOUR HEART: REFLECTIONS FROM AN ONGOING JOURNEY

RODNEY K. SISCO

Wheaton College, Director of the Office of Multicultural Development

Never lose the groove in order to find a note.

—Victor Wooten[1]

"Take Five" is an essential jazz composition by the Dave Brubeck Quartet on the recording *Time Out* (Columbia Records, 1959). It has an incredible vamp that draws the listener into its unusual 5/4 time signature. The composition is in a collection of tunes that have unusual time signatures (hence the album name *Time Out)* that, when released, was one of the biggest-selling jazz singles. "Written in the key of E-flat minor, it is known for its distinctive two-chord piano vamp; catchy blues-scale saxophone melody; inventive, jolting drum solo; and use of the unusual quintuple (5/4) time, from which its name is derived."[2] As a piece of music (on the original recording), it displays both a consistency and artistry in developing the theme. The piano and bass lay down the consistency, holding steady the backbone of the piece; equally important are the saxophone and drums, with the artistry or the playfulness of moving around the theme. Consistency and artistry are the foundations in serving in a single context for a long time. The consistency is the base that facilitates the flow of the artistry. The complexity of music pales in comparison to the complexity of understanding diversity in contemporary society. Just as listening to a complex composition requires focus and diligence, so too does the conversation of diversity. Longevity in Christian higher education for me has been to find that balance of consistency and artistry akin to finding the groove of a song.

More than a century ago, W. E. B. DuBois offered this perspective of the times in which he lived: "The problem of the twentieth century is the problem of the color line, the relation of the darker to the lighter races of men in Asia and Africa, in America, and the islands of the sea."[3] Unfortunately, as we are in the second decade of the twenty-first century, we have carried forward the same problem in society in general and, specifically, within Christian higher education. The social development, sociological grouping, economic movement, interpersonal relationships, physiological distinctions, religious movements, and participation in the workforce of ethnic minorities are just a few of the topics that can be found in doing any quick search in academic journals today. Many others could talk about the challenges, problems, and failure at predominantly white academic institutions (including most of our Christian colleges and universities) to completely diversify and be inclusive at all levels of the institution. An outcome of the education offered by Christian colleges should be to develop students who, being centered on Christ, focus on social justice, understand the complexity of the world in which they live and the interconnectedness of multiple identities, and are able to live and learn with people from diverse backgrounds. In my life experience, it has been the desire to groove in both consistency and artistry, addressing issues of diversity and inclusion, that has facilitated a productive tenure in Christian higher education. Along the way, there have been a few specific insights that have contributed to my resiliency and can impact the longevity of others serving in Christian higher education.

FINDING THE "WIN"

Righteous indignation is real; there are times when the arc of social justice is on your side and you really want to lash out. However, the question is, what does that lashing out actually accomplish? As educators, our challenge, though daunting, is to win others over, defy limitations, change stereotypes, and allow our institutions to flourish as beacons of Christian wisdom and learning. New York DJ Jay Smooth has described the difference between referencing someone as being racist versus describing their words and behavior as being racist.[4] The former creates all kinds of defensiveness and limits the ability for others to learn; the latter provides an opportunity to point out which specific words or behaviors were problematic, and why. An additional challenge is understanding the importance of recognizing times when we are called to speak the truth in love powerfully and unapologetically, balanced by a willingness to listen to and dialogue with the opposition. However, reaching our goal will also, at times, involve recognizing those whose foreclosed ideas will never allow them to move forward and with whom peaceful disagreement is the best approach.

The analogy has been made many times that transforming Christian higher education is the equivalent of changing the direction of an aircraft carrier, or that change is glacial. Candidly wonderful ideas sometimes take time. Time to transform our campuses into intentionally Christ-centered, diverse, inclusive institutions that are also focused on unity. Unity does not mean that we are all the same but rather that we have the freedom to be uniquely who we are called to be, with our very differences that focus on one Lord. "Finding the win" means we enter conversations and situations with the question "Can you help me understand?" as opposed to "What is wrong with you, and how could you ever have done that?" Focusing on the win requires that we choose wisely what we address and how we address it. When others chose to emphasize what your predecessor used to do, the win is to acknowledge that individual's giftedness and be grateful for how the Lord used them, but then to reflect upon your unique giftedness and how the Lord will use you in the present season. A picture of the season of the win reflects finding and celebrating white allies as well as more voices of color effectively steering the institution in a new direction. Focusing on the win requires time, which allows us the opportunity to see those victories transform the shape and the course of our institutions in ways that lead to a Christ-centered, inclusive academic community. The artistry of my service has been finding my unique "wins."

SHARED RESPONSIBILITY

When I first started at Wheaton, I asked questions along the lines of why students of color were not choosing to come to Wheaton, what influenced those decisions, and what colleges they chose to attend. I soon found that the administration never really thought of those questions; in fact, the assumption was that the creation of the multicultural admissions counselor position would ensure that students would automatically come to Wheaton. Initially it was viewed as my responsibility to bring students to Wheaton and ensure that they stayed at Wheaton. In my years of experience, I've encountered many who have similar dual-appointed positions and are perceived to be the only resources allocated toward the success of the recruitment and retention of ethnic minority students, faculty, and staff.

In my context, I soon began to focus on the fact that the success of students of color was the responsibility of the entire college. The success and thriving of students is a combination of multiple factors, including students feeling at home, students finding programs that engage them, students having academics that challenge them, and the campus being made up of women and men who understand cultural competence as an institutional responsibility. One singular department cannot be responsible for all of that, especially when it's done with a limited budget. The concept of having one department be responsible for all of diversity initially comes from a misperception that diversity is nothing more than an add-on to the institution as a whole. It also contributes to the burnout of those responsible for that position within a few years. The strength of developing a truly robust community requires the recognition that diversity must be infused at all levels. The recruitment and retention of students, staff, faculty, and administration is facilitated by how well the institution as a whole lets candidates know that they have a place where they can thrive. Claremont Graduate University researcher Daryl Smith provides a model for holistic evaluation of the institution by addressing four domains:

- *Access and success.* This dimension relates to an institution's undergraduate and graduate populations by field and levels, student success (e.g., graduation rates, persistence, and honors), and pursuit of advanced degrees and transfer among fields.
- *Campus climate.* This dimension encompasses the type and quality of social interactions among students, faculty, and staff, as well as individual and group perceptions of institutional commitment to diversity.
- *Educational and scholarly mission.* This dimension involves the availability of courses with significant diversity content, but also diversity course-taking patterns, faculty engagement with diversity issues, and student-learning outcomes related to diversity.
- *Institutional vitality and viability.* This dimension can be described by the following characteristics: increasing the racial/ethnic diversity of faculty, a public examination of the institutional history of diversity issues and incidents, strategies being employed to address diversity, the centrality of diversity in the mission and planning process, the monitoring of the work being done on diversity, the perceptions of the public and other constituents of the institution's commitment, and the governing board's engagement on the issue.[5]

These four domains make it clear that an entire university culture is being developed that engages all members of the community to bring about success in this domain.

The shared responsibility may take time to build; in my context, I started with two friends, the dean of students and the director of human resources. We would periodically have meals together or simply find opportunities to talk. We would talk about diversity at the college, the challenges for people of color to come into the Wheaton setting, and how we could encourage campus change. Both individuals had people in their past who had begun their journeys, and our conversations continued those journeys. Both made it their point to encourage and challenge me to be a better professional on the campus. Our relationships flourished as we then served on campus committees together and ultimately served on the president's Diversity Council. The Diversity Council is a multidivisional campus task force (including all vice-presidents of the college) that serves to monitor, assess, and report to the president on issues of Christ-centered diversity within the Wheaton College community and recommend a vision for Wheaton's multicultural mission. Diversity at Wheaton has become a shared responsibility. My task has focused on tying this shared responsibility to the larger mission of the college.

YOU ARE NOT ALONE: COMMUNITY

In an article by Henri Nouwen titled *Moving from Solitude to Community to Ministry*[6], he reflects upon the importance of following the example of Christ, who over the course of his ministry took time alone to be with the Lord and also to be in community, and then from the community of his apostles he was able to do ministry that transformed the world. It's important to remember that we are never alone. When I started at Wheaton I was the sole nonwhite director at the college. My first year on staff, one of my former professors (and eventually mentor), Alvaro Nieves, a Latino sociologist, honored me with a comment that we needed to spend time together. Additionally, a new African American woman joined the Psychology Department. In my first few years, if I was ever struggling, unaware of what to do and what to say and attempting to think through the theory behind my praxis, I sought out one of these two individuals. Alvaro encouraged me to engage outside of the college for other resources to help me in this question of diversity in Christian education. He, along with John Lee and Hank Allen, are the editors of one of the few academic texts addressing racial and ethnic minorities in Christian higher education.[7] Al reminded me that I was not alone in Christian higher education and he encouraged me to find others that could serve as resources and colleagues. He, along with others, challenged me to look for settings that would support my work.

In addition to the important role of these two friends and colleagues on my campus, two colleagues who were not people of color were also encouragers. They were open to conversations about the challenges and struggles of the Wheaton setting and helped provide me with opportunities to think outside of Wheaton. The list of those who were sources of support would take a chapter in itself, but I here I would like to highlight the National Black Evangelical Association (NBEA, an organization that allowed for further exploration of faith and ethnicity); the National Christian Multicultural Student Leaders Conference (NCMSLC, which provided a forum to network with others in the student development arena); the CCCU's original Office of Racial/Ethnic

Diversity, which has transformed into the current Commission on Diversity and Inclusion (and provided multiple contexts for engagement with diverse faculty and staff across the CCCU); and of course Hasana, my wife (who listens to my complaints, gives wise counsel, prays with and for me, and partners with me along a journey to develop a true community). It is the awareness of being in community that has contributed to my ministry and allowed me to stay, knowing that I was never truly alone.

Part of not being alone is focusing on self-care. I have found that I need to build times of reflection into my academic life, as well as provide the same for those who are my staff. Reflection is my time of solitude to get alone into the Word of God and to reflect critically on the call for my work at Wheaton. The move to community is time of both reflection and renewal with resources (meaning, friends and colleagues), both on and off campus, who help reframe and review our work. I have found support in the conferences and workshops that have provided me with opportunities for service, hosting, and presenting at the National Christian Multicultural Student Leaders Conference (NCMSLC), the New Professionals Retreat of the Association of Christians in Student Development (ACSD), diversity colloquiums, and the Racial Harmony Task Force of the Council for Christian Colleges & Universities (CCCU), as well as multiple speaking engagements on other campuses because of networking at one event or another. I have found that when I care for myself, when I keep up with reading, Scripture, rest, and personal development, I have a wealth that allows me to serve others, sustaining me through the many emotionally challenging conversations that make up my life at Wheaton. Finally, in terms of self-care, it is important to also seek out those who can benefit from encouragement, support, and mentoring. I've had success because many have poured into me and I have attempted to pour into others. The artistry has been in connecting with others, including my pouring into those who are new.

ONE'S UNIQUE CALL

As a prisoner for the Lord, then, I urge you to live a life worthy of the calling you have received. Be completely humble and gentle; be patient, bearing with one another in love. Make every effort to keep the unity of the Spirit through the bond of peace. There is one body and one Spirit, just as you were called to one hope when you were called; one Lord, one faith, one baptism; one God and Father of all, who is over all and through all and in all.

—Ephesians 4:1–6 NIV

Longevity includes playing out complex themes. The shortest way to give the reasons behind my longevity within Christian higher education, and specifically at Wheaton College, is in understanding that I've been called by the Lord for such a time as this to serve in this context. Each of us has to know the unique call we have been given and the unique gifts that allow us to fulfill that call. Knowing that the Lord has directed our steps allow us the freedom to say no when someone else has grand ideas for our work or office, particularly when resources—either physical, fiscal, or emotional—are limited.

The spirit of the living God uniquely calls and uniquely qualifies each of us to serve. Scripture is replete with examples of women and men whom most would assume could not do anything. As just a few examples: Moses stuttered and he was a murderer; Abraham was too old, by the assessment of most people; David was far too young and an adulterer; Peter had a short fuse; Naomi was a widow; both Gideon and Thomas doubted; and the only training Amos had was tree pruning. Yet each of these individuals was called in Scripture by God to do creative and amazing things, and each did so, proving that it is not earthly standards that determine success, but rather God's call and our response to that call. These words are not intended to offer an easy out for the responsibility of preparation—continued study, professional development, engagement in the professional organizations of our discipline, and creative thinking regarding the use of gifts in a specific institutional setting are all important. However, my faith is the foundation that binds me to a specific call to serve the Lord currently at Wheaton College.

Recognizing my call has provided strength for the journey. Clearly knowing that the Lord has set me on this task helps me when I find myself in times of isolation, those times when I feel as if I'm the only person who understands what I'm going through. For many years, I was the only nonwhite person with the title of director at my institution. There was an awkward feeling of knowing that I was welcome in the community, but not quite the same as everyone else. I balanced that sense of isolation with a sense of dual consciousness: recognizing my own ethnicity and the importance of my ethnicity to who I am, while also working in an environment that was primarily Anglo and needing to be able to speak in the way that my peers would normally speak.

That awareness of a calling provided the strength to translate experience from a different cultural perspective in a manner that others could hear and receive. That calling has granted me patience when I've explained my experience only to have my words dismissed with the question, "That didn't really happen to you, did it?" It has also granted me perspective when I shared for close to an hour about the experience of students of color to faculty and administrators, only to receive responses such as "Everybody has challenges," "Aren't you being a little too sensitive?," or "Maybe race has nothing to do with it." My call helps me to discern, when dealing with such microaggressions and more, the best approach to encourage growth, especially when it includes holding the speakers accountable. Similar to the scriptural examples, my call gives me the voice to speak because I know that I have been challenged to speak, empowered by the Lord. I understand that it is my responsibility to recognize and counter the work of the evil one. The unique calling of the Lord on each of our lives allows us to rest assured in that call and to serve boldly in our campus settings.

Finally, in terms of the call, I am inspired by the recognition that the call of the Lord on my life, and for my institution, has had an impact even beyond my institution. The strong diversified multicultural programs, significant recruitment programs, and the proliferation of senior diversity officers now present in Christian higher education were not present on the landscape of our campuses at any significant level in the early 1980s. Part of my call at Wheaton has been the impact of Wheaton College on other Christian colleges. The call has been to push my institution so that it would encourage other institutions to grow as well. Connecting with the CCCU and ACSD, challenging both of those contexts to address diversity, meant taking what I have learned in my Wheaton experience and encouraging others to develop their own plans for their contexts. The joy of the call is being able to look and see others who have taken what we've started and have excelled, which adds a new calling for us as well. The call is recognizing the responsibility to state clearly—and then to evaluate—what we expect in order to determine whether we are meeting those goals. Such a call must reflect both consistency and artistry.

CONCLUSION

I started this chapter by referencing a piece of jazz music that I hope readers will find and listen to; it reflects a joyous groove that embodies serving in Christian higher education in terms of both longevity and impact. The music Christ placed in my heart pushes me to both consistency and artistry. The consistency has been in developing a sense of shared responsibility between the institution and me—that diversity is the responsibility of all of us . . . and is at the heart of institutional mission. Consistency has also been in my recognition that my unique call facilitates the continued strength needed to serve within Christian higher education.

Similarly, a sense of artistry allows each of us to assume creative ways to go about our work. We do not follow the plans of others but allow our unique gifts to empower the way we find the "win," live in community without feeling alone, and live into the spirit-led call that is uniquely ours. Serving for more than three decades in Christian higher education has been a process of finding my voice and groove to influence my setting and beyond by being consistent and yet flexible. I have stayed at Wheaton College because Wheaton provides me with an opportunity to impact not only this campus but also others through the gifts I have been given.

In specific, my gifts and calling have allowed me to serve students (students of color and ethnic majority students) and help them find a safe place to engage in conversations of understanding Christ-centered diversity and their own ethnic identity; to be of assistance to faculty as they wrestle with how to bring diversity to the classroom; and to provide encouragement and direction to the institution as a whole in seeking to become a more intentionally Christ-centered, culturally diverse living and learning educational community. My prayer for you, the reader, is that you are able to find your unique voice and to do so over a long period of time, influencing the lives of students and colleagues and transforming your institutions into more holistic, Christ-centered, diverse, and inclusive academic communities. I also pray that you will find your groove and live into it fully.

FOR DISCUSSION

1. In your spheres of influence, what is a "win"? What does success look like for you in your setting? What factors are necessary for you to reach a win? How are you uniquely called to be artistic in serving in your role?

2. How does your work impact the mission of your institution? To what extent do you sometimes feel you are alone on your campus in your role? If that is rarely the case, with whom do you share the responsibility of your role? What assets or resources do you have outside of your campus that sustain and nourish you? How can you be consistent in the application of your work?

3. Have you sometimes experienced microaggressions or some other types of discrimination? How would you encourage new employees in your setting to address this if such things happen to them?

4. Who has poured into your life at your campus currently? Into what other lives are you investing within your institution to support them personally and professionally? How do you care for yourself?

5. In what ways have you sought the Lord for your unique call for your work? Have you asked the Lord about the unique "song" that can be developed in your heart for your work?

6. How will you nurture the new professional who is asking questions about diversity and longevity at your institution? What will your contributions be either in encouraging them to flourish or discerning whether it is time to leave?

NOTES

1   Victor L. Wooten, *The Music Lesson: A Spiritual Search for Growth through Music* (New York: The Berkley Publishing Group, 2006) 13.

2   "Take Five," Wikipedia, accessed May 7, 2017, https://en.wikipedia.org/wiki/Take_Five.

3   W. E. B. DuBois, *The Souls of Black Folk: Essays and Sketches* (Chicago: McClurg & Co., 1903), 10.

4   Jay Smooth, "How to Tell Someone They Sound Racist," YouTube, accessed May 7, 2017, https://www.youtube.com/watch?v=b0Ti-gkJiXc.

5   Daryl Smith, *Diversity's Promise for Higher Education: Making It Work* (Baltimore: Johns Hopkins University Press, 2009).

6   Henri Nouwen, "Moving from Solitude to Community to Ministry," Fellowship Bible Church, accessed May 7, 2017, http://www.stdavidschurch.org/filerequest/3565.pdf.

7   D. John Lee, Alvaro Nieves, and Henry Allen, *Ethnic Minorities and Evangelical Christian Colleges*, ed. D. John Lee (Lanham, MD: University Press of America, 1991).

VOICES OF OUR FRIENDS

SPEAKING FOR THEMSELVES

Introduction

WHITE ALLIES STRIVING TO BE AWARE AND ENGAGED

ALLISON N. ASH, MDIV

Wheaton College, Dean of Student Care and Graduate Student Life

ALEXANDER JUN, PHD

Azusa Pacific University, Professor of Higher Education

In the end, we will remember not the words of our enemies, but the silence of our friends.
—Martin Luther King Jr.

We begin this introductory chapter of this section by citing a quote often attributed to Martin Luther King. The work of racial reconciliation and anti-racism is a lonely, painful, yet necessary journey down a troubled path for many people of color. For those who regularly battle overt and covert racism or macro- and microaggressions from colleagues, church members, leaders, and even subordinates, their struggle for justice emerges for the sake of survival. A common misunderstanding about diversity and equity work is that people of color are the ones responsible to make change. Rarely do those in the dominant white majority consider racial justice *their* issue.

To understand the perspectives and dynamics around issues of racial diversity, I (Jun) have collaborated with another colleague to address the great lengths that some white people go to in order to defend, justify, and rationalize privilege and dominance.[1] Issues related to diversity such as racial injustice are everyone's problem, and thus everyone ought to be part of the solution.

For the past few years, we (Ash and Jun) have focused our research on the role of white allies because the voices of white people are a necessary part of the solution to racial discord. Specifically, we have been conducting research on the role of white people who intentionally engage in racial justice advocacy and antiracist work in both secular and Christian higher education institutions.

Drawing from our research findings, we have developed a visual representation of what we term the "Awareness and Engagement Continuum" (Figure 1), which we have presented to colleagues but introduce for the first time in this book.

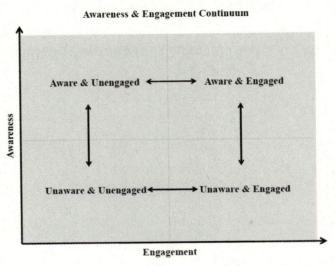

Figure 1. Awareness & Engagement Continuum. Demonstrates changes in engagement and awareness as a person experiences development as an advocate for social justice.

The Awareness and Engagement Continuum best captures what we have found to be a pattern of racial justice journeys among white people we have studied. Within the four quadrants, the bottom left emerged from our assumption that most white people begin by being both unaware and unengaged. The ultimate goal and prayer is for individuals to become both aware and engaged (upper right quadrant), though we acknowledge that there is not an agreed upon, set, or measurable outcome in this quadrant, but rather an aspirational mind-set of critical consciousness as it pertains to racial justice. We caution many would-be allies of the bottom right quadrant (unaware yet engaged): being positioned in that quadrant leads to some of the most unpromising of results, and often hurts people of color through words, attitudes, or actions by well-intentioned yet uninformed white colleagues. Several authors share their own struggles of this reality in the essays that follow, recognizing their crucial role in raising awareness among white people, including themselves.

The chapters in this section represent the reflections of three upper-level administrators and one tenured professor who share their own journeys with racial identity and diversity. These narratives are deeply personal, vulnerable, and offer much in teaching others about the process of wrestling daily with privilege. Their stories explain how they leverage both their whiteness as well as their positional leadership and authority to disrupt and dismantle the systemic racism that permeates Christian higher education.

Given that we employ qualitative methods in much of our research, we would be remiss if we did not acknowledge some emergent themes from the four essays that follow. We note that the authors talk about becoming aware of racial injustice as a process that occurred over time. This process included an awareness of racism as a social problem, as well as stages of their own racial identity development. The authors also comment on the struggle of staying engaged in the face of wanting to quit and the privilege that these sentiments reveal. Allison Ash and Sarah Visser, in particular, share of their own fragility and reference the work of Robin DiAngelo,[2] and Ash and Kristin Paredes-Collins address the complexities associated with multiracial identity or heritage, while at the same time identifying, presenting, or passing as white. Sarah Visser and Brian Howell share personal stories of painful racial incidents on their respective campuses and their subsequent attempts to encourage and support others along the way.

We acknowledge the complexities of having a section on white allies, but simultaneously stress its importance. First, the white narrative has been dominant in higher education and other narratives have been silenced. For this reason, the reader may question the use of stories from white people in a book about racial diversity. However, we hope that the reader will see the stories as forms of counter-narratives to the prevailing narratives that dominate higher education, in which white is the norm and against which everyone is often compared.

Second, one could argue that white allies receive this distinct ally label only when others have named persons as such. In other words, one cannot be a self-proclaimed white ally. The chapters in this section include stories of the successes and failures of white people who are attempting to be faithful to God's call to do justice, love mercy, and walk humbly. We acknowledge that whether or not these efforts constitute "ally-ship" is best assessed by those who regularly experience the kinds of injustices that the authors are seeking to remedy, with the ultimate judgment reserved for God alone.

Third, while we desire to share the stories of white colleagues who embrace their own positionality and struggle to fight with and for their colleagues of color, we are acutely aware of the dangers of coming across as celebrating white saviors who, at the end of the day, have the hidden privilege of choosing to engage in the work or not. Some scholars have referred to this process as decentering whiteness. This concept is a call to remove whiteness from the center of society and within our own hearts and minds, and replace the center with multiracial values. In order to do so, everyone ought to be engaged in this work of reconciliation, including our white brothers and sisters who need to be both aware and engaged. We need white colleagues to look at diversity work as mirrors to self-examine their identity rather than as windows used to gaze upon the challenges faced by Christians of color. It is critical for white Christians to shift their gaze and look internally at personal assumptions and biases toward a goal of critical consciousness and a solidarity with minority colleagues. This encouragement is especially true for leaders of Christian colleges and universities. As the leadership goes, so goes the rest of the institution. We hope this section serves as a catalyst for some people and an encouragement to others to begin or continue engaging in racial justice work.

This work is both important and urgent. Racial micro- and macroaggressions continue to persist on campuses across the country for minority students, faculty, and staff. Implicit biases that lead to microaggressions remain unchecked or uncritically examined, and white normativity continues to be tantamount to Christianity in Christian colleges and universities by well-intentioned people who love the Lord and would never knowingly or maliciously cause harm to their neighbor. One example is the problematizing of minority groups by questioning why in multiethnic spaces all the blacks or Asians seem to be congregating together, without ever acknowledging that whites have been exclusively gathering together for generations. The problem is that these unquestioned defaults in our thinking of normativity reveal our inherent assumptions about what is not only natural but what is Christian.

White people may respond to this section of the book on white allies in at least three possible ways. The first response is to continue with the status quo. Some will read this exhortation as a call to action for "them" and not take it as a personal appeal. Perhaps by not talking about racial injustice and the role that members of the white community can play, the problem will just go away. But it won't. It requires collaborative work from all parties. When one part of the body suffers, the entire body will suffer. We must see racial injustice as our collective problem.

A second response is to become or remain defensive. It is important to remember that the authors' descriptions of concepts like white privilege and normativity are a criticism against a system that has developed and grown over centuries, not a criticism of any particular individuals. We hope that the readers' perspectives could be shaped by the stories and insights from the authors to embrace the notion that this not you against me, but you and me against the problem.

The third and final response is to more fully recognize that there is a problem and commit to honest self-reflection and earnest engagement. Many of us who work in Christian ministry know what it means to be in community. We know what it means to hear the message of the gospel time and again before finally understanding and coming to grips with our own shortcomings, failures, and sins. Coming to this realization takes some people longer than others, but eventually, hopefully, we all recognize that we have a problem and we need a savior.

We acknowledge that for some people we are merely preaching to the choir, yet even the choir needs to be reminded of the gospel. It may be that even some long-standing members of the choir have been singing off-key for years. They might be unaware yet quite engaged. Choir members need to surround themselves with other members with a better sense of pitch and tone so that they can accurately hear themselves and improve their overall contribution to creating music that draws others closer to the kingdom.

It is important that we continue to live courageously. Our hope is that this section of *Diversity Matters* will help readers to recognize brokenness of individuals and of systems that perpetuate the problem of partiality and racism in society broadly, and Christian higher education specifically. Having conversations and critical reflections of identity, such as those related by these chapter authors, takes tremendous courage. It exposes some of our deepest fears about race discussions. We will make mistakes. Winston Churchill has often been credited as saying that the definition of success is to go from one failure to the next without losing any enthusiasm. Within the structural hierarchies of colleges, it is important for humble and courageous white faculty and administrative leaders to address ongoing racialized patterns within majority culture institutions. It is for such a time as this that colleagues across the country should engage in winsome discussions like these in order to unite rather than divide.

NOTES

1   Christopher Collins and Alexander Jun, *White Out: Understanding White Privilege and Dominance in the Modern Age* (New York: Peter Lang), 2017.
2   Robin DiAngelo, "White Fragility," *The International Journal of Critical Pedagogy* 3 (3; 2011): 54–70.

Chapter Ten

IDENTITY, AWARENESS, AND ENGAGEMENT: UNDERSTANDING MY WHITENESS

ALLISON N. ASH, MDIV

Wheaton College, Dean of Student Care and Graduate Student Life

We shall not cease from exploration, and the end of all our exploring will be to arrive where we started and know the place for the first time.

—T. S. Eliot, *Four Quartets*

Our lives begin to end the day we become silent about things that matter.

—Martin Luther King Jr.

"I don't understand why you're leading this group. It's just another example of a white person coming in and taking over. Why do white people have to lead everything around here?"

The room was silent as the other six students looked at me, appearing uncomfortable with their classmate's candor. I could tell that they were on the edge of their seats waiting to see what I, their leader, would say in response. In that moment, I felt a range of emotions and was tempted to respond defensively. My supervisor had asked me to lead a group that was meant to be a supportive and growing environment for people to share their stories and talk honestly about issues of race and diversity. It so happened that I was the only white person—and also the leader—of the group. I don't remember exactly what I said in the moment, but I think I told the student that I did not intend to take over, but to facilitate the group and help everyone in the process.

I left the meeting feeling frustrated, hurt, confused, angry, and defensive. That night, I had thoughts of quitting as the leader and asking my supervisor to find someone else to fill that role. Only later did I realize that my reaction revealed the very privilege I possessed as a white woman. As I prayed and reflected on the day, I realized that if I was going to quit over that comment, I had no place at the racial reconciliation table. The student's concern was not about me, but about something much larger. I suddenly knew that if I wanted to take part in helping, I needed to try to understand things from the student's perspective.

Part of what happened in that small group exchange was that this student decided to speak up about the reality of white leadership, privilege, and power at the school. Before that first meeting, I had not thought about how the group would feel about having the only white person be the leader of the group as they discussed difficult and sensitive racial and cultural issues. I had not considered how it would be for this student and others to have yet another white person in charge, calling the shots, and making decisions on their behalf. And I definitely had not thought about the fact that the other students were probably thinking exactly what this particular student was thinking, but had been reticent to say anything.

Writer bell hooks explains that, historically, slaves could be punished for observing the white people they served: "To be fully an object then was to lack the capacity to see or recognize reality."[1] The student speaking up about this group dynamic was seeing and recognizing reality: that yet another white person was going to tell these young people how things were going to be. That act of courage forced me to face my own whiteness in a new way and to understand how my presence came with a history. I learned to recognize what it meant not only to be a person working for racial justice but to be a *white* person engaged in this work.

Conferences, books, seminars, and classes have all been key sources of training for me in working toward racial justice and reconciliation. My hands-on work of social justice engagement has taken many forms: from seeking to make structural and systemic changes within educational institutions, to focusing my research and writing on improving efforts at diversifying Christian higher educational institutions, to being present with students and staff who may simply need to vent about the pains of experiencing racism on their campuses. As much as I could discuss these efforts, I could talk as much, if not more, about my failures and the ways in which I fall short at making significant changes in my spheres of influence. Each aspect of training, along with the successes and failures of engaging in advocacy, has helped me know what it means to be an advocate.

However, the lessons such as the one I described previously, along with other key personal moments of understanding my white identity, have been some of the most important aspects of my engagement in social justice. Without fundamentally understanding my own racial history and story, all of the practical training and knowledge would be like columns and pillars of a house lying in a pile of rubble, disconnected from the home's foundation. Without understanding my unconscious assumptions and biases that accompany my engagement in justice work, I believe that I have the potential to unintentionally do harm instead of good.

As I have explored the journey of my racial consciousness and development in this chapter, the foundations for my engagement in racial justice advocacy began to emerge. There are stories of mistakes, successes, and confusion about how to engage in this work, yet each speaks to the issues inherent in the work of diversity.

FROM CONFUSION TO CONVICTION

When my mother had to register my brother, sister, and me into a racial category for the US Census, she would check "other" and write in "Heinz 57." I recall her explaining this racial categorization to her friends when I was a little girl, but I didn't understand her creative category until I began to see and understand the racial diversity of my family.

As a child when we would visit my father's side of the family, I remember sitting on the laps of aunts, uncles, and my grandfather who had brown and caramel skin, unlike the white skin of my mom's side of the family—skin that looked much like mine. It wasn't until my sister asked one time, "Dad, is Aunt Net black?" that I realized my skin color was different from Aunt Net's skin color. I don't remember my father answering my sister's question that day. We didn't talk about the fact that his grandmother was black and that many of my aunts, uncles, and cousins are black. It wasn't until a few years later, at large extended family gatherings, that I met relatives who had darker skin than Aunt Net. When I saw their dark skin and coarse hair, and I saw my light skin and straight blonde hair, I realized that we were not the same. In those moments, I noticed for the first time that some of the members of my extended family were black and I was white. Skin color, ethnicity, and identity are intertwined in complex ways for me, as they are for many others.

From the time I was a child sitting on Aunt Net's lap and meeting my black relatives, I began unconsciously searching for my own racial identity. Although I grew up in a small, rural, white farming community in West Michigan and later attended a predominantly white college, I found myself searching to understand more about race and diversity throughout high school and college. As a child I wrote poems about Martin Luther King Jr.; in college, I was drawn to friendships with the few African American classmates I had; and I always seemed to experience more intense anger and outrage than my fellow white classmates when I learned about injustices like slavery and segregation.

While I was in seminary, I took ethics, systematic theology, and New Testament classes related to race and justice, and my search for racial identity converged with the theological understanding of the mandate for justice.[2] In these classes, I learned about things like the construction of whiteness through early US immigration policy, which forced citizens to biologically prove their whiteness in order to become citizens;[3] about *legal* forms of discrimination that prohibited black qualified Americans the right to home ownership in desirable areas;[4] and about black liberation theology from reading authors like James Cone.[5] I began seeing Scripture through a different lens: the gospel was not only a message of personal and individual salvation but included a message about the redemption of unjust evil structures that perpetuate a system of privilege and oppression (Matt. 20:1–16).

The process of racial and theological awareness raised enough courage and curiosity in me to ask my mother and father, my aunt, and my grandfather the difficult questions about our family's identity. At the prompting of my questions, I finally began learning about my family's racial categorization, a subject we had not broached in the past. From these conversations, I learned that my great-grandmother was African American and my great-grandfather's registered race on his birth certificate was white, although his marriage license said, "Colored."

I also learned that although my father was light-skinned and had passed for white throughout most of his life, his own sense of racial identity has been complex. On the one hand, growing up, he felt mostly accepted by people in his rural, white farming community. He described how he was accepted on playgrounds and included in sleepovers. On the other hand, he understood that people in his community knew that he was part black, which resulted in his fear of rejection and sense of inferiority. He told me one time, "Our neighbors really embraced my family, but I guess maybe we were our own worst enemy, trying to think that we were okay, but we just couldn't really believe that we were as good as the German, Polish, Italian, or Jewish neighbors." My father's fears became a reality when his high school girlfriend's parents made her break up with him because they "didn't want to have black grandchildren."

Eventually, when my mother and father attempted to discuss this racial history with my great-grandparents, they wouldn't talk about it. Even my grandfather denied his own race and distanced himself from many of his darker-skinned relatives. My family had painful experiences with racism: like the time my mother received an anonymous harassing phone call while engaged to my father, and the angry caller said, "Are you really going to marry that 'n word'?" My great-grandfather had been arrested for simply riding on a train. Regarding my great-grandfather's arrest, a relative told me that he had never recovered.

"He was never the same after that," she said. Lodged into this part of my family's imagination was the lie that white was superior and that, no matter how hard they tried to deny their race, they simply could never attain the whiteness that they desired.

With the convergence of discovering the racial complexity of my family and their encounters with racism, alongside a growing awareness of social injustice and an emerging understanding of the theological mandate for justice, I found myself becoming angry, confused, and convicted. I was angry at the injustice in the world, confused about what I was supposed to do with that anger, and yet convicted that I had to do something positive with it. I did not know what it was going to look like, but I knew that the gospel of Jesus called me to make some kind of positive change toward a more just society. Although I had strong convictions about seeking justice and engaging in antiracism advocacy, I had little understanding of my own white identity.

I would later learn that the process of understanding my own racial history—the things that I bring to the table as a white woman—would be one of the most important steps in understanding how to create positive change without doing damage to others along the way.

UNDERSTANDING WHITENESS

Understanding my whiteness began with me wanting to deny it. After learning about my family's diverse racial heritage, I thought that I had a leg up on other white people because I was not "totally white" and I understood racism and injustice through hearing about the experiences of my family firsthand. However, I eventually learned that although I experienced strong emotional connections to this important familial narrative, my experience of walking through life as a white woman created for me a distinctly different reality.

I have heard people of color say that white people fighting for justice who don't understand whiteness and their own identities can do as much damage as anyone in the fight to end racism. They have explained that it is possible for people to think they understand what needs to be done, but remain unaware of all of the complex dynamics of power and dominance that may be at play. I agree. These unconscious realities have the potential to perpetuate oppressive conditions without the "helper" even knowing. As some friends of color have said to me, "If someone is blatantly racist, at least I know where the person stands. Someone who has unconscious biases and attitudes but thinks he or she is actually helping to make positive change can do a lot of damage."

I admit that in these early days of engaging in antiracism advocacy I made damaging mistakes. It was through these mistakes that I finally began learning about what it meant to be white—not a textbook knowledge of whiteness (for example, how early immigration policies had constructed whiteness), but a deeply personal and sometimes painful awareness of what it meant that I was a white person who had unconscious privileges and biases.

An example of one of my mistakes was when I was the director of chapel at a seminary. Looking back at that point in my life, I now understand that I was in an early stage of white identity development—the stage that Janet Helms calls disintegration.[6] As I stated earlier, I had become reticent to identify as white because I didn't want to be the *bad guy*. I wanted to stand alongside my family and express my anger with and for them because of the racism they experienced. I didn't want to be associated with the group that was racist against them.

At the same time, I had a deep commitment to advocate for racial justice. I wanted to use my leadership position as a way to diversify our chapel services and reflect the racial composition of our campus so that *all* students, faculty, and staff would have a sense of belonging in worship.

Indeed, striking a balance of awareness and engagement is a challenging and delicate dance. At one chapel service, throughout the message we projected images of Jesus the speaker had chosen. In my opinion, the images created a powerful and moving dynamic and the entire chapel service was a success. However, a few days after the chapel, an African American friend who was also a student expressed to me her disappointment in the service. "Allison, every image of Jesus was a white man," she said. "Couldn't there have been some different images to reflect the diversity of those attending chapel?"

I felt the temptation to defend myself and explain that I hadn't chosen the images (which was true), but honestly I knew that even if I had reviewed them, I would not have suggested any changes. I was not conscious of the fact that all of the images of Jesus were white when I was participating in the chapel service that morning.

This experience taught me four critical lessons: First, it revealed to me my privilege as a white person of being able to view my race as the norm through the religious symbols that reflected me. Some scholars call this "White Normativity"[7]—the idea that the way white people understand life and society is accepted as the norm or *just the way things are*. I could not escape the fact that I had been molded by society's categorization of me which told me I was a part of that norm. The idea of white normativity lived inside of me and had the power to manifest itself in and through me, doing damage to the people I was leading.

Second, and more frightening, the experience made me aware that my privilege was *invisible* to me. As much as I wanted to enter into the pain of my family's experiences of racism, and as much as I was committed to creating chapel services that were inclusive of all people, I simply did not see the damaging unconscious assumptions that intermingled with my desire to do good. I learned that I could have a pure heart before God, confess my sin, love people deeply, want to make positive change, and still unknowingly hurt people through my unawareness. I learned that good intentions were not enough.

Third, understanding the invisible ideology of white normativity that lived inside of me meant that stripping myself of my whiteness was not a possibility. Being white—or black, or any other race—was not a categorization that I could choose any more than my father and his family could choose whether or not they would pass as white, or whether my great-grandfather was categorized as white at birth or "colored" by the time he was married. I began to understand something I did not have a label for at the time: the social construction of race. Even though I embraced the historical reality of the diversity of my family, I realized that I walked around every day in a white body that is afforded privileges whether I recognize those privileges or not.

Lastly, I learned that standing in solidarity with my family meant doing the tough work of self-examination to *embrace* my identity, to become aware of my privilege, and to begin seeing the ways in which I had unknowingly been complicit in the things that grieved me about the experiences of my family.

My attempt to diversify worship as the director of chapel was one of my earliest efforts to consciously advocate for racial justice within an educational setting. Perhaps that is why it was so painful to learn that in my eager desire to do something to help make things better, I actually did the opposite on that particular day. But this incident served as the foundation of understanding my own white identity and, consequently, engaging more deeply in the future.

The following experiences along the continual process of understanding my white identity have been critical in my engagement in social justice advocacy.

GETTING IT RIGHT AND WRONG AND RIGHT AND WRONG

Early in my marriage, I had a conflict with my husband Jeff. We were both out of a steady job and we were on a tight food budget. We had guests staying with us from out of town, and we decided to buy a nice pork roast. I realized after our guests left that I had forgotten to cook the roast. In fact, it was past the expiration date, and it was spoiled. When I realized what had happened, I was furious with myself for spending the money and for the waste of this expensive meal.

Jeff tried to make me feel better by hugging me and telling me that it wasn't a big deal, that everything would be fine. He and I quickly learned that this comfort was not what I wanted. I proceeded to tell him that I needed to be angry and that he should stop trying to fix something that couldn't be fixed. He then understandably felt hurt and betrayed after having tried to extend a comforting hand only to be rejected.

Other times, however, when I explained a frustrating situation to Jeff about something at work or with a friend, he remained silent. At times during his silence, I expressed frustration and said things like, "Well? What do you think? Do you have any advice?" Needless to say, Jeff was very confused. I know that Jeff and I have both felt confused throughout our marriage when we are attempting to figure out how to support the other person; we have both wondered if we should listen, engage, be silent, or step back.

The process of entering into racial justice or reconciliation as a white person has, for me, felt similarly confusing at times. I have heard sentiments like, "If you're not fighting to end racism, you're a part of the problem . . . ." However, as evidenced in the opening story, there are other times where I have jumped in and engaged in antiracism work only to feel criticized for that engagement. Sometimes I want an equation for exactly what to say and what to do at exactly the right time. But just as there was and still is no equation for the ways in which my husband and I know how to navigate each other's needs in particular circumstances, there is no perfect equation or formula for a white person advocating for social justice. Although at times simply listening to another person's story is what is needed, at other times, just listening with no action perpetuates a cyclical problem of dialogue without engagement.

My chances of knowing how and when to listen, engage, or retreat increase as I learn more about my own racial history and personal story. For example, learning about individualism in white evangelicalism[8] has opened my eyes to understand that my identity has largely been fashioned to see myself as an individual and not a member of a racial group. Understanding this reality helps me recognize that hindrances to effective engagement in racial justice work is related not only to my individual sinful nature, but also to the racial and cultural norms that are embedded in the worldview of my racial group. Consequently, I am conscious of the racial lenses through which I look when I encounter injustice. Instead of jumping in and offering a solution that reflects an individualistic worldview (e.g., we only need to get individual people to confess their individual sins), I may focus efforts at changing the systems and structures that hinder the progress of racial justice (e.g., helping change campus structures that perpetuate white normativity).

The awkwardness of not knowing what to say or not say, as well as when to engage or when not to, has tempted me to retreat from engaging in racial reconciliation. Sometimes it just feels too hard. Again, I reveal my privilege to talk about how hard it is to choose to engage in racial reconciliation, whereas my colleagues of color engage for the sake of survival. As author Peggy McIntosh has explained, white privilege is "an invisible package of unearned assets which I can count on cashing in each day, but about which I was 'meant' to remain oblivious."[9]

Without understanding my privilege, I may see retreating from the work of racial justice when things get tough just like I would understand walking away from any other commitment in my life. However, while I have the ability to walk away from the work of racial justice without any personal cost or damage, I am reminded that the failure to end racism has little direct impact on my daily life. From a personal standpoint, I am mostly free from the damaging effects of racism in my educational institution, Christian community, and society at large. This freedom is a privilege. As a white person, I can afford not to be involved because making that decision won't directly affect me. Yet when I begin to understand it as a privilege and not just another freedom, like the choice to stop serving on a church council, I can—and must—make conscious decisions not to retreat, even though the work is difficult.

Early in my work for racial justice, I wondered why racial conflict was so painful and why I was so quickly tempted to walk away from the costly work of racial justice. When my husband and I had those conflicts early in our marriage, we did not walk away from the first difficult discussion saying, "Well, this is just too hard. I'm done." Yet, as evidenced in the example at the beginning of this chapter, I was tempted to quit leading the small group at my school after a student challenged my authority as a white person. Why?

Understanding what author Robin DiAngelo calls "white fragility" has helped me comprehend this sensitivity. White fragility is the idea that for white people "even a minimum amount of racial stress becomes intolerable, triggering a range of defensive moves . . . such as anger, fear, and guilt."[10] As a white person, I have existed in a safe racial milieu where I have mostly been protected from racial stress. I am used to being liked and being around people who generally appreciate my leadership. Part of my identity—especially my professional identity—has been shaped by a cycle of my reaching out to help others, the recipients appreciating my help, and them typically expressing that appreciation. When I began engaging in activities like leading the small group of students where I was the only white person, challenging racial dynamics and cultural misunderstandings existed. These dynamics and misunderstandings challenged a significant part of my identity—that people generally like me. Instead of being the person who was the helpful leader, I discovered that I could easily make mistakes, hurt others, and not be appreciated for my efforts.

Understanding the reality of white fragility has helped me ask God to open my eyes to my own fragility and to make me mindful about why I may feel defensive or how to respond to those feelings. Although my gut reaction is to feel defensive when I have racial stumbles, stumbling is part of the process of being a white advocate. Thinking that I can be an advocate without making mistakes is like telling a toddler to learn to walk without ever falling down. It is simply not possible.

A racial stumble can become what author and speaker Brenda Salter McNeil calls a *catalytic moment*, that moment of disequilibrium when my preconceived notion of what is right, wrong, good, and bad is thrown into disarray and I am faced with a painful event. Salter McNeil explains that catalytic moments are painful but they also present opportunities.[11] The times of disequilibrium can reframe my thinking.

If I allow these moments to help me understand that working toward racial justice includes getting it right and getting it wrong as well as apologizing, rejoicing, being humbled, and being frustrated, then instead of allowing a well-intentioned action that has caused another pain to end in my withdrawal, I can respond appropriately. I can listen, apologize, learn, and stay engaged. Expecting total comfort along the way is not possible, just as feeling ignorant, embarrassed, or grieved because of my own mistakes never feels good. Ever. But allowing my discomfort to teach me instead of defeat me is critical in this work.

REMAINING

Perhaps one of the most profound, catalytic moments in the New Testament is the Apostle Paul's conversion and calling to preach the gospel in Acts 9. Through a medical and spiritual crisis (i.e., blindness and the inability to eat or drink for three days, combined with the obliteration of Paul's previous theological understanding), God literally opened Paul's eyes to the reality that Jesus was the son of God and that Paul was called to preach this message to the "Gentiles and kings and the people of Israel" (Acts 9:15 ESV). God brought Paul to a place of profound disequilibrium in order to make Paul aware of what he needed to know to fulfill his life's work and ministry.

Understanding my own complex racial heritage, jumping in to engage in advocacy work only to make mistakes, and recognizing how my own privileges and unconsciousness have, at times, created in me a disequilibrium, are all part of the process. God has used such disequilibrium to open my eyes to my own blindness and to obey God's call to work for racial reconciliation.

Those of us who desire to be white allies must embrace our own stories with wisdom and self-awareness, understand our racial history humbly and honestly, and allow the sometimes painful experiences of disequilibrium to be catalyzing moments of growth, humility, courage, and commitment to remain in the gospel-centric work of racial reconciliation.

FOR DISCUSSION

1. What is your racial, ethnic, or cultural story?

2. In what ways do you feel that your race affects the way you approach racial reconciliation?

3. If you are a white person, what are some ways you have felt stuck in trying to know the right thing to do as an advocate engaged in racial justice and reconciliation?

4. How have you been criticized for the ways that you have engaged in racial justice advocacy? What were your reactions or feelings as a result of that criticism?

5. What steps are you currently taking to engage in racial justice or reconciliation, as well as to increase your own racial consciousness?

6. When you hear the term "white privilege," what kinds of feelings are evoked in you?

7. In what ways does—or could—your biblical understanding form a vision and a strategy for engaging in racial reconciliation?

8. What is one step that you can take to increase your own racial consciousness? To increase your engagement in racial reconciliation?

NOTES

1 bell hooks, "Representations of Whiteness in the Black Imagination," in *White Privilege: Essential Readings on the Other Side of Racism*, ed. Paula S. Rothenberg (New York: Worth Publishers, 2012), 21.

2 Obery Hendricks, *The Politics of Jesus: Rediscovering the True Revolutionary Nature of Jesus' Teachings and How They Have Been Corrupted* (New York: Doubleday, 2006).

3 Richard Delgado and Jean Stefancic, *Critical Race Theory: An Introduction* (New York: New York University Press, 2012).

4 Jacquelyn D. Hall, "The Long Civil Rights Movement and Political Uses of the Past," *The Journal of American History* 91 (4; 2005): 1233–63, doi: 10.2307/3660172.

5 James H. Cone, *A Black Theology of Liberation* (Maryknoll, NY: Orbis Books, 2010).

6 Janet E. Helms, *Black and White Racial Identity: Theory, Research, and Practice* (New York: Greenwood Press, 1990).

7 Woody Doane, "Rethinking Whiteness Studies," in *White Out: The Continuing Significance of Racism*, ed. Ashley W. Doane and Eduardo Bonilla-Silva (New York: Routledge, 2003), 3–18.

8 Michael O. Emerson and Christian Smith, *Divided by Faith: Evangelical Religion and the Problem of Race in America* (Oxford: Oxford University Press, 2000), 2.

9 Peggy McIntosh, "White Privilege: Unpacking the Invisible Knapsack," in *White Privilege: Essential Readings on the Other Side of Racism*, ed. Paula S. Rothenberg (New York: Worth Publishers, 2012), 121.

10 Robin DiAngelo, "White Fragility," *International Journal of Critical Pedagogy* 3 (3; 2011): 54.

11 Brenda Salter McNeil, *Roadmap to Reconciliation: Moving Communities into Unity, Wholeness, and Justice* (Downers Grove, IL: InterVarsity Press, 2015), 42.

Chapter Eleven

FROM DENIAL TO SOLIDARITY: FINDING MY PLACE AS A WHITE ALLY

Brian Howell, PhD
Wheaton College, Professor of Anthropology

Let us all hope that the dark clouds of racial prejudice will soon pass away and the deep fog of misunderstanding will be lifted from our fear drenched communities and in some not too distant tomorrow the radiant stars of love and brotherhood will shine over our great nation with all their scintillating beauty.
—Martin Luther King Jr., *Letter from a Birmingham Jail*

Love takes off masks that we fear we cannot live without and know we cannot live within.
—James Baldwin

Vince was a first-year student in the first row of my first class on the first day of my first semester as a professor at Wheaton College.[1] He was a biracial guy (black and white) from St. Louis, the city from which I had just arrived, having attended graduate school at Washington University. He was a friendly, outgoing student who was thrilled to be at Wheaton, just like me. We clicked.

He also arrived, like many students, ready to assume that in a Christian community, race would not matter. Only Jesus would matter. He assumed that as he bonded with the men on his floor, met with women of his sister floor, and pursued friendships of all kinds, social differences would become, if not meaningless, at least unimportant.

By the end of his first year, Vince was more than a bit disappointed. He'd had a student touch his hair, patting him on the head like a poodle, declaring it "poofy." He had people imitate (and grossly exaggerate) his very subtle urban accent. He had people ask him for "his" music and want to borrow his clothes, so they could have a "rap battle." Small things. Each was a reminder to Vince that he was different, and that some differences were not as respected as others.

In the following years, Vince responded by adopting a strong black persona; an afro nearly a foot across; sports jerseys from FUBU, a hip-hop apparel company, and the "bling" that was popular among black urban youth in the Midwest at that time. He leaned into the identity that was, he had learned, unwelcomed in a predominantly white school. At the same time, he found ways to engage his peers, rally other black students, and try to grow, even in the face of various obstacles.

Vince was one of the first students I would see going through this sort of process, but he certainly was not the last. Thankfully, Vince brought me along on this process with him. He shared openly in my office, sometimes nearly in tears, as he related the most recent insult, the experience of a black friend, or his own questions about identity as a black man in Christ. I learned a lot from Vince.

Because I have *had* allies in learning about race and racism, I have learned why and how to *become* an ally in the antiracism work in Christian higher education.[2] I have come to see that engaging race and racism is not an "issue" that affects some groups, or that some people are called to address, but is fundamental to what it means to love one another well; what it means to be part of God's work to bring shalom and redemption; what it means to love our neighbor (Luke 10:25–37) and put others' interests ahead of our own (Phil. 2:4).

These experiences with Vince have become part of my life at my institution. Learning to listen to the experiences of others has allowed me to find a voice to speak or offer support to others on their journey. As I have learned to be vulnerable about my own mistakes, and my own ignorance, I have been able to create space for more healthy conversations, and productive action, around issues of race.

LEARNING TO LISTEN: FINDING RESOURCES FOR THE JOURNEY

Having grown up in a small city in Southeastern Washington State, I had a few Asian American friends, and there were several Latino students in my high school, but for the most part, my world was racially homogenous. I certainly did not get much help within that context to understand racial issues prior to college. For me, going away to college across the country was a profound shift in perspective, and I was eager to learn about the wider world.

I did not attend a Christian institution as an undergraduate. Instead, in 1987, I flew to a secular liberal arts college in Connecticut to join a community that I would come to realize was known for political activism and progressive politics. I received a good education in all the conventional ways, but even more profoundly in issues of diversity and race. Not that I set out looking for these lessons. As a politically conservative student from eastern Washington, I resisted much of what I heard.

Some narratives of discrimination and oppression made sense to me. When Asians and Asian Americans talked about the ways their culture was denigrated, or how the immigrant experience had shaped their understanding of the United States, I could wrap my head around it. I could see the differences in language and culture. But when African Americans and other black people in the United States spoke about racial discrimination, I didn't get it. *Your family has been here for generations*, I would think. *Slavery has been over for 100 years, and the Civil Rights movement solved the lingering problems*, I would tell myself. Here were students at an elite New England college—recruited by the institution and given, from my perspective, all kinds of concessions and preferential treatment—complaining that they were discriminated against. It just didn't make sense.

I did try to find answers to my questions, but this engagement wasn't always easy. I vividly recall one evening when I attended a meeting sponsored by SOAR (Students Organized Against Racism); the program was a discussion on Affirmative Action held at Malcolm X House, the black student housing on campus. I can't recall if or what I contributed to the conversation, but I recall a moment when one of my peers, a Puerto Rican woman of African heritage, stood to talk about her frustrations as a minority woman in the United States and on campus. She pointed a finger directly at me, one of the few white men in the room, and said something like "Because *you* have had everything handed to you on a silver platter and have oppressed me my whole life!"

I'm probably exaggerating the exact words, but this accusation is what my twenty-year-old mind took in and exactly how it felt in the moment. I certainly understood that racism was real to this woman and the many others in the room. I understood that there was *something* going on, something that I still didn't understand. I also learned that I was the problem. I had no moral ground to say or think or do anything except receive an accusation. I felt stereotyped, condemned, and dismissed. Needless to say, I left that meeting, and many others, frustrated, alienated, and resistant to the words I heard.

From college, I joined Teach for America and moved to Los Angeles, where I worked in a fifth-grade class of mostly black and Latino students. I began to understand more of the issues at play in race, but honestly, I continued to see concerns about contemporary racism as overblown, easily explained by other factors (such as class and culture), and I continued to resist much of what I heard from my black colleagues, students, and their parents.

Perhaps my greatest shift came while I was living in St. Louis for graduate school. By then I had been married for several years to my wife, Marissa Sabio, a Filipino-American who taught English as a second language (ESL) and Spanish in public and private schools. I had begun to experience life as a father of kids with that ethnically ambiguous look that would, at times, elicit some odd reactions from strangers (with questions about adoption, babysitting, and even suspicions of abduction). Most significantly, I had been part of an innovative congregation in St. Louis working toward racial reconciliation in a deeply racially divided city.[3] William and Jenna Wallace were the leaders of our small group, along with a white couple.[4] They were spiritually mature, fun, compassionate people who, as African Americans a generation older than me, had lived a life very different from mine. As this couple became something of a mentor to me, I could see more clearly how race and racism had shaped their lives.

If there was something of an epiphany in my own journey of racial development, it was when Jenna described how her supervisor treated her at work. She shared the subtle degradations, the missed promotion, and racial comments that made it clear that her blackness was at the root of these issues. William shared experiences returning from Vietnam, about life in a segregated neighborhood, and his often negative interactions with police. As I would listen to these stories, our relationship made it possible for me to ask questions—even some dumb questions—and receive patient and compassionate answers. I learned to laugh with them about the funny things black folks do, and the odd ways of white people. This couple was a gift from God that he put right in my living room every Wednesday night.

It was more than relationships, however, that enlarged my ability to grasp the significance of what people told me. As a graduate student in anthropology, I was learning to read the symbols and significance of the world around me, and I was coming to appreciate the importance of research and insights gained from a variety of fields. I could see that learning to listen to the people around me, as well as becoming familiar with the extant literature, was indispensible to my ability to speak about matters of race.

No single story from William and Jenna, no single anecdote from another black church member, no definitive article or book that I read convinced me that my earlier views about race were wrong, but taken together they changed me. I saw that racism, from its most virulent forms in slavery and Jim Crow, or anti-Chinese laws, Japanese internment, and the lynching of Mexicans in the Southwest, had not disappeared but had evolved.[5] I learned that racism and discrimination affected individuals differently and showed up in many guises for Latino/a, Asian, black, Native, women, or disabled people. I also learned that my earlier attitudes—my resistance to their stories in college and early professional life—were simply wrong. Even students of color at an elite New England college, or black people who had achieved professional success experienced the quotidian racism of verbal slights, small humiliations, and (often unintended) discrimination. My eyes were finally opened to the ways racism mattered in American life.

Thus, when I showed up at Wheaton College in 2001, my thinking about race was in a very difference place from where it had been when I graduated from college ten years earlier. But in spite of this growth, my undergraduate experience left me with the expectation that I should not insert myself into conversations on race. These were better addressed by faculty of color and administrators, many of whom were more adequately positioned to take the lead in matters of race and diversity. Although I had done a bit of writing on race, my research was in the anthropology of Christianity. I was not teaching classes specifically devoted to race and ethnicity. Most importantly, I was a white, Anglo-Saxon, Protestant man. I grew up in a family that owned Tupperware specifically devoted to holding Velveeta cheese, for heaven's sake. I often felt like the whitest person ever. I did not come into Wheaton thinking that I would have a role in conversations about race beyond shutting up, listening, and—frankly—getting out of the way.

Wheaton, however, turned out be a rather different place than my own undergraduate university. Certainly, I was a very different person from my eighteen-year-old self, but the Christian context dramatically affected the expectations of incoming students. Like Vince, some students of color came to Wheaton with high hopes that a common Christian identity would overcome racial and cultural differences. They rarely arrived at Wheaton expecting to confront difficult racial politics. Often they came with a pretty strong appreciation for, or at least understanding of, "white culture"—at least the evangelical variety. These students of color were, like many Wheaton students, fairly conflict averse, tending to associate such hard discussions with division and a lack of Christian love. As underclass students of color, they were quite unlikely to point an accusing finger at a white peer.

By their senior years, however, I could see that many were frustrated, exhausted, and just done. They were sometimes still reluctant to point a finger in blame, but they were often tired of talking, tired of explaining the same issues, tired of receiving the same sorts of pushback again and again.

In my anthropology classes, I had the opportunity to talk about race to my captive audiences of majority and minority students, and I knew that I could not shy away from the difficult truths about inequality, cultural and structural racism, and microaggressions.[6] But racism was not my specific area of expertise, and I had to learn where and how to bring in these conversations as well as be ready for the complications that would come with it. I had to learn, and continue to develop, my ability to speak on matters of race.

FINDING A VOICE: LEARNING TO SPEAK TRUTH IN LOVE

There is no doubt that one of the great barriers for white people to engage conversations about race is fear.[7] We fear making a mistake. We fear this mistake
will lead to misunderstanding. We fear, most of all, being perceived as a racist.
This conversation becomes an area where white people live with a kind of "stereotype threat," fearing that others (particularly people of color) may assume
we are racially insensitive, so we become more cautious, tense, and resistant in
those very moments where we most need to engage. (And, in a cruel twist, we
consequently become more likely to make mistakes.)[8]

At the same time, we must learn to speak. Learning how, when, and why we
white Christians can speak about race becomes part of our work as members of
a diverse body where we are called to bear one another's burdens, act justly and
do mercy, and be salt and light in the world.[9] Like people of every background,
white people are part of a context in which racial classification shapes us all in
complex ways. We owe it to ourselves, and our students, to learn to speak well
about race. For myself, I have had to learn how to speak to what my own experience has been as a white man learning about race. First, this topic requires a
fair bit of humility as I address continued mistakes and gaps in my own understanding. It also requires practice, putting myself into situations where I can
learn, listen, and sometimes speak on what I've come to learn about race.

In speaking of my own experience, I've had to be honest about my own
background. As someone who has been through a fairly classic version of
"white identity development," there are times in my past where I have denied
racism, rejected people's stories, or been far too eager to solve what I perceive
to be the problems.[10] But admitting mistakes in the past is relatively easy compared to confessing my ongoing missteps. I recall a faculty development seminar at Wheaton when the speaker asked us to share experiences in which we
felt we had made racial missteps with our students or colleagues. I had been at
Wheaton for more than eight years at that point, and was known as someone
who cared about issues of race and diversity. I raised my hand. I shared a story
of a time when I had an introductory anthropology class of about forty students, four of whom were black. At Wheaton, 10 percent is pretty high for one
class. These were not students who had come as friends, or even sat next to each
other in class, but knowing we would be talking about race later in the semester,
I was pleased to have more than just one black student. Several weeks into the
course, one of those students approached me in the dining hall. She said she
was enjoying the course and was glad she'd decided to take it. I replied, "Yes, I'm
glad you guys are in the class, too."

At this admission, the room of my peers both gasped and laughed. Fortunately, that was pretty much what I did when speaking with this student as well. She and I were able to laugh and I apologized for lumping her in with her black classmates as some kind of club for black students, and it became a running joke as she and I got to know each other through future classes. But it was, needless to say, embarrassing and potentially hurtful to her. I could have also shared the several occasions in which I consistently confused the names of the two Asian American women in the class. (I often do this to blond women, too, but that doesn't make it any better.) I could also have mentioned the time I assumed that the only black faculty member in the music conservatory must be the jazz professor. (He taught composition and played classical clarinet.) There is, and I suspect will be, no shortage of humiliations I could share.

I can say, however, that these gaffes and missteps each provide me an opportunity to learn and grow. They have given me a sensitivity to others, and have made me more approachable to students and colleagues when I share these stories (or even when they witness them), provided I can respond without defensiveness or denial. Like every white American I know, I have breathed deeply the air of racial superiority, stereotype, and hierarchy. I have had to unlearn what comes so naturally in our culture, and I may never be wholly redeemed in these matters, this side of heaven.

Much of learning to speak about these matters has come through practice. I have, through the topics I present in class, the events I attend, and even the churches my family and I have joined, deliberately put myself in positions to engage matters of race. I admit that in terms of my professional life, including conversations of race is easier in an anthropology classroom than it would be in your typical physics class. However, there are certainly courses I teach in which race is not easily incorporated into the syllabus. My engagement with race is something I may need to bring in creatively, not as a formal part of the course, but rather as one of those parts of life that find their way into our courses.

I have certainly used the "devotion" time of some courses to talk about matters of community, love, and race as they have surfaced on our campus and in the world. During the Ferguson unrest of 2014, taking place only a few hours away from our campus, many students of color were distracted and alarmed by all that they saw on the news. I knew that I needed to take time in class to, at minimum, pray for that community. I also chose one day to devote considerable time for students to speak about their feelings around this event. It was scary for me, as the professor, to allow a conversation that could (and did) become emotional and contentious, but it was also my responsibility as a faculty member to create a space where students could share their frustration, fear, anger, and sadness over these events, even if their classmates couldn't quite understand what they were saying.

What surprises me as I have learned to speak about race is how helpful some of this would prove to be to my students, and even my colleagues, of color. For my students, I discovered that many of them were just beginning their process of understanding their racial identity as a part of their emerging adult life. Given their wide variety of backgrounds and experiences, many students were confused by the difficulty of communicating the nature of their experiences as minorities in the United States to their white peers. As they heard me saying things from the front of the classroom that resonated with their experiences—articulating things they had said many times before to limited or hostile reception—they found themselves empowered, validated, and encouraged. For some of these students, particularly those in their first year, this could be the first time that someone in a position of authority—particularly a white man—was saying that their experiences were worthy of discussion. For many, especially those who had gone to majority white high schools, it was the first time a teacher had led a discussion of race, affirming what they knew as complex, important, and real.

Such conversations are not only helpful for students of color, of course. White students also need their white faculty to speak out. Beverly Daniel Tatum, a well-known author on matters of racial identity and education, said:

> As a black woman who has been teaching about racism for almost twenty years, I have learned how desperate white students are for positive images of whiteness. In the process of learning about racism, white students are forced to confront their whiteness in ways that most have not done before,—to recognize their racial privilege and the assumption of White superiority that has been so interwoven in most of their educational experiences.[11]

Tatum went onto note that many white students, as they confront racism, feel shame, sadness, and anger. As a white faculty member, I am in a position to empathize with these feelings, speak to them, and respond to them out of my own personal experience. Just as all students need role models to help them navigate into adulthood, white students in particular need mentors who can show them a way through the often confusing landscape of contemporary racial politics.

I recall one young white woman from the South who was one of my top students: brilliant, engaged, and motivated. She confronted her family's and region's racial legacy by throwing herself into antiracist activism. When a painful racial incident occurred on campus, she was quick to join with students of color, and was mindful to follow their lead, prioritize their stories and suffering, and self-consciously engage as an ally. Nevertheless, some of her friends of color told her to back off. They needed their own space in which to process, and they began to cut her out of some of their work.

She sat in my office, crying, wondering what she had done wrong. We prayed and talked, but mostly I assured her that I understood what she was feeling. I, too, had walked through this difficult terrain of emotions in a complex and broken world. I was able to help her step back and see a bigger picture that included painful historical realities of white oppression and dominance. But mostly I was able to provide a safe place for her to wonder aloud about what she was doing, analyze how her friends were responding, and ask questions that didn't feel very safe to ask.

To be clear: I certainly don't want to suggest that my voice, as a white man, was more important than those of my colleagues of color. Whenever I have spoken about race, in the classroom or elsewhere, I remain acutely aware that I am in a privileged position to choose if and when I would think about race, and that my experience is always removed from a firsthand experience of being disadvantaged, stigmatized, or marginalized by racial hierarchies. The very presence of black, Asian, and Latino/a faculty, even those who may not teach, research, or speak about race often, is a powerful witness of possibility to students of color. Even more, I can always see that my colleagues of color engage race and racism in ways that are qualitatively different than what I can. But that doesn't change the fact that I must understand these issues and learn to speak; that I simply have a responsibility as a Christian to do so.

Learning to listen and finding my voice has led me to become an advocate who does not always wait to step in where injustices occur. When a racial incident rocked our campus in 2012, it was important for the faculty to make a formal statement recognizing the severity of the event. My colleagues of color, many of whom were caring for students, and themselves personally wounded, could trust that I would lead an effort to draft a statement and bring it to the floor of a faculty meeting. They didn't have to ask; it was the right thing to do.[12] Similarly, as I have heard from many students about the lack of historical and cultural awareness of their peers, when the opportunity for curricular reform came up at our institution, I sought out service on the committee that would focus on a diversity requirement. I knew that, as a white man, I had a kind of (unearned) legitimacy; I would be perceived as "neutral." (If they only knew!) If the committee was composed only of people of color, the very sorts of assumptions that make such curricular reform necessary could undercut the legitimacy of the work. I could ally with my colleagues of color to support and advocate for these crucial changes.

Without an intentional commitment to inhabit these spaces, it would be easy to avoid them. One of the most significant aspects of what is often called white privilege is the ability to simply avoid those contexts where our whiteness is visible.[13] We often find it awkward, or uncomfortable, when we notice there are few other white people around, wondering if we're welcome, or if we should even be there. We may shy away from discussions of race, thinking that is "their" issue, and not something we should address. Only by making the decision to move into these spaces have I overcome my own discomfort, gained from the wisdom of people of color who regularly feel their minority status, and learned to articulate how race and racism affect us all.

CONCLUSION: TO LOVE ONE ANOTHER

Learning how to listen and speak well has been—and is—an ongoing process. Like many white people, I avoided speaking frankly about race for a long time, traumatized by early negative experiences, and silenced by the fear of saying the wrong thing. At the same time, as I have grown in my understanding that the kingdom of God is at hand, I have become convinced that *not* speaking into the brokenness we have around race in the United States is simply not an option. As so many of the essays in this volume testify, the church's inability to love one another well across the socially constructed divides of race have left wounds on the body of Christ and damaged our witness in the world.

My wife and I try to subject all our choices—where we live, where our children go to school, the church we attend, how we live out our vocations—to our sense of call and service in the gospel. Naturally, each person has to follow God's leading in these things, leading to as many different configurations of Christian life as there are Christians. But to the extent that my wife and I are convinced that racial justice is a part of the gospel, it has always been a part of our decisions as well. As a highly educated, relatively wealthy white person, it is easy to avoid those places, communities, and circumstances that would challenge the dominant narrative of white normativity in the United States. Thus I have to choose to do otherwise.

Like so much in the Christian life, learning to be a white ally is a calling to abandon the easy and wide road. It is a calling to pick up others' burdens and bear them as our own. It is a calling to humbly allow others to correct, admonish, and guide us as we learn to listen and speak. Such work is part of what it means to live in the light of the coming kingdom, where "every nation, and all tribes, and people, and tongues, [are] standing before the throne and before the Lamb." (Rev. 7:9 NASB). Learning to walk with my brothers and sisters of color, learning to listen well, and learning to speak in ways that serve them and the kingdom has been a source of great growth for me, and a tremendous joy. May we all find grace in the journey.

FOR DISCUSSION

1. If you are white, what are some of the fears or experiences that prevent you from engaging conversations about race? What are the fears you have heard others express? If you are a person of color, how have you observed white Christians avoiding conversations about race? Why do you think it makes them uncomfortable?

2. Are there aspects of the author's experience with which you can identify? How has your own process of racial identity formation overlapped or diverged from that of the author?

3. In considering the process of learning to listen, what are some ways that you have learned to listen, or felt listened to, when it comes to matters of racial differences?

4. In finding your voice, what are some things that you find helpful from those trying to facilitate conversations about race? What inhibits these conversations? What do you do (or wish you could do) in facilitating healthy conversations about race?

5. Whether you are white or a person of color, what are some ways you might put yourself into new positions or places, on your campus or elsewhere in your life, to be stretched to engage conversations about race in new ways?

NOTES

1   With permission, I use Vince's real name here. He remains a good friend and source of wisdom for me on questions of race and antiracism work in the church.

2   This notion of ally-ship running both ways is taken from Gary R. Howard, "White Man Dancing: A Story of Personal Transformation," in *Becoming and Unbecoming White: Owning and Disowning a Racial Identity*, ed. Christine Clark and James O'Donnell, vol. 13, Critical Studies in Education and Culture Series (Westport, CT: Bergin & Garvey, 1999), 219.

3   Brian M. Howell, "Power and Reconciliation in an Urban Church: The Case of New City Fellowship," in *This Side of Heaven: Race, Ethnicity, and the Christian Faith*, ed. Robert Priest and Alvaro L. Nieves (New York: Oxford University Press, 2007), 293–308.

4   Pseudonyms are used here to protect the identity of those involved. See Howell, "Power and Reconciliation in an Urban Church: The Case of New City Fellowship."

5   I take this language of the "evolution of racism" from the work of Bryan Stevenson and the Equal Justice Initiative. See Bryan Stevenson, *Just Mercy: A Story of Justice and Redemption*, reprint edition (New York: Spiegel & Grau, 2015). Also, "Equal Justice Initiative," *EJI*, accessed June 24, 2016, http://www.eji.org.

6   Regarding racism in everyday life, see Jane Hill, *The Everyday Language of White Racism* (London: Blackwell, 2008). For work dealing specifically with the concept of "microaggressions," see Derald Wing Sue, *Microaggressions and Marginality Manifestation, Dynamics, and Impact* (Hoboken, NJ: Wiley, 2010).

7   See Beverly Daniel Tatum, "Talking about Race, Learning about Racism: The Application of Racial Identity Development and Theory in the Classroom," in *Racial and Ethnic Diversity in Higher Education*, ed. C. S. V. Turner et al. (Needham Heights, MA: Simon & Schuster, 1996), 150–69.

8   There is a great deal of sophisticated research on *stereotype threat* and how it affects the performance and psyche of individuals in various situations. It is most often experienced by visible minorities, including women, in situations where cultural and racial stereotypes often prevail, but can be experienced by any individual depending on context. For an immanently readable overview of this literature from a social psychology perspective, see Claude M. Steele, *Whistling Vivaldi: How Stereotypes Affect Us and What We Can Do*, reprint edition (New York: W. W. Norton & Company, 2011).

9   Gal. 6:2; Mic. 6:8; Matt. 5:13–16.

10 There are a number of resources to understand white racial identity development and the scholarly discussion around these ideas. For a helpful overview of this literature, particularly as it intersects with higher education, see Vasti Torres, Mary F. Howard-Hamilton, and Diane L. Cooper, *Identity Development of Diverse Populations: Implications for Teaching and Administration in Higher Education* (San Francisco: Jossey-Bass, 2003).

11 Beverly Daniel Tatum, "Lighting Candles in the Dark: One Black Woman's Response to White Antiracist Narratives," in *Becoming and Unbecoming White: Owning and Disowning a Racial Identity*, ed. Christine Clark and James O'Donnell, Critical Studies in Education and Culture Series, vol. 13 (Westport, CT: Bergin & Garvey, 1999), 56.

12 I did bring this statement to a number of trusted colleagues of color for review, but they told me at the time that they were glad for a white faculty member to take the lead. I would note, of course, that in such incidents, I would always defer to a person of color if he or she felt it were best initiated by someone within that community.

13 A widely read and frequently cited piece on white privilege is Peggy McIntosh, "White Privilege: Unpacking the Invisible Knapsack," *Independent School* 49 (2; 1990): 31–36. See also Stephanie M. Wildman, "The Persistence of White Privilege Whiteness: Some Critical Perspectives," *Washington University Journal of Law & Policy* 18 (2005): 245–66.

Chapter Twelve

THE EVOLUTION OF A WHITE SCHOLAR-PRACTITIONER

Kristin Paredes-Collins, PhD

Pepperdine University, Dean of Enrollment Management

In July 2016, as I write this chapter on being a white ally, I mourn the loss of Philando Castille and Alton Sterling: two more black men whose lives were cut short by the hands of police officers in the United States. Yet I do not necessarily feel like a white ally; I do not deserve to be called one. Yes, I have worked to develop consciousness connected to my racial identity and my white privilege, while actively working toward access, equity, and inclusion for students of color in higher education. I understand the value of diversity in higher education and I care deeply about creating a diverse learning environment for students. The majority of my scholarly work has focused on the disparities between students of color and white students in the higher education environment.

Despite my efforts to advance diversity, I am still very shielded from the reality that students of color experience on Christian college campuses. I attend diversity-related conferences with students and promise that I am an advocate on their behalf when I am behind closed doors. Even then, I largely shy away from having the tough conversations about race and privilege with many around me. I still fear saying the wrong thing.

I feel like my advocacy comes in the form of words on paper that few will ever read, at least those who need to. I preach to the choir. By nature, I am someone who hates uncomfortable situations. I have been known to flee an awkward family event where a new significant other is introduced.

I am an introvert who happens to work in a very extroverted industry: university admissions. Before large recruitment events where I am speaking, I typically hide out in the restroom to avoid awkward interactions with prospective families prior to my address. Sometimes I feel like I hide behind my distaste of awkwardness—I let this be an excuse not to engage in the toughest, and perhaps most important, conversations about race and privilege with those around me.

Thus I feel like I can just barely be called an ally. In fact, I am a theoretical ally more than I am practically anything else. But I am committed to moving beyond being an ally with a keyboard. I am committed to refining my voice, using it where I have influence, and continuing to learn. If there is one thing that I am very confident about, it is this: knowing that I have not yet *arrived* to some final or greater level of critical consciousness, nor will I ever. Instead, I know that I have so much to learn and I am willing to do so.

WHO AM I?

I am white. I am Mexican American. I am multiracial. I have light skin and my family name is Paredes. The word *paredes* means "walls" in Spanish, but for much of my educational and professional experience, more people wondered if I was Greek than Hispanic. I grew up close to the maternal side of my family, with a predominantly white family identity. I attended predominately white schools and went to white churches. I thought I knew what it meant to be Mexican because we ate tacos for more meals than we didn't, and I knew how to properly pronounce a variety of food-related words in Spanish. Even then, I struggled with learning Spanish.

English was my father's second language, and my grandparents gained access to the United States via sponsorship practices that have long since disappeared. I grew up several hours from the Mexican side of my family, whom we visited a few times a year. I have vivid, beautiful memories of attending a wedding in the Crystal Cathedral as a child and a family reunion in Tijuana, where the colors and the people and the food were more beautiful than anything I had ever known. These few experiences and interactions provided me with the illusion of knowing what it meant to be Mexican. I would have proudly called myself Mexican before I would have referred to myself as white. But, I most certainly would never have considered myself to be a minority. And why would I? I looked white, I lived in a white community, I attended a white church, and I attended white schools. I *was* white.

My first opportunity to live and learn in a more diverse community was as an undergraduate at a Christian university, where I enjoyed rich growth academically, spiritually, and intellectually. In the years during and following my undergraduate experience, I began to explore my identity as a Mexican American woman, which finally stretched beyond my lifelong love of Mexican food. Because I lived closer to my Mexican grandparents (Nana y Papacito), my time spent with them had a newly revived vigor—the language barrier had melted and I yearned to hear the stories of their youth when they grappled with life in Southern California as immigrants.

With the combination of their rich and painful stories and my burgeoning career in university admission work, I was confronted with the disheartening reality of the roadblocks to access of and equity in higher education (and beyond) that many historically underrepresented students experience. Through my continued exposure to such inequity, my research interests in the areas of access, equity, and campus climate for diversity at Christian institutions were born. I took on the role of a *practitioner scholar*, committed to the experiences of underrepresented students, faculty, and staff at predominantly white faith-based institutions.

An ally is sometimes understood to reference someone in a dominant position who is committed to issues of justice; as a multiracial woman, I face the intersection of power on many levels. However, my ability to operate as a white woman also places me in the position of having the opportunity to explore what it means to be an ally. I have spent most of my professional career working in admissions and enrollment management. I have also served as an associate editor for an academic journal, and I see my practice and scholarship rooted in issues of access, admission, and campus climate. This chapter includes vignettes about my identity development, my experience as an administrator, and the role of scholarship in the life of an administrator.

REUNIÓN DE LA FAMILIA

When I was fifteen, my family traveled to Tijuana for my great aunt's birthday. Because the entire extended family planned to attend, the event would also serve as a family reunion. I had never been to Mexico, and I was simultaneously excited and nervous. As we made the drive from Northern California, I distinctly remember being overwhelmed by the idea that I was going to be in Mexico meeting family for the very first time. This feeling of excitement heightened as I reflected upon the meaningful relationships I had with cousins and aunts and uncles on the white side of my family.

Ten hours after my parents picked me up from school, we crossed the border into Mexico. As we drove to the family home, which was not too far from the border, I was struck by how the neighborhoods were everything my beige suburban home wasn't. The homes had huge gates and the windows were barricaded with bars. I had never seen so many bars in my life. I wondered, *Were we safe here? Is this a dangerous place?* My mom was also nervous about safety. In preparation for making this visit, my parents had even borrowed a Club, one of those steering wheel devices that promised to prevent a car from being stolen.

As we turned toward our final destination, we drove into the most beautiful neighborhood I had ever seen—the buildings were like colored sugar: oranges, yellows, greens, turquoises, and blues. When we left our car and walked to the huge gate, the feeling of danger and lack of safety emerged yet again. And then I saw this enormous mansion: it was surely the biggest and most beautiful home I had ever seen my entire life. It was six stories tall, with what seemed like dozens of rooms. There also seemed to be a hundred people inside, and a dozen types of mole and every other type of Mexican food I could imagine.

Everything was different than I expected it to be, including the food. I had grown up eating tostadas with a flat tortilla and a layer of beans, meat, shredded cheddar cheese, sour cream, and guacamole. But here, the tostadas were tiny and puffy, and the fried tortillas were filled with ground meat, potatoes, onions, carrots, and cotija cheese. Until that moment, I couldn't conceive of Mexican food not including sour cream, melted cheese, and guacamole. But this was different, and even better.

Prior to this experience, a great deal of my identity as a Mexican American was connected to food—and this was a whole new world. Everything seemed simultaneously exciting and confusing . . . yet distinctive. There was no water to drink, only soda. There seemed to be no language barrier, even though there were significant language differences. I do not remember having any trouble communicating with my cousins and the other people there who were my age, and the same was true for my brother and sister.

On our way to Tijuana, I had taken emotional cues from my mom, but the moment I was there, all of my attention shifted to my dad. This is how my dad grew up, this is the home that my dad visited, and how he used to eat tacos and tostadas. This was his family. Being there was a window into my dad's youth. I entered the experience being nervous and afraid, and left reflecting on the fact that I didn't know what it meant to be Mexican at all. I sensed that I had been missing out on something important.

I also felt like I was missing out on family. Everybody seemed to know a lot about me, and I didn't know anything about them. Growing up, I always thought it was "cool" that my dad spoke Spanish and that he knew all the very best taquito places. But in Tijuana, I wondered if my dad, as well as Nana and Papacito, ever felt like they were missing out. In Tijuana, they seemed bigger, whereas back in Southern California, their life seemed relatively small—though now, of course, I know that this is not the case. The moment we left Mexico, I wanted to return, and I was disappointed that we never did.

Before this experience and whenever I had to fill out an official form that asked for my racial identity, I had always put Mexican/Hispanic. I was very proud to be Mexican; I just didn't know what that meant. I didn't feel strange about it until I started applying to college and I was offered a large diversity scholarship from a Christian college in California; I felt uncomfortable. Because I had been raised with a "pull yourself up by your own bootstraps" mentality, I wanted to receive a scholarship because of my academic record, not because of my paternal background. I turned down the diversity scholarship and went to a different college with a predominantly white student body and student experience that I could relate to.

DIVERSIFYING THE STUDENT BODY

I started processing my identity more seriously when I began working with a team of admission counselors at my alma mater the year after I graduated. As an admissions counselor, I was responsible for recruiting a broad spectrum of domestic students from an assigned territory to submit an application. The team of counselors was given a directive to visit a diverse combination of "feeder" schools. We had a list of places that we received applications from in the past, and we were expected to develop a list of high schools that included suburban and urban schools, large publics, small privates, religious schools, and charter schools in cities I had never visited and knew nothing about.

My very first territory included the Midwest, the mid-Atlantic, and the Bay Area in California. I followed the rules and developed lists of schools and scheduled visits where I planned to recruit students. By the second city I visited, I realized that I could pull up to a school with my car still running, assess the school's appearance, and guess what the student population would look like.

These experiences had a profound impact on my identity because they forced me to reconcile many previously cemented thoughts and feelings. In high school and college, I perceived that I went to a "regular" high school with "regular" people, in a "regular" middle-class neighborhood and community. I assumed that everybody had the same opportunities and access that I had; in reality, however, I lived in an affluent white community where I had spent most of my primary and secondary years in private schools. Consequently, I knew little about difference or diversity. Even as a college student, I perceived little meaningful difference in background or access. But when I started visiting high schools around the country, I began to see schools with more than four thousand students that had only two guidance counselors. In contrast, most private high schools had one hundred students per guidance counselor.

The discrepancy was immense. At one private high school I visited, the counselor said, "We have eighteen students coming today and your institution is at the top of at least half of their lists." As the students walked in, the counselor would greet each person by name. But immediately following that visit, I walked into the guidance office at a large, urban public school, where the counselor couldn't possibly know all of the students by name because the ratio of students to each counselor was unrealistic.

I sat in hundreds of rooms—conference rooms, classrooms, offices, lobby areas—to meet groups of students. Often students from majority white neighborhoods with wealthier high schools had lists of questions prepared in advance; they knew what to ask and were engaged in the process of selecting a college. Students from poorer schools would often stare at me with their eyes wide open as soon as they turned to the tuition page of my pamphlets and brochures. Their brains seemed to shut off at that moment because they perceived that there was no way that they could afford to go to a school like Pepperdine University. At that time, tuition was approximately $36,000 annually.

I initially delivered the same presentation at every school. Despite quickly recognizing the differences between the audiences, I didn't know how to adapt at that point. I had received no preparation or training to represent the university in these various settings before I headed out on the road—not even a conversation. Yet after my first travel season, when it came time to read applications, I realized that although diversity was identified as a priority in the application review process, there had been no actual conversations about why admitting a diverse incoming class was important.

Our entire admissions process revolved around which applicants we were admitting, without any consideration of race. Eventually, we employed a very race-conscious admission process. After a few weeks of reading applications, I began to understand the realities of the situation. The feelings I had while visiting high schools were substantiated in the application review process, and I began to see the differences in the applications from students who did not have the same access to preparation or advanced coursework. Not all students of color came from poor backgrounds, by any means. But I realized, firsthand, the inequity in the college application process.

During my second year, I visited more schools and was more intentional about focusing on larger public schools in urban areas. I began to adapt the message for different environments and groups of students. In my third year as the associate director, I chose to invest more attention on hiring and training counselors.

At that time, I was also enrolled in a master's program where I, for the first time, researched access and equity for underserved and underrepresented students in higher education. My professional experience influenced the direction I took with my graduate program, focusing specifically on similar issues in the college admissions process.

As I trained new counselors, I described some of my own experiences over the past few years. I did not want these younger counselors to begin their careers with as little preparation as I had. So we talked about diversity, equity, and lack of college preparedness among certain groups of students.

In my final year as associate director, I started a PhD program. Due to the intensive nature of doctoral work, I made the connection between being a scholar and a practitioner. After spending time studying the literature, I wanted to understand the experience of underrepresented students who were attending Christian colleges. Although I had several friends in college who were students of color, we weren't particularly close. I had never heard the real story behind their experiences at a predominantly white Christian institution.

AUTO-ANNOTATED BIBLIOGRAPHY

To understand these stories, I researched, wrote, and published papers related to the experiences of students of color. Simultaneously, as I advanced professionally, my work dramatically informed my research and my research informed my work. In this section, I will highlight some of the ways these interactions occurred.

My first paper in my first class was an evaluative study that explored the relationship between institutional priorities for diversity and minority enrollment at four institutions that were members of the Council for Christian Colleges & Universities (CCCU). I used public resources to gather descriptive data on minority enrollment and institutional commitment while developing a coding system to construct an analysis of each institution's actual priority for diversity. The degree to which the universities embodied themes such as intentionality, environment, and demographic awareness substantiated their placement within a typology of institutional commitment. The typology then gave each college or university a classification of high, moderate, or weak institutional commitment.

Overall, it was clear that most of these institutions had not yet made a clear commitment to diversity. The paper I wrote in that class, titled "Institutional Priority for Diversity at Christian Institutions,"[1] and every publication afterward became a central part of my development as a scholar practitioner and an ally. Eventually, I transitioned to the role of directing the office of admission at Pepperdine, where I continued to use the same policies in reviewing every application. In my first year as director, we enrolled the first class of incoming students in which 50 percent were students of color.

People were amazed that we made such a significant jump in diversity while still maintaining a strong academic profile. Given that we did not have a clear institutional directive to achieve such a high level of diversity, I was worried that

I would get some backlash, but it never came. Instead, there was a bit of an "as long as you make the class, it doesn't really matter how you get there" mentality. By that time, however, I was well aware of the fact that we had not "arrived" to some level of institutional diversity-related success; all that we had really achieved was significant compositional diversity. In my final years as director, I expanded my scholarship and deepened my understanding of campus climate.

In a subsequent qualitative case study, I explored multiple perspectives of the campus climate at a faith-based university in another state that was known to have a particularly strong commitment to diversity. I wondered what it was like to be an underrepresented student or faculty member at that institution. After interviewing faculty, staff, and students of color, it was clear that there was both a positive and a negative side to each story, despite the institution's clear, biblical rationale as to why diversity mattered. First, while the participants agreed that their institution had a strong commitment to diversity and the senior administration was on board with moving forward, most noted that campus still felt mostly white. Instead of being integrated into the campus community, people of color seemed to have to adapt in order to survive. Second, while people had recognized a tangible increase in diversity over the past few years, many reported feelings of invisibility, aloneness, or self-consciousness about their differences.

In a book chapter titled "Thriving in Students of Color on Predominantly White Campuses: A Divergent Path?,"[2] I highlighted one of the participants in this interview. When I asked Katrina, a black student in her third year, to describe her transition to a predominantly white institution as a first-year student, she used words like "unbearable" and articulated how invisible she felt on campus. Katrina reported that it had been difficult to make meaningful relationships with white students on campus. She didn't feel as if she fit in, and she perceived that her white peers found it challenging to see past the color of her skin. In her words:

> Sometimes, people can get lost in how you're saying it and never hear you and never see you for who you are. That hurts. So in that way, yes, I feel judged. I feel discriminated against. Has anyone ever outright called me the N-word? No. Has anyone ever made motions or said, "You can't sit at this table?" No. But I feel it, and I shouldn't have to.

This project was particularly challenging for me. When I listened to Katrina, I found myself nodding to her answers—as if I had any idea what it was like to experience those feelings in a college environment. I thought back to my own high school and early college experiences where I knew, in those years, I could never have imagined being best friends with Katrina. She would have felt "too different," and I knew I preferred to surround myself with people who were more like me.

From then on, I started to think more critically about diversity on college campuses (or lack thereof) and how spiritual growth and development might be affected. This convergence was largely due to my own interest and advocacy in building positive campus climates on predominately white Christian campuses. I knew at this point that our Christian campuses were racially homogenous—even when they had commitments to diversity—and that students of color, in general, felt like they didn't fit in with the majority culture on campus. I also theorized that the spiritual environment on these campuses was designed for the majority culture. For the next several years, all of my research focused on the intersection of race and spirituality, at both Christian and non-sectarian schools.

In one study, I utilized data from the College Students' Beliefs and Values survey, a longitudinal dataset from the UCLA Spirituality in Higher Education project. As a doctoral student at UCLA, my husband had worked on the spirituality project, and we were eager to explore the racial differences in students' spirituality at CCCU member institutions. We found that, among all CCCU students, seniors demonstrated significant growth on the spiritual identification scale (involvement and interest in spiritual and prayerful activities) and their religious commitment decreased during college.

These findings were not too surprising. We also found that white students scored significantly higher on the religious commitment scale than nonwhite students, and nonwhite students scored significantly higher on the ethic of caring scale. The religious commitment scale included the following items: "I seek to follow religious teachings in my everyday life; I find religion to be personally helpful; My spiritual/religious beliefs are one of the most important things in my life." The ethic of caring scale, in contrast, was less individualistic and more altruistic in nature and included the following: "It is important to me to help promote racial understanding, reduce pain and suffering in the world, and try to change things that are unfair in the world." This study, which resulted in a journal article titled "The Intersection of Race and Spirituality: Underrepresented Students' Spiritual Development at Predominantly White Evangelical Colleges,"[3] represented a sort of "aha" moment for me.

Eventually, my focus shifted toward white evangelical attitudes about race. The research and commentary I came across was both staggering and convicting. In one chapter,[4] I synthesized a great deal of research to demonstrate the importance of cultivating a positive climate for diversity at Christian institutions. I noted the following:

> Demonstrating an increased awareness of the campus climate for diversity, white evangelical attitudes toward race, and how the climate for diversity can impact spirituality for all students and for students of color would represent a nominal response to the research. A more thorough response would involve the application of best practices from peer and aspirational institutions and a commitment to biblical values related to diversity and inclusion (i.e., the table metaphor).[5]

In that particular chapter, I offered four pathways to cultivating a sense of belonging among students of color (i.e., establish infrastructure, promote intentional engagement, enact methods to assess the environment, and implement intentional leadership), while also increasing positive cross-racial interactions on campus and redefining white evangelical norms on campus.

One of the things that kept emerging over and over again in this research was the importance of fostering a sense of belonging for students of color. In a culminating quantitative study,[6] I used structural equation modeling to explore once again the relationship between the campus climate for diversity and spirituality among twenty-five hundred students at twenty-one CCCU member institutions.

The findings were equally heartbreaking and unsurprising. Indeed, the campus climate for diversity predicted spirituality for both white students and students of color. This finding indicated that the campus climate for diversity impacts spiritual growth among *all* students. However, the data also indicated that the direct causal paths to spirituality were different for students of color versus white students: sense of belonging emerged as the single direct predictor of spirituality for students of color, whereas overall satisfaction emerged as the single direct predictor for white students. Additionally, white students had a significantly higher sense of belonging and satisfaction than students of color. The data were clear: we are not serving all of our students well.

INTERACTIONS WITH STUDENTS

After leaving my university and the field of admissions for several years, I later returned as the dean of enrollment management. In my first few months, I was disappointed to find that the consciousness around admissions had diminished. I had naively hoped that the increased compositional diversity on campus had been a significant step toward a positive campus climate.

A few months after I returned, I attended a diversity-related retreat with about a hundred students, almost all of whom were students of color. Because students had been encouraged/required to invite friends, faculty, and staff to this particular retreat, they did not find it strange to have me in the group. The topic of the retreat was the power of language and the things that people say, both verbally and nonverbally. The format was very interactive and participants had many opportunities to hear a variety of different voices, opinions, and personal experiences regarding the topic. It was both challenging and cathartic for these students; because they were finally not in the visible minority on campus, they discussed what was really going on. The day we departed for the retreat there was a blackface incident on campus in a residence hall. The offending student also made derogatory comments about black history month. The timing and subject matter of this occurrence gave a lot of texture to the conversations at the retreat.

There were large breakout discussions, smaller breakouts, one-on-one conversations, and other opportunities for interaction in a variety of formats. I decided to be very engaged and broadly shared my experiences as a multiracial, white-looking adoptive mother of a Mexican son who looks very different than me. Some students commented that it was the first time they felt an administrator was legitimately contributing to the conversation in a meaningful way.

In one of the group breakout sessions, we met with people in self-selected identity groups. I was a part of a multiracial group that was connected to foster parenting and adoption in a variety of ways. After some initial conversations in our group, we were paired with another group for deeper discussion. We had to name our groups, and the one we joined had chosen as its name: "Black men who attend college and are treated like thugs."

We had a long time to talk about various issues and responded to facilitated questions and scenarios. At one point, I asked the group: "How bad is it really at this school?" The responses included stifled laughs to one comment: "How long do you have?" One male student simply responded, "It's really bad, Kristy; it's really bad."

Their stories included everything from the classic classroom scenarios where the one black student in class is called on to speak on behalf of all black issues, to microaggressions where students were questioned about their posture in class. Students with dreadlocks had been asked to leave buildings when they were studying late at night. They also told stories of roommates destroying personal property and not being held accountable.

I wasn't surprised by a single story or experience they shared, but it was the first time I had a serious discussion about overt racism and microaggressions with a group of college-aged black men. I had talked about the same issues and experiences at length with colleagues, friends, study participants, and others my age, but it was the first time I'd heard it from a group of students at my home institution.

When you care so much about diversity and campus climate, it is very easy to allow your care and effort to instill a false sense of security, as if all is right with the world. For me, taking positive steps forward made me feel like I was doing my part: I perceived myself to be an ally within my sphere of influence. However, when I heard those stories, I was challenged to acknowledge how little I knew about what actually happened on my own campus.

Those conversations with students reminded me that my sphere of influence could and should extend far beyond just getting students through the door. In fact, composition and climate are deeply intertwined.

CONCLUSION

My journey is not complete, but I feel compelled in my current phase to continue to advocate and educate around the fact that diverse learning environments benefit everyone, even if they are difficult to create or maintain. Learning environments are an ecosystem of cross-pollinated knowledge; when they are homogenous, everyone in the environment suffers. When we admit a class of students, it is never a comparison of equal test scores, leadership experiences, gender, race, and so on. Instead, we are shaping a class of students with the intent of building the strongest ecosystem possible. My job is to continue to educate my team about this process, as well as the larger field of college admissions. Balanced ecology requires affirmative action, a reality that still makes people uncomfortable because of a failure to see the larger system. In addition, I see it as my responsibility as a Christ-following scholar-practitioner to extend my advocacy into all of my spheres of influence.

As I noted in the introduction of this chapter, in many ways, I feel like a theoretical ally. It is easy to play a behind-the-scenes role in this work of advocacy. However, the data tell a different story that will require a bolder, more courageous approach. I want to step out from behind the keyboard to continue to listen and to speak out loud in and beyond my spheres of influence.

FOR DISCUSSION

1. How and why is diversity in the academic setting important and valuable?
2. What effective ways could be used to talk with colleagues about affirmative action and/or race conscious admission policies?

3. How would you describe your own campus climate for diversity?
4. In what specific ways do you sense that diversity affects your home institution?
5. How might a diverse student body benefit all students, staff, and faculty?
6. How can higher education administrators make an impact in and beyond their sphere of influence?

NOTES

1   Kristin Paredes-Collins, "Institutional Priority for Diversity at Christian Institutions," *Christian Higher Education* 8 (4; 2009): 280–303.

2   Kristin Paredes-Collins, "Thriving in Students of Color on Predominantly White Campuses: A Divergent Path?," in L. Schreiner, M. Louis, and D. Nelson, eds., *Thriving in Transitions* (Columbia: University of South Carolina Press, 2012).

3   Kristin Paredes-Collins and C. S. Collins. "The Intersection of Race and Spirituality: Underrepresented Students' Spiritual Development at Predominantly White Evangelical Colleges," *Journal of Research on Christian Education* 20 (2011): 73–100.

4   Kristin Paredes-Collins, "Cultivating Diversity and Spirituality: A Compelling Interest for Institutional Priority," *Christian Higher Education*, special issue with guest editors Alexander Jun and Mari Luna De La Rosa, 12 (1–2; 2013): 122–37.

5   Ibid., 130.

6   Kristin Paredes-Collins, "Campus Climate for Diversity as a Predictor of Spiritual Development at Christian Colleges," *Religion & Education* 41 (2; 2014): 171–93.

Chapter Thirteen

LIVING THE QUESTIONS: THE CONVOLUTED PATH FROM FEAR-FULL SHAME TO COURAGEOUS HOPE

SARAH VISSER, PhD

Calvin College, Vice-President for Student Life

Be patient toward all that is unsolved in your heart and try to love the questions themselves, like locked rooms and like books that are now written in a very foreign tongue. Do not now seek the answers, which cannot be given you because you would not be able to live them. And the point is, to live everything. Live the questions now. Perhaps you will then gradually, without noticing it, live along some distant day into the answer.

—Rainer Maria Rilke, *Letters to a Young Poet*

For now we see in a mirror, dimly, but then we will see face to face. Now I know only in part; then I will know fully, even as I have been fully known.

—1 Corinthians 13:12 (NRSV)

I fell in love with social science as a first-year college student. I distinctly remember my first psychology course and the introduction of developmental stage theory. Something about the orderly patterning of time and behavior appealed to my "Type A" personality, which meant that I quite naturally began to search for any and all signs of growth in myself and those around me. I consumed the writings of Erik Erikson, Jean Piaget, and Lawrence Kohlberg, eager to better understand the behavior patterns and age-related stages that captured the *typical* human experience. I'm what some would call a sense-seeker. I like things that make sense, that fit into neat categories, and that distinguish structures and systems from one another. That's the logic-oriented left-brained side of me.

I also love story. I love the way it captures hidden characteristics and uncovers context. Story allows us to peer more deeply, beyond what is immediately visible. It reminds us that there is power in personal experience. It relishes the nuances, the exceptions, the underlying truths. It's the *why* and *how* behind the *what*. Story feeds the empathetic, intuitive right-brained side of me.

Early in my academic journey, I remember experiencing a visceral bewilderment the first time these two loves collided: development and story. I say "collided" because my entrance into the work of social justice and diversity wasn't exactly graceful. In fact, if I were asked to trace my initial awakening to systemic injustice, I'd blushingly admit that I came upon it rather haphazardly. It was awkward. It was uncomfortable. It threatened my "I like to be in control" equilibrium. On the outside, I appeared to have it all together. I was a good student. I was outgoing and loved the social aspects of collegiate life. I was adept at taking simple human interactions and finding complicated ways to intellectualize them. And I had already been given the label "student leader," despite the fact that I was much more accustomed to following than influencing. Gregarious? *Yes.* Driven? *Certainly.* Overly optimistic? *Perhaps.* Culturally cognizant? *Not a chance.*

FRAGILE BEGINNING

As an eighteen-year-old white woman from a small homogenous town in the Midwest, it's safe to say that I was oblivious to dynamics of difference on my campus. At the end of my first year of college, I made a last-minute decision to apply for a resident advisor role for my sophomore year. In a surprising twist, I was selected and placed as RA in an intentionally diverse living-learning community. Doing so meant that in addition to supporting forty young women through the ups and downs of residential campus living, I was responsible for facilitating regular diversity-related conversations and fostering Christian community with others who were quite different from me. To say that I felt intimidated by this assignment is a severe understatement. I remember entering the year feeling completely inadequate, naive, and honestly not sure how I had ended up where I was. My insecurity increased as the year wore on.

The more stories I heard, the more I realized that the developmental theories I had quickly gained an affinity for were flawed. I started to see that there is not a *single* story of human growth. Despite my best attempts to order my community, I had yet to meet someone whose cognitive development unfolded in perfect, orderly succession, integrating all the achievements of earlier stages into a coherent and complete pattern. And the more I studied abstract theory that sought to make sense of human experience, the more skeptical I became. Upon closer inspection, the theories and ideas that had captivated me now seemed shallow, myopic, and blatantly biased. Despite my best efforts to construct learning in the midst of diverse community, the complex narratives all around me threatened to deconstruct all I thought I knew.

I suppose one reaction to this season of disequilibrium would have been righteous indignation. Why had I never been exposed to histories other than my own? Why was the idea of privilege a new concept to me? But in all honesty, I didn't experience righteous indignation. I experienced shame. Confronted with the ugly truth of my privilege, I was swimming in white guilt.

Sociologist Brené Brown has spent the majority of her professional career researching shame and vulnerability. She suggests that there are three things that cause shame to intensify in our lives: secrecy, silence, and judgment.[1] Brown uses the metaphor *web of shame* to describe the "layered, conflicting and competing social-community expectations . . . that dictate who we should be, what we should be, and how we should be."[2] Prior to my awakening to racial and economic injustice, I assumed that I was well within bounds when it came to being who, what, and how I should be. Once confronted with systemic injustice, I questioned everything. Shame corroded the part of me that believed that I was capable of change and empowered action.

Brown points out that this is the distinguishing factor between guilt and shame. Guilt can have a positive effect because it often motivates us to move beyond discomfort, to correct negative behaviors, to make amends, to repent. She points out that when we experience shame, "We feel disconnected and desperate for worthiness. Full of shame or the fear of shame, we are more likely to engage in self-destructive behaviors and to attack or shame others."[3] Early on, I confused guilt for shame. I believed that guilt defined who I was, and as a result, I was hesitant to tell my story. Even worse, guilt prevented me from really listening to the stories of others. I was accustomed to learning environments that were generally comfortable, and this new awareness of injustice and inequity meant that I was no longer insulated from race-based stress.

In fact, I was a textbook case of what Robin DiAngelo has termed *White Fragility*,[4] described as "a state in which even a minimum amount of racial stress becomes intolerable, triggering a range of defensive moves."[5] In the midst of attempting to lead my peers, I often opted for silence, avoidance, and fear. Though my role required me to model constructive engagement across racial divides, I was often unsure of how to respond in constructive ways to the reality of my own privilege and power. This is a pattern that persists in my narrative, and its sustained presence in my own journey allows me to see it more clearly in other whites. Back then, a budding awareness of my own propensity toward shame and white fragility catalyzed a paradigm shift. As I prepared to depart campus at the end of that sophomore year of serving as an RA in that diverse living-learning community, I remember feeling deeply changed. My experiences had instilled in me a sense that something wasn't whole about the way we live, breathe, and work together. I sensed that my own brokenness was deeper than I had originally thought. I started to see myself in new and unmistakable ways. It was the first time I recall being cognizant of my privilege.

In *A Hidden Wholeness: The Journey toward an Undivided Life*, Parker Palmer writes about the things that inhibit mindfulness.[6] He suggests that when we face a question, dilemma, or decision that we know needs resolution, the spiritual resources we need to resolve it are often blocked by "layers" of inner "stuff" like confusion, habitual thinking, fear, and despair. And even though we have this inherent sense that the people we're close to could probably help us uncover our inner voice, exposing the problem or issue to others means we run the risk of being judged, of being invaded by assumptions, of being alienated by unsolicited advice. Consequently, we often distance ourselves from others and choose to walk alone, privatizing our questions. Parker described the consequences of taking this approach: "[A]t the very moment when we need all the help we can get, we find ourselves cut off from both our inner resources and the support of a community."[7]

I've heard it said that when you live in community—authentic community—there are people who tell you who you are in ways that you cannot turn away from. When I came to the point where I could not turn away, I began to sit with the tension of questioning—not because I was obsessed with deconstructing my life or analyzing the truths I had encountered but because the process of asking why and wading through some of the discomfort, guilt, fear, and pain that surfaced brought me to a new understanding of God's redemptive work in the world. I began to understand that my privilege means that I can walk away from these conversations and this work anytime I want to, but my identity in Christ means that I mustn't. I thought of how I could so easily slip into using Christian lingo to preach that we don't *need* to talk about this because we're all created in God's image and so we are somehow above the fallen-ness of this world. I began to see that my approach was profoundly short-sighted—that by trying to smooth over the complexity of humanity and our brokenness, I was minimizing the profound role of God's grace, redemption, and reconciliation. I was, in effect, snubbing God's invitation to join the party. I caught the first glimpse of what it might mean to be an agent of renewal.

CONNECTING THE DOTS

Once I accepted this invitation to "join the party," the next step for me was trying to figure out how to connect these new questions to larger systemic issues. And so I delved into exploring these topics during my graduate studies. Who am I? How does the intellectual connect with the spiritual? How does God's concept of justice intersect with the idea of social justice? How does all of this relate to my vocation and calling?

I began to intentionally seek out opportunities to learn from those who were different from me. I enrolled in classes taught by faculty of color. I selected paper topics that critiqued epistemological racism. I attended cultural events, lectures, and town halls in an effort to hear from those whose backgrounds and opinions differed from my own. It was a season of rigorous learning and intellectual curiosity. It was also a season characterized by awkward interactions. For the first time in my life, I found myself an occasional outsider. I'd enter venues and conversations that other whites assumed did not pertain to them. I was prone to speaking too much or too little, and often when I spoke, I used the wrong words. Although my external mannerisms displayed warmth and genuineness, I was often insecure and fearful on the inside.

Just when I thought I was making true progress, I'd blunder terribly. Despite the awakening I'd experienced as an undergraduate, my postbaccalaureate self was so focused on thinking the right thoughts, saying the right words, and enacting the right behaviors that I missed the people right in front of me, crashing around like a bull in a china shop. And just when I thought I'd learned to resist the urge to avoid discomfort, I was confronted again with my innate desire to fix and to solve.

While I was working as a graduate assistant at a small, private, highly selective institution in Southern California, an event occurred that garnered significant attention, both on campus and in the local and national media. The campus was on the tail end of a season of significant unrest, most of it stemming from a series of racialized incidents over the previous three years. These events included things like defaced white boards, insensitive comments in public spaces, and graffiti in the campus commons. The tipping point was a prank-turned-disaster. During the winter holiday, a student's art project—an eleven-foot cross—was stolen by a group of student athletes and set ablaze, a symbolic act that generated intense reaction, though the students later claimed they weren't aware of the antiblack racist symbolism of cross-burning. In the months following the cross-burning, there were rallies, protests, teach-ins, and think tanks. There were policy changes, revised mission statements, and overhauled curricula. And in the midst of all of this, there were students, navigating a campus culture that was at times hospitable, at times isolating.

I spent hours with students, talking through what happened, discussing campus culture, and more importantly, listening to their stories of alienation,

betrayal, guilt, shame, and anger. Despite all of my newfound intellectual prow-
ess, despite my experience leading trainings, doing research, and facilitating
discussions, I saw that this was personal—not just for the students, but also for
me. I allowed myself to feel deeply, to sit with the pain in a way that acknowledged that I was broken and that I was part of the larger brokenness of this
world. I had to engage with a posture of humility, fully aware of my inadequacy.

Henri Nouwen once wrote:

> Compassion is hard because it requires the inner disposition to go with
> others to place where they are weak, vulnerable, lonely, and broken. But
> this is not our spontaneous response to suffering. What we desire most is
> to do away with suffering by fleeing from it or finding a quick cure for it.[8]

A few years down the road, as I engaged in my doctoral research tied to the
work of diversity and its implications for higher education, I still found myself
more comfortable engaging with the intellectual, choosing the head over the
heart. And yet I've learned again and again that I will only be an effective agent
of renewal if I am willing to get at the heart of the matter.

NAVIGATING BORDERLANDS

In the months and years that followed, there were other incidents. And I often
found myself in the middle of conversations—one-on-one meetings with students who were hurting, heated administrative sessions where we strategized
responses, and volatile student leadership training sessions. In each situation, I found myself wanting to fix what was happening; I wanted the conflict
resolved. Yet, truth be told, I had no idea how to resolve it. In fact, I knew
that the only possible source of resolution—Jesus Christ—was not known
or even acknowledged by the vast majority of my students and colleagues. I
often found myself expressing my concerns to God: "How do I do this work
here without acknowledging that you are at the center of it?" The answer was
simple: "Keep looking. I am in the center of it. Even here." And so my paradigm shifted once again.

It was during this season that I first came across the work of Gloria Anzaldua,
a Chicana who introduced the concept of "border thinking."[9] According to
Anzaldua, border thinking embodies a double consciousness that creates "a
change in the way we perceive reality, the way we see ourselves, and the ways we
behave."[10] She describes her experience navigating the borderlands between her
indigenous upbringing and her elite education. Rather than bemoan her insider-
outsider identity in both spheres, she instead calls readers to new ways of making

meaning. Anzaldua recognizes the inherent value of living without borders, embodying the crossroads. She asserts that this approach to living fosters "a new story to explain the world and our participation in it, a new value system with images and symbols that connect us to each other."[11] She believes that many who live within the borderlands have a capacity to see deeper realities below the surface. Although Anzaldua's work is secular, I could not help but catch the faith-full truth of her message. In the midst of navigating various borderlands— Christian/secular, personal/professional, scholar/practitioner—it was suddenly very clear to me that the metaphor of the borderlands beautifully captures the sort of paradoxical living that Christians are called to embrace. The challenge lies in the fact that I'm not particularly good at processing paradox or holding creative tensions. Richard Rohr captures this sentiment well in his book *Falling Upward* when he writes, "We are better at rushing to judgment and demanding a complete resolution to things before we have learned what they have to teach us. This is not the way of wisdom."[12] At times, wisdom seems elusive.

In the aftermath of the significant bias-related incidents on my previous campus, I was part of a small planning team charged with developing a comprehensive diversity training for 150+ student leaders at my institution. Many of the student leaders were resident advisors and peer mentors under my span of care. Given the racial tension on campus, it was particularly weighty to be involved in planning and facilitating the training that year. Following several years of unrest, the large diversity training event was controversial from the start. Over the previous few years, students had heavily critiqued the college's approach to diversity training. Students of color felt that it was geared toward white students who often had very limited exposure to engaging issues of privilege and identity. Many white students felt that it was unnecessary and divisive to focus on difference. Because we believed it was important to involve students and staff across the spectrum of experience in the planning process, we contracted a nationally renowned facilitation expert to help guide the daylong training session. A few hours into the event, it became apparent that things were not going well. Students from all vantage points were sharing their lived experiences on campus, and our guest facilitator was (surprisingly) not aware of the strong emotional dynamics in the room. Through he didn't intend to, his approach minimized certain voices and fed the resistance and frustration of many of the student participants. At the lunch break, our planning team collectively processed what was happening and made the difficult decision to politely excuse our guest and spend the afternoon transparently processing with the large group about what had transpired.

Our four-person planning team formed a panel at the front of the ballroom where the event was being held and engaged students in open dialogue about the cultural dynamics we were witnessing and experiencing. I can honestly say it was one of the most trying experiences of my young professional life. It was daunting and fear-inducing to sit in front of 150+ articulate student leaders who saw the administration as a major obstacle to the process of creating an inclusive campus, and it's worth noting that this critique came from both students of color and white students. In that moment, despite the fact that I wanted to run for cover or bury my head in the sand, I committed to staying present by listening and seeking to understand their frustration and concerns, rather than attempting to justify our actions or responses. Three hours later, I wrapped up the session by offering a humble apology to the students. I explained that despite our best intentions, the impact of our collective leadership and institutional structures was contributing to the problems they had identified. I owned the fact that "we can do better, and we need to." The subsequent weeks and months saw many follow-up conversations with students, colleagues, and administrators. It was an emotionally exhausting season. As a white woman, I discovered that my position of privilege afforded me opportunities to examine institutional processes without appearing as though I had an "agenda." I committed to advocating on behalf of my colleagues of color, engaging challenging conversations in my department, in division meetings, and with executive leaders.

Near the end of that year, after significant movement on all sides, there was a particular day when an African American student was in my office processing a recent conversation he had with a white sophomore student leader. He recounted how this leader had come to realize his privileged position on campus and was experiencing some painful guilt and shame. The student leader in my office shared his pleasure at witnessing the other student's discomfort and explained that he finally felt like white students were getting to experience a taste of what he had experienced every day of the past four years. I recognized my eighteen-year-old self in the tale he recounted. I listened intently to his narrative and then asked a simple question. "At the end of the day, what is it you hope for this college and its constituents?" When he paused, uncertain of how to reply, I shared a metaphor that seemed to capture what I saw happening.

I explained that it seemed as though the college was almost like a house that had rampant structural damage and was rotting from the inside out, although none of this was visible to the outside world. So, while from the outside everything appeared to be quite stately and impressive, those who dwelt inside saw the decay, heard the moaning rafters, and worried about the structural integrity. Using this metaphor, it seemed that what had transpired over the past year had exposed the home's realities. For the first time, people were peeling back the wallpaper and seeing the decaying wood underneath. And as more and more of the truth emerged, folks started to worry about the safety of remaining inside the house. Eventually, there was a collective sense that the house was condemned and needed to be torn down.

In meeting after meeting, brave souls found themselves courageously stepping away from the safety of the home and some dared to throw rocks at the windows, shattering what appeared to be pristine. I explained that we had come to a point where at long last, the condemned house had crumbled to the ground, and what we were experiencing was the simultaneous heartache and relief that accompanied the process of deconstruction. But I pointed out that the true "end goal" was not that the house had crumbled, nor that we could now stand around the rubble and allow it to remain as a shrine of dysfunction and decay. Instead, if progress was to be made, it was time for the real work to begin. It would require *everyone* to begin the arduous task of clearing the debris, carefully attending to the scrapes and bruises that occurred as we handled sharp edges and jutting nails. And eventually, it would involve a rebuilding, a co-creation of a new house that was structurally sound, open to all, and integral in design and function. I offered my perspective that the real work required all of us, and I concluded by asking if he was a willing worker.

Not only was he willing, he became a staunch advocate for collective action. Although the metaphor served its purpose in rallying students to partner in the work of reconciliation, it was also a humble reminder to me of the importance of moving beyond mere rhetoric toward empowered action. In the months and years since that conversation, I've reflected on it often. Beyond the obvious metaphor, it also illuminates the primary snare that I've been prone to be entangled in along the way: the need to be in control.

FEAR-FULL CONTROL

In 1990, Peter Senge published a book called *The Fifth Discipline*.[13] It was a breakthrough book in the field of management because it changed the way people thought about organizations. Following the Industrial Revolution, companies and organizations across a variety of sectors, including education, became more and more machine-like. Founders designed the machine, put it together, and got it up and running. Next came the managers, those who operated or controlled the machine. They were followed by the line workers, those who worked to enact the machine's purpose. In this assembly line scenario, everything is about control. A good machine is one that its operators can control. If something in the organization is broken and needs change, they bring in someone who can fix it. The ability to control is how we keep fear at bay. But here's the thing Senge realized: organizations aren't machines; they're *living* organisms, made up of *living* people, and treating organizations and the people within them like machines actually keeps them from changing. We bring in mechanics when what we really need are gardeners. We keep trying to *drive* change when what we need to do is *cultivate* change.

Fear is a basic instinct, a primal reaction. There are many things in our culture that contribute to fear—chief among them are loneliness and alienation. We are culturally fragmented across all kinds of social and political differences. This fragmentation is a natural outcome of a culture obsessed with individualism. We lack connection to both our past and our present. We yearn for communal connection. To the extent that we lack community, we lack courage. As Brené Brown has observed, "Awareness is knowing something exists; critical awareness is knowing why it exists, how it works, how our society is impacted by it, and who benefits from it."[14] Another name for critical awareness is critical consciousness, which involves beginning to understand the link between our personal experiences and larger social systems. It's what happens when understanding the deeper context increases personal agency, the sense that we are called to respond, to lead.

When we lead from fear, we create distance in our organizations and relationships. We focus on individual goals. We disempower and restrain others, and we get stuck in an "us versus them" mind-set. Fear doesn't like strangers, people who don't look like us or act like us. Fear is terrified of the unknown. Fear makes us think we have nothing to say. It causes us to avert our eyes and check our hearts at the door. Fear seduces us into silence, holds us hostage, stifles opportunity. As Pulitzer Prize–winning novelist and essayist Marilynne Robinson has noted, "Fear is not a Christian habit of mind."[15]

When I reflect back on my journey, I see snapshots: my eighteen-year-old self reeling from the sting of saying the wrong thing again; my graduate-student self desperately trying to escape pervasive cognitive dissonance; my early-career-professional self sitting humiliated and ashamed in front of a crowded ballroom. Even now, my thirty-something self resists owning the unpleasant aspects of my story. Time and again, I'm confronted with the realization that I have an overwhelming need to be validated as an ally, to get it right, to be the hero. But the truth is, most of the time, I feel like a fraud. In my attempts to control, I quite often let down the people who are counting on me. Whether I want to be or not, I am responsible for and connected to the pain of these stories. It's what makes this work so vulnerable.

But here's where redemption takes the spotlight: as I am confronted with the very things I have tried so hard to avoid, something begins to shift in my soul. Instead of accusation, I begin to hear truth. Instead of failure, I see opportunity.

Instead of dismissal, I experience invitation. Instead of brokenness, I witness healing. The question is not whether the people around me are willing to follow a flawed leader. The question is whether or not I am willing to lead with courageous hope. It's not the presence of fear that matters but rather our response to it. God is not the author of fear. He is the answer to it.

EMBODIED HOPE

Each of these milestones in my journey taught me to trust my own experience, to welcome imperfection as an opportunity to learn, to embrace my limitations, and to willingly admit that just when I think I've made progress, I blunder. Along the way, I've started to realize that I have to own the work by owning my story. Over the past few years, I've started to notice that the scenery is changing; the paradigms I once clung to continue to shift. It isn't always instantaneous, and old scenes sometimes crash-land back into the landscape of my life. I've come to believe that this work cannot be done in isolation, and yet I believe we all have to do our own work, to walk forward in grace and humility. This is what community looks like.

I've come to terms with the fact that I so often engage this work with a desire for conflict resolution instead of conflict transformation. I'm slowly learning to start from a place of inquiry, to live into the questions. How does my experience shape the way I see others? What might I be missing that others are seeing? What if the experience that others share (including my students) was true? What would that mean for my approach to living, loving, and leading? How am I pursuing "being" instead of "doing?" These questions are slowly emerging into answers—profound hope and spiritual transformation.

Hope invites questions. Hope grows something new out of something old, abandoned, without purpose. Hope instills courage that breaks down walls. Hope compels us to cross boundaries. Hope obliges us to live out of conviction, to build affection. I believe that hope is the central thread of Christian leadership, and it is at the core of this work.

FOR DISCUSSION

1. When you reflect on your personal story, are there moments that you would characterize as "collisions" or that led to bewilderment? How have these shaped your narrative?
2. When have you witnessed a positive impact of guilt that led to growth and change?
3. What steps could you take to identify the causes and impacts of "White Fragility" on your campus?

4.   What borderlands have you navigated? How did the experience change the way you perceive reality? How did it change your behavior?
5.   What metaphors have been instrumental in the development of your personal understanding of racial justice?
6.   What questions do you have that remain unanswered? What are the fears that keep you from moving forward in courageous hope?

NOTES

1   Brené Brown, *The Gifts of Imperfection* (Center City, MN: Hazelden, 2010).
2   Brené Brown, *I Thought It Was Just Me (but It Isn't): Making the Journey from "What Will People Think?" to "I Am Enough"* (New York: Gotham Books, 2007), 17–18.
3   Brown, *The Gifts of Imperfection*, 41.
4   Robin DiAngelo, "White Fragility," *International Journal of Critical Pedagogy* 3 (3; 2011): 54–70.
5   Ibid., 57.
6   Parker J. Palmer, *A Hidden Wholeness: The Journey toward an Undivided Life: Welcoming the Soul and Weaving Community in a Wounded World* (San Francisco: Jossey-Bass, 2004).
7   "The Clearness Committee: A Communal Approach to Discernment in Retreats," Center for Courage and Renewal, accessed May 8, 2017, http://www.couragerenewal.org/clearnesscommittee/.
8   Robert Durback, ed. *Seeds of Hope: A Henri Nouwen Reader* (New York: Doubleday, 1997).
9   Gloria Anzaldua, *Borderlands: La Frontera—The New Mestiza* (San Franciso: Spinsters/Aunt Lute Book Company, 1987).
10   Ibid., 102.
11   Ibid., 103.
12   Richard Rohr, *Falling Upward: A Spirituality for the Two Halves of Life* (San Francisco: Jossey-Bass, 2013).
13   Peter Senge, *The Fifth Discipline: The Art and Practice of the Learning Organization* (New York: Doubleday, 1990).
14   Brown, *I Thought It Was Just Me (but It Isn't)*, 93.
15   Marilynne Robinson, *The Givenness of Things: Essays* (New York: Farrar, Straus, and Giroux, 2015), 125.

CURRICULAR/ COCURRICULAR INITIATIVES TO ENHANCE DIVERSITY AWARENESS AND ACTION

Introduction

THE OTHER SIDE OF DIVERSITY

REBECCA HERNANDEZ, PhD

*George Fox University, Associate Vice-President of Intercultural
Engagement and Faculty Development*

> At a local hospital, there were three nurses working in different departments. The first is
> asked, "What are you doing?" and replies, "Checking in this patient." The second is asked,
> "What are you doing?" The reply is "Feeding my family." The third is asked, "What are you
> doing?" and replies, "I'm here to make a difference in the health of our community."
> —Greg Bell[1]

When we talk about diversity, it is common to hear detailed aspects of various situations that bring anxiety, fear, and even anger. Yet another side of diversity—the beauty, creativity, and strength—is at the core of the next few chapters in this section. These authors, who work with and for Christian colleges and universities in varied roles, directly with students or in support of students, share their learning and experience in program development and implementation across various areas of campus life.

In the provided vignette, Bell points out how different people see what they are doing differently based on their visions of the roles they play. Diversity work is challenging, given that those called to lead this work must try to build and call others to a vision of diversity that reflects the heart and mind of Christ in all who call themselves Christ followers. Likewise, when moving beyond the obvious tensions between cultures on Christian campuses, genuine diversity can only be achieved through attending to matters of the heart.

The previous chapters in this book have conveyed stories of pain that are juxtaposed with those of individuals and institutions that have been tenacious in honoring a deep-seated commitment to mission, purpose, and calling. Many of these voices have made clear that honoring differences and embracing diversity is God's work, reflecting his nature and character, and that we have been invited into that work, as difficult and as exciting as it can be. Despite the complexities, to be involved with what certainly is kingdom work is nothing short of a blessing.

In this section of *Diversity Matters,* we explore the hard and creative "work" of this blessing, the action steps of programming where most practitioners live. Those of us who hold responsibilities for addressing campus culture issues in order to better serve and equip all students love the busyness of planning events, developing programs, and identifying speakers. Part of what contributes to the exciting nature of this work is seeing students challenged . . . and sometimes stretched in ways that cause them to experience resistance or anger. Over time, those students often grow and change in their identity development and cultural competency knowledge, embracing the desire for a sense of community that is broader and more complex than what they experienced back home. They mature and develop in our institutions, many for the better, and we proudly watch them graduate into careers and responsibilities that really do "change the world," or at least one small part of it. They are better people, and better representatives of Christ's kingdom, because they came to our institutions and we know—again—that this is God's good work.

The picture is not always so rosy, however. We create diversity videos and get complaints from students of color expressing frustration and hurt that the messages conveyed are not their reality—the pain of their present experience defines their reality. And yet we see the longer view and the changes that, while slow, are happening day-by-day and month-by-month on our campuses. We hear from majority culture students who are "sick and tired" of all this politically correct talk, and they ask why we can't just stop talking about color and differences, citing verses like "we are one in Christ"—even as they cite the verse incorrectly, we believe. By that I mean, they seem to want everyone to be "like me." To look like me, think like me, and act like me. Of course, the "me" in this scenario denies the differences—gender, race, life experiences, and culture— that God has built in each of us. It's easier to desire this, and yet such is not the reality of our experiences.

Similarly, many faculty on our campuses determined to engage in hard topics such as racism and justice brace themselves for harsh critics from multiple sides; yet other faculty members just want to "teach their subject matter" and not be distracted with talk about diversity.

So on a good day we celebrate that we have made a difference in one student's life or we have programmed a well-received chapel, and yet we know that the work started long before that day. Most of us understand that before a performance of any kind—a music concert, theatre performance, or a sermon delivery—a period of preparation is needed. Practice, rehearsals, feedback, and, as for this book, lots of editing go on before any public unveiling. It is like the growth of a plant from a small seed: lots of care, fertilizer, light, and water are needed before a crop can be harvested. That kind of preparation, sometimes hidden and sometimes visible, is needed for the growth of plants as well as ideas and programs.

I recently read a business book that offered a visual imagery of success concepts in a unique way. Titled *Water the Bamboo*, this book uses the giant timber bamboo as a metaphor for success.

> This giant timber bamboo can grow 90 feet in 60 days—that's a foot and a half a day! Some claim that you can hear it grow. . . . However, what's even more amazing about giant timber bamboo is that once it's planted, it takes at least three years to break through the ground. Timber bamboo farmers water the seed and tend to it faithfully, even though there's no visible evidence of growth for years.[2]

We know that, like the giant timber bamboo, much of the action we see in diversity-related programming happens underground, or first in the quiet private places across our campuses, before the public unveiling. The classroom seems the most obvious place, but that's not always the place where the constructive rub of one person against another is easily found. The more personal places can be in the residence halls, the dining hall, the chapel programming, or in the other day-to-day dimensions of campus life that promote learning. It's those "daily living spaces" where tensions grow and the work of understanding and change is needed. But it is important to note that this work of change begins with a commitment to the vision statements of our colleges, and the vision of those who lead by position, like the president, resident directors, campus chaplains, and faculty. These individuals are responsible for setting an inclusive climate if the vision is to be fulfilled. Although the work can be challenging, our campuses are also places of reward and building of deep relationships with others.

KNOWLEDGE AND CONTENT

I have often been surprised when people assume they know about diversity, cultural competency, white privilege, ethnic identity, race relations, systems oppression, and other related topics. Because they heard a talk once about it (usually not from someone well educated in the area) or saw a movie related to diverse cultures, they view themselves as being knowledgeable enough.

What we know about growth and change is that we plan for it, train for it, make changes in our spheres of influence, and then check that the desired growth and change has actually occurred. Short- and long-term strategies that lead to the fulfillment of the mission of the institution—to be a welcoming place for all students as we are image bearers of Christ—are needed. As I think of my own institution, we have a promise that "each person will be known" that we try to fulfill every day. The amplified version of this institutional commitment is expressed as follows:

> It's the hope each student brings to the college experience. To be known by name. To be understood, valued, encouraged, and uplifted. At George Fox, to be known means that professors and staff connect with students in authentic ways—personally, academically, spiritually—recognizing that we all come to this place with different backgrounds, life experiences, and dreams for the future. To be known means that students not only learn new ideas, they share their own. To be known means to be heard.
>
> When a student feels what it's like to be known in this way, they become inspired. And that's when real change happens. Knowledge moves from the mind to the heart. Careers turn into callings. Faith turns into action. And that's why we begin with a simple promise, that each student will be known.[3]

Fulfilling this promise means every employee focuses on knowing the students with whom they interact. Focusing on "hearing" students means developing skills to listen effectively and to engage with students where they are. Having an open stance of learning about others is critical. These skills and vision for inclusive diversity relate to all aspects of the institution because knowing and being known is an important value of Christian higher education.

There are visible ways that we engage diversity—cultural celebrations, chapel services, and public and private declarations of support from leaders. These are good places to start and they must continue; however, institutional systemic inequalities and policies, practices, classroom curriculum, and hiring must also be addressed at the same time. That's why this process is so hard! To illustrate ways in which this challenge can be addressed, the programs featured in this section illustrate how specific spheres of influence across a campus can each contribute to the overall diversity strategy of change in higher education. Both the long-term work and the immediate work are necessary for change to occur and for each of us in Christian higher education to stay engaged and encouraged.

Consider the following quote from Bell's *Water the Bamboo*:

The other fascinating fact about this bamboo —which is useful for our analogy —is that you can plant other crops above the bamboo for those three years that it's working its way to the surface. So, you can be working on your bamboo, but also planting corn, beans, and any other crop that will help sustain you in the meantime. When you're watering those crops, you're also watering your bamboo.[4]

With that image in mind, the four chapters that follow focus on diversity-related initiatives and implementation—heart matters as well as academic training. Each chapter includes examples and questions that encourage us to collaborate: the cocurricular (e.g., student life, global student programming, multiethnic programming, spiritual development, the chaplain's office) with the academic curriculum. Budget cuts and limited financial and personnel resources can stymie efforts. Such challenges, of course, can also become opportunities to dream about the array of possibilities that could emerge on each respective campus.

In the first chapter by Lisa Ishihari, the Director of Chapel Programs at Biola University, we turn to the connection between spiritual development programming and campus partnerships for fulfilling genuine diversity goals. After all, one distinction of our campuses within Christian higher education is our unity in Christ. With a foundational commitment to more fully reflect the Kingdom of God and the diversity yet unity of the Trinity, this chapter guides us through the redemptive work of Christ crucified for all nations (Rev. 7), and the unity we can and should experience as the body of Christ (1 Cor. 12). Other issues such as diversifying campus programming; change and implementation; partnerships and collaborations; and how students, faculty, and staff can participate in the spiritual formation of all students are also explored. The invitation to discern and cooperate with what God is already doing individually and corporately calls us to respond.

Next, Jennifer Shewmaker's chapter addresses the work of faculty in advancing the commitment to diversity on our campuses. Specifically, she details the goals of recruiting, hiring, and retaining faculty of color to reflect the growing diversity of the student body on her campus, Abilene Christian University. This hiring goal is similar to that of many Christian and non-Christian colleges. What she highlights about the work her institution is doing in diverse faculty recruitment and retention can provide helpful insights to faculty and leaders on other campuses.

The chapter written by Yvonne RB-Banks at the University of Northwestern (Minnesota) emphasizes three specific steps and sources of support that she believes are crucial if Christian institutions are to more effectively support people of color who join our communities in staff, administrative, or faculty roles. From the perspective of a long-term faculty member and administrator, this chapter explains why she stayed and recommends specific and concrete steps that can encourage other faculty of color to stay as well.

The last chapter features vignettes from three Christian institutions that have made commitments and invested resources to address specific issues related to diversity. The first, by Jenny Elsey at George Fox University (GFU), sets the stage with specific steps GFU has taken to change its culture, structure, and practices to become a more diverse and welcoming campus for all its students. The examples of identifying large goals and developing specific strategies to achieve those goals is exciting and, I believe, offers realistic and hopeful insight for other institutions to follow.

The second vignette by Glen Kinoshita of Biola University features the annual Student Conference on Racial Reconciliation (SCORR), the longest running diversity conference in Christian higher education. This conference, now in its twenty-second year, brings students together with some of the best speakers and practitioners in Christendom to engage in learning and conversation around diversity and racial reconciliation in the context of our Christian faith. Glen describes how the conference has grown and changed over time, and the challenges and joys of guiding these changes while staying true to its original goal of racial reconciliation.

Finally, the last vignette is a timely and timeless story of how one institution has begun to focus attention on a group of people that has been marginalized in the past, and found ways to offer support that has allowed the university to become a place of help and hope for that same group. Dina Gonzalez-Piña, formerly of Fresno Pacific University, describes the story of the Samaritan scholarship, a program focused on serving undocumented students with funding and program support at Fresno Pacific. As an example that could be replicated on other campuses, this vignette illustrates how one institution located in the Central Valley of California has made changes to fulfill its call to serve a vulnerable group of students.

Each of these chapters highlights the multiple practices of "doing" diversity work on Christian college campuses in the United States. This work can be challenging but, as will be evident from these pages, there are many efforts underway to fulfill our Christian calling to prepare our students well, and I'm thrilled to be a part of it!

> … To act justly, to love mercy, and to walk humbly with your God.
> —Micah 6:8 (NHEB)

NOTES

1   Greg Bell, *Water the Bamboo: Unleashing the Potential of Teams and Individuals* (Portland: Three Star
      Publishing, 2009), 309.

2   Ibid., 102.

3   George Fox University, "Be Known," accessed May 11, 2017, http://www.georgefox.edu/be-known
      /index.html.

4   Ibid., 102.

Chapter Fourteen

LEADING CHANGE THROUGH DIVERSITY IN SPIRITUAL DEVELOPMENT

LISA ISHIHARA, MDIV, MA

Biola University, Director, Chapel Programs

And it is my prayer that your love may abound more and more, with knowledge and all discernment, so that you may approve what is excellent, and so be pure and blameless for the day of Christ, filled with the fruit of righteousness that comes through Jesus Christ, to the glory and praise of God.
—Philippians 1:9-11 (ESV)

It was that time of year again at Biola University. Time to select the student leadership for worship teams! We were looking for students who love the Lord, are competently skilled, and are open to growing through training. Mike Ahn, the Director of Worship and Formation, commented, "People look at my job and they think audition day is the best because you get to listen to music all day. You get to be Simon Cowell or Alicia Keys! What people don't know is that listening to eight auditions in a row is incredibly grueling because I'm not only listening to people, but my 'people pleaser' comes out and I don't want to let people down." Our reality is that we have to say *no* to people more than we can say *yes*.

At Biola University, a commitment to offering diverse worship styles, genres, and expressions of worship has been a core value of our chapel programming. We want to more fully reflect the image, diversity, and beauty of our God. Although finding teams that are pastoral, competent, have chemistry, and have the ability to lead our campus in new approaches to worship feels impossible at times, it can be a reality, particularly through practicing patience and celebrating *small* wins as building blocks for a diversified approach to spiritual formation and ministry.

I remember, in particular, one Saturday morning when our student leaders piled into Sutherland Auditorium, filled with anticipation about our musical auditions for potential worship teams. A team led by Carla Veliz was up next. She opened in prayer and then invited us, people from different places, to sing together in different languages. The praise song rang out, "Lord you are good and your mercy endureth forever. . . . People from every nation and tongue. From generation to generation. We worship you, hallelujah, hallelujah," followed by singing the chorus in Spanish, "*Te adoramos hoy, Aleluya, aleluya, Te adoramos hoy, por quien tu eres, Te adoramos hoy, aleluya, aleluya.*"[1] The worship director turned to me and I saw his eyes welling up with tears, not just because the music was beautiful, or that the singing was in another language, but because the sense of worship in a broader context was so profound. He later mentioned that the drummer, who was the solitary white and male member of the team, had particularly inspired him. Although the drummer didn't know any Spanish, he entered fully into this worship experience with a heart full of praise. In that sense, the drummer was the "first follower."[2] The worship leader may initiate change, but it is the first followers who facilitate changing the culture.

The worship director summarized why the experience had been so powerful for him: "I can't believe I get to be a part of this! We get to introduce people to a different way and diverse expressions of worship." Watching God do this work in Mike, giving him a glimpse and a vision of what a multicultural worship experience could be, was paradigm shifting for our programming. What changed for Mike? He began to realize the importance of taking a risk and moving toward change. He needed to experience a deeper sense of worship in his own heart and spirit, in order to believe that it was possible for the broader student body. Mike began to realize that it is only when we taste and see that we can lead and pave the way for others, or become the "first followers" to further the movement by "courageously stand(ing) up and join(ing) in," changing the culture.[3]

In this chapter, we will consider practical strategies for inclusive spiritual formation ministry and engagement, as part of the distinctly Christian redemptive work that can shape the culture of our campuses.

WHAT MAKES CHRISTIAN HIGHER EDUCATION DISTINCTIVE?

Christian higher education seeks to produce graduates who are Christ-like, living and loving as Jesus did for God's kingdom purposes. These colleges and universities are committed to biblically grounded scholarship and service that empowers women and men for kingdom work.[4] Such central goals are accomplished by offering an integrated education in which both curricular and cocurricular approaches develop our students in mind and character. Foundational to a distinctively Christian approach to higher education is the redemptive work of reconciling people to God, to others, and to all of creation, thereby demonstrating the power and love of God to a world that desires to flourish yet finds itself broken.

THE REDEMPTIVE CALL: UNIFIED DIVERSE WORSHIP ON OUR CAMPUSES

In Genesis 1:28, God gave the cultural mandate to fill the earth with his glory, reflected in the people of God who have been created in his image. As the story of the Tower of Babel is recounted in Genesis 11, the Lord confused the languages and dispersed the people over all of the earth. According to the narrative, the people living at that time tried to establish themselves and create their own security apart from God by building a tower that would be "in the heaven" close to God; in doing so, their goal was to make a name for themselves and not be scattered. But God confused them by removing their ability to communicate, resulting in dissonance with God and with each other in contrast to the union that had been intended in creation.[5]

Parallel circumstances of this narrative in Genesis 11 can be found on our campuses when common language, understanding, and unity are lacking and we think our way is better than God's. In its purist form, times of community worship represent opportunities for the people of God to be united in spirit with one another, celebrating who God is and flourishing in fulfilling his kingdom purposes.

One aspect of this process involves redemption between believers and a restoration of the union between them and God. As Dr. Brenda Salter McNeil has elaborated, "Reconciliation is an ongoing spiritual process involving forgiveness, repentance, and justice that restores broken relationships and systems to reflect God's original intention for all of creation to flourish."[6] Thus reconciliation not only calls for a unity that respects the beauty of differences as embodied in intercultural competence and integrity, but further invites us into a deeper relationship with God and one another. This deeply meaningful work is part of what makes Christian higher education distinctive, as those on our campuses are transformed both spiritually and relationally.

Because spiritual formation and worship are at the heart of Christian believers living and working in community, this chapter identifies a variety of practical considerations, strategies, and possible diversity initiatives that can be integrated into an institution's already-existing plans or serve as a foundational piece for developing new short-term and long-term programming.

STRATEGIES FOR INCLUSIVE SPIRITUAL FORMATION MINISTRY AND ENGAGEMENT

Spiritual Development or Campus Ministry Departments can be strategic allies and ministry partners for numerous other offices in advancing the mission and vision of Christian colleges and universities. The personnel in these departments typically hold primary responsibility for providing pastoral care, campus spiritual programming, and training and educational programming for students. However, because the staffing arrangements and expectations of campus pastors and campus ministry teams vary from campus to campus, the following recommendations will likely need to be nuanced based on the specific institutional context. In large part, the six primary recommendations that follow emerge from the experience gained over the past decade at Biola University in Southern California, which aims for its six-thousand-plus students to "think biblically about everything."

1. Articulate Clear Diversification Goals and Align Them with Other University Initiatives

Defining measurable diversification goals and initiatives is important to the success of efforts in this area, as is the case with programming of any kind. Clear and specific language is important; for greatest impact, the language related to diversity goals should be aligned with the institution's vision, mission, and values. When possible, common language related to diversity goals should be included in communication from senior leadership to the campus community. Synergistic goals to advance existing initiatives and to identify new niches for spiritual formation are powerful when collaboration is developed with other areas of campus life (e.g., Multiethnic, Diversity, or Cross-cultural Engagement Departments). Communicating a commitment to diversification demonstrates to all students that their well-being is an institutional priority.

Consider your structure and partnerships. As a Spiritual Development Department, do your staffing structure and partnerships enable you to minister and equip the campus in areas of diverse spiritual formation? Such programmatic initiatives typically include ministries of musical worship, prayer services, small groups, affinity groups, spiritually formative partnerships, and bringing diverse speakers and educators for conferences and special events on your campus.

The question should be asked: With whom and how is the Spiritual Development Department on your campus aligned with the institution's diversity initiatives? One example of a synergistic partnership is the Office of Spiritual and Intercultural Life at George Fox University. With a focus on the holistic student experience, student diversity cocurricular programming is a priority for the spiritual life staff, enabling them to collaborate and create ministry opportunities together in an organic way. A shared physical location in the same building creates opportunities for informal conversations as staff stop by a nearby office for quick "What do you think about . . . ?" conversations that encourage movement toward common outcomes.

Advocate for financial stability and sustainability. Given the tuition-dependent nature of nearly all Christian colleges and universities, access to adequate resources for the work we feel called to do cannot be taken for granted. Creating partnerships and aligning diversity goals with the mission and vision of the institution are therefore imperative in order to sustain key programs and services. Because the trends related to birthrates and high school graduation rates document the wisdom—if not imperative—of Christian institutions becoming more inclusive, a financial case can be made for supporting diversity initiatives. Younger donors and others in touch with the changing demographic realities may well be interested in supporting well-designed programs that support greater diversity on our campuses. That being the case, are you strategically connected to the decision-makers either in your area or other influential relationships to encourage advocacy for greater funding to support a spiritually formative program that diversifies worship and reconciliation programming? Clearly it is important to document the demographic shifts now underway in your region or nationally, and to publicize small wins . . . even the stories of individual students who are being served well by key programming. Diversity work moves forward incrementally through everyday attitudes and behaviors, and this work will only advance when investments are made that will benefit coming generations of students.

One major staffing "win" on many Christian college campuses in recent years has been the designation of a chief diversity officer, with the establishment of an office that includes a budget line for diversity initiatives. However, various challenges toward the goal of hiring more faculty and staff of color—and a lack of willingness for various reasons to evaluate and change the systems and structures that continue to perpetuate systemic inequalities[7]—hinder the goal of creating a redemptive campus culture. Numerous studies have documented that accountable structures, empowered interdepartmental diversity taskforces,[8] and incentive-based programs can impact the culture and leadership structure.[9] Given that much work still needs to be done, these areas also represent bridging opportunities for Spiritual Development Departments to articulate shared outcomes and programming initiatives with partners in Diversity Departments.

2. Collaborate Strategically with Partners and Allies

The process of growth and change will vary from campus to campus, given the distinctive features of structure, resources, and personnel in place. The process and theory of implementation used by individual leaders will differ based upon their education and experience. In addition, the cultural background of individual leaders will inform their execution of change, in conscious or uncon-scious ways. Leaders from majority-culture predominantly white institutions (PWIs) tend to execute from the top down; in contrast, leaders from minority cultures (including female leaders) more typically implement change commu-nally through influential relationships. Leading and implementing change by establishing a diverse guiding coalition can be very effective; however, doing so requires a time investment, education, and resources in order to sustain the change process.[10]

As I look back and begin my tenth year of serving as the Director of Chapel Programs, I am impressed by the extent to which collaborative relationships have been extremely effective in accomplishing goals that have been import-ant to my role. From chapel planning collaborations to diversifying speakers in our chapel programming, to empowering worship leaders from diverse back-grounds, collaborative partnerships have provided different perspectives and allowed us to access supportive funding.

My most effective and mutually beneficial collaborations have been those that have built connections between curricular and cocurricular departments in ways that allow us to share the expenses of honoraria, travel, and lodging.[11] For example, as coeducators, I have partnered with academic departments across campus to bring in noted individuals who speak in our morning chapel, at a student lunch, then address a classroom setting, and conclude the day with a presentation in our evening chapel. I have also collaborated with depart-ments pioneering new university initiatives and administrative departments, such as the President's Office, alumni, and advancement, to share speakers for events or conferences on campus. As finances become tighter, we have been "pushed to reduce costs, improve the quality of products and services, locate new opportunities for growth, and increase productivity."[12] Collaborative part-nerships have increasingly become one of our most effective ways to bring outside perspectives and diverse education to our classrooms and other campus programming.

Flip the script when no allies are in sight. When I started in this posi-tion, there were zero collaborative partnerships supporting diversity work on campus. Similarly, some of you may feel like you are alone and as though no one is interested in partnering with you. Recently, when I was feeling less hopeful, the Vice-President for Student Development, André Stephens, suggested to me: "Lisa, I wonder how you can flip the script?" Exactly how is that done? Is there one person or department you can start with? One meeting you can get on your calendar? Could you bring in a speaker for an event or chapel that an academic department could mutually benefit from? Be generous and willing to cover the expenses for the first partnership as you are able and "try it on for size." It's an investment. Step out and ask God to help you find a way. Small relational wins matter and increase your network of connections!

3. Diversify the Visible Perception and Experience of University Gatherings

Executing diversity initiatives through all-community or convocation-style programming is important for changing the visible fabric and perception of the university. The Spiritual Development and Campus Ministry Department can be strong advocates in this growth process.

Diversify chapel programming. When I was hired as the Director of Chapel Programs, our team was tasked with evaluating and implementing a spiritual development cocurricular education. We wanted to maintain the high caliber of preaching the Word of God, while also bringing in local pastors and continuing to feature our esteemed faculty. However, our selection of speakers at that point was primarily from the mainstream Protestant majority culture. As a woman of color, I was very aware that women and people of color were significantly underrepresented in our annual chapel schedule, and I was concerned about the lack of diversity in worship leaders, musical styles, and denominational liturgies that our students were missing out on.

Careful tracking of key indicators over the past decade reflects the impact of intentional efforts toward greater diversity in settings that are both symbolic and substantive. During the 2005–06 academic year, 6 percent of Biola's chapel speakers were people of color. During the year (2008–09) that I was hired as Director of Chapel Programs, the speakers of color increased to 19 percent, and that percentage grew to 40 percent in the 2015–16 academic year. Another example of intentionality bringing about change is Biola's Word Chapel Series, held each Monday. During the two academic years 2014–16, we invited speakers from various academic disciplines, ministry-related occupations, and local pastors to present the Word of God to our campus community; 45 percent of these chapel speakers were people of color and 55 percent were from the white majority culture. Additionally, 42 percent of these chapel speakers were female and 58 percent were male.

Many people have expressed appreciation for the progress we have made in more fully reflecting the diversity of God's kingdom in those who educate our students. Sitting under the biblical teaching of an array of gifted men and women has changed our university culture and the students' capacity to receive from people and experiences different than their own. Even when not all students agree with positions taken by the speaker, their ability to engage critically indicates that education, engagement, and transformation have occurred.

Ethnic diversity in chapel speakers is particularly important because our students get a glimpse of diverse perspectives and the possibilities of who God has created them to be. Even on campuses where the vast majority of students are from the dominant culture, diverse speakers open up the world and introduce students to new ways of thinking about biblical principles and the relevance of key passages and topics. Chapel services and convocations then become what Dr. Brenda Salter McNeil has advocated: the flourishing of a diverse humanity, in a communal expression of worship where we can be transformed through the shared experience of filling the earth with God's glory.[13]

Diversify and equip student leadership. Because the culture of our campus is receptive to students leading students, changing the visible fabric of Biola has meant diversifying our student leadership. Reflecting the diversity of our student body in our chapel and ministry team student leadership therefore became a high priority at our university. Our graduate interns, who now oversee eighty volunteer student leaders from diverse backgrounds,[14] include 80 percent (four out of five) people of color and 20 percent majority culture (one out of five); 60 percent are female and 40 percent are male. Our undergraduate interns include 60 percent (three out of five) people of color, 40 percent majority culture (two out of five); 60 percent are female and 40 percent are male. We believe that as student leaders from diverse backgrounds lead in public ways on campus, the dreams and aspirations of all students for leadership positions on campus will become more empowered and normative.

Both substantively and symbolically, worship leading in diverse expressions on campus has been central to our diversity initiatives in chapel programming. I quickly learned during my first year as the Director of Chapel Programs that the students had amazing hearts and strong desires to lead others into authentic worship. Many of our student leaders at that time came from our mainstream majority culture and attended medium-sized local evangelical churches where they sang Hillsong and Chris Tomlin worship songs and contemporary compositions of traditional evangelical hymns. I was also very aware of our lack of diverse student leadership and diverse worship styles. I began to diversify our worship leading expressions by partnering with key staff in our Diversity Programming Department to empower student-led worship in our gospel choir, on the hula worship ministry team, and spoken word poets who shared their stories. Over the years, these teams were enfolded into all aspects of leading in chapel services.

In addition, I was able to hire an assistant director who focused specifically on investing in and diversifying our worship leadership. We have found that it takes great care and a significant time investment to equip, empower, and continue to support students from diverse backgrounds as they guide worship in chapel. From leading songs in Spanish to featuring songs with an EDM (electronic dance music) track or a worship set led by the gospel choir, continual training in wisdom and contextualization, belief, and encouragement in times of feedback is critical to our leaders. We believe in investing in the progress and development of our diversity initiatives, which requires a commitment of both financial and personnel resources.

Provide an invitation to spiritual maturity in student leadership. In our good and important work, opportunities arise that clearly invite us to model a spiritually mature process for growth in areas of diversity. As students from diverse backgrounds engage one another in our visible public ministry, their differing perspectives and internal tensions can arise and become very uncomfortable. In these critical, seemingly insignificant moments, our choices and their choices matter. It is our priority to equip and resource our student leaders in ways to engage the world and people who are different from them. The following spiritual exercise of prayer and reflection for diversity leadership training has been a helpful preparation in my own personal devotions; it may also be a tool for leadership in student or staff meetings, especially when conflict is present.

1. *Prayer of offering.* Begin the first few minutes by reading Romans 12:1–2; then ask the members to offer themselves to God and all that they bring with them. This is a time to invite them to offer themselves fully to God, who can hold all of their cares and concerns.

2. *Prayerfully reflect.* Take a moment to prayerfully reflect on the words of Proverbs 4:23, "Keep your heart with all vigilance, for from it flow the springs of life" (ESV). We all have robust internal worlds that hold our conscious and unconscious responses and reactions. God made us as thinking, feeling, human beings created with the capacity for complex relationships. So pay attention to what is being experienced in the moment, including the positive, neutral, and negative thoughts and feelings that flow out of our hearts.

3. *Consider their part and my part.* Take time to consider: Exactly what happened? From *their* perspective, what did the other person(s) do? What did I do? What is the tension? What is the conflict?

4. *Prayer of honesty and prayer of confession.* This prayer of freedom, based on Psalm 139:23–24, can provide a means to say exactly what we are thinking and feeling to a God who can hold all things. Pray silently asking God, "What is going on in my heart right now with you, with others, with my life, my situations?"[15] Honestly talk to God about what you think about the people and circumstances that you find yourself in and confess any challenging feelings or sin that you consciously or unconsciously have.

5.   *Invitation—What is God doing? How can you cooperate with him?* Prayerfully
     consider the words of Hebrews 4:12. How is God growing and changing me
     to cooperate more with the redemptive work he is already doing? Ask God
     to increase your capacity to love, be patient, bear the burdens of others, and
     walk in the sufferings of your sisters and brothers.

Our hope for our student leadership is that they will rely on the work of the
indwelling Holy Spirit to teach them a process of hospitality, forgiveness, and
kindness when working in and through difficult situations in work and ministry.

Diversifying the visible fabric is a temporary Band-Aid. The reality is that
surface-level changes can be made rather easily to chapel and university gatherings.
Essentially, such changes are a Band-Aid, buying the institution time to address
the systemic inequalities in structure, hiring of faculty and staff, and investing
both personnel and finances in order to bring about justice and equity as part of
healing relationships that have been damaged. Surface changes are like "flipping
a house" but only painting the outside. External visible diversification initiatives
must be accompanied by internal systematic change. Only when our students,
faculty, and staff experience a hospitable community life and diverse educational
and worshipful engagements will our campuses more fully model the goodness of
God's intention for believers dwelling together in unity (Psalm 133:1).

4. Be Creative with Faculty, Staff, and Student Diversity Initiatives

Many of our campuses are serving students of color who are thriving in part
through involvement in affinity clubs, small groups, residence life programs,
and missions trip teams. In fact, research has documented the importance of
such organizations and activities, which "appear to offer minority students
more social options, enhancing their integration and comfort on campus."[16] Yet
we must acknowledge that some students who come from diverse backgrounds
do not experience these gatherings as inclusive environments that open doors
of opportunity for their personal development.

Recognize the importance of affinity groups. The availability of affinity
groups has proven to be effective in enhancing students' identity development and
sense of belonging on campuses.[17] Research in corporate America has evaluated
the experiences of women and people of color, demonstrating that mentoring programs are more effective in opening opportunities than other programs, such as
diversity awareness training,[18] because they are designed to address a recognized
area of inequality.[19] In response to these research findings, what if Christian college
campuses hosted mentoring and affinity groups where students could come and
be seen, heard, and known not only by each other but by faculty and staff who are

further along on the journey of life? Either formally or informally, mentorships and sponsorships could be arranged that encourage individuals to be invested in the growth and success of individual students, likely contributing to greater levels of personal and academic success for students of color.[20]

Biola University's Director of Diversity Initiatives and Assessment has developed affinity group programming[21] that empowers a group of faculty and staff from a specific affinity group to create an educational and ministry collective to support, empower, and equip our students from diverse backgrounds. Our students of color need "authentic professional human beings who are worthy of emulation. . . . They need models who exhibit professional behavior, a sense of commitment and purposefulness, and a sense of autonomy and integrity in a world that generates enormous stress."[22] Our students "value most highly academic advisors who serve as mentors—who are accessible, approachable, and helpful in providing guidance that connects their present academic experience with their future life plans."[23] Corporations such as JPMorgan Chase & Co. and Apple have illustrated the power of such affinity groups as being formative in creating an inclusive environment for employees of diverse backgrounds.[24] Similarly, affinity groups on the campuses of Christian colleges and universities represent opportunities for mentoring and empowering our students.

Recognize the added contributions of mentors of color. Staff and faculty of color regularly play an additional role of caring for students of color who have often been the recipients of unconscious bias, racism, and microaggressions on campus. While this giving of themselves is done for the sake of the students' growth and success, the additional investment of time and resources typically comes at their own expense. In the search for successful, sustainable mentoring programs, some institutions offer a level of financial compensation or other incentives for this additional workload.[25] While mentoring can be costly—potentially involving release time for mentors and mentees, travel to meetings, and training for both groups— the expense generally pays off.[26] Even the modest investment of covering the cost of meals with students, or a fund to purchase pizza for small group discussions, signals that the institution is investing in students of color who may feel marginalized or misunderstood on a predominantly white campus. There are many creative options that faculty, staff, and students could collaborate on with a little financial investment and personnel support.

5. Develop and Promote People Who Can Implement the Vision

A few years ago, I hired an Assistant Director of Chapel Programs. It became apparent that he had the skills and ability to diversify our worship leading program in a way that would allow our increasingly diverse student body to flourish. He is very good at mentoring our student leaders to contextualize; he coaches them in times of trial and times of success. He is innovative and is willing to take calculated risks to diversify our programming. We needed to invest both time and more resources in our worship leaders who come from different backgrounds, which has the ripple effect of investing in our students of color. Because I wanted to ensure that he would remain a member of our leadership team, I advocated for his promotion to Director of Worship and Formation so that he could have the authority and freedom to lead his own department. He has flourished and enabled our leaders to flourish in this expanded position of influence on our campus. As administrators and managers, we hold the potential of creating positions and promoting qualified people of color into places of power and authority. By doing so, we change the culture and break through existing barriers and ceilings.

In addition, we have a responsibility to expand our definition of effective leadership to include other cultural norms and perceptions. In comparison to my male colleagues, for example, I often find myself carrying the added burdens of being a woman, and someone who appears younger than I am. I have wondered why there are so few Asian American women in the leadership of Christian colleges and universities. Could it be that unconscious bias toward Asian Americans appearing young and being perceived as conscientious employees rather than effective leaders has played a role in their underrepresentation? I would offer that broadening the perceptions of what constitutes effective leadership may yield some surprising results, while also advancing the extent to which Christian higher education models kingdom values.

6. Regularly Assess Your Programs and Ministries

Assessment! Assessment! Assessment! The assessment process enables us to collect data and make adjustments and changes that will benefit our students and our institutions. It will help give us a more accurate picture of who is being reached and who is being lost or overlooked. Assessment will help us discern if a program is effective or if it needs to be eliminated for a season. Every semester, our department uses a variety of instruments and measures such as class assignments, prayer projects, and experiences related to the spiritual disciplines to collect data. Based on the results, we make adjustments for the next semester and academic year to complete our assessment cycle.

Assess the diversity of spiritual development programming. Ministries on campus and off campus are often spiritually formative opportunities for growth for our students. Many of our programs are steeped in a historical tradition or a liturgy of how we have always done ministry at our institution. Given this, our programs may be places of unintentional exclusion for students from outside the dominant culture. Unconsciously, have we forgotten to diversify our hospitality and education? Have we considered how our campus ministries and campus ministry offices are inviting or uninviting for students of diverse backgrounds? As we assess our campus ministries, it can be helpful to consider the following:

1. To what extent are we showing hospitality to students of all backgrounds? Consider what would make different groups of students feel welcomed. If you don't know, ask them. Our students can give us a wealth of information and insight into their felt and actual needs when they are given an attentive hearing.

2. To what extent do our ministries on campus and off campus demonstrate our diversity values or raise awareness? Who do our ministries reach and provide care for? Consider the needs of the diverse populations on your campus and how to initiate ministries that provide hospitality, care, and provision for those groups.

3. Who participates in our programs? Do the various ministries attract a diverse group of students? Or does the same demographic of students participate in certain ministries year after year? Do we have enough varied opportunities to attract a diverse group of students? How are we recruiting and marketing our ministries? Do we communicate in a way that diverse populations feel invited and can find communal experiences of acceptance and shared purpose?

4. Assess your training modules. Who is your audience? Are the modules being offered geared toward your majority culture (i.e., white middle- and upper-class students)? Also, do you have diversity training modules? If you do, what is their focus? To what extent, and in what ways, do your white students recognize their privilege? How can you be intentional about training students of all backgrounds? If you don't know where to start, Biola's annual SCORR (Student Congress on Racial Reconciliation) Conference, a nationally recognized resource for colleges and universities, is designed to equip students in the basic foundations of diversity education. Additional tools include Biola's online resources[27] and assessments such as the Intercultural Effectiveness Survey, the Intercultural Development Inventory, and the Intercultural Conflict Style Inventory.[28]

5. What is missing on your campus? What spiritually formative needs are not being met? How might God be inviting your ministry into a new horizon of possibilities?

As campus ministries are assessed and student experiences come to light, many opportunities for pastoral care will become evident. Listening and showing compassion may be the most influential gift we can offer to our diverse student body. Campus ministers have the opportunity to be present and incarnate the love of God that motivates and moves us into action and advocacy.

CONCLUSION

God is at work on our campuses. Let us continue to lead and care for our students in spiritually formative ways, embracing our redemptive calling to reflect the diverse likeness of God.

As Paul wrote to the church in Philippi, let this be our prayer for each of us personally and for our campuses: "And it is my prayer that your love may abound more and more, with knowledge and all discernment, so that you may approve what is excellent, and so be pure and blameless for the day of Christ, filled with the fruit of righteousness that comes through Jesus Christ, to the glory and praise of God" (Phil. 1:9–11 ESV). May the redemptive work of God continue to transform the movement of Christian higher education, educating and empowering all of our students to become who God has created them to be and to impact the world for our Lord Jesus Christ. Amen.

FOR DISCUSSION

1. In what ways do you view your work as a coeducator in diversity leadership to be moving toward a kingdom ethic of reconciliation that not only calls for a unity embodied in intercultural competence and integrity, but further invites us into a deeper relationship with God and one another?

2. With whom and how is the Spiritual Development Department on your campus aligned with the institution's diversity initiatives? Are they strategically connected to the decision makers either in their area or other influential relationships in ways that will enable them to advocate for greater funding to support a spiritually formative program that diversifies worship and educates the student body in reconciliation ministry?

3. In what areas of your work do you need to ask the question: How can I "flip the script"? Is it looking for partners and allies? Is it investing in collaborative, mutually beneficial relationships? Is it dreaming about the possibilities of a new inclusive ministry idea outside the box?

4. In what areas are you assessing your diversity growth goals (e.g., chapel programming, campus ministry programming)? How are you demonstrating your successes and setbacks? To what extent are you making significant progress in reaching and exceeding those goals? How can you more

comprehensively expand your goals? Does anything need to change so that you can more fully attain your goals?

5. How are you changing the visible fabric and felt experience of the campus in your spiritual and pastoral ministry?

6. Think of a situation where you had conflict over a conscious diversity issue. How did you respond? What was going on in your thoughts, feelings, and emotions? Take a moment to honestly ask God, "What was going on in my heart at that time with you, with others, with that situation?" Then prayerfully consider: How is God growing and changing you to cooperate more with the redemptive work he is already doing with this situation and this person(s)?

7. How can you invest and empower those serving and leading students of underrepresented groups on campus? How can you advocate, promote, and compensate those who are carrying additional burdens to move these diversity initiatives forward?

8. Where and how can you expand your definition of effective leadership to include other cultural norms and perceptions of effective strong leadership?

NOTES

1 Israel Houghton, "You Are Good," Integrity's Praise! Music, Capitol CMG Publishing, 2001, http://us.search.ccli.com/songs/3383788/you-are-good; Eddie Ramirez and Israel Houghton, "Eres Fiel," Integrity's Praise! Music, Capitol CMG Publishing, 2001, http://us.search.ccli.com/songs/5776214/eres-fiel.

2 Derek Sivers, "First Follower: Leadership Lessons from Dancing," YouTube, posted February 11, 2010, https://www.youtube.com/watch?v=fW8amMCVAJQ.

3 Ibid.

4 As one example of this commitment, the mission of Biola University is "biblically centered education, scholarship and service—equipping men and women in mind and character to impact the world for the Lord Jesus Christ." "Mission, Vision and Values," Biola University, accessed June 23, 2016, https://www.biola.edu/about/mission.

5 Brenda Salter McNeil, *Roadmap to Reconciliation: Moving Communities into Unity, Wholeness and Justice* (Downers Grove, IL: InterVarsity Press, 2015), 24–26.

6 Salter McNeil, *Roadmap to Reconciliation*, 21–22.

7 Systemic inequalities may include established norms in hiring practices, promotion qualifications, lack of access to decision-making positions of power within the institution, recruitment bias, systemic cultural preferences, and so on. Because we all have biases and preferences, this is an opportunity to honestly reflect on where those biases might be unintentionally influencing our work and decision-making.

8 Frank Dobbin and Alexandra Kalev, "Why Diversity Programs Fail," *Harvard Business Review*, accessed May 9, 2017, https://hbr.org/2016/07/why-diversity-programs-fail.

9 Alexandra Kalev, Frank Dobbin, and Erin Kelly, "Best Practices or Best Guesses? Assessing the Efficacy of Corporate Affirmative Action and Diversity Policies," *American Sociological Review* 71 (2006): 611, doi: 10.1177/000312240607100404.

10   John P. Kotter, *Leading Change* (Boston: Harvard Business Review, 2012), 59. Kotter suggests four key characteristics of a successful guiding coalition: (1) position power, having enough key players on board so that the process doesn't get blocked; (2) expertise, having various perspectives of discipline, experience, nationality, and so on relevant to the task so that educated intelligent decisions can be made; (3) credibility, having trusted members so the employees will buy in; (4) leadership, having proven leaders to drive and sustain the change process.

11   My curricular and cocurricular partnerships have included the President's Office; Multiethnic Programs and Development; Talbot School of Theology; the Center for Christianity, Culture and the Arts; the Center for Christian Thought; the Center for Marriage and Relationships; the Institute for Spiritual Formation; the Apologetics; Sociology; Psychology; Communications; Art; Theater; Worship and Music Department; the Conservatory; the Alumni Office; Global Student Programs and Development; the Student Government Association; and the Student Missionary Union.

12   Kotter, *Leading Change*, 3.

13   Salter McNeil, *Roadmap to Reconciliation,* 23–26.

14   Our diverse hiring practices and training for student leaders includes consideration of gender, year in school, on-campus housing, commuter students, major, denominational affiliation, veterans, first-generation college students, ethnic background, international background, and disabilities.

15   John Coe, "Daily Prayers for Intentional Formation," Talbot School of Theology at Biola University, accessed September 20, 2010, https://static.biola.edu/studentlife/media/downloads /SpiDevResources/dailyprayersintention110826pickett.pdf.

16   Kimberly A. Griffin et al., "Making Campus Activities and Student Organizations Inclusive for Racial/ Ethnic Minority Students," in *Creating Inclusive Campus Environments: For Cross-cultural Learning and Student Engagement*, ed. Shaun R. Harper (Author: National Association of Student Personnel Administrators, 2008), 125.

17   "Student Development Theory Resource Guide: Application in Fraternity/Sorority Advising," Association of Fraternity/Sorority Advisors (Fort Collins, CO, 2012), http://www.afa1976.org/. In student development theory, Chickering's theory of identity development identifies "developing mature interpersonal relationships" as a foundation for developing students' identities in fraternities and sororities.

18   Dobbin and Kalev, "Why Diversity Programs Fail."

19   Alexandra Kalev, Frank Dobbin, and Erin Kelly, "Best Practices or Best Guesses? Assessing the Efficacy of Corporate Affirmative Action and Diversity Policies," *American Sociological Review* 71 (2006): 591, 593–94, 611, doi: 10.1177/000312240607100404.

20   Joe Cuseo, "The Case for Faculty-Student Mentoring," accessed June 17, 2016, http://uwc.edu /sites/uwc.edu/files/imce-uploads/employees/academic-resources/esfy/_files/case_for_faculty-student_mentoring.pdf.

21   Our campus currently has five affinity groups: Chocolate Chat for black female students, Iron Sharpens Iron for black male students, Latinas Connect for Latina students, Taro Talk for Asian American students, and White Identity Formation Group for white students.

22   Cuseo, "The Case for Faculty-Student Mentoring."

23   Ibid. Cuseo sites the following studies in order to draw this conclusion. See his article for further reference: Winston, Ender, & Miller, 1982; Winston, Miller, Ender, Grites, & Associates, 1984; Frost, 1991; Gordon, Habley, & Associates, 2000.

24   "Diversity Initiatives," JPMorgan Chase & Co., accessed January 10, 2017, https://www.jpmorgan chase.com/corporate/About-JPMC/corporate-initiatives.htm; "Inclusion and Diversity," Apple, accessed January 10, 2017, http://www.apple.com/diversity/.

25   Jane Hyun, *Breaking the Bamboo Ceiling: Career Strategies for Asians: The Essential Guide to Getting In, Moving Up and Reaching the Top* (New York: HarperCollins, 2005), 65.

26   Kalev, Dobbin, and Kelly, "Best Practices or Best Guesses?," 594.

27 See Biola University's Student Enrichment and Intercultural Development Department for ideas and examples: https://www.biola.edu/mepd/resources.

28 The IES is the most economical assessment tool (http://www.kozaigroup.com/intercultural-effectiveness-scale-ies/). The IDI is helpful measurement tool of intercultural development with a pre- and posttest to assist in how a person changes his or her understanding of difference (https://idiinventory.com). The ICS inventory assists in learning how to mediate conflict (http://www.icsinventory.com).

Chapter Fifteen

BUILDING BELONGING: FOSTERING DIFFICULT CONVERSATIONS AROUND DIVERSITY

Jennifer W. Shewmaker, PhD

Abilene Christian University, Executive Director of Adams Center
for Teaching and Learning, Professor of Psychology

A young female student stands in the doorway of her dorm room, wearing an ACU t-shirt, a dark charcoal mask on her face. She and a friend recording her both giggle. Just a normal picture of college life, and then, across the screen, appear the words, "This is why Black Lives Matter exists." The girl in front of the screen says, "I am a strong black woman," and then pops a pair of oversized, bright red, plastic lips in her mouth. Much giggling ensues, and the video ends.

This video went viral on social media in November 2016, with stories popping up in the national media, and Abilene Christian University (ACU) was thrust into the spotlight as an example of tension in race relations on college campuses. As I watched the video and resultant fallout, I, along with many who love ACU, felt sick and anxious. Faculty, staff, students, alumni, and supporters all wondered how our university would respond, how we as a community could support one another, how we could begin to heal old wounds and the continuing pain that had been exacerbated by a few seconds of thoughtlessness, how we could foster the difficult conversations that needed to happen in order to move from a racially separated and segregated past to representing a campus community that is truly "a world house of learning" for all students, as described by Rebecca Hernandez in laying out her vision for Christian higher education.

As we continue to work through the issue of racial reconciliation within our institution, we have found that fostering honest, open conversation is difficult, but vital. The faculty and staff at ACU have not figured it all out, and we continue to struggle with racial tensions, just as our entire country does. But ACU is committed to moving forward, in love and courage, to embrace the unity of Christ together.

A CHANGING STUDENT BODY

ACU, similar to many postsecondary institutions, has an increasingly diverse student body. In five years, we have gone from about 20 percent identifying as "other than white" to 40 percent identifying as such. While these students have been encouraged to join our community, it is clear that our job does not end with simply achieving a different balance in student demographics. In fact, noted scholar Daryl Smith, in her book titled *Diversity's Promise for Higher Education*, makes a powerful case that diversity initiatives must move beyond what she terms as "structural diversity."[1] Rather, recruitment of a diverse student body must be combined with effective measures to provide a campus environment in which all can succeed and thrive throughout their college experience. Providing an education that supports the academic and relational success of all students depends on building and maintaining an inclusive campus community, and this means that all members of the community need to feel valued and supported. Because our student body is changing, it is important for ACU, both individual faculty and staff and as an institution, to consider our history as an institution in the South that has aligned with a predominantly white theological tradition, the biases that have permeated our culture, and how these influences affect our students' ability to benefit from having a sense of belonging on our campuses.

SENSE OF BELONGING AND UNDERREPRESENTED POPULATIONS

As our student body has changed, it is important for us as faculty and staff to think about what those changing realities mean for us an institution. One of the key issues is the fact that our students of color, a growing population, may not feel a sense of belonging on our campus. Research conducted by Terrell L. Strayhorn, Director of the Center for Higher Education Enterprise and Professor of Higher Education at Ohio State University, documents that a sense of belonging is key to academic success for college students. He defines the construct of a sense of belonging as "the students' perceived social support on campus, a feeling or sensation of connectedness, the feeling of mattering or feeling cared about, accepted, respected, valued by and important to the group or others on campus."[2] Strayhorn frames this sense of belonging as "a basic human need,"[3] which is especially significant for college students for several reasons. For one thing, traditional college students are at a developmental stage in which they are seeking to solidify their identity and are susceptible to peer influence. Strayhorn notes that sense of belonging may be especially import-ant for students who are from underrepresented groups and therefore may feel marginalized on their college campuses.[4] In addition, being a new member of a community, such as an entering college student, may heighten the need for a sense of belonging.[5] It is vital for faculty and staff to understand that our first-year students, already vulnerable due to their age and stage of life, are likely to feel a lack of belonging on campus if they are from underrepresented groups. Faculty, administrators, and staff need to be aware of these dynamics and act intentionally to provide those students with a sense of belonging.

Helping all members of a campus community experience having a sense of community is important not just for incoming students, but also for new faculty. The first years after receiving a faculty appointment are challenging for almost everyone who enters the profession. However, new faculty from under-represented groups—which may relate to gender, race, nationality, socioeco-nomic class, or disability—face unique challenges relating to certain aspects of their identity. One of the problems frequently encountered by nonmajority faculty is stress due to subtle discrimination,[6] such as the feeling of having less support than others and a sense of isolation.[7] Faculty of color also tend to expe-rience students' questioning of their authority and knowledge more than their majority colleagues,[8] and the perception of unequal expectations that create an unequal burden of obligation to work harder than their majority colleagues and prove themselves again and again.[9] Understanding these challenges presented to underrepresented faculty, being willing to openly discuss such challenges, and intentionally providing all faculty with the support they need to thrive is a responsibility that the university has acknowledged and accepted by choosing to make diversity and inclusion a key component of our strategic plan. Figuring out the best ways to make these things happen is a work in progress.

INSTITUTIONAL CONTEXT FOR THE WORK AT HAND

Abilene Christian University was founded in 1906 with links to the Churches of Christ and the mission of providing a Christian education for students in West Texas. This heritage has influenced the diversity, or lack thereof, within our community in important ways; it has also presented us with several chal-lenges when creating an environment that contributes to a sense of belonging for all students.

Tanya Smith Brice, Dean of the School of Health and Human Services at Benedict College in South Carolina, notes that the Churches of Christ even today are typically racially segregated, and she argues that this was purposeful from its origins.[10] Brice describes the historical context by observing that, in contrast to the independent development of historically black denominations, the white members of the Churches of Christ established the black congrega-tions within those holding the same theological tradition in order to maintain separation between the races, and even used scripture to support the segregation and subjugation of black people.[11] Church historian and minister Wes Crawford also notes this paternalistic separation, noting that even as the Civil Rights movement of the 1960s advanced, black and white Churches of Christ grew further apart and at this point in time typically function independently.[12]

Attempts at racial reconciliation have been made, both within the Churches of Christ as a whole and within specific institutions such as ACU. For example, in the 1990s ACU's president, Royce Money, publicly denounced the history of racism within both the Churches of Christ and our university, and asked for forgiveness.[13] Despite the steps that have been taken, a book written by ACU professor Douglas A. Foster, titled *The Story of the Churches of Christ*, emphasizes the importance of continued intentionality: "Many leaders in Churches of Christ continue to work to bring reconciliation and inclusion, but there is still much to be done."[14]

More than a hundred years after its founding, and almost thirty years after Money's public apology for historical racism, ACU is seeking to develop an environment that supports unity rather than separation. Having established an Office of Multicultural Affairs, an Intercultural Effectiveness Team, and a variety of groups serving multicultural students, ACU has taken significant steps to model a commitment to inclusion. These intentional steps gained traction in the mid-2000s, when ACU established United By Faith, a multicultural reading group of faculty, administrators, and staff that met in each others' homes to talk about racial reconciliation. Conversations about race on campus have been ongoing, although much of our work has been within silos, with little coordination. The challenge that we confront is how to develop consistent, connected programming, policies, and actions that support diversity. How do we move from saying we want to provide a place for hard conversations about race, a place of unity, a place of support and belonging for all students to actually doing the hard work to make that happen? And specifically, for the purposes of this chapter, how can faculty development be a vibrant part of that initiative, given the central role of the faculty in creating a learning climate that feels safe and affirming for all students? In the spring of 2016, ACU released its most recent strategic plan, *In Christ and in Unity: Our Vision in Action*.[15] One of the five pillars of the new strategic plan is a focus on diversity. The plan states that, even as we celebrate our growing diversity, we must be aware that doing so will entail a commitment to intentionally building the deep relationships and sense of belonging that have been cherished by faculty, students, and staff from the dominant culture since the university's founding. The adoption of diversity as a primary part of our strategic plan has allowed ACU to move forward with the honest, open conversations about race that are required to make further progress. One of the first actions taken as a part of the new strategic plan was the appointment of a Diversity Task Force, which was tasked with preparing a diversity plan that considers organizational structure and best practices and recommends an integrated and unified approach to diversity. Central to the work ahead is a variety of programs related to the faculty. Thus, this chapter focuses on ways that faculty development programming at ACU's Center for Teaching and Learning can serve as a central point for difficult but important conversations about diversity and inclusion on the campuses of Christian colleges and universities.

FACULTY DEVELOPMENT PROGRAMMING AND DIVERSITY

As an institution, ACU has struggled with the best way to promote effective community with an increasingly diverse student body, and to increase the representation and support of faculty members from underrepresented groups. Being located in the southwest region and being aligned with a church tradition that has historically been racially separated has only added to the complexities of how best to make progress in an area that receives wide verbal support but has met with limited success. As the leader of the Center for Teaching and Learning, I believe that such centers can provide a grounding place to host conversations on difficult topics, offer education regarding teaching strategies for supporting all learners, and build alliances across dispersed programs being run by a variety of offices on campus, thus providing consistency and systemic support for all of these efforts. This chapter focuses on the programming that has been offered through ACU's Center for Teaching and Learning focused on faculty development. I offer this perspective based on my responsibility, over the past five years, of creating and providing faculty development services, first as the Director of Faculty Enrichment and currently as the Executive Director of the Adams Center for Teaching and Learning.

Specifically, my colleagues and I have been developing programming and partnerships in two areas aimed at ensuring an inclusive environment across our campus. First, as a center for faculty development, the Adams Center offers programs to support faculty members from underrepresented groups, working to provide equity in opportunity for development as a teacher, scholar, and leader. These conversations also provide opportunities for faculty members from majority groups the opportunity to understand the perspectives of their colleagues. Second, our programs designed to assist faculty in providing a welcoming and supportive classroom environment for all students have implications both in terms of pedagogy and course content.

CURRENT FACULTY DEVELOPMENT PROGRAMMING

The Adams Center focuses on three key areas to providing training and support regarding diversity and inclusion. These areas include programming specifically for academic leaders, sponsored conversations about inequity, and educational sessions for all faculty.

Focus One: Academic Leaders

The Adams Center's primary mission, as a center for teaching and learning, necessarily focuses its work on the academic side of the university. Therefore most of the center's programming was developed for academic leaders and related to the importance of diversity and addressing explicit or implicit biases, both institutional and personal, that can undermine the university's stated commitment to having all community members experience a sense of belonging. A pilot program, called Blind Spots, was developed in the fall of 2014 and implemented for the first time in the spring of 2015. Initially offered to academic leaders in four sessions, each ninety minutes in length, the program focused on the topic of implicit bias and how such bias can hinder the success of students and faculty from underrepresented groups. The open, honest, and practical conversations that occurred led to many breakthrough moments of deep honest sharing among faculty and administrative leaders on our campus.

The curriculum that guided the four Blind Spots conversations was based on research and best practice in the fields of diversity, social psychology, and faculty development. Incorporating sharing of information and readings, active learning experiences, and products of reflection, the series provided a variety of experiences that allowed participants to build knowledge and skills in identifying bias within themselves and others, and the tools to reduce bias and its impact on the ability to treat all people with respect. A foundational source of reading was the book *Blind Spot: The Hidden Biases of Good People,*[16] which emphasizes that every person has implicit biases, or blind spots. These beliefs are outside of our awareness yet cause us to attribute characteristics to particular groups of people.[17] Such blind spots can hinder our ability to authentically engage with colleagues and students who are different from us, and can contribute to underrepresented groups feeling like they are marginalized on our campuses.

One example of the kind of "aha" moment that occurred among these academic leaders happened as the group was asked to generate a list of the ways in which our current student body is different from that of fifteen years ago; additionally, they were asked to discuss changes that might be in our future. At our university, we have experienced a rather dramatic shift in terms of the percentage of students who self-identify as being white—from 82 percent in 2008 to 60 percent in 2015.

As the group talked about the biases and assumptions that may keep students of color from feeling as if they belong on campus, one said, "You know what I've been thinking about, is the stories that we tend to tell about the heroes of our university. What do they all have in common?" In that moment, each of us in the room realized that our hero stories, so often shared with students, were almost always about affluent white men. In response to this insight, I asked everyone to come to the next session ready to answer the question: What are different or new stories that we can tell about ACU, and how might those stories promote connection among all faculty, staff, and students? Because our campus culture is driven by storytelling and narrative, it is imperative that we begin to connect the kinds of stories told and the kinds of heroes promoted with our spoken value of diversity.

We spent time brainstorming about a variety of stories that might be shared, from the tales of trailblazers Dr. Billy Curl and Larry Bonner, the first full-time African American undergraduate students to attend ACU, to the founding of the Hispanos Unidos student organization in 1991 by a group of students who wanted to provide representation and inclusion for Hispanic students. We mulled over different ways to hear stories from a variety of students, with several leaders mentioning that our conversations had encouraged them to seek out the voices of a wider variety students they encountered in different venues. One idea that resonated was hosting a monthly student lunch, being careful to select a diverse group so as to hear different perspectives. This kind of thoughtfulness about hearing new and different voices was something we felt was a direct outgrowth of being willing to talk honestly about the biases and assumptions that the leadership of our university has historically held.

Focus Two: Support for Conversations about Inequity

The Adams Center regularly hosts open faculty conversations related to books or films that address issues of inequity. In the past few years, these groups have read books such as *Whistling Vivaldi: And Other Clues as to How Stereotypes Affect Us* by Claude Steele,[18] and *Hispanic Realities Impacting America: Implications for Evangelism and Missions*. Reading and discussing these books together has provided a safe place for open conversation about bias and diversity. As we discussed the description of stereotypes and stereotype threat in *Whistling Vivaldi*, one faculty participant offered this honest admission: "I didn't know about stereotype threat, it didn't occur to me that thinking that others believed something negative about you could impact the way you can perform in class."

Another group discussed the concept of microaggressions. In the book *Reconciliation Reconsidered*, William Lofton Turner defines microaggressions as "brief and commonplace verbal, behavioral, or environmental indignities, whether intentional or unintentional that communicate hostile, derogatory, or negative racial slights and insults toward people of color."[19] One example offered in the book was occasions when a compliment feels more like a subtle insult to the recipient. The high level of trust within the group allowed a male professor to comment that this idea was confusing to him. His African American female colleague shared an example and her perspective saying, "I've had people say to me, 'You're so articulate.' That feels insulting because it implies that they didn't expect me to be articulate." When the questioner then expressed surprise, members of the group talked through their own experiences and points of view, which allowed everyone to grow in their understanding. This kind of open exchange and the clarity it brings can only occur when we provide opportunities for honest conversations about diversity within our communities.

Focus Three: Partnership with Multiple Offices on Campus

The Adams Center works with several offices across campus to provide programming to enhance the work of faculty with an increasingly diverse student body. A partnership with the Halbert Institute for Missions, which promotes cultural competency, has allowed us to cohost guest speakers who have addressed issues such as recruiting and retaining minority faculty, improving campus climate to support faculty and student diversity, building cultural intelligence, strategies for improving the ability to work within a multicultural environment, and developing practices to build relationships with those from different cultural backgrounds.

Working together with the Center for Heritage and Renewal in Spirituality (CHARIS), the Adams Center offers monthly lunch sessions in which faculty discuss and process aspects of our faith background. Through these sessions, the participants are challenged to consider the ways that our religious tradition has responded to issues of race, gender, and unity and more effective avenues to promote mutual respect and reconciliation.

We also work with the Center for International Education (CIE) to develop and provide programming for faculty members regarding the challenges that international students face on our campus, as well as effective methods of instruction and classroom management that work most effectively in aiding these students. The CIE develops these sessions, which not only promote greater understanding of students from culturally and linguistically diverse backgrounds but also offer faculty members specific techniques that they can use to increase a sense of belonging in the classroom. For example, in one session, the CIE staff noted that international students are often not called on in class because faculty members cannot pronounce their names. The presenter then gave faculty members brief instruction on how to say common names for those nationalities most highly represented on our campus. Faculty members also learned and practiced acceptable ways of approaching international students to ask them how to pronounce their name. This may sound like a minor issue, but when many faculty members avoid calling on students because they are hesitant to pronounce their names, the students can sense being marginalized in the classroom.

We have also invited experts from both inside and outside of the university to provide instruction regarding the use of teaching strategies to support belonging and best practices for certain populations. Examples of sessions provided to faculty include resources for working with populations such as international students, LGBTQ students, first-generation students, and culturally and linguistically diverse students. These sessions provide practical teaching solutions, including examining curriculum to include readings from a diverse array of authors, providing techniques and learning opportunities such as active and cooperative learning, and the use of inclusive technology.

Over the past two years, the Adams Center has developed an ongoing partnership with ACU's Office of Multicultural Affairs (OMA) in order to provide education and support regarding teaching a student body that is becoming increasingly diverse. This partnership has proven useful in having an informed voice speak into the practices of teaching, given that the director of OMA is very active in developing relationships and talking with students from traditionally underrepresented groups about their needs and experiences.

During the 2014–15 academic year, the OMA director hosted a series in which faculty viewed and discussed a film created by the OMA office about the experience of black students at ACU. In the film, titled *There's a Difference*,[20] the producers explore the diversity of the thoughts, appearances, and experiences among black students at ACU. Their goal of the filmmakers was to allow a variety of students to describe what being black means to them, and how their identity informed and affected life as students on our campus. This film, which is now available publicly on YouTube, allowed the ACU community to have glimpses into the experiences of black students who came from differing socioeconomic backgrounds, family educational backgrounds, regions, and nationalities.

During the 2015–16 academic year, the OMA director hosted a three-part series of lunch sessions for faculty called "Making Meaning of Diversity in Higher Education." Over the course of these sessions, faculty (1) were provided with information regarding trends in higher education in regard to diversity; (2) discussed the ways that diversity affects our own campus and the challenges that we face in providing an environment that engages and provides a sense of belonging for all students; and (3) explored the challenges of broaching discussions about diversity and inclusion, such as faculty not wanting to be pressured to be "politically correct." In the series, as the OMA director told the stories of students on our campus and shared their words and struggles, the importance of having these difficult conversations in order to nurture and support all students became more compelling.

NEW INITIATIVES

At ACU we are continuing to look for ways to provide an environment that supports engagement and belonging for all students. New initiatives that are currently in development focus on providing support for underrepresented faculty members and continuing to develop faculty in their ability to serve and create a place of belonging for all students. In the spring of 2017, the Adams Center began hosting a series titled "The Hospitable Classroom," sharing strategies for working with students who have typically been underrepresented at ACU. (This series will continue into the 2017–18 academic year.)

We plan to develop targeted resources designed to serve underrepresented faculty, including programs and retreats for these faculty members, along with instruction by experts in the fields of diversity or leadership, multiday conferences, and other similar programming for all faculty members, with a focus on diversity, inclusion, and belonging. It is important to provide financial support for faculty and other emerging leaders to attend events such as the Texas Women in Higher Education (TWHE) conference, the Council for Christian Colleges & Universities' Multi-Ethnic Leadership Development Institute and Women's Leadership Development Institute, the American Association of Blacks in Higher Education annual conference, and the Southwest Center for Human Relations Studies' Annual National Conference for Race & Ethnicity in American Higher Education.

We believe that our partnership with campus offices such as the Office of University Access, the Halbert Center for Missions, CIE, and OMA will continue to grow and provide important insights and resources for faculty seeking to offer an environment that supports the full engagement of all students in the educational experience offered by our university.

CONCLUSIONS

As we consider the work that has been done to enhance the sense of belonging and engagement on the part of all members of the ACU community, it is clear that although we have made progress in recent years, a great deal of important work remains to be done. Our campus community values relationships, and programs that build upon our distinct faith heritage and history will be most likely to succeed. Bringing diversity into the strategic plan is a huge component in being able to move forward and have the honest conversation about bias that is vital for us to move forward.

Other institutions seeking to develop programming that supports under-represented groups and expands inclusive environments would likewise benefit from examining their own individual setting, history, and needs. Based on our experience, I offer several recommendations when developing diversity programming. First, contemplate the institutional language and ethos. What kinds of words, narratives, and images connect with those on your campus? At ACU, we are a culture that values storytelling. Thus, when we establish programs, it is important for us to consider how we work the concept of story into new programs. What are the specific cultural values of the institution where you serve? What kinds of programs are most likely to resonate with your community?

Second, consider the pockets of strength currently within your community. Are there departments, programs, or colleges that have effective diversity programs, either small or large? In what ways are those programs successful? In what ways might you build upon those areas of effectiveness to develop wider programming for the institution? What people across campus are known to be "magnets" for students of color, and what creates that catalytic effect? As we have worked to shape programs that enhance a sense of belonging, we have built on strengths that already exist within our community. Using this approach has allowed us to glean information about what types of approaches work well, what challenges have been faced, and what strategies may be most successful in our setting.

Lastly, it is imperative to build partnerships both across the institution, with other similar institutions, and with community partners. The partnership that the Adams Center for Teaching and Learning has developed with the Office of Multicultural Affairs has benefitted both, providing support and opportunities for growth. Establishing partnerships within your own institution can build connections and promote synergy that move the mission of offices, centers, or groups forward.

Our response to the blackface video described at the beginning of the chapter followed these three guidelines. The president sent an email to the university community to clarify what had happened and that this behavior did not represent ACU's values, holding an all-campus meeting during daily chapel to discuss the incident and our response. In addition, the Office of Multicultural Affairs organized a public opportunity for students to share their own stories and feelings after the chapel event. Campus leaders, students, faculty, and staff listened for two hours while students of different races and backgrounds shared their experiences at ACU. It was difficult to hear some of the stories being told, and a challenge to know the best way to respond. But as a result, our community has committed to having the hard conversations about racial tension and reconciliation and not backing away from honest examination of our own challenges. To be the Christ-centered, vibrant, engaged community that we aspire to be at ACU, it is imperative that we face these trials and learn how to best promote a sense of belonging for all. Through understanding our distinctive faith heritage and regional setting and how those have impacted our culture, building upon our strengths, and forming partnerships, our heartfelt commitment is to increasingly model unity within the midst of growing diversity. At the heart of our work at ACU is the teaching of Jesus, who told the story of the Good Samaritan—a person offering love, grace, and belonging to someone very different from himself—defining what it means to be a neighbor living in true community with one another. So we, too, at ACU want to always be a place of love and belonging, a place where each person who joins our community can find caring neighbors on every side.

FOR DISCUSSION

1. What is the history of racial separation or reconciliation in the faith tradition for your institution? Are there ways that this heritage challenges or promotes a sense of belonging for culturally and linguistically diverse students and faculty on your campus?

2. How might you better understand the sense of belonging felt by culturally and linguistically diverse students and faculty? Would a campus climate survey or focus groups provide helpful information?

3. Are there particular groups on your campus that you believe do not experience a sense of belonging? What makes you think that?

4. Does your institution have a center for teaching and learning? If so, how does it support underrepresented faculty and students? Are there new or additional ways you think such a center might serve as a hub for conversations and training regarding diversity?

5. What offices or centers within your institution might provide important information or trainings to support culturally and linguistically diverse students and faculty? How might you build partnerships among these groups to provide new services?

6. Are there community groups that might be helpful in building new programs, trainings, or understanding on your campus? How might you further those partnerships?

NOTES

1   Daryl G. Smith, *Diversity's Promise for Higher Education: Making It Work,* 2nd ed. (Baltimore: Johns Hopkins University Press, 2015).

2   Terrell L. Strayhorn, *College Students' Sense of Belonging a Key to Educational Success for All Students* (New York: Routledge, 2012).

3   Ibid., 33.

4   Ibid., 34.

5   Ibid., 38.

6   Caroline Sotello Viernes Turner, Juan Carlos González, and Kathleen Wong (Lau), "Faculty Women of Color: The Critical Nexus of Race and Gender," *Journal of Diversity in Higher Education* 4 (4; 2011): 199–211. M. Kevin Eagan, Jr., and Jason C. Garvey, "Stressing Out: Connecting Race, Gender, and Stress with Faculty Productivity," *Journal of Higher Education* 86 (6; 2015): 923–54.

7   Tiffany D. Joseph and Laura E. Hirshfield, "'Why Don't You Get Somebody New to Do It?' Race and Cultural Taxation in the Academy," *Ethnic & Racial Studies* 34 (1; 2011): 121–41. Turner, González, and Wong, "Faculty Women of Color."

8   Caroline Sotello Viernes Turner, Juan Carlos González, and J. Luke Wood, "Faculty of Color in Academe: What 20 Years of Literature Tells Us," *Journal of Diversity in Higher Education* 1 (3; 2008): 139–68.

9   Turner, González, and Wong, "Faculty Women of Color."

10 Ibid.

11 Ibid.

12 Wes Crawford, *Shattering the Illusion: How African American Churches of Christ Moved from Segregation to Independence* (Abilene, TX: Abilene Christian University Press, 2013).

13 Douglas A. Foster, *The Story of the Churches of Christ* (Abilene, TX: Abilene Christian University Press, 2013).

14 Ibid., 34.

15 "In Christ and in Unity: Our Vision in Action," Abilene Christian University, accessed May 10, 2017, http://www.acu.edu/content/dam/acu_2016/documents/acu-strategic-plan-2016-21.pdf

16 Mahzarin R. Banaji and Anthony G. Greenwald, *Blindspot: Hidden Biases of Good People* (New York: Delacorte Press, 2013).

17 "Project Implicit," Harvard University, accessed May 10, 2017, https://implicit.harvard.edu/implicit /faqs.html.

18 Claude Steele, *Whistling Vivaldi: And Other Clues to How Stereotypes Affect Us* (New York: W. W. Norton & Company, 2010).

19 William Lofton Turner, "Seeking Higher Ground: Bringing to Light Microaggressions That Impede Progress on the Road to the Beloved Community," in *Reconciliation Reconsidered: Advancing the National Conversation on Race in Churches of Christ*, ed. Tanya S. Brice (Abilene, TX: Abilene Christian University Press, 2016), 147.

20 Faith Abili, *There's a Difference* (Abilene, TX: Abilene Christian University Office of Multicultural Affairs, 2015), film.

Chapter Sixteen

INTERLOCKING CROSSROADS: STARTING CONVERSATIONS ABOUT COMPLEX MATTERS

Yvonne RB-Banks, EdD

University of Northwestern, St. Paul, Professor of Education

> I speak to the Black experience, but I am always talking
> about the human condition—about what we can endure,
> dream, fail at and survive.
>
> —Maya Angelou

This quote by Maya Angelou reflects well my experiences since I entered the halls of Christian higher education eighteen years ago. At the time, I marveled at the opportunity to bring my whole self to my career. Having spent sixteen years working in public education, I was ready to live into the dream that had been in the back of my mind for a long time. I wanted to have the freedom to teach from a Christ-centered perspective in order to prepare future professionals to work in the field of education. My expectations were high regarding the benefits of working in an institution where my faith would be foundational to my scholarship, research, and teaching. I also looked forward to what could be accomplished together when working alongside believers who were unshakable in their faith.

Looking back, I realize that I had given a great deal of thought during that transition from the public school system to what it would mean, as a Christian, to teach in a Christian university. However, I had given only limited thought to considering the complexities of being an African American female entering a new arena as a teacher and administrator. I am still amazed that although I came from the South and was raised in a social context characterized by barriers related to race, gender, and class, I never considered that such social biases would be part of the culture in a Christian institution.

I since have learned how naive I was about the ways in which the diversity of my personhood would shape my experiences in this new environment. Even as of this writing, I am still the only female African American scholar on the faculty of the institution where I serve. Going through the steps of being promoted from director to dean on my campus, I have had to reconsider the best approach for addressing the intersections of diversity for people of color working in Christian higher education. After spending eighteen years in this context, I am convinced that leaders need to take specific actions to bring about the diversity work that our campuses require. Such work cannot be done in isolation or designated to one person or department. Rather, this work of diversity must incorporate the engagement of many, especially those on the frontlines and at entry points into our Christian institutions.

Leadership in terms of taking on and promoting diversity work is essential to the effectiveness of our efforts, in addition to holding our Christian communities accountable. As an important starting point, understanding the work of such scholars as Kimberlé Crenshaw on the impact of intersectionality is critical to changing the experiences of people of color in these settings. Crenshaw has emphasized the importance of requiring this work to be based on a new prism of understanding if the goal of recruiting and retaining people of color (students, staff, faculty, and administrators) is to be achieved. Describing the concept of intersectionality, Crenshaw observed:

Intersectionality is thus a critical lens for bringing awareness and capacity to the social justice industry in order to expand and deepen its interventions. Intersectionality was initially conceived as a way to present a simple reality that seemed to be hidden by conventional thinking about discrimination and exclusion. This simple reality is that disadvantage or exclusion can be based on the interaction of multiple factors rather than just one. Yet conventional approaches to social problems are often organized as though these risk factors are mutually exclusive and separable. As a consequence, many interventions and policies fail to capture the interactive effects of race, gender, sexuality, class, etc. and marginalize the needs of those who are multiply affected by them.[1]

Although the concept of intersectionality has drawn from many sources and been defined in many ways, the literature consistently recognizes the complexity of diversity. The dimensions of this complexity are illustrated in the following diagram[2] and may explain why the concept of intersectionality has not been well understood, even within the context of higher education.[3]

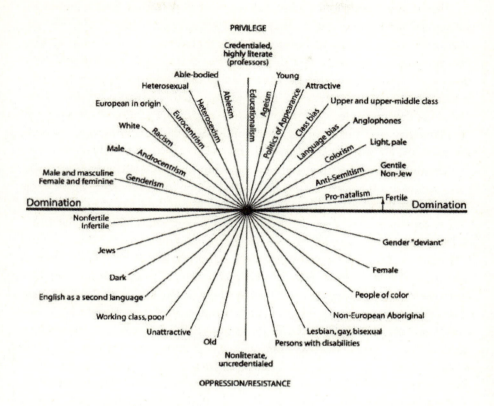

It is important for leaders to know that the intersections of various identities have historically represented places of change that often come through tensions, requiring action by broader society. Because the matter of diversity in Christian higher education is at such a place of tension, and perhaps even at crossroads that requires action, leaders will need to make fundamental decisions about how to move forward. Our campuses can continue down the same path regarding diversity, putting forth well-meaning efforts, or we can seek a new path that offers ideas for needed change and effective growth. Clearly, an understanding of the impact of diversity on a campus is required if constructive change is to occur. As can be seen by the diagram above, diversity does not exist in a singular frame; therefore, reconsidering the topic through the lens of intersectionality offers a starting point for conversations that are relevant not only to people of color but to the well-being of Christian colleges and universities. By understanding and using the concept of intersectionality to address matters of diversity, leaders can construct ways for those in community to better understand and support one another.

This chapter, which describes various experiences that have represented crossroads during my tenure in Christian higher education, identifies themes that can be generalized and applied to efforts that impact students, staff, faculty, and administrative leaders. Specifically, three contributing factors that anchored me to remain over these years may have value and implications for others who are committed to diversity work. The hope behind this writing is to start a conversation that moves forward the efforts of leadership regarding diversity. Why? It is time to move from often segmented well-meaning work, with no clear path, to work that is connected, intentional, intersecting, and sustainable.

The three factors that have been valuable to my own continued investment in a sector of higher education that many people of color have found to be lonely, if not unwelcoming, are (1) mentoring to build relationships, (2) learning engagements and opportunities for professional development that foster intellectual growth regarding the social context and the impact of diversity, and (3) ensuring the presence of resources that are essential to fostering a path of growth tied to a richly diverse campus community. Throughout the chapter, I will reference the concept of *interlocking complexities* of diversity, recognizing that no one issue, or one sector, in this complex set of realities stands alone. Therefore, the agenda proposed in the sections that follow can offer a good start to what I see as key needs and solutions for strengthening our work in the area of diversity across our campuses. The three areas discussed in this chapter have far-ranging application across various sectors of a campus. For example, the three areas outlined impact the work of enrollment management in recruiting students of color, the work of student development in supporting the social/emotional needs of students of color to improve retention, and the work of human resources in hiring and intervention practices that assist in retaining staff, faculty, and administrators of color. Research supports that the responsibility for embracing and affirming diversity needs to be widely owned across any organization if that work is to be successful.[4]

WHERE ARE WE HEADED?

Addressing the commitment of Christian colleges and universities to respond constructively to changing demographics will require more than well-meaning platitudes to remove barriers. The work of diversity requires road maps that connect to the social and emotional needs of our community members, engaging our intellects beyond stereotypes about other people groups regarding race, gender, and socioeconomic status/class. Why? Because who our students and employees are, as individuals, can't be compartmentalized into a color box. And who we are as people of color entering Christian higher education can't be addressed through selective engagement, which is another form of compart-mentalization. How we engage across campus life should reflect a deep valuing and respect for what each person brings as strengths from the various dimensions of our lives.

Where we are headed, and how well we respond to the challenges facing Christian campuses, will depend largely upon the leadership of our institutions. Effective leadership will require taking thoughtful steps and creating opportunities that signal a commitment to promoting dialogue, learning, and support across the entire community. Designing and implementing sustainability plans that allow our campuses to be places of respect and learning for all will be reflected through an institutional commitment of targeted resources, rather than viewed as a negotiable commodity. It will be the work of leadership to promote learning from and with diverse communities, as well as individuals, to signal that a theologically based commitment to diversity is part of the fabric of the institution.

WORKING AT THE CROSSROADS: A PART OF MY STORY

Finding myself quickly at a crossroad upon entering a Christian institution was not a part of the story I had initially planned. Being faced early in my career with a decision about whether to stay or leave was the mark of a crossroad. I knew that I could not mentor students, teach, effectively contribute to committee responsibilities, or serve within the community without bringing my whole self to the table. In other words, I could not leave my race, birth order, culture, dialect, public school education, class, gender, or widowhood outside of my interactions, suggestions, thought processes, or daily contributions—nor would I attempt to do so. Who I was and who I am are all tied to various categories that define my personhood; all such categories contribute to my lived experiences.

Those of us who are people of color come from richly diverse lived experiences, yet upon entry into the world of Christian higher education, we often find ourselves challenged. Our lived experiences can at times get relegated to one or two demographic boxes on a hiring form, and for some of us we may even get ignored when we push pass unspoken norms of who we are expected to be within our new cultural setting. It is only when respect for diversity is viewed as an asset rather than a frustrating distraction that our campuses will be able to make sustainable progress.

Reflecting back on my years of working at a Christian university, I have come to appreciate how experiences in three areas have been important to my continued investment and involvement in this sector of private higher education. Specifically, I have found support and encouragement through experiences of mentoring, learning engagements and opportunities for professional development, and the availability of resources to support programs and services that I know to be important to my institution. I refer to these areas as my anchors. In thinking about specific ways that a commitment to diversity can be reflected across a campus, I encourage campus leaders and other individuals who want to proactively support diversity initiatives to incorporate programming that addresses these three areas.

When challenges are seen as opportunities, innovative ways to create new solutions can take shape in the form of needed actions. With discussions and ongoing conversations about diversity occurring with fresh urgency across the United States and on Christian campuses, leaders have an opportunity to provide direction that can bring about beneficial outcomes.

THREE ANCHORS TO SUPPORT DIVERSITY

There is no such thing as a single-issue struggle because we do not live single-issues lives.
—Audre Lorde[5]

Based on my experiences and training over many years, mentor opportunities continue to be one of the most powerful ways to anchor people to an organization. From my own experience, two mentoring experiences were instrumental in shaping my career path. During my immersion as a new schoolteacher, after having moved to a new state, being paired with an experienced educator grounded me for what was ahead in my career. Specifically, my experience of working in public schooling for sixteen years took me from the classroom to the district-level, with key responsibilities for running programs, hiring, and training teachers. Similarly, as a new professor entering Christian higher education, I appreciated the support that I received from two individuals, one a peer-mentor and another a senior administrator, who guided me through the early years of my career with measureable outcomes; from director to dean and from the rank of assistant professor to full professor.

Clearly, there is a benefit to ensuring mentoring opportunities for young professionals and perhaps especially for people who do not naturally fit the dominant culture of the institution. Now in my role as consultant, for example, as I work with organizations seeking to bridge cultural experiences, I recommend giving particular attention to the on-boarding of new employees and emphasize that mentorship should be included.[6]

Various studies have documented that mentoring, whether that be in the form of formal or informal relationships, is especially important for people of color entering an organization.[7] Such mentoring relationships can help new students, faculty, and administrators address barriers that may be unseen and enhance their sense of belonging. In my personal experience, having a mentor became my first anchor when I entered Christian higher education. This opportunity was put into place by my senior dean at the time, who made it possible for another faculty member to come alongside me in ways that, now looking back, kept me at my institution. This faculty member, who now serves as a department chair, proactively listened to encourage and engage about what was important to me. This mentoring involved a range of touch points, from things as simple as checking in when grading deadlines loomed, to being intentional to sit with me during faculty meetings, to more complex matters such as occasions when students challenged my scholarship or authority in the classroom.

Having someone be a phone call away to process such events was a tangible form of support that kept me centered on who I needed to be, and gave me confidence regarding what I did not have to defend because of my personhood. She became my anchor, and in times of deep hurt and confusion, she offered insight; I viewed her to be, in the term now commonly used, an "ally." This mentor provided many spaces over the years for me to express—sometimes in very raw ways—my painful disappointment in my fellow brothers and sisters in Christ. She understood and could name the embedded microaggressions and barriers I faced upon my arrival and beyond. She openly declared that such actions were wrong and, without my initially knowing it, she used her social capital to share with the administration some of the incidents that were occurring. She took professional risks by openly mentoring and advocating on my behalf. As we have continued to be friends over the years, she has conveyed to me how this mentoring relationship was equally as beneficial to her. Our relationship moved beyond the walls of the institution many years ago, extending to support for our families and sharing the lessons of raising children, even as we experienced very different socialized constructs.

The art of mentoring, when designed and embraced well, can be beneficial to both parties. The special efforts taken on my behalf by my mentor and administrator had a tremendous impact on my career path inside and outside my institution. For mentors (as anchors) to be effective in this role, they must be prepared, believe in biblical principles regarding diversity and social justice, and have both training and their own support systems to be effective in addressing the challenges faced by those from diverse backgrounds. The encouragement here is for leaders to understand the importance of their role in promoting formal and informal mentoring across campuses, with particular attention to counteracting some of the isolation that may be initially experienced by people of color upon entering an unfamiliar organizational culture.

Another "anchor" that proved to be extremely important early in my professional journey was the availability of professional development opportunities.

Various initiatives to increase my learning were made available not only in my area of scholarship but also in professional experiences that connected me with other administrators of color. These experiences contributed to my willingness to proactively take on more diversity-related work, despite the complexities involved. Such actions came out of my increased awareness that strategies to improve the campus climate for people of color needed to be personalized. I found myself asking, "If not me, then who? Given that this is a part of my lived experience, who else should be doing this work to bring about needed change?" With this conviction and the support of the provost at that time, I was able to benefit from learning opportunities that helped me to develop professionally.

One such opportunity for professional development came through participation in the CCCU's Women's Advanced Leadership Institute, which brought together approximately thirty senior leaders from across Christian higher education.[8] Networking with that group of talented professionals, combined with the content of sessions that were led by highly effective cabinet-level leaders, encouraged and challenged me to continue to learn and grow professionally. Over the years, I was able to participate in several CCCU conferences, always with the support of my primary administrative leader, who without hesitation provided funding for my involvement. What unexpectedly grew out of those experiences were several benefits, such as learning much more about the essential leadership skills that took me from director to dean. My scholarship was enhanced through networking that provided avenues to publish, research engagements, and insights from other scholars and administrators of color that grounded me in "best practices" that I now use in my consulting work.

Clearly, this second anchor of professional development (learning opportunities) is essential to attracting and retaining people of color in faculty and administrative roles on our campuses, and particularly so in terms of developing future leadership. Without access to such opportunities, other colleagues across Christian higher education have echoed similar sentiments and themes regarding the limitations and isolation of working in these settings. These themes are consistent with the three priorities identified from my own professional experience: specifically having access to someone who acts as a guide and mentor, to relevant professional development opportunities that support scholarship and networking engagements, and to resources that are critical toward reaching the goal of greater diversity in this sector of higher education.

A third "anchor" that was important in sustaining my commitment to continue investing my life in Christian education relates to having confidence that an assurance to diversity work existed along with resource allocation for programming, personnel, and projects. However, even as the budget signals what is important to those who hold positions of institutional leadership, money is not the only kind of resource that sends signals. Identifying and tapping nonmonetary opportunities as resources represent an avenue to be considered. For example, there is much to be gained through developing coalitions and partnerships, and through reaching out to people who have expertise to offer based on their own experiences. Similarly, reaching out to local communities of color and finding ways to affirm expertise and opportunities for equal partnerships can signal that the institution is serious about diversity.

The experiences of the CCCU's diversity conferences, the Multi-Ethnic Leadership Development Institutes, and previous related research projects signal that a wealth of resources and networks can be shared across campuses when there is a common commitment to embracing diversity. Too often, when budgets are tight, little more than one event, one conference, or one speaker being brought to campus becomes a symbolic representation of a verbalized commitment to diversity. In contrast, when steps are taken in the areas of mentoring, professional development opportunities, and ensuring resources to support diversity initiatives, progress is made. Additionally, individual and collective outreach that involve networking across diversity communities can benefit both people of color and Christian higher education collectively, while potentially requiring little monetary investment.

I am sure that my story would be quite different, had my early years in Christian higher education not been supported by these three key experiences—mentoring, professional development, and the provision of resources in areas that signal institutional support for the goal of honoring and supporting diversity. While these three anchors are critical both substantively and symbolically to advancing our institutions, ongoing conversations and evidence of commitment by the leadership of our campuses must provide the vision, accountability, and interlocking actions in order to effectively make progress.

ONE PERSON: THE IMPORTANCE OF LEADERSHIP

> Leaders must learn to face difficult issues and reconcile differences among factions of their followers … seeking to stay the course.
> —Arthur Padilla[9]

Successful diversity efforts across campuses can be advanced through the integration of the three anchors that I found to be critical in my professional journey, parallel with the journeys of many other people of color in Christian higher education: being supported through mentoring, having opportunities for professional development and networking, and ensuring that resources are available to support diversity work. Overarching these three specific strategies and steps, making progress in this area also requires the clear and proactive support of those holding leadership responsibilities on our campuses. Leaders can provide vision and urgency to the change process with some constructive first steps and strong conversations, starting with being more educated about the topic as part of their own professional development.

As a starting point to developing a campus-based action plan, it is important to have senior institutional leaders who "get it" and are courageous enough to talk about diversity with all its intersections and interlocking complexities. Specifically, it is important that leaders understand the living impact of socially constructed norms in this country—and any other country—that underlie biases. Leaders must therefore also "understand it" and communicate that understanding in ways that influence the development of diversity initiatives. Based on my experiences, the impact of what leaders understand and relatedly *do* to act upon that understanding is key to success when working cross-culturally. Yet it should be noted that such progress often requires hard and sometimes painfully sensitive discussion about co-laboring in a community where race, culture, and gender are often at the core of misunderstandings. Consequently, it is important for those holding roles at the frontline of diversity work on our campuses to believe deeply in the educational and relational value of such work, keeping in mind the special mandate we have as Christians to model Christ's call to honor the dignity of those representing "every nation, tribe, people and language" (Rev. 7:9 NIV).

Two primary lessons I learned early in my professional career from watching and listening to leaders I respect centered on what effective leaders do with what they know. Simply stated, it is quite possible to "learn" something and to "know" something, but if that knowledge is not integrated into the decision-making process in ways that impact change for others, it continues to be simply head knowledge. I often recall the words of a particular leader from my early years in the public school system: "Don't try, do!" That leader's influence planted the seed that carries the important distinction between "trying" and actually "doing" the important work that stands before us. In the midst of busy lives, the notion of "trying" can be a safety net for failure, especially when the desired outcomes do not have a direct impact on the individual leader involved. The more effective alternative mind-set is entering a situation in which the status quo is unsatisfactory and being so committed to making change that failure to do so would be unacceptable. This is the kind of "can do" and "must do" attitude that needs to undergird the commitment of individuals in various sectors of influence across Christian colleges and universities.

One person, especially someone in a role of institutional leadership, can communicate with conviction and support programmatic steps that create ripple effects that contribute to building a culture of inclusiveness for all community members. What I have witnessed is that leaders who set this tone and embody a commitment to diversity encourage others to do the same. As recommended steps based on my experience in Christian higher education and now as a consultant to organizations seeking to more fully embrace a commitment to diversity, change efforts are most effective when leaders

- articulate a compelling vision for the importance of diversity based on theological and educational convictions;
- ensure that efforts of planning for diversity campus-wide move beyond comfortable short-term initiatives;
- set the tone and convey accountability of those given the responsibility for developing various facets of this work;
- encourage widespread ownership that contributes to campus-wide synergy for change that empowers others to speak about matters of diversity;
- ensure that those holding specific spheres of responsibility (e.g., student affairs, human resources, academic affairs, chapel/spiritual life) are working to address barriers that have hindered the development of a campus climate that welcomes all students and employees; and
- provide clear support, both in words and resourcing, for identifying and engaging the tools needed to do the work.

CONCLUSION: MATTERS OF DIVERSITY ARE COMPLEX MATTERS

Everywhere around us and within us we experience complexity and diversity.
—Margaret J. Wheatley[10]

When I am conducting diversity engagements, I often guide teams to consider the complex intersections and the impact of race, gender, and social economics on various aspects of society, even on organizational culture and within family structures. In doing so, I emphasize that none of the social concepts commonly used to identify people can be understood in isolation. That point seems to come across clearly whenever I ask, "Can you see me only as African American, or female, or speaking with a southern dialect, or without dreads, or without . . . ?" Campus leaders can raise similar questions by asking constituent groups questions such as "How can we authentically model the kingdom of God without our brothers and sisters of color present in the community?

What do we leave out of community experiences when we are lacking in diversity? What is missed in broader learning engagements without diversity?" In Christian higher education, we have access to tools that can help us see those around us as having been uniquely designed by a loving God, and gifted to represent God's nature and character in the world around us.

As I enter a new chapter in my career as a consultant who retains a relationship with a Christian university, I have become increasingly aware of the complexity of diversity and of new intersections related to this matter. Yet in the midst of that complexity, I also know that if leadership is truly interested in making our campuses welcoming, engaging, and life-changing places for all community members, this work is essential. I can't stress enough that when used concurrently, the three anchors described in this chapter can bring affirming and amazing change.

From the onset of my career in Christian higher education, it has been my hope that more leaders would take action to change the cultural ethos on our campuses for people of color coming aboard. We have the choice of either continuing to discuss and debate, or actually taking steps to make the necessary changes around this issue of diversity. As Christians we have a power source, the cross of Christ, to draw from in terms of how we should live and work together. Discussing the complexities and sensitivities that relate to diversity can only occur if we listen deeply in new ways to each other and not allow our social constructs to become barriers. It is important to recognize that those of us who bring diversity to our campuses also bring a wealth of assets to share. By doing the complex work needed, we can create new insights and pathways into matters of diversity. We can challenge our campus communities to develop new and better ways—starting with what is outlined here—to prepare the entire community for taking ownership of this cultural shift. We can choose to accept no less than creating a campus culture that is welcoming and embracing to all our brothers and sisters in Christ. This work can be messy, but progress will be made only if agreement is reached that failure is not an option. As our model and guide, we can look to Jesus, who willingly stepped into moments that were messy and intentional on our behalf.

FOR DISCUSSION

1. In what ways would your institution likely change if efforts toward improving diversity are successful? What do you envision to be the best possible changes? What areas of concern might emerge if such changes occur?

2. How will you know when your institution, as a community, has reached an acceptable level of inclusion for all employees and students? To what extent do you think there is such a thing as an "acceptable level" of diversity?

3. What cross-cultural experiences are offered on your campus, or through your institution, as opportunities for professional development? In what ways could these opportunities help individuals better understand the impact of social biases?

4. What immediately comes to mind when you think about opportunities across CCCU institutions within your region that could foster collaboration and be resources to support (and anchor) people of color in ways that keep them in Christian higher education?

5. What are some examples of intersectionality that relate to individuals on your campus who represent nondominant groups? To what extent have you heard reports of microaggressions, and in what specific ways are such reported incidents addressed?

6. In terms of the educational environment being offered to students on your campus and/or across much of Christian higher education, what is missing due to the underrepresentation of other "voices" in conversations and discussions?

7. Thinking back to someone who influenced your life through mentoring, what exactly made that relationship powerful? How might that knowledge be beneficial in mentoring others, perhaps specifically individuals from diverse backgrounds?

NOTES

1   Kimberlé Crenshaw, "A Primer on Intersectionality," accessed May 9, 2017, http://www.whiteprivilege conference.com/pdf/intersectionality_primer.pdf.

2   "Intersectionality Image," accessed May 9, 2017, https://rosswolfe.files.wordpress.com/2013/12 /oppression12.jpg.

3   "Intersectionality and Matrix of Domination: Nineteen Wikipedia Articles," accessed May 9, 2017, http://www.markfoster.net/struc/intersectionality-wiki.pdf.

4   "Best Practices in Achieving Workforce Diversity," U.S. Department of Commerce/Benchmark Study, accessed May 9, 2017, https://govinfo.library.unt.edu/npr/library/workforce-diversity.pdf.

5   "Audre Lorde Quotes," Goodreads, accessed May 9, 2017, http://www.goodreads.com/author /quotes/18486.Audre_Lorde.

6   Oracle, Human Capital Management, *Leveraging Differences to Drive Success: 5 Best Practices for Building a Diverse Workforce/an Inclusive Workplace* (Redwood City, CA: Author, 2014).

7   Audrey J. Murrell, "Five Key Steps for Effective Mentoring Relationships," accessed May 9, 2017, http://nl.walterkaitz.org/FiveStepsInMentoring_Murrell.pdf.

8   "Women's Advanced Leadership Institute," Council for Christian Colleges & Universities, accessed May 9, 2017, http://www.cccu.org/ConferencesAndEvents/CalendarOfEvents/2015/6/2015 _AdvancedWLDI.

9   Arthur Padilla, *Portraits in Leadership: Six Extraordinary University Presidents* (Westport, CT: Praeger, 2005), 61.

10 Margaret Wheatley, *Leadership and the New Science: Learning about Organization from an Orderly Universe* (San Francisco: Berrett-Koehler, 1994), 149–51.

Chapter Seventeen

MOVING FROM THEORY TO PRACTICE

REBECCA HERNANDEZ, PhD

George Fox University, Associate Vice-President of
Intercultural Engagement and Faculty Development

Who do you think Paul is, anyway? Or Apollos, for that matter? Servants, both of us—servants who waited on you as you gradually learned to entrust your lives to our mutual Master. We each carried out our servant assignment. I planted the seed, Apollos watered the plants, but God made you grow. It's not the one who plants or the one who waters who is at the center of this process but God, who makes things grow. Planting and watering are menial servant jobs at minimum wages. What makes them worth doing is the God we are serving. You happen to be God's field in which we are working.

—1 Corinthians 3:5–9 *The Message*

One of the greatest joys I have experienced in my work is my connection with colleagues across the country who have been similarly called to help lead diversity change in their institutions. Although the challenges are great in these roles, we also find joy because we believe this work brings our campuses closer to fully modeling God's vision for Christian community, as expressed through the body of Christ on earth. To illustrate how various parts of the body are contributing to the work of the whole, I called on several outstanding colleagues to share examples of how they are focusing attention on certain aspects of this work in their institutions. Similar to the image of giant water bamboo[1] growing both below and above the ground in ways that change the landscape, it is encouraging to see growth in both the roots and fruit of such efforts across Christian higher education.

Before presenting these examples, I would offer the following cautions about simply attempting to copy these programs without some assessment work of your own campus environment. Not every program works the same on each campus, and various factors should be considered before implementing a program one has read or heard about. Here are some issues to consider:

1. *Context matters.* Each of these efforts has been developed and implemented in a time and place. The mission, ethos, and campus leadership all matter. To make progress, it is important to be aware of the roots that have formed a campus environment, including its values, vision, and mission. What ties Christian higher education together, and differentiates us from secular institutions, is our unique foundational belief in God, the Bible, and the redeeming grace we have received through the death and resurrection of Christ. But there is more to the context than that. For example, at George Fox University, where I currently serve, our Quaker roots emphasize our commitment to peace, justice, and reconciliation work more passionately than perhaps is the case at other institutions.

2. *This work requires tenacity.* It is challenging and requires time and perseverance, often over a period of years, to see significant impact and fruit on a given campus or more broadly. Two of the programs showcased in the sections that follow have been in place for a decade or more, and that "long obedience in the same direction" (to borrow from the title of Eugene Peterson's book) has allowed for refinements and a long-term impact that has changed the campus culture in significant ways. Developing such programs requires both attentiveness to the realities of a campus culture as well as strategic thinking to move an institution in new, and at times controversial, directions.

3. *This effort requires collaboration.* It is simply a fact that most of the good work being done does not happen in isolation, but rather by working across and within multiple units on campus. Someone with vision can develop a compelling vision of a better future in a certain area of campus life, and other individuals and units embrace that idea, for the betterment of wider networks within and often beyond the institution.

4. *Assessment is needed.* How do we know if these programs are beneficial and document as such? Excellent resources and evaluation tools are available and can be helpful both in documenting the impact of specific programs as well as refining and polishing ideas for greater effectiveness in the future. Although the standard assessment tools are important, in the work of diversity, additional perspectives and measures need to be considered. For example, we need to ask questions such as "Whose voice matters most? Is this change good for students and the institution? Are these changes good even if the value isn't immediately clear to those directly impacted?" An institutional commitment to ensuring that our campuses include and value every individual member (students, staff, and faculty) requires that the impact of specific programs and services be documented.

In the following sections, three specific programs are described that illustrate the constructive work now underway across Christian college campuses. Each of these programs was developed in response to a perceived need, and guided by the passions of individuals who have been tenacious about furthering the work of diversity in a specific dimension of campus life. It is my hope that these models can illustrate various lessons that can be gleaned from the envisioning and implementation processes of multiple related initiatives across other campuses.

First, Jenny Elsey, Associate Dean of Intercultural Life at George Fox University, describes five specific steps that have been implemented strategically at that institution to advance the work of changing the campus climate to be more welcoming to diverse communities and to encourage respectful discourse across differing perspectives. Other campuses may benefit from learning how these steps have been incorporated into an effective process of institutional change.

Second, we focus attention on the long-term commitment of Glen Kinoshita, Director of the Imago Dei Initiatives at Biola University, who envisioned and has championed Biola's hosting of the Student Congress on Race and Reconciliation (SCORR) conference for more than twenty years. For thousands of students, faculty, and diversity leaders across Christian higher education, SCORR has offered a place to connect, learn, and grow with like-minded believers. This annual conference stands as a testimony to the impact that one person can have, not only on a campus but also on the movement of Christian higher education across North America.

A third example of effective programming is offered by Dina Gonzalez-Piña, the former Assistant Dean of Multicultural Ministries and an adjunct professor at Fresno Pacific University who now works nationally as the Ethnic and Gender Equity Specialist with the Mennonite Central Committee. This section describes the Samaritan Scholarship program that Dina launched in 2000. This scholarship program story was begun in response to the Fresno community's request to care for an even more vulnerable group—undocumented students in the Central Valley of California. In contrast to the institutional approach of the programming at George Fox University and the national scope of the SCORR conference vision, the impetus for the Samaritan Scholarship program emerged from the demographic and political changes evident in the local community. As described here, the biblical response offered through this scholarship initiative has supported the educational journeys of dozens of first-generation students who otherwise had very limited access to higher education.

Strategies for Campus Climate Change

JENNY ELSEY

George Fox University

In the spring of 2016, George Fox University participated in a program developed by a group of community leaders in the city of Portland to provide more than fifty paid internships specifically for students who came from an ethnic-minority background. Soon after a campus-wide announcement was made, we began to receive the question "Isn't this reverse racism/discrimination?" Although this response did not represent the sentiment of the majority of our student population, it did highlight a challenge that I have seen repeated in every predominantly white institution (PWI) where I have worked. The same sentiments take other forms, such as questions like: "Why don't we have a white heritage month?" "Why can't we have a white resource center?" or "Doesn't [multicultural programming] work against our unity in Christ?"

The challenge that PWIs face in the work of diversity typically can be placed somewhere along a continuum that focuses on providing direct support for individual minority students on one end and creating a more inclusive campus culture on the other. Even as the support of individual minority students is necessary to bolster retention and graduation rates, it is also important to focus on campus culture and climate in order for all students to experience the benefit that diversity brings to a campus. This focus is particularly important, given that many institutions have only a handful of staff members dedicated to this type of work and support; additionally, it is important for institutions where the ethnic minority population has begun to reach a critical mass.

Developing multicultural competency on a PWI offers a variety of challenges that are both visible and invisible. These challenges take various forms in established campus cultural norms, as reflected in policies and traditions that often assume a four-year residential environment for students. However, many campuses are shifting toward populations that include a high percentage of commuters, transfers, and nontraditional students. And because the CCCU member institutions have been historically white, ethnic minority students often quickly sense that the college experience was not designed for them. This reality is particularly problematic when these students also represent the sub-populations of commuters, transfers, and nontraditional students.

So how can deeply embedded institutional assumptions and ultimately the campus climate be changed? At George Fox University, we have begun that process by developing a five-part strategy that includes (1) leveraging institutional culture, (2) identifying and cultivating a network of white allies, (3) implementing programs that celebrate and educate, (4) encouraging cultural humility, and (5) helping our white majority student population find their role in the work.

LEVERAGING INSTITUTIONAL CULTURE

At George Fox, we promise that each student will be known—personally, academically, and spiritually. As a newcomer to the university a few years ago, I quickly learned that this promise drives the institution's initiatives and its daily work. It also became apparent that not all of our students—and particularly those from our ethnic-minority population—were experiencing the benefits of this promise. As Daryl Smith encouraged in her book *Diversity's Promise for Higher Education*, rather than fighting to establish an entirely new culture, our team began to use the "Be Known" culture as the starting point. The primary goal at first was to enhance the understanding of faculty, staff, and students from the majority culture that there were students who did not believe the "Be Known" promise applied to them. The next step was to work with the community to understand how these students wanted to be known. In part, we were told that the students wanted to acknowledge that their race and ethnic identity affected their daily lives.

The response from the institution to these steps to change the institutional culture has been primarily positive. The initiative struck a chord with faculty and staff, given that helping students "Be Known" was something that they deeply cared about, felt personal ownership over, and embraced as a driving force to their work. Using this approach allowed us to articulate a collective vision for the future of the university that built and celebrated the contributions of faculty and staff.

IDENTIFYING AND CULTIVATING A NETWORK OF WHITE ALLIES

It quickly became apparent upon my arrival to campus that the culture of George Fox University is built on relationships. One of my first goals was to identify which voices on campus were "heard" by the broader community, and those who were already supportive of initiatives addressing racial/ethnic diversity that we wanted to implement. One source of great encouragement was finding faculty members and staff who embodied both.

When I identified colleagues who could support diversity initiatives, I began the work of developing those relationships. One of the first challenges that emerged was an awareness that although we may have shared values and convictions, we sometimes had different mandates and represented different institutional contexts. There was a delicate balance of practicing my own cultural humility and working to honor my colleagues' institutional knowledge while also advocating for new thoughts and ideas that might have challenged a majority culture's way of thinking, yet spoke to the needs of our ethnic-minority students.

To cultivate our white allies, our team created a series of training workshops for staff and faculty. We strategically implemented the workshops with departments that were most open, and as people demonstrated a desire to go deeper in their understanding, follow-up sessions and conversations were initiated.

Finding and cultivating white allies is also important among the student population. Our institution faces an additional challenge in being situated in a homogenous community, with our student body largely reflecting the surrounding demographics. Although this pattern is shifting nationally and on campus, many students admit that they have not had the opportunity to interact with diverse populations prior to coming to campus.

We attempt to cultivate white ally-ship in the student body through three strategies: a multicultural leadership program, campus-wide educational programming, and linking multicultural competency back to the workforce.

Recognizing that relationships are the gateway to change is particularly accurate in what I have witnessed with my white students. Unless they grew up in a multicultural environment and/or home, most of these students begin their journey as allies through the friendships they form with students from a different ethnic background. Friendship is not enough, however. There must be a willingness to share painful experiences and a willingness to be uncomfortable in validating those experiences. This becomes one part of the space we intentionally create in the multicultural leadership scholarship program (Mosaic Scholars) at George Fox. The scholarship recruits multiethnic students, but space is specifically reserved for a handful of white students who demonstrate a desire and a level of competency to engage in conversations regarding diversity.

One of the learning outcomes of the scholarship program, identity development, creates a space for students to share their stories and to hear stories outside of their own experience. I remember during one activity we asked students to share their responses to a prompt. When asked to name something they learned, one student raised a hand and told us "Shannon here is from a small town. She was telling us about how overwhelmed she was when she first arrived on campus because of how big it was. All I have been thinking about since I arrived on campus was how small this place was compared to the city I grew up in. It never occurred to me that someone else could have a totally different experience!" Although this moment was lighthearted, it paved the way for the group to begin to engage in other discussions about how their lived reality differed from one another.

Campus-wide educational programming is another piece of the strategy we have employed. One reason for doing so is to take the burden of educating others off the shoulder of our ethnic-minority students. Although experiences such as the one I described earlier regarding the multicultural leadership scholarship program are important, it is equally important to prevent racial fatigue. The Mosaic Scholars program is designed so that all students have an equal part in the learning experience. Therefore it is important for student life administrators and/or other staff and faculty to advance the conversation where personal relationships might leave off. Ethnic-minority students need to have opportunities where they can point others toward continued learning after sharing their personal experiences, rather than feeling like they alone are the educators.

One such program that has become an annual tradition at George Fox University is the Colored White Panel. This event consists of a diverse panel of faculty, staff, and students who are asked to address the issue of white privilege. Attendees are invited to write their questions down for a moderator to sort based on similarities, crossover, and occasionally appropriateness. A handful of leading questions are used to prime the conversation, but the majority of the evening is given to questions from the audience. One important aspect of the evening is that the timing coincides with one of Fox's spiritual formation programs, Shalom, with chapel credit given to students who attend. The organizers felt that these pieces were important, to communicate the spiritual significance of the work and to emphasize the need for broad involvement in the conversation.

IMPLEMENTING PROGRAMS THAT CELEBRATE AND EDUCATE

I have found that there is a need for a rhythm to multicultural programming. Specifically this involves moving between events that celebrate the diversity in our community and events that educate the community on the justice issues inherent in the work of diversity. In applying Nevitt Sanford's theory of challenge and support,[2] campuses that only celebrate diversity often alienate their ethnic minority students, which can lead to feelings of cultural appropriation, while campuses that only push the difficult educational topics slip into a "preaching to the choir" mode, which can alienate the students who need to hear the message the most.

So while our campus hosts events such as World's Got Talent, which highlight various cultures through music, art, dance, and spoken word, and a Multiethnic

Progressive Dinner, we intentionally design these celebratory events and others to contain some form of educational component, even if passive or underlying. In 2015, the intern in charge of coordinating the World's Got Talent event expressed her interest in "pushing the boundaries" of the event. As an ethnic-minority student herself, she was tired of having 200+ people "consume the cultural expressions of her peers" with little or no thought given afterward to their daily lived experiences on campus. So we sat down and talked about her goals for the event and what would be feasible and/or appropriate for the venue, with consideration given to the history and traditions of the event. In the end, we added two new elements: the first was a passive programming component in which the intern took advantage of a captive audience by printing posters containing quotes that highlighted a community's responsibilities toward justice and to recognize the marginalized and vulnerable; the second was an invitation to the university's ethnic clubs and organizations to provide snacks at intermission while simultaneously providing information about their clubs.

ENCOURAGING CULTURAL HUMILITY

Jody Wiley Fernando begins her book *Pondering Privilege*[3] with "an appeal to cultural humility." She describes cultural humility through a series of examples that highlight a willingness to admit one's lack of knowledge, expand one's worldview, learn from others, and stand in solidarity with others. Fernando writes that this approach made sense to her, and it occurred to me that the same would be true for the evangelical community with whom I worked.

I often hear my white colleagues express a frustration with the need to be "PC," or politically correct. Diversity is often seen as a secular and liberal agenda. Using the framework of cultural humility, however, I found a way to explain to my colleagues something that I have believed all along: justice, and framing justice around the work of diversity, is a matter of spiritual formation. Cultural humility promotes a posture that quite frankly resembles characteristics highly valued within our Christian ethos, including those of servanthood, humility, grace, and not thinking of ourselves higher than we ought.

So, then, how do we promote cultural humility on our campuses? George Fox has one of the most unique examples that I have seen. Not only are the university's Spiritual Life Office and Multicultural Life Office philosophically connected; they are also structurally connected. This has resulted in a direct focus on issues of diversity in our chapel and spiritual formation programs. It has been important to highlight how our spiritual life impacts the work of diversity and vice versa. Although both offices have agreed that multicultural programs will eventually outgrow the structure, spiritual life has intentionally leveraged its standing within the university to highlight the work and message of diversity.

HELPING OUR WHITE MAJORITY POPULATION FIND THEIR ROLE

I recall an interaction with one of my white students who asked, as she was processing out loud with me, "Are there any white role models within diversity?" Her lament was that although she did not want to co-opt the experience of ethnic minorities as a white person, she knew of no white role models she could mirror. In her experience, white people were the perpetrators and she felt a sense of helplessness in trying to move toward an unfamiliar narrative. She wanted to know, "How can I be different? Who can show me the way?"

I do not want to disregard the need for white majority campuses to listen to their ethnic minority leaders. Quite often the voices of those on the margins are missed while trying to solve the problems of a biased system. We have seen too many instances of the white savior complex, swooping into communities and telling them what they need without adequately listening to those who live in the daily realities.

This is not what I am advocating in the suggestion that we need to help our white students find role models in this work. However, similar to the need for our ethnic minority students to see themselves reflected in various professions and leadership roles, our white students need to see themselves reflected in the work of diversity. In my narrative, therefore, I have been challenged to include examples of white allies who have demonstrated an ability to leverage their privilege for a greater cause, listen (and even step aside when necessary) to their minority counterparts, and actively seek to challenge and educate themselves. I pointed this student to the voices of Peggy McIntosh[4] and Tim Wise.[5] I referred them to staff and faculty allies on campus. Moving forward, I'll be recommending the works of Jody Wiley Fernando.

Student Congress on Racial Reconciliation (SCORR)

GLEN KINOSHITA
Biola University

The first conference of what was to become known as the Student Congress on Racial Reconciliation (SCORR) took place in February of 1996 on the campus of Biola University. The original intent of the conference was based on the need to create a space for those desiring to connect with others who daily navigated being students of color, as well as those who valued an appreciation for diversity within the context of a predominately white institution. The vision statement of SCORR indicates that it is "to be an annual gathering where attendees experience instruction that broadens their perspectives, dialogue that enhances critical thinking, and artistic expression that inspires creativity."[6]

In these early days, the conference was predominately regional, serving Christian colleges and universities in Southern California. The feel of the gathering was intimate, as conversations addressed topics such as promoting diversity in a Christian context and addressing systemic injustices. Those who yearned for such dialogue found a place where they could be free to explore and think deeply.

As time progressed, the demographics of those attending the conference began to shift. Several departments on Biola's campus, as well as other institutions represented at the conference, began requiring student leaders (e.g., student government, residence life, etc.) to attend SCORR. Challenges arose in that many student leaders were either new to the conversation or had not given much thought to topics relating to diversity. Because much of the content was unfamiliar, some participants experienced cognitive and emotional dissonance, expressing that they felt confused or guilty when conversations addressed ethnic identity development or framed diversity issues as being systemic in nature. The challenge faced by the conference organizers then became that the SCORR attendees had shifted to comprise those new to the conversation, as well as those who yearned to go deeper, and sought for ways to implement structural change on their campuses.

As a result, I expanded the conference to utilize a developmental perspective referred to as "sequencing," which essentially programs according to the current developmental level of the student. Diane Goodman explains this developmental perspective, suggesting "that change occurs through particular sequences. As one's current perspective or way of being becomes inadequate, this creates a sense of disequilibrium, and the impetus to move to new ways of seeing and being."[7] Goodman further described the concept of sequencing by citing the work of Harvard scholar Robert Kegan:

> He maintains that growth unfolds through alternating periods of dynamic stability, instability, and temporary rebalance. Individuals need a sense of "confirmation," an environment of support, before moving on to situations of "contradiction," conditions that challenge current meaning-making systems. They then need a context for "continuity," which allows for transformation and re-equilibrium. A sequence of confirmation, contradiction, and continuity can provide a framework for designing and responding to issues in social justice education.[8]

By utilizing this sequencing method, we constructed workshop sessions into tracks structured around this model.

The "confirmation" phase, as described by Kegan, is appropriate for those new to the conversation on diversity. Sessions for those in the confirmation phase consisted of introductory concepts of intercultural competence and establishing why addressing issues of equity and inclusion is important. A crucial aspect at this level is establishing the biblical foundations that establish the value of diversity from a theological perspective. In addition to establishing these foundational concepts, the confirmation phase is also used to stimulate the process of continued growth in SCORR participants. Movement into the next phase, "contradiction," may also require dialogue and personal connection with faculty, student development professionals, or student peers who can coach students to think deeper while establishing strong rapport with one another in the process.

The contradiction phase engages the dissonance that conversations on diversity and justice often evoke. Conference sessions designed for those in the contradiction phase address issues of systemic injustice, such as power and privilege, while also allowing participants to engage in dialogue on topics such as biblical justice, internalized racism, and other forms of oppression. The process used to stretch and challenge participants during the contradiction stage involves integration of thought and emotion in learning, with facilitators carefully managing the affective domain. In the "continuity" phase, students are urged to continue the process they started during the contradiction phase. Goodman has described this step in the process: "In the continuity phase, our goal is to help students integrate and apply their new knowledge and awareness. They are seeking to recreate a sense of equilibrium."[9] Movement that integrates critical thinking into action and leadership results in the continuation of learning that is needed in our institutions.

Over the years, I began utilizing a more collaborative approach that involved the student development deans and directors who sent student leaders to SCORR. We discussed that wherever possible, it is important for students to engage topics of diversity prior to attending SCORR, as well as to debrief afterward, thereby conveying the point that diversity, equity, and inclusion are leadership values. Regardless of the level of the participants' understanding, one goal of the program is to provide a safe learning environment for each person. The importance of offering a safe learning environment has been emphasized by Nathalie Kees: such an environment "offers challenges, both intellectual and emotional, within an atmosphere of support, curiosity, cooperation, encouragement, and caring. Above all, a safe environment provides clear and realistic opportunities for success to all students."[10] As we made adjustments to encompass various developmental levels, the feedback from students new to the conversation improved. Providing a SCORR conference program recognizing the stages of sequencing is an ongoing learning process that we are committed to continue. The vision will remain to engage in transformational growth as a lifelong process for the glory of God. These elements in our vision are encompassed throughout the conference, whether for confirmation, contradiction, or continuity.

Another significant element through the years has been the presence of the arts. Music from various cultures, especially as it relates to worship, is embedded throughout SCORR. Other expressions of creativity such as graffiti art, dance, spoken word poetry, and drama are present every year. We have been challenged by speakers such as Richard Twiss, Brenda Salter McNeil, Soong Chan Rah, Judy Peterson, Efrem Smith, and Lisa Sharon Harper. On average, fifteen to seventeen Christian colleges and universities from across the country send delegations to SCORR, in addition to attendees from the Biola community, with annual conference attendance now averaging 900 students and staff. The future of SCORR will no doubt encompass sessions for faculty and staff, which will further broaden the scope and impact of the conference.

The Fresno Pacific University Samaritan Scholarship Story

Dina Gonzalez-Piña

Ethnic and Gender Equity Specialist, Mennonite Central Committee National Office
Adjunct Professor, Fresno Pacific University

The story of Fresno Pacific University (FPU) choosing to make "Samaritan Scholarships" available to undocumented students begins California's Central Valley. The city of Fresno is a community where the neighboring farmlands are rich and able to produce food for the state, the nation, and the world. In the minds of some Americans, this region is known as the food basket capital of the world.

Although primarily white farmers own the Central Valley that surrounds Fresno, it is the immigrant Hispanic community that works the land, often in 110-degree heat, giving of themselves to produce its crops. It is well known in the region that approximately 80 percent of the labor force in the farm-working community is undocumented.[11] No one with any kind of education, English language skills, or vocational skills would choose to work in this physically demanding agricultural work.

It was in the year 2000 that a group of local high school counselors approached
Fresno Pacific University advocating for educational access on behalf of their
talented undocumented students. At that time, most California postsecondary
institutions would accept undocumented students only if they chose to pay tuition fees as "out-of-state" students, representing a hurdle that was impossible
to surmount for some of the most vulnerable and economically impoverished
students, who have come to be known as "dreamers." Although the local public
university had invested in these students, most of these students were unable to
pursue their career goals unless they were able to secure a scholarship or financially commit to the high cost of education.

What the high school counselors who approached Fresno Pacific University
did not know at the time of their request was that FPU had adopted an internal
policy in response to California's concerns over "the browning of America."
The institutional policy at that time asked that if an employee suspected any
student of being undocumented/illegal, a report was to be made to the administration. How do you move a faith-based educational institution from a place
of patrolling and hostility to a place of welcome and embrace? That process
required a combination of prayer, relationships, education, negotiation, and
lots of patience. It took ethnic Latino staff to cast a new vision that included
these students.

In order for this new vision to be implemented, numerous meetings were
held within the university, beginning with the admissions team wrestling over
this situation that brought together matters related to policy, financial need, and
institutional vision. Once the admissions recruiters/directors were in agreement regarding a commitment to support undocumented students to attend
FPU, the next step was to move toward convincing a few of the administrative
leaders, all of whom were white, to consider the need to provide educational
opportunities to those living in the local community.

Making progress on this issue within the institution required several meetings and actively engaging a variety of people in a cross-cultural dialogue and
experience. A small number of us (Latino and white) joined a local "Voices of
the Valley Tour" that was directed by the Mennonite Central Committee (MCC),
an organization that works on issues related to immigration and faith. This tour
consisted of encountering the immigrant undocumented farm laborers in their
agricultural work settings to hear their hopes and dreams for their children.
These workers also shared with the group their challenges in seeking proper
documentation with the broken immigration system. Another critical step in
moving our institution forward was providing opportunities for key administrators to meet with potential undocumented students, who told stories of personal

struggles and racism faced by members of immigrant communities as they sought acceptance and opportunities. One result of those dialogues was a deeper commitment to the university becoming a place of biblical compassion and justice, rather than a place of indifference or judgment regarding their situation.

In 2001, Fresno Pacific University established a program of offering two full-tuition Samaritan Scholarships each year to two students who meet established criteria, in response to the request of the community and the institution's commitment to its biblical values (see the university website for criteria).[12] The first student to graduate from FPU after receiving this scholarship continued his education at Duke University and now serves as a practitioner in the impoverished farm working community of Firebaugh, California. To date, FPU has graduated more than fifty Samaritan Scholars with degrees in almost all of the thirty-plus majors offered at the university. The students who have been supported through Samaritan Scholars funding have a graduation rate of 100 percent in four years or less. These students, who have been one of the institution's best investments, have graduated with academic honors, and have been some of the best athletes, musicians, and academic scholars. Many of these Samaritan graduates have continued to complete master's degrees in fields such as business, social work, education, and chemistry; some have completed doctoral studies in areas of the health sciences. A few have been able to successfully navigate through the legal process and have obtained their residency and citizenship. In the past years, these undocumented students have been able to travel abroad with academic cross-cultural programs offered through the university. Over two summers, twenty undocumented students from Fresno Pacific University have been able to participate in study abroad programs in Latin America (Colombia and Guatemala).

Living out the scriptural mandate of Matthew 25:35 ("I was a stranger and you took me in" NHEB), FPU has provided for these students an opportunity to continue their academic dreams, to deepen their spiritual faith, to develop peer relationships, and to be "seen." For other institutions that might be interested to create a program like the Samaritan Scholars, what follows is a list of suggested action steps.

First, find out what your campus might already be doing in this area. Meet with the professionals in the admissions office and ask if they have an application process for undocumented students, what resources are available, and whether admissions counselors have been trained and assigned to serve this specific population. Additionally, you might want to ask if your institutional recruiters have developed a relationship/partnership with local immigrant church congregations that serve families with these specific needs.

Second, find out what the authorities in your community are saying to high school students who are undocumented. High school counselors, local ethnic pastors, and local ethnic leaders are positioned to offer helpful guidance in terms of postsecondary institutions that are welcoming of undocumented students. If such students are not considering or currently attending your institution, it might be that they are unaware of being welcomed on your campus.

Third, know your state laws as they pertain to funding undocumented students. Although some states have allocated resources (in-state tuition, grants) to support the education of undocumented students, others have not.

Fourth, in conversation with the financial aid director at your institution, be aware of whether aid might be committed to funding scholarships for these students. If there is institutional willingness and concern to support undocumented students, meeting with staff in the Advancement Office could open doors to donors who have a burden or passion to make higher education accessible to these students. In concert with key institutional leaders, find acceptable ways to pursue the creation of a similar scholarship fund to serve generations of future students.

FOR DISCUSSION

1. Take an inventory of the variables in your context—history, mission, demographics, and community—and discuss what works for and against diversity initiatives. What aspects of the context at your institution can help lend to great diversity initiatives? What might potentially become a stumbling block that should be considered?
2. What lessons can you learn from these examples from three different institutions? What are the parallel values you share with other like institutions?
3. With what people, groups, or departments on campus can you collaborate to affect positive diversity change? What can you work on now?
4. What can be done at your institution to broaden the campus culture and climate to help all students experience the benefit that diversity brings?
5. How can you promote cultural humility on your campus?
6. What visions or missions are already in place at your institution that can be used to help promote further diversity initiatives?

NOTES

1   Greg Bell, *Water the Bamboo: Unleashing the Potential of Teams and Individuals* (Portland: Three Star Publishing, 2009), 309.
2   Nevitt Sanford, *Where Colleges Fail: A Study of Student as Person* (San Francisco: Jossey-Bass, 1968).
3   Jody W. Fernando, *Pondering Privilege: Toward a Deeper Understanding of Whiteness, Race, and Faith* (Minneapolis: NextStep, 2016).

4   Peggy McIntosh, "White Privilege: Unpacking the Invisible Knapsack," in ed. P. S. Rothenberg, *White Privilege: Essential Readings on the Other Side of Racism*, 4th ed. (New York: Worth Publishers, 2012), 121–25.

5   Tim Wise, *White Like Me: Reflections on Race from a Privileged Son* (Berkeley: Soft Skull Press, 2011).

6   "SCORR Conference: Vision," Biola University, http://studentlife.biola.edu/diversity/scorr/about/.

7   Diane J. Goodman, *Promoting Diversity and Social Justice: Educating People from Privileged Groups* (New York: Routledge, 2011), 34.

8   Ibid., 35.

9   Ibid., 39.

10 Nathalie Kees, "Creating Safe Learning Environments," in *Teaching Diversity: Challenges and Complexities, Identities and Integrity*, ed. William M. Timpson, Silvia Sara Canetto, Evelinn Borrayo, and Raymond Yang (Madison, WI: Atwood Publishing, 2003), 56.

11 Caitlin Dickerson and Jennifer Medina, "California Farmers Backed Trump, but Now Fear Losing Field Workers," *New York Times*, February 10, 2017, A10, https://www.nytimes.com/2017/02/09/us/california-farmers-backed-trump-but-now-fear-losing-field-workers.html?_r=0.

12 "The Samaritan Scholarship," Fresno Pacific University, https://www.fresno.edu/students/student-financial-services/types-aid/scholarships/samaritan-scholarship.

AUTOETHNOGRAPHIES

EMERGING LEADERS AND CAREER STAGES

Introduction

THE FACES BEHIND THE NUMBERS

KATHY-ANN C. HERNANDEZ, PhD

Eastern University, Professor, College of Business and Leadership

As a research methodologist trained in positivistic paradigms, I was taught about the credibility of numbers. In fact, in conversations relating to the status of minorities in terms of leadership, and in particular black women in higher education, I am well versed in data, especially as it relates to someone like me who faces a triple threat of being immigrant, black, and female.[1] However, as compelling as numbers are, they do not tell the full story. They cannot show faces—faces like mine and the seven other contributing authors to this section. Each of us has committed to stepping out from behind the data to make ourselves visible. We seek to give readers of this volume a close-up view of our lived experiences as minorities positioned in predominantly white institutional contexts. Stories like ours are part of a growing anthology of experiences of people of color in higher education who are choosing to lend our voices and break the silence—choosing to make known the challenges we face as outsiders within the academy.[2,3]

At the same time, we recognize that our stories represent a somewhat privileged perspective. Unlike many other minorities in higher education, each of us has benefitted from the rich nurturing of attending a leadership development institute, with ongoing connections throughout the following year. Yet by virtue of where we are positioned at this stage of our individual careers, this input continues to affect us in different ways. In the chapters that follow, we reflect on how our status as minorities in the academy, as well as the supports that we have received or not received along the way, have both challenged and inspired our leadership strivings. We also offer suggestions for colleges and universities to take proactive steps to create institutional contexts that support the leadership development of people like us.

Our collective story began in June 2015 when we first met for the four-day Multi-Ethnic Leadership Development Institute (M-E LDI) in a picturesque retreat setting near the Canadian border of Washington State. Each of us found ourselves there, in some cases through our own efforts and/or the recommendation or advocacy of others, as a participant in this institute sponsored by the Council for Christian Colleges & Universities (CCCU). Through this experience, we benefitted from time set aside to intentionally strategize for our personal leadership development. The institute began a yearlong experience of working through a self-constructed professional development plan under the guidance of the LDI resource leaders and conference organizer. Two required elements of our plans were further immersion in the leadership literature and participation in a shadowing experience with a self-selected senior-level leader at another CCCU campus.

In addition to being a part of the larger Multi-Ethnic Leadership Development Institute cohort, the authors in this section are also among the seventeen participants who elected to be involved in a nine-month collaborative research project focused on the influence of mentorship[4,5] and sponsorship[6] as potentially salient elements in leadership development.[7] Specifically, each participant identified and worked with at least one sponsor during the 2015–16 academic year. For this research project, we employed the qualitative research methodology known as collaborative autoethnography (CAE). CAE involves researchers "[working] in community to collect their autobiographical materials and to analyze and interpret their data collectively to gain a meaningful understanding of social phenomenon."[8]

This anthology is a product of such reflections and provides intimate accounts of the challenges and opportunities we face at the intersection of our different identities. In combination, our stories resonate with the theoretical contributions of legal scholar Kimberlé Crenshaw,[9,10] who argues that individuals differently positioned by virtue of the combination of their various socio-identities—for example, race, gender, and immigrant status—can find themselves prey to marginalization. In actuality, it is the intersection of these various socio-identities and not any one element alone that presents significant challenges to our leadership aspirations. Moreover, drawing on the work of critical race theorist Patricia Hill Collins,[11] these stories highlight the challenges we face as we occupy the liminal space of being outsiders within the academy. We are part of the higher education landscape but are often outsiders to the predominant organizational culture within these spaces that can provide the "constellation" of developmental relationships to support our leadership strivings.[12] These eight individual stories organized into four groups illustrate that we each experience our context differently, yet the stories taken together suggest some commonalities that can be useful in centering our voices around areas to be targeted by individuals seeking to support the leadership development of people like us.

The first two chapters feature the work of Leah Fulton and Kevin Williams. Both Leah and Kevin are in the early career stages of juggling work and family while entertaining the option of further graduate studies. Until recently, Leah has served as the associate dean of intercultural programs and services at Bethel University in Minnesota. She is also the mother of three young children. In a piece entitled "A New Rite of Passage: Integration, Agency, and the StrongBlackWoman," Leah reflects on the hard lessons she has had to learn to achieve leadership success. She writes candidly about her struggles to overcome the prevalent archetype of the strong black woman, while travelling a path to leadership without much professional support. Likewise, Kevin Williams, who—until a recent transition to another Christian college—served as the assistant director of residence life at Messiah College, is the father of three young children. In his chapter, entitled "Potholes on the Professional Journey of a Developing Leader," Kevin adds his perspective as a black male and reflects on how the stereotypical expectations of this identity colors his leadership experiences and motivations.

The next two chapters by Aisha N. Lowe, Associate Professor of Education and Associate Dean of the Office of Academic Research at William Jessup University, and me (Kathy-Ann C. Hernandez), a professor in the College of Business and Leadership at Eastern University, reflect on our midcareer aspirations as black women in Christian higher education. We independently retrace the path we have travelled to this destination and consider the ways in which our statuses continue to shape our experiences and perspectives. Whereas Aisha is native born and has occupied predominantly white spaces for most of her life, I am an immigrant who is still coming to terms with what it means to be a black person in the United States. Having once occupied the status of majority in my home country of Trinidad and Tobago, I make a case for positioning oneself in the place of others of difference as a useful step for understanding and addressing the nuances of diversity. My chapter is entitled "Embracing the Perspective of the Other." Offering another perspective, Aisha discusses how she has learned to turn a perceived position of disadvantage as a minority into one of advantage by harnessing "The Power of the Only."

Chapters Twenty-Two and Twenty-Three feature the work of Gladys Robalino and Rukshan Fernando. Gladys is currently serving as the chair of the Modern Language Department at Messiah College, and Rukshan is the associate dean of the School of Behavioral and Applied Sciences at Azusa Pacific University. Both Rukshan and Gladys are in a transitional phase of their career, having recently stepped up to new responsibilities. Gladys never envisioned holding a professional position other than serving as a faculty member and scholar in the academy. However, when she was asked to serve as interim chair of her department shortly after attending the Multi-Ethnic Leadership Development Institute in 2015, she found herself engaged in deep intrapersonal reflection on her reluctance to lead. She shares this internal dialogue in her chapter entitled "Navigating the Transition to Administrative Leadership." In contrast, as the second of only two males contributing to this section, Rukshan discusses how the combination of his statuses as immigrant and male has uniquely positioned him at the intersection of cultural ethnicity and gender to view his experiences through a distinct cross-cultural lens. In the chapter entitled "I Don't Belong Here: A Circle Leader in a Square University," Rukshan describes some of the systemic institutional challenges people like him face in their leadership aspirations.

The final two chapters feature the work of Rebecca Torres Valdovinos, director of the English Language Institute at George Fox University, and Roberta Wilburn, associate dean for graduate studies in education and diversity initiatives at Whitworth University. Both women have invested their careers in higher education. Rebecca, in a moving chapter entitled "A Lifetime in Search of a Sponsor," describes the challenges she experienced as a fourth generation Mexican American and later as a single mother raising four children. With refreshing honesty, she vividly recounts the arduous path along which she limped without clearly identified support networks to ultimately develop leadership strivings. Likewise, Roberta, an African American woman who has spent more than thirty-five years in higher education—with ten of those being in Christian higher education—shares the lessons she has learned along the way. Drawing from these past experiences, Roberta describes how she has utilized these lessons to propel her forward in her leadership aspirations. Moreover, she writes with a view to inspiring the next generation of black women to continue to more courageously step into broader leadership in her chapter entitled "Going to the Next Level: Opportunities and Challenges Facing African American Women Leaders in the Academy."

What we hope these chapters communicate beyond numbers is a vivid account of our collective positioning in the landscape of higher education. We hope to convey a sense of who we are, our faces, and our lived experiences so that readers of this volume may come to see us and know our collective struggles and victories. In doing so, we hold up our stories as testimonies that can inspire others in their leadership aspirations and development. But more importantly, we hope that these stories can lead the way to difficult conversations, to door-opening encounters, and to informed actions that more fully enable people like us to survive and thrive in the context of predominantly white institutional spaces.

NOTES

1   Kathy C. Hernandez, Faith W. Ngunjiri, and Heewon Chang, "Exploiting the Margins in Higher Education: A Collaborative Autoethnography of Three Foreign-Born Female Faculty of Color," *International Journal of Qualitative Studies in Education* 28 (2015): 533–51, doi: 10.1080/09518398.2014.933910.

2   Gabriella Gutierrez y Muhs, Yolanda Flores Niemann, Carmen G. Gonzalez, and Angela P. Harris, eds., *Presumed Incompetent: The Intersections of Race and Class for Women in Academia* (Logan, UT: Utah State University Press, 2013).

3   Christine A. Stanley, "Coloring the Academic Landscape: Faculty of Color Breaking the Silence in Predominantly White Colleges and Universities," *American Educational Research Journal* 43 (2006): 701–36, doi:10.3102/00028312043004701.

4   Kathy E. Kram, *Mentoring at Work* (Glenview, IL: Scott, Foresman, and Company, 1985).

5   Paul B. Lester, Sean T. Hannah, Peter D. Harms, Gretchen R. Vogelgesang, and Bruce J. Avolio, "Mentoring Impact on Leader Efficacy Development: A Field Experiment," *Academy of Management Learning & Education* 10 (2011): 409–29.

6   Sylvia A. Hewlett, *Forget a Mentor, Find a Sponsor: The New Way to Fast-Track Your Career* (Boston: Harvard Business Review, 2013).

7   Lynn M. Gangone and Tiffani Lennon, "Benchmarking Women's Leadership in Academia and Beyond," in *Women and Leadership in Higher Education*, eds. Karen A. Longman and Susan R. Madsen (Charlotte, NC: Information Age Publishing, 2014), 3–22. See also Barbara Kellerman and Deborah L. Rhode, "Women at the Top: The Pipeline Reconsidered," in *Women and Leadership in Higher Education*, eds. Longman and Madsen, 23–40.

8   Heewon Chang, Faith W. Ngunjiri, and Kathy-Ann C. Hernandez, *Collaborative Autoethnography* (Walnut Creek, CA: Left Coast Press, 2013), 24.

9   Kimberlé W. Crenshaw, "Demarginalizing the Intersection of Race and Sex: A Black Feminist Critique of Antidiscrimination Doctrine, Feminist Theory, and Antiracist Politics," *The University of Chicago Legal Forum 1989* (1989): 139–67.

10 Kimberlé W. Crenshaw, "Mapping the Margins: Intersectionality, Identity Politics, and Violence against Women of Color," *Stanford Law Review* 43 (1991): 1241–99.

11 Patricia Hill Collins, *Black Feminist Thought: Knowledge, Consciousness, and the Politics of Empowerment* (New York: Routledge, 2008).

12 See, for example, Monica C. Higgins and Kathy E. Kram, "Reconceptualizing Mentoring at Work: A Developmental Network Perspective," *The Academy of Management Review*, 26.2 (2001): 264–88, http://www.jstor.org/stable/259122.

Chapter Eighteen

A NEW RITE OF PASSAGE: AGENCY, INTEGRATION, AND THE STRONGBLACKWOMAN

LEAH FULTON, MA

Bethel University, Interim Director of the Bethel Experience,
Common Ground Consortium Fellow

> Proving myself capable of taking care of everything and everyone in my sphere of existence was, I thought, a rite of passage into full Black woman hood.... The StrongBlackWoman is a legendary figure, typified by extraordinary capacities for caregiving and suffering without complaint.... Strong is a racial-gender codeword. It is verbal and mental shorthand for the three core features of the StrongBlackWoman—caregiving, independence, and emotional strength/regulation.
>
> —Chanequa Walker-Barnes, *Too Heavy a Yoke*

I began to emulate the StrongBlackWoman as a nine-year-old girl. Relatives had moved into our home, which meant that I was no longer the youngest in the household. By the time I started college, four cousins, my grandmother, the church missionary, and one family friend had lived in our home. With each guest, I was expected to cook, clean, change diapers, and give up my bed when necessary without complaint. Taking care of other people before ourselves is a practice ingrained in the hearts, minds, and ultimately the actions of black women from the time we are little girls. Be it family, friends, colleagues, or the church community . . . giving, serving, sharing, extending—even overextending—is not only a standard practice, but an expectation. It is learned through the actions of other black women, and it is reaffirmed by the words of people around us. Though it is never explicitly referred to as such, you could call it a rite of passage.

While individuals who are neither black nor female may also find themselves being overextended, there is a distinctive nuance found in the collective characterization of black women that distinguishes these experiences. The sheer combination of being black and female results in the expectation to fulfill this complex, as Walker-Barnes says, "[the StrongBlackWoman] is a cultural myth that defines—and confines—ways of being in the world for women of African descent."[1] While StrongBlackWoman is not a sustainable way of being, neither is it a simple thing to undo.

On July 6, 2016, Philando Castille was shot and killed by police fifteen miles from my front door and five miles from the Christian university where I worked. In the weeks following his death, I received a flood of text messages and emails from friends, colleagues, and church members asking how I was doing. As a diversity professional, I felt a measure of shame to admit that my most salient sentiment was gratitude. Not gratitude for the thoughtfulness of my community, but that the timing of Philando's death (over summer break) meant I could avoid processing the raw emotions felt by many of my students, particularly students of color. I was incapable—and unwilling—to uphold the StrongBlackWoman mantle. It wasn't merely my role in multicultural affairs that caused the flood of concern from my community, but the intersectionality of my identities—my roles as African American woman, Christian, diversity professional, wife to an African American man, and mother to three African American sons—that collectively created cause for concern. The geographic triangle between the site of Philando's death, my home, and my place of employment represented an inescapable convergence of my life's characteristics.

My identity is an ever-present reality that I did not choose and cannot change, yet I carry it with me every place I go. It shapes both the way I see the world and the way the world sees me. Instead of regarding my identity as a liability, I embrace it. It has become a source of agency—strength, courage, and wisdom. I find agency in my faith, setting boundaries, and the very identities that are sometimes regarded by others as deficits. I am learning how to navigate successfully through vocation, family life, and education as a black woman who embraces the proud legacy that comes with my identity while rejecting the premise of the StrongBlackWoman.

VOCATION

While serving in an associate dean role, I had concluded a series of disciplinary meetings with a white student when he said to me: "When I first found out you were a black woman, I thought, 'Can't I catch a break?!'" Without ever having met or spoken to me, this student had drawn conclusions about who I was. His comments were not surprising, given my keen awareness of the ways in which black women are characterized in American society. In a 2004 *Boston Globe* article by Vanessa Jones, she addresses the various stereotypes placed on black women. She highlights the angry black woman (ABW) in particular:

"You see this character so often in movies," Wyatt says. "They're always telling somebody off. The media plays a very strong role in perpetuating the stereotype." Today the ABW is so ingrained in society that the tag gets slapped on any African-American woman in a position of power.[2]

I learned at a young age that words like sassy, angry, and intimidating are often-times used to characterize black women, so I was especially mindful of how I interacted with people. Word choice, mannerisms, and my appearance were factors that I attempted to manage in order to keep the majority culture comfortable without alienating my own cultural community; however, I quickly learned that my attempts to manage my self-image could not protect me from the pervasive nature of racism.

In part, I experienced racism when I spent two years in a dual student development graduate assistantship. One role was with a scholarship program in the Office of Multicultural Development, while the other role was in Residence Life supervising two campus apartment buildings that primarily housed juniors. The fire department was called to my buildings on multiple occasions, typically because students would inadvertently set off the smoke detectors after storing oven mittens in the broiler. During each visit the firefighters seemed to assume that information should be obtained from the first white male resident they saw. I had to repeatedly assert myself as the professional in residence in order for the firefighters to address me. This kind of disregard for me as a professional by medical and emergency staff continued in my subsequent role.

After sending a student to the hospital for medical evaluation, it took my supervisor, a middle-aged white female, to convince law enforcement to discontinue their conversation with the white male student they had engaged and address me, the dean who had requested their presence. Upon arrival at the hospital, despite having communicated my role to desk staff, I sat for nearly five hours before a doctor stopped to speak with me. He told me: "Oh! I didn't think anyone from the university would be available. I just thought you were a relative."

While professional colleagues in my assistantship could describe a variety of challenges they had faced, none of them had experiences quite like mine. For example, one student always stopped me at his front door. During safety checks I realized he had a Confederate flag hung just inside his room. This and other exchanges made it clear that many of my students did not know how to engage with me as either an African American woman or as an authority figure.

In each position, I received responses from my leadership such as, "Leah, this isn't a hill to die on" or "I'm sure they didn't mean anything by that." While other actions from the leadership at my university demonstrated care for me as an individual, their statements demonstrated either a lack of ability, a lack of awareness, or both, to traverse the racialized dynamics of my encounters. I convinced myself that the best way to care well for myself and ease the discomfort of both my students and my colleagues would be for me to employ minimization.

Minimization is an orientation on the Intercultural Development Inventory (IDI) continuum administered by IDI, LLC. According to IDI's website, "The Intercultural Development Inventory® (IDI®) assesses intercultural competence—the capability to shift cultural perspective and appropriately adapt behavior to cultural differences and commonalities."[3] Minimization is a transitional orientation on the IDI spectrum that emphasizes similarities between cultures while ignoring differences. Minimization may look like color-blindness among members of dominant cultural communities; however, when employed by members of nondominant cultural communities, IDI describes minimization as having an approach of "go along to get along." It is a coping mechanism used to maintain the status quo and not upset the dominant cultural community. Even when cultural values or expressions clash, nondominant community members will behave as if nothing is wrong; in other words, they "go along to get along."

In my professional life, I used this approach as a coping mechanism. For fear that majority students and colleagues would see me as a race baiter or an angry black woman, I suppressed my genuine cultural expression for the sake of their comfort. My behavior did not reflect cultural competence or Christian love. Instead, it was a reflection of StrongBlackWoman-prioritizing other peoples' comfort above my own genuine identity. It ultimately cost me opportunities to grow in my leadership capacity as well as to influence students, which was particularly ironic given that I was working as a professional in the field of student development.

While I began to reject the StrongBlackWoman complex and the harmful practice of minimization prior to the completion of my assistantship, it is an ongoing battle that requires multiple strategies over time to deconstruct. I employ agency through maintaining relationships with other women of color who model a healthy sense of self. These women speak truth into my life, which is especially valuable while working for a predominantly white institution.

After a number of years in Christian higher education I came to a sobering realization. Diversity work is often interpreted as politically liberal, inherently secular, and humanly divisive. It can be perceived as something antithetical to unity and Christian faith by people within the body of Christ. That perception can pose major problems for both designated diversity professionals as well as people who represent diverse populations, such as women and people of color. In organizations where there are mixed or negative feelings about the work of diversity, those sentiments are sometimes projected onto the personhood of the professionals themselves. Those feelings can play out in the refusal to work cooperatively with diverse professionals or undermining the competence of diverse populations. The consequences can be detrimental to the emotional, physical, and spiritual well-being of those on the receiving end.

My identity is inextricably tied to diversity. Consequently, it can be difficult to separate myself from the negative perceptions that people have about it. Difficult as it may be, it is necessary for black women and other diverse populations to find language that calls out the nuanced nature of carrying particular identities while not internalizing the negative perceptions of others. This represents another strategy for exercising agency, which is key to the success and well-being of diverse professionals in the workplace—especially in relation to their home lives.

FAMILY LIFE

I value the growing use of the phrase "work-life integration" rather than "work-life balance." The latter seems to imply that there is always room to add more; in contrast, the former recognizes limitations. Relevant to my efforts of establishing a new rite of passage characterized by well-being, healthy work-life integration is an important step in the process.

After nearly four years of marriage, my husband and I were both ready for children. Upon completing my master's degree and graduate assistantship, I accepted an associate dean position at a small Christian college eight hours away from our nearest relatives. It was a counterintuitive decision in light of our plans to have children. Both of us had been reared in communities where the matriarchs of our families cared for us during the day. Childcare centers and home daycares had never been part of our lives, but they soon would be.

We became a family of five in less than three years. Pickup and drop-off times, childcare costs, and work responsibilities outside of traditional office hours intensified our transition into parenthood. With an expanding professional portfolio and a growing family, finding a healthy work-life integration has been an increasingly difficult task.

In her book *Lean In*, Sheryl Sandberg refers to statistics indicating that working moms spend, on average, five hours more per week than their working partners on domestic responsibilities. She goes on to discuss the value of staying in the workforce despite family demands and childcare expenses.[4] Even with an amazing spouse who does bath time, bedtime, haircuts, diaper changes, and so much more, I still found myself shouldering the bulk of cooking, laundry, and comforting for our young children. Resisting the StrongBlackWoman with small children and a budding career was difficult. My portfolio grew tremendously throughout the course of my role as associate dean. I became the committee cochair for a new scholarship program, successfully implemented a cultural center in collaboration with campus partners, and was given supervisory responsibility for a full-time and a part-time position. With each new responsibility I sought out resources—mentors, webinars, and other professional development opportunities. Taking advantage of available resources was vital for my own ability to steward those new responsibilities well and assuring university leadership that I was more than capable of managing my new responsibilities. However, nothing could prepare me for rearing children in a state that has been recognized as having some of the worst racial disparity gaps from education and healthcare to employment.[5]

After the birth of our first son, upon observing my husband's hands-on approach to fatherhood, one pediatrician commented: "What a great helper you have! Does he have other children?" In response to what I understood as stereotyping, I thought, *How can I entrust my children's health care to providers who carry such biases about their personhood?* Subsequent experiences with educators and health care providers made this question a recurring theme.

In childcare settings when my sons were the only black children in the classroom, teachers characterized them as dancers and athletes, two longstanding troupes that confine the identity of black people to that of entertainers. I intentionally offered to spend time in their largely homogenous classrooms in order to broaden the educational experiences of the children. My initial offer was met with an invitation to read a book during Black History Month. I agreed to read a book and recommended that people of color be invited to contribute outside of cultural heritage months. I went back in March to play my violin for the class.

Such attitudes and consequential perspectives contribute to another subtle form of challenge for people of color—microaggressions. Derald Wing Sue defines microaggressions as

> Commonplace verbal, nonverbal, behavioral, environmental indignities whether intentional or unintentional, that communicate hostile, derogatory, or negative slights and insults to target persons based on their race or other marginalized group membership.[6]

Though microaggressions are oftentimes unintentional, their impact is no less harmful. Physically, my experiences with microaggressions have resulted in unhealthy internalized coping mechanisms including grinding teeth as well as an inability to sleep or produce milk for my nursing infants. Emotionally, encounters with microaggressions have led to the sobering realization that I cannot protect my children from the ways that society will perceive them. Whether at home, at work, or in public, they will—just as I do—carry these identities that they did not choose but cannot change.

Stereotypes and microaggressions represent a snapshot of sinful attitudes and behaviors that are worthy of lament. They reflect the broken nature of our fallen world. On one hand, StrongBlackWoman would excuse, ignore, or pretend that these realities have no bearing on her. On the other hand, if I am not vigilant, lament can consume me. Instead of being overwhelmed by lament, I give it a proper place and then I move forward with agency.

Hebrews 12:1 says, "Therefore, since we are surrounded by such a great cloud of witnesses, let us throw off everything that hinders and the sin that so easily entangles. And let us run with perseverance the race marked out for us" (NIV). When I conceptualize those who make up that great cloud of witnesses, I imagine members of the early church standing shoulder to shoulder with saints like my grandmother, who sang hymns to get through difficult times. Through her, I learned the power of confessing our need for God and relying on him to sustain us.

Setting boundaries flies in the face of StrongBlackWoman, yet doing so is critical to exercising agency. While I gladly embrace the responsibility to orient educators, health care providers, and others to the nuanced personhood of each of my children, I do not take responsibility for teaching them best practices related to culturally responsive methods in their own professional fields. If I have any chance of undoing StrongBlackWoman, I need to be selective about the spaces I leave my children in as well as where I spend my cultural capital and emotional energy.

StrongBlackWoman grossly exaggerates many of the legitimate qualities that black women have embodied for generations. Maintaining relationships with other black women and learning more about those who have been trailblazers and pioneers empowers us to tap into the rich legacy from which we come. Although I cannot protect my children from the ways in which society will perceive them, through exercising my agency, I can help them tap into their own.

EDUCATION

I completed my master's degree prior to having children. The multicultural affairs component of my assistantship provided me with a cultural community through which I found support. My insistence to write a master's level thesis as part of my degree program was met with hesitation and eventually with silence.

The value of a thesis, my advisor told me, was minimal unless I planned to pursue doctoral studies. It was the second of my three-year MA program before I found a network and outlet for scholarship. I published my first article in partnership with colleagues on that very same campus. I conducted research on the ethnic history of the college and contributed to the development of the institution's first living-learning community. The active pursuit of opportunities to grow as a scholar and finding spaces where I could offer and receive support were key to my success. Throughout my studies, I experienced a number of gendered and racialized experiences, such as observing the extent to which my advisor worked with a male classmate as he wrote his thesis. Upon my graduation, my advisor apologized that he had not taken the time to invest in me. My own experience as a master's-level student at a Christian college provided context for the kinds of experiences my students faced. Feeling invisible in the curriculum or tokenized in the classroom were real sentiments that deserved to be acknowledged; however, after we lamented those realities, I called my students to exercise agency through action. My steadfast desire and commitment to pursue doctoral studies, a journey upon which I am now embarking, represented one of the ways I modeled this principle.

Seasoned higher education professionals had communicated the necessity of a terminal degree. They made it clear that possessing the right skills and knowledge without a terminal degree would result in missed leadership opportunities. While I had always contemplated doctoral studies, I had accepted social norms that obliged me to wait until my children were school-aged; however, when I found myself on the horizon of a career transition, doctoral studies resurfaced.

I had participated in the Multi-Ethnic Leadership Development Institute (M-E LDI)—a year-long leadership development program for emerging leaders of color at CCCU institutions. I came out of the summer institute with a clear sense of priorities: health, margin, and sustainability. This was how I would define well-being. Less than a semester into the fall after the M-E LDI, it was clear that my priorities were incompatible with my professional role, but I was unsure about next steps. Following the summer institute, I prepared for a fall semester "shadowing" visit on another campus (as part of the year-long program); those days proved to be a catalyst experience for discerning my next steps.

My mentor for the visit was a senior-level leader at another Christian college. Conversations with my senior-level leadership mentor during the shadowing visit and with other women leaders on her campus provided the opportunity to explore the possibility of an impending career change and a commitment to prioritize my own well-being. During those conversations, I also felt confirmed that doctoral studies should be my next step. Before I returned home I had already started my application and signed up to take the Graduate Record Exam. I had two weeks to begin, complete, and submit my materials. Although my network of sponsors and mentors was diverse, there was one consistent cautionary tale that came specifically from African American women. Whether it is fair or not, there is a longstanding narrative that African Americans have to work twice as hard to earn half as much respect or notoriety as our non-black peers. I was repeatedly encouraged to pursue a PhD over an EdD. "A PhD is more credible than an EdD in some circles. Don't limit yourself" was the advice I received from fellow black women in a sign of solidarity. In addition to keenly desiring the professional knowledge that would be gained by pursuing a PhD, the academic platform of earned credibility was important, and I took that advice to heart.

I continued to draw upon that solidarity with other women of color when— just weeks after submitting my PhD application—I realized I was pregnant with my third son. My advisor, a working mother and woman of color, offered honest and direct feedback. She continued to advocate for me in the process of securing assistantship opportunities and made herself available until I decided to defer enrollment for one year. StrongBlackWoman may have driven me to move forward to prove a point, but for the sake of healthy work-life integration, I chose not to do so.

The pursuit of my PhD represents my desire to provide leadership to institutional functions outside of diversity that impact marginalized populations— especially people of color. While I hold diversity roles in high regard, I hope to operate as a partner to people in designated diversity roles while providing oversight for other areas of campus life. If the attainment of a doctorate is required in order to access the proverbial tables where university-wide decisions that shape culture and impact people are made, then I am willing to pursue it. Modeling healthy work-life integration and creating a culture where others can do the same is another essential element of my aspirations to work in senior-level leadership. Because I have never before faced the level of demands that will be required for me to meet this goal, bringing StrongBlackWoman under my authority is all the more important.

CONCLUSION

Although I have worked with countless students struggling to keep their faith, one in particular stands out. Years after she left the Christian college campus where we met, she reminded me of the words I had spoken to her:

"My hope is in Jesus. Just because people do wrong doesn't change who God is." She would cite those words, years after our conversation, as she continued to wrestle with the suffering of black and brown people across the country at the hands of law enforcement. Hope in God offers proper perspective about the world around us, not permission to ignore, deny, or abandon it.

My response to the inquiries about my well-being following the death of Philando Castille was: "I am numb. It's the only way I can remain functional." The shooting death of a legally armed black man (literally close to home) by a police officer contributes to a centuries-long legacy of terror and uncertainty for many black Americans. Neither the caregiving of StrongBlackWoman nor operating as a law abiding citizen are sufficient to rescind the pervasive consequences of being black in America. *What does that mean for my husband, my children, and my students? What does that mean for me?*

In retrospect, numbness was a default coping mechanism that demonstrated the lingering influence of StrongBlackWoman. Living in a state of perpetual numbness is neither sustainable nor is it God's intention for his people. Instead of numbness, he offers fullness of life. Experiencing the life that God intends means breaking stride with the harmful persona of StrongBlackWoman, embracing the true legacy of black women, finding and implementing agency, and maintaining a healthy work-life integration. These principles represent a new rite of passage that honors black women and recognizes that while we are strong, we are also fully human.

FOR DISCUSSION

1. What expectations (either self- or other-imposed) impede your ability to set healthy boundaries?
2. What does healthy work-life integration look like for you? Are you experiencing health in your own work-life integration? If not, what are the barriers?
3. How do your race, culture, and gender impact the ways in which you experience work, life, and education (for better or worse)?
4. To what extent do you have a community where you can talk freely about the complexity of your identity and its impact on your lived reality?
5. How can your institution intentionally support professionals with marginalized identities experience healthy work-life integration?
6. On your campus, what interventions are in place to support diverse professionals and students?

NOTES

1   Chanequa Walker-Barnes, *Too Heavy a Yoke: Black Women and the Burden of Strength* (Eugene, OR: Cascade Books, 2014).

2   Vanessa E. Jones, "The Angry Black Woman: Tart-Tongued or Driven and No-Nonsense, She Is a Stereotype That Amuses Some and Offends Others," *Boston Globe*, April 20, 2004, accessed May 15, 2017, http://archive.boston.com/yourlife/articles/2004/04/20/the_angry_black_woman/.

3   "The Intercultural Development Inventory (IDI) Products," IDI, LLC, accessed January 20, 2017, https://idiinventory.com/products/.

4   Sheryl Sandberg, *Lean In: Women, Work, and the Will to Lead* (New York: Knopf, 2013).

5   "Educational Equity: Closing Gaps," University of Minnesota, accessed January 20, 2017, http://gap.umn.edu.

6   Derald Wing Sue, *Microaggressions in Everyday Life* (Hoboken, NJ: Wiley, 2010); "Microaggressions: More Than Just Race," *Psychology Today*, November 17, 2010.

Chapter Nineteen

POTHOLES ON THE PROFESSIONAL JOURNEY OF A DEVELOPING LEADER

KEVIN L. WILLIAMS JR., MA

Assistant Director of Residence Life, Special Interest Housing, Messiah College

> If there is no struggle, there is no progress.
> —Frederick Douglass

I have been working in Christian higher education for twelve years, first as an admissions counselor fresh out of college, and now serving as Assistant Director of Residence Life. I am also a black man, husband, and the father of three children. Based on my observation and experience, the professional journey into Christian college leadership for many who are not part of the dominant culture is packed with challenges that are shaped by cultural influences. For black men and women, this journey becomes even more complex when navigating work and family life against stereotypical narratives.

These challenges have certainly been true for my journey, and I know from friends and colleagues that I am not alone in this. In fact, much of the leadership literature emphasizes the importance of being stretched, taking risks, making decisions, and proactively accepting new roles and responsibilities. The steep uphill climb can test our muscles but ultimately strengthens us. While on that journey, it is also important to deal with, and successfully move beyond, a variety of potholes that can be a very real part of the route in front of us. Related to the focus of this book, dominant narratives related to race and gender can seem like cavernous potholes that cause high-potential individuals to stumble and fall.

Despite the challenges, exemplary leaders have learned how to assume a posture of "adaptive capacity"[1] and actually embrace challenges as learning opportunities. Leadership scholars Warren Bennis and Robert Thomas discuss these characteristics in their book titled *Leading for Lifetime*, noting that individuals can actually became stronger through embracing the learning that comes with

"crucible moments" such as those encountered in steep climbing and precipi-
tous pothole experiences. In fact, the difficult parts of the journey often equip
leaders and develop in them the ability to empathize and guide others, even as
the joys and small victories keep them forging ahead.

For men of color, the journey toward academic leadership is packed with a
particular set of considerations and cultural influences. In the following sections, I reflect on four kinds of potholes that have influenced my own professional journey, also identifying the strategies I am employing to navigate them
successfully. Each strategy helped me understand that leadership is a dynamic
tension that requires constant maintenance. Whether navigating promotions,
work and life balance, job transitions, or sponsorship, any combination of these
potholes can derail individuals who may be gifted and even called into broader
levels of influence.

POTHOLE 1: PROMOTED AND WONDERING WHY

My first professional role in the academy began shortly after graduation, when
I was hired into a part-time admissions counselor role at my alma mater. After
being in the position for about eight months, I was offered options to expand
my scope of responsibility and found myself leaning toward taking a position
that had the title of Coordinator of Multicultural Recruitment. I moved into
full-time admissions work, enjoying the role in part because it allowed me to
invest my talents and energy on behalf of a place that I loved.

As part of the transition process, I attended one of our weekly staff meetings where my coworkers were informed about my promotion. During the walk
back to our offices, a colleague, who was a white female, made the comment to
me: "I was interested in that position. Now you are going to make more money
than me!"

Her comment caught me off guard, partly because I was troubled by her
emphasis on the words "you" and "me." Was there no sense that she could offer
some affirmation for my promotion? Did I only get the job because of my skin
color . . . or was it because I was genuinely better qualified for the promotion?
Was I not supposed to make more money than she was making? Was she more
interested in the money or the position? Would we now be at odds with each
other over my promotion? All of these questions raced through my mind.

My response during this interaction reflected the tensions that people of
color can sometimes experience when being promoted in a setting where they
are also a minority. Such tensions often emerge from the disadvantaged status of
African Americans, and males in particular, within the cultural context of our
nation and college campuses . . . and particularly those that are predominantly

white institutions (PWIs). A 2016 book titled *Advancing Black Male Student Success from Preschool through Ph.D.* documents various factors that contribute to the uphill struggle both personally and professionally:

> For generations, black boys and men have occupied the lowest rungs of almost any quality of life indicator used to assess health, well-being, and success across myriad sectors. For example, black males have extremely high rates of homicide and rising rates of suicide. They are also less likely to have health care coverage. Black men have the lowest rates of employment of any racial group in the United States.[2]

When I hit the "pothole" of questioning and some level of self-doubt in facing the scenario described previously, I made an intentional decision to believe in myself. A quote attributed to President Theodore Roosevelt has been helpful to me in similar situations: "Comparison is the thief of all joy." I determined that it was important to trust the judgment of those who had selected me for this new role, and I focused on performing the job with confidence, to the best of my ability. Another aspect of the perspective I assumed was coming to view my skin color and life experience as assets that uniquely equip me to have a different voice and perspective than others. Being proactive to seek out ways to learn new skills and enhance my abilities has opened doors of opportunity on my campus that will enhance my career trajectory in ways I could only have imagined.

POTHOLE 2: DISCONFIRMING THE STEREOTYPE

In 2012, my family packed up and headed off to my new job at another Christian college in a bordering state. It was a long drive, which allowed for plenty of time to reminisce with my wife about what brought us to this move. She and I had met at the college where I had been working for the previous seven years. The car ride represented a transition from my admissions-related role as the Coordinator of Multicultural Recruitment to a new role in student development as a residence director. After completing my master's degree, I desired to be in a role where I could invest in the lives of students throughout their college journey by mentoring and walking alongside them. So I had prayed that if it was God's will for me to become a residence director, God would orchestrate the events accordingly.

My prayer included a desire that those closest to me would also be given a similar vision for how I could use my commitment to students' development and my relational gifts more fully. Two years after praying this prayer, my wife came to me and said, "Whatever the Lord is telling you to do, I am ready!" Her supportive attitude allowed me to pursue the role of a residence director with confidence, a fact that we celebrated on that day of reminiscing as we drove to my new job and our new home.

Although the role of a residence director seemed an ideal fit for my skills and interest, it wasn't until I entered the role that I realized how challenging the job would be in terms of managing my time. In admissions, there was an ebb and flow to the work. There were travel seasons, late night calls, and office hours. In this new role, I was learning what it meant to be "on call" in caring for students during evenings and nights, while also trying to find a rhythm that worked in helping care for our three-year-old and two-year-old children.

Many African American males need to learn how to responsibly meet their family obligations, in part because they have not been raised in a stable family unit that included the father in the home as a role model. The statistics emerging from US Census Bureau data[3] and other related reports are shocking, and have implications for the role modeling that I want to offer to our students and college community regarding healthy parenting and family life. According to a report issued by the Population Reference Bureau,[4] 41 percent of all births in the United States as of 2010 were to unmarried parents, an increase from 33 percent in 2000. A disproportionate share of those nonmarital births have occurred within the African American community. In fact, 72 percent of African American births in 2010 occurred outside of marriage, in contrast to 36 percent of white births.[5]

Some individuals perceive raising children to be an easy task for men because "behind every hard-working man is an even harder working woman." Although there is some truth to that adage, the fact remains that a husband's responsibility is to be fully mindful of the needs at home, even if a stay-at-home mother supports his professional aspirations. Work and life balance is difficult for everyone. Those who are single and those who are married—with or without children—all struggle to balance career with personal life. And the task of being a good father can be daunting when that role has not been modeled during the formative years of childhood and youth.

I have always desired to be a family man, not just in name but also in the way I live my life before others. Growing up as an African American male, I frequently heard comments that men who look like me do not take care of their families. Again, the statistics about my sector of the US population are sobering. Many African American men are incarcerated; in fact, a 2015 *New York Times* article titled "1.5 Million Missing Black Men"[6] documented that more than one out of six black men between the ages of 25 and 54 had essentially disappeared from daily life in the United States either from early death or incarceration. From within this age group, one in twelve (a total of more than 600,000) is behind bars, compared with one in sixty of nonblack men in the same age group.

Being well aware of these demographic patterns, part of my vision has been to show other young men that it is possible to have a family and to accept the related responsibilities. As much as it depended on me, I made a commitment early in my career that I would be a man who loved my wife and was a full partner with her in raising our children, while also providing financially and emotionally for the needs of the family.

Often, though, our commitments are tested with the real demands inherent in higher education. My desire do a good job in the arena of work and family quickly pulled me in different directions. My first time of being "on call" as a residence director, for example, made me realize how little I understood about what would be expected. Out of my desire to respect my wife, I initially made the decision that I would sleep on the couch in the living room to avoid awakening her if I received a call in the middle of the night. While this decision was well intentioned on my part, it was not what she wanted or expected of me. Along the way, I have learned the valuable leadership lesson that communicating clearly and thoughtfully, as well as managing my time well, is important both at work and at home.

Additionally, I have tried to find ways of involving my family in my job so that they would be visible on campus. In part, I have wanted students and colleagues to see me as a father and a husband, not the "black guy." It is equally important that my children see me at work and being respected as a professional. In leadership, perception and image are important, but it is important that the image projected is true to the reality of daily life. Talking with trusted colleagues is a good way to assess public perceptions of your life and work, thus allowing for midcourse corrections in navigating the campus climate.

POTHOLE 3: BEING THE FIRST

Because I desire to be a wise and well-informed leader in higher education, I have become increasingly committed to the goal of pursuing doctoral studies. My father has been a champion of this goal, even from the day of my graduation with a master's degree in higher education administration from the University of Akron. One of his first questions was, "You're going for a PhD next, right?" The tensions of having multiple desires and responsibilities was already evident at that point, given that I had been married only for a few years, we had a young child, and we were expecting a second. My plate was feeling very full.

A variety of questions required soul-searching for answers: Would another degree be detrimental to my career, given my limited work experience? As a new husband and a first-generation college student, was I ready to handle the academic challenge of a PhD program? As an African American male in pre-dominantly white spaces, what signals would I be sending if I invested a significant amount of time and money in pursuing a doctoral degree? As I have mulled these questions, and as a result of others speaking into my life, I have come to more fully appreciate the importance of role models and advisors, particularly for first-generation, ethnic-minority emerging professionals.

Because of the intentional commitment I have made to be a good husband and father, the decision-point for me related to the timing that was best to begin doctoral studies—not whether, but when. My desire to complete my education grew, along with my confidence, when I met an African American man who, while caring for two children, was working in higher education and pursuing his PhD. We both held the same commitment to creating a family unit that was strong and nurturing. Because he seemed to have time for family and was adept at balancing work and life, I have taken active steps to explore the application process to begin doctoral studies. As many have noted, the terminal degree is "the coin of the realm" in higher education, and earning a PhD is important not only for the knowledge to be gained but also to allow me to serve with greater expertise as a role model for the generation of African Americans coming behind me.

POTHOLE 4: THE VALUE OF MENTORS/SPONSORS

Meeting the African American professional who was attentive to his family while also pursuing his PhD happened at a critical point when I was pondering next steps in my academic career. His presence as a role model and his ability to speak into my life proved to be pivotal. Yet like many of my ethnic-minority colleagues across Christian higher education nationally, I see almost no one in leadership who looks like me on the campus where I have served for five years. Despite that troubling vacuum, white allies have been good friends and advisors when I have reached out to seek guidance about my desire to develop my leadership capacity. For example, through a conversation with the president of my alma mater, I learned about the Leadership Development Institutes being offered through the Council for Christian Colleges & Universities. I applied for the Multi-Ethnic Leadership Development Institute (M-E LDI) via the CCCU website, was accepted, and attended.

Spending most of a week interacting with a team of ethnically diverse resource leaders and colleagues from other Christian institutions filled my mind and heart with hope. I was able to see and hear from other leaders who looked like me as they shared about having similar experiences. At M-E LDI, I also learned the importance of having people speak into my life who contributed at a level beyond being role models and, in fact, beyond being mentors. As part of our curriculum, we learned about the concept of sponsorship as contrasted with mentoring.

The concept of sponsoring has become much more visible in the leadership development literature in recent years through the research and writing of Sylvia Ann Hewlett, which is best captured in a 2013 Harvard Business Review book titled *Forget a Mentor, Find a Sponsor*. Writing from the perspective of the corporate world, Hewlett identifies sponsorship as "the new way to fast-track your career"[7] and offers this description of a sponsor:

> A *sponsor* . . . is someone who takes an interest in you and your career, but not out of altruism or like-mindedness. A sponsor sees furthering your career as an important investment in his or her *own* career, organization, or vision. Sponsors may advise or steer you, but their chief role is to develop you as a leader. Your role is to earn their investment in you. Indeed, throughout the relationship, you're delivering outstanding results, building their brand or legacy, and generally making them look good.[8]

The importance of linking emerging professionals with mentors has been well documented in the literature[9] and reaffirmed through research with early participants in the CCCU's Multi-Ethnic Leadership Development Institutes.[10]

Having been introduced to the concept of sponsorship, I realized that I had been blessed to know several leaders who could be emulated as role models, and I could identify a few mentors. However, no one in my life had been serving as an intentional sponsor. Through a research project that emerged from our M-E LDI group, I was asked to identify a sponsor, and we have been working closely together to ensure that I am growing in areas that enhance and expand my ability to serve effectively within Christian higher education.

I'd like to close this chapter with some words of advice for others who are navigating various potholes that emerge on the journey toward leadership. It is important to remember that others have gone before you, some of whom can step in to serve as mentors or sponsors on your journey. When faced with doubt in the midst of transition, trust those who have hired you and your ability to do the job well. When responsibilities for family life and work life seem to collide, or when the stereotypical images that are portrayed are inconsistent with who you are, seek clarity of expectations and be true to the best of all that God has built into you. When there seem to be no mentors or sponsors in your corner, take a step back to reassess your lenses and then look again. Kindred spirits who want to be supportive can be found in other ethnic-minority groups as well as among white allies.

Finally, take encouragement in the words of the Apostle Paul in Ephesians 2:10 that each person has been created wonderfully and individually as "God's workmanship," with good works already laid out for us to walk into. While the potholes on this journey may seem large, they can actually represent places to take stock for a period until new lessons are learned that allow us to more effectively navigate the terrain of leadership in Christian higher education.

FOR DISCUSSION

1. Imagine you are in a demanding position in higher education (which may be your current reality or aspiration if you are reading this book) and married with two children. You made a lateral move to enter into a new role on your campus or elsewhere within higher education. Although this is a good move because it fits your skill set and interests, you must live in the residence hall, where your work-life balance needs to be readjusted. In your previous position, you left work at 5:00 p.m. and simply went home, but that is impossible with your new responsibilities. What do you do? To what extent do you go with the flow because it's a new position and you do not know what to expect? To what extent, and in what ways, can you guard your family time? How do you determine priorities?

2. What practices does your institution have that discourage healthy family practices? If certain unhealthy practices are identified, what could you do individually or with others to urge that those practices are revamped?

3. What individual comes to mind who has been a role model in your professional life? To what extent have you been mentored by someone in leadership? What aspects of a mentoring relationship have been most helpful for you?

4. Based on Hewlett's definition of a "sponsor," as described previously, in what ways might sponsorship be more advantageous than mentorship? Are you aware of any sponsorship relationships on your campus? What could you do to identify a sponsor, or to take proactive steps to be a sponsor to someone coming behind you (a student leader, employee, etc.)?

NOTES

1   Warren G. Bennis and Robert J. Thomas, *Leading for a Lifetime* (Boston: Harvard Business School Press, 2007).

2   Shaun R. Harper and J. Luke Woods, eds., *Advancing Black Male Student Success from Preschool through PhD* (Sterling, VA: Stylus Publishing, 2016), 3–4.

3   US Census Bureau, "*Family Structure and Children's Living Arrangements 2012,*" Current Population Report, July 1, 2012.

4   Linda A. Jacobsen, Mark Mather, and Genevieve Dupuis, "Household Change in the United States," *Population Bulletin* 67 (1; 2012), http://www.prb.org/pdf12/us-household-change-2012.pdf.

5   Ibid., 11.

6   Justin Wolfers, David Leonhardt, and Kevin Quealy, "1.5 Million Missing Black Men," *New York Times*, April 20, 2015, http://www.nytimes.com/interactive/2015/04/20/upshot/missing-black-men.html ?_r=0.

7   Sylvia Ann Hewlett, *Forget a Mentor, Find a Sponsor: The New Way to Fast-Track Your Career* (Boston: Harvard Business Review, 2013).

8   Ibid., 20.

9   Caroline S. V. Turner and Juan Carlos Gonzalez, eds., *Modeling Mentoring across Race/Ethnicity and Gender* (Sterling, VA: Stylus Publishing, 2015).

10 Heewon Chang, Karen A. Longman, and Marla Franco, "Leadership Development through Mentoring in Higher Education: A Collaborative Autoethnography of Leaders of Color," *Mentoring & Tutoring: Partnership in Learning*, 22 (4; 2014): 373–89.

Chapter Twenty

THE POWER OF "THE ONLY"

Aisha N. Lowe, PhD

William Jessup University, Associate Professor of Education,
Associate Dean of the Office of Academic Research

As a woman of color in higher education, I have grown used to being "the only"—the only person of color and/or the only woman in rooms of power. The situations in which I have found myself are not unique to higher education. The novelty of having someone like me in leadership can also be seen in business, health care, K–12 education, and many other arenas.

National statistics in the United States tell the story: according to the monthly household survey conducted by the Bureau of the Census for the Bureau of Labor Statistics in 2015, African Americans accounted for 11.7 percent of employed persons sixteen years of age and older but were underrepresented in management (7.3 percent).[1] Out of twenty-two categories of management types across industries, African Americans were underrepresented in fifteen of those categories, with the lowest rates being as chief executives (3.6 percent), and as managers in advertising and promotions (0 percent), computer and information systems (5.6 percent), industrial production (5.1 percent), agriculture (0.9 percent), and construction (3.3 percent).

This being "the only" is a very familiar experience for me. As a fourteen-year-old girl, I entered my predominantly Caucasian, private high school in San Francisco, and for the first time found myself as "the only" in classrooms. My high school had traditionally been attended by the wealthy elite of the Bay Area and was undergoing a purposeful transition to increase diversity. I entered ninth grade in 1991 as a member of its most diverse class to date. Representing that diversity were five of us in my entering class: an African American female, a mixed-race African American and Filipino female, a Latino male, a Chinese male, and me (another African American female). Five students of color in a class of forty was a new record for my high school, and we would soon learn how difficult this transition would be for the school community. Many of the culture clashes we experienced were just that—clashes of culture. For example, a white male student could not understand why my African American female classmate was appalled when his hacky sack landed in her nachos and he did not apologize. Our Caucasian teachers wondered why we remained standing when they took the class outside to sit in the grass, and why we did not partake of the food provided for school events. These differences in upbringing and practices created distinctions among us and further highlighted our "onlyness."

Then there were the microaggressions. We were often asked to represent the "black perspective" in class discussions. We were advised away from pursuing our education at elite private institutions in the college counseling process. We were even told openly by white classmates that the only reason we were attending the school was because of affirmative action; they let us know that they felt we did not deserve to be there. These were challenging experiences for me as a young girl, still developing my own identity and having to do so in a hostile environment.

Yet we, and our parents, brought our "onlyness" to bear on that community and catalyzed great change at my high school. Our parents met with the administration when disturbing incidents took place to help them understand why certain practices were discriminatory and why certain occurrences were rooted in white privilege and racism. We students formed the first-ever support group for students of color and created intercultural events and activities for the student body. We challenged assumptions and provided new archetypes as we fully engaged in the school environment and wove our cultures and perspectives into class discussions and the broader school culture. Twenty-five years later, one of the school administrators who at the time was observably opposed to these efforts now speaks highly of how our efforts helped create a more inclusive and dynamically rich atmosphere for learning. "You guys really transformed the school for the better. We need to capture and celebrate that history and honor the great work you did," she said one evening at a board meeting, on which I served for six years.

Thankfully, my high school embraced the challenge of achieving true inclusion and began to engage the school community in necessary difficult conversations. School leadership brought in speakers to discuss race, racism, and privilege with the students. They also brought in experts to train the faculty on culturally responsive pedagogy. Today my high school is a very different place. Diversity, inclusion, and white privilege training is an essential element of professional development for faculty and staff. The school is now explicit and strategic about its commitment to a student body that reflects the rich diversity of the city in which it resides, and remains an accessible option for all students, despite rising costs. With a student body that is now 25 percent students of color, my high school is the kind of place I would want my future children to attend.

Still, the metamorphosis of my high school was not an easy process and it was a transition that came at some emotional and psychological costs for those of us, as students of color, who led the charge. "Onlyness" is always costly. And yet those costs to us have yielded a much greater reward—a school community transformed for the better that will benefit many more students of color and, in fact, all students for generations to come. Although the experience was difficult at the time, the benefits and opportunities afforded to us and to the school community are part of the positive side effects of "onlyness." Today I have a great fondness for my high school. I proudly served on its board of trustees and led another transition of establishing an alumni association, which is now thriving. Despite the burden of being "the only," I would not change a thing about that experience. I grew as a person in that space of conflict, and it is there that I began my leadership journey.

"ONLYNESS" IN THE UNIVERSITY

When I served on my high school's board of trustees as a student representative during my junior year of high school and again as a graduate, I was the only black face in the room. That experience of being "the only" continued with me to Stanford University, where I yet again experienced that status in many classrooms and, during graduate school, as "the only" in my doctoral program. I have continued to live in that same space in faculty meetings and as an administrator at the private Christian college where I now work, "the only" within the faculty council that works in concert with the provost.

At my university and in many other settings, discussions about the persistent diversity gap in leadership occur frequently. Numerous books and research studies have investigated and discussed the importance of diversity and advocate that diversity be embedded as nascent.[2] Taking a diverse and global view of society and its institutions, these theorists argue that the organizational and societal contexts in which leadership is exercised requires greater diversity.[3] In their book *Black Faces in White Places*,[4] Pinkett and Robinson discuss the competitive world of business and the difficulties African Americans face as they pursue greater leadership in their "onlyness." Those difficulties are echoed in a 2015 book written by academics in the Christian academy, *Black Scholars in White Space*.[5] Whether viewed through a lens of educational attainment, economic development, global competitiveness, leadership capacity, or social justice and equity, diversity has become an imperative.[6]

Often lacking in this discussion, however, are the benefits and opportunities of those challenges and what being "the only" can provide. In open environments and for those seeking to embrace diversity (even when flawed in those attempts), a role as "the only" can provide leadership influence and access that a person of color might not otherwise be afforded. Yes, that can be the dreaded "token" role. However, even though the token role is at times rooted in short-sighted intentions, it can provide access to decision-making tables. Although as a person of color I sometimes resent this role, I have learned to embrace those token opportunities as open doors of access that can be beneficial on my leadership path and provide entry for other colleagues of color.

I have also recognized my "onlyness" as an opportunity to be an ambassador of my race. While this burden to represent blackness is not always welcomed by professionals of color, I recognize it more as an opportunity to showcase my talents and shift others' understanding of what blackness is. I have learned to embrace my "onlyness" as an opportunity to shatter the stereotypical perspectives that others may hold. As my colleagues interact with me and see my leadership in action, and as my students sit under my tutelage and learn from me, I am hopeful that their perspectives are shifting. In such interactions, I become a lived experience of what black people are like that they can reference as they combat the limited and diluted images presented to them in popular culture. Instead of the myths perpetuated by the media, my colleagues and students experience in me someone who is intelligent, strong, insightful, skilled, and able. In being all that God has made me to be, I serve as the blueprint for what a black Christian woman is, both as a person and as a leader. The power of this influence is invaluable.

I have also embraced the essential importance of bringing my unique perspective into rooms of power. Research has documented that when college students have racially diverse friends and classmates, and engage in discussions with racial- and opinion-minority members, students' integrative complexity is positively impacted.[7] As Kim Box discusses in her book, *Woven Leadership: The Power of Diversity to Transform Your Organization for Success*,[8] diversity is a secret weapon to be productively exploited in order to build more successful organizations.

MAKING "ONLYNESS" WORK

I learned at a young age the burdens of being "the only," and I have faced the challenges of racism and prejudice in many arenas over the course of my career and life. Those challenges have strengthened me, producing perseverance, character, and hope (Rom. 5:3–4). In the midst of those difficulties, I have employed a few strategies that have transitioned my "onlyness" from a burden to an asset.

Let Your Credentials Speak for You

As any academic will tell you, the path to higher education is one of learning, developing expertise, and earning degrees. As a professor or administrator in higher education, you have earned that role and deserve to walk in that space. Own that role, and the quality of your academic preparation, with boldness and confidence.

Ask and You Shall Receive

At my university, I was recently named the associate dean of the office of academic research, a role that grew out of an appointment as director of that same office. I was placed in this role because I asked for it. When the previous director retired, I recognized that I had the experience and expertise to assume the director's role. I was pleased to learn that my provost wanted me to fill the role. "You were my first choice," he remarked, "but I knew you already had so much on your plate and I didn't want to overload you." I was happy to assure him that I was up for the challenge. If there is a leadership role you desire to fill, put yourself out there. It is important to advocate for yourself.

Be the Voice

As people of color, we sometimes resent having to educate others about our experiences and needs. But if we do not speak for ourselves, who will? Why not embrace being the authors and arbiters of our own experiences? I am not ignorant of the burden and costs of that duty, but I choose to focus on the benefits. People of color bring a unique voice. We must use our voices to bring new perspectives and push our institutions to be more open and accessible. Be present, fully involved, and vocal—join the meetings when asked; sit on the search committees; take on those additional responsibilities; express your concerns.

Redefine Your Experience

The most important strategy I have used to navigate my experience as "the only" has been choosing a specific perspective related to my experience: I have chosen to redefine my experience as one of privilege, embracing the benefits of accessing otherwise limited environments through the door of my unique perspective and carrying the mantle of diverse leadership. The seeds of this perspective were birthed in me as a high school student, working with my friends and our parents to diversify our school. That seed grew further at Stanford as African American female faculty members modeled the process for me. That seed continues to grow today as I now play roles I previously observed from afar.

While my perspective of my experience is key—and my boldness to ask for what I want and be confident with my voice are essential—none of what I bring matters in a closed, inaccessible environment. Therefore I encourage institutions and leadership to know your people of color and women well (or whomever "the only" is on your campuses). Know their skills, abilities, and desires and tap them for leadership opportunities. Furthermore, when leadership opportunities arise, solicit participation far and wide. Directly and explicitly ask your "only" and "few" faculty and staff if they would like to fulfill those roles. Empower people to step forward by showing them you want them to do so.

FOR DISCUSSION

For those experiencing "onlyness" . . .
1. How have your childhood experiences with being the "only" shaped your perceptions of being in that space?
2. Have you experienced positive outcomes from being the "only" in an environment? How did your reaction to the environment help make that a positive experience?
3. How have you had to advocate for yourself as the "only" on your campus or in your school or department? How can you?
4. How have you used your vantage point as the "only" to help advocate for others? How can you?
5. How and when have you found it difficult to voice concerns or present new ideas? Are there ways that "onlyness" has served as a stumbling block in those attempts? Are there ways that "onlyness" has served as an asset in those attempts?

For institutions . . .
6. Are you aware of whom on your campus might be experiencing this "onlyness"?
7. Have you provided a safe space for those faculty and staff to reflect on their experiences of "onlyness" and its impact on them?
8. What avenues and vehicles exist at your institution that can help transform "onlyness" into a positive, asset-based experience? What can be created?
9. How can you better ascertain the skills, abilities, and desires of your "only" faculty and staff?
10. How does your internal promotion process work, and is it a truly open and transparent process that allows anyone to throw his or her hat in the ring?
11. How might you specifically encourage your "only" faculty and staff to pursue promotion opportunities?

NOTES

1 "Labor Force Statistics from the Current Population Survey," accessed May 11, 2015, Bureau of Labor Statistics, http://www.bls.gov/cps/cpsaat11.htm.

2 Jacky Lumby and Marianne Coleman, *Leadership and Diversity: Challenging Theory and Practice in Education* (Thousand Oaks, CA: SAGE Publications, 2007).

3 Jean Lau Chin and Joseph E. Trimble, *Diversity and Leadership* (Thousand Oaks, CA: SAGE Publications, 2014).

4 Randall Pinkett and Jeffrey Robinson, *Black Faces in White Places: 10 Game-Changing Strategies to Achieve Success and Find Greatness* (New York: AMACOM Division, American Management Association, 2010).

5 Anthony Bradley, *Black Scholars in White Space: New Vistas in African American Studies from the Christian Academy* (Eugene, OR: Wipf and Stock, 2015).

6 Damon A. Williams, *Strategic Diversity Leadership: Activating Change and Transformation in Higher Education* (Sterling, VA: Stylus Publishing, 2013).

7 Anthony Lising, Mitchell J. Chang, Kenji Hakuta, David A. Kenny, Shana Levin, and Jeffrey F. Milem, "Effects of Racial Diversity on Complex Thinking in College Students," *Psychological Science* 15 (8; 2004): 507–10.

8 Kim Box, *Woven Leadership: The Power of Diversity to Transform Your Organization for Success* (Gold River, CA: Authority Publications, 2011).

Chapter Twenty-One

EMBRACING THE PERSPECTIVE OF THE OTHER

KATHY-ANN C. HERNANDEZ, PhD

Eastern University, Professor, College of Business and Leadership

You never really understand a person until you consider things from his point of view.... Until you climb inside of his skin and walk around in it.

—Harper Lee, *To Kill a Mockingbird*

I did not fully think of myself as being black until a few years after I came to the United States for a second time in 2000. Having spent most of my early life growing up in the twin-island Republic of Trinidad and Tobago, the most important socioidentity marker for me was that of being Trinidadian, or "Trini," as we say. Yet many of the encounters I have had in the past seventeen years of living in the United States and working in Christian higher education have led me to question and think critically about the sociocultural reality of what it means to be a black person in the United States.

I am married to an African American man, and we have two daughters who were born here in the United States. I am aware that though we are all "black," we are not all the same kind of black. In some ways, I think this variation among my own family circle is a good, though imperfect, analogy for beginning conversations about the multiplicity of black experiences in the United States.

In the book *Disintegration: The Splintering of Black America*,[1] Eugene Robinson makes a case against monolithic constructions of black identity. He describes four black Americas: (1) the *transcendent elite*, those blacks who through wealth and/or influence have seemingly transcended racial/ethnic categorizations; (2) the *mainstream* middle class, which now accounts for a majority of black Americans; (3) an *emergent* community, composed of mixed-race families and black immigrants from Africa and the Caribbean; (4) and the *abandoned*, a large underclass residing mostly in urban areas and some poor neighborhoods in the rural South. I would fit into the emergent category as a first-generation immigrant black person now living in the United States. However, neither my daughters nor my husband share this lived experience that I have described elsewhere[2,3] as a fluid identity. It is an identity that allows immigrants like me to move in and out of minority/majority categorizations. We have known what it is to occupy majority spaces, but in this new context we must also learn to occupy minority spaces.

At the same time, drawing on the work of Kimberlé Crenshaw,[4,5] a leading legal scholar on critical race theory, I recognize that I am more than my cultural-ethnic identity. As Crenshaw and Patricia Hill Collins,[6] another black feminist scholar, articulate, the combination of two or more socioidentities, the intersection, creates potent challenges for such persons as they navigate leadership positions in predominantly white spaces. As an immigrant from the Caribbean who now works in a predominantly white Christian university, I have experienced and continue to experience challenges as I occupy the space at the nexus of my cultural ethnic, gender, and spiritual identities.

NAVIGATING THE US/THEM DISTINCTION

I first came to the United States in 1996, when I attended a small Christian university in Michigan to pursue a master's degree in educational administration. I stayed only for about nine months, and then I completed the remainder of the program online and with summer visits for the next two years. One of my first classes was on campus planning. As part of the course, we carpooled for a field trip to Chicago to see the campus site of Northwestern University. Not having a car, I was invited by my white professor to drive along with him. As we made our way through Gary, Indiana, I noticed that we had driven from a seemingly affluent neighborhood and entered what appeared to be a low-income neighborhood. I also noticed that this low-income neighborhood appeared to be predominantly black. I was thinking these things to myself, when I heard my professor mutter almost to himself in disgust, "I don't understand *these* people. Why can't they keep their properties better?" Then, as if suddenly remembering that I was in the car, he turned to me and said apologetically, "Oh, but I don't mean you! You are different because you are from the Caribbean." In that moment, I did not know what to think or say. Inside, I was conflicted; I felt happy that he had not included me among *these* people, but at the same time, I was deeply troubled by his characterization of people who looked just like me.

That incident happened almost twenty years ago, but as I write these words, I must admit that those conflicting feelings still rage on within me. Moreover, I have heard similar stories echoed among other black immigrants[7] who must learn, as I have been learning, to navigate the *us/them* distinction. It is a nettlesome space to occupy. On one hand, the us/them distinction might be perceived as a position of privilege among a marginalized group—considered a more palatable construction of blackness. On the other hand, it creates walls of distrust as we try to find and understand our precarious position within the African American community. Moreover, we are challenged to find a safe space to talk openly and candidly about the stressors we encounter in making the sociological and psychological leap from majority to minority status and coming to terms with this "new construction of blackness."[8]

At the same time, my status as an outsider/insider has led me to ask some difficult questions. At my current university, which has long been committed to social justice and diversity, data has been compiled by the office of institutional research for the 2014–15 academic year, and it documents that among undergraduate students who selected to identify with a racial ethnic group, 46 percent identified with a race other than white, compared with 54 percent who identified as white or non-Hispanic.[9] In contrast, only 20 percent of the faculty identify as people of color. At present, among full-time faculty there is not one African American male. The few male faculty members are immigrants mostly from Africa and the Caribbean. Recognizing the pervasive negative stereotypes that are challenging to African American males, it is disheartening for me to think that in our campus setting we have not been more intentional in creating space for counterexamples of African American masculinity for our students.

Why is it the case that we have black male immigrant faculty but no African American male faculty? When I ask myself this question, I often wonder about my own hiring. The truth is that I question how much the combination of my various identities was salient in my hiring: my name, Kathy-Ann Hernandez (I have kept my paternal last name, and I am the product of African and Hispanic ancestry); my immigrant status; my gender; and the hue of my skin. These are troubling concerns.

TEMPERING ANGER INTO ACTION

Like the rest of the coauthors in this section, I was part of the Multi-Ethnic Leadership Development Institute in 2015. One year later as I sat to write this chapter, I admitted to one of the institute's resource leaders that attending the institute had made me angry. It was analogous to the opening of a Pandora's box—the furies had been let out and there was no putting them back in. I left the institute thinking more intentionally about the reasons why my university was not more diverse, especially at the faculty and leadership levels. Moreover, although I have not aspired to take on formal leadership roles, I felt like a heavy mantle of responsibility had been laid on me to begin to create a vision for myself to work toward taking on formal leadership responsibilities: "If I don't advocate for people like me, who will?"

At the same time, my identity as a woman—caught in the conundrum of the working wife and mother to two young kids—left me feeling the time squeeze to assume Superwoman status. I was not in doubt of my leadership abilities. In fact, I was confident in my ability to lead from the margins as a tempered radical effecting change in the classroom, through the committees on which I sat, and in leveraging small wins.[10,11] I just did not want to take on Sheryl Sandberg's clarion cry to *lean in*[12] to my job when, for the present, I knew that leaning into my family responsibilities was the better choice for me.

However, navigating the work-life balance or work-life integration challenge is a complex and multilayered proposition when examined through the lens of culture and spirituality. Within my own cultural context, the role of women as wives and mothers is deeply rooted in unique historical and sociological realities. Specifically, within the Caribbean and African American community, religiosity remains salient and plays an influential role in clearly defined gender roles based on biblical considerations. Black women have played and continue to play pivotal roles as the spiritual progenitors and matriarchs in black families, often raising their own children and grandchildren in the absence of fathers and/or mothers. At the intersection of my spiritual, ethnic, and gender identity, I was conflicted. Should I aspire to a formal leadership position with a fierce determination to color the administrative landscape at my university, or should I choose to remain comfortable in the faculty position, which I had so intentionally carved out for myself?

In addition to these internal struggles, I was angry that more than a few of the administrative leaders were white and seemed, at least from my perspective, to have been appointed clandestinely and primarily on the basis of likability—or a penchant for not rocking the boat—rather than competence or qualifications. Had qualified people of color not been considered, or were there none to be found? Why had there not been open internal calls for candidates interested in being considered for certain leadership positions? And what was it about the organizational culture that supported unquestioningly what appeared to be injustices? As I thought about the "leadership" of Christian higher education as a result of readings and conversations during the Multi-Ethnic Leadership Development Institute, these questions disturbed me.

THE BURDEN OF BEING A BLACK FACULTY MEMBER

In the summer of 2015, I was surprised to be asked to serve on a very important university committee, given that I consider myself as someone who likes to lead quietly and not in center stage. Yet, when I received the call from one of the key administrative leaders, I felt certain that he did not even know me by face or name. So although I should have been honored to receive such an invitation, I was suspicious. As we spoke over the phone about the composition of the committee, I soon learned that not only would I be the only faculty of color serving, but that all the other committee members would be tenured faculty. I quickly did the math and realized that because there were only a handful of tenured minority faculty of color at my university, it was no surprise that the lot fell on me. I was still processing this information when I heard my caller say, "The choice to ask you to serve has nothing to do with filling a check box or quota. We are looking for the best people to do the best job." When I hung up the phone, I was even more convinced that extending the invitation to me had *everything* to do with checking that box.

I declined the opportunity to serve on the committee for several reasons. For one thing, I was being asked in May to serve during the summer months when I was on a nine-month contract (extending from Septempter to May), and I was already committed to heavy travel plans for the summer. Second, as one of the few faculty members at the university with young children, I had decided to guard my summer months to spend quality time with my children. Finally, I could not get rid of the nagging question in my mind: "Had I been invited to serve based on what I could contribute to the committee, or to satisfy appearances of diversity and inclusion?"

However, even as I grappled with the question of whether to accept, I felt the burden to say yes simply because I knew it was important to have a minority perspective on that committee. There were contributions that I could make—a *black way of knowing*[13] that the other members of the committee could not possibly bring to the table. So before making the decision to decline, I called two other faculty of color and asked them if they would consider serving if I proposed their name in my stead. They also declined. I understood why. Like me, they were weary of being called upon time and time again to fulfill this role in multiple committees on campus—the black-person role. As others have articulated,[14] the decision of faculty to say yes to service within the context of a predominantly white institution is wearisome because doing so often feels more like an obligation than a choice. Conversely, saying no creates another kind of stress, including the feeling of being a traitor to the cause.

ADOPTING A MULTIFOCAL LENS

Growing up in Trinidad, I always had role models of people in key leadership positions who looked just like me. I was a member of the majority group. The color of my skin was of marginal significance in my determination to achieve social mobility in life. I admit that there was *shade prejudice*—a lighter complexion was perceived as more aesthetically pleasing than darker complexions and some hair texture as *good hair* and *bad hair*. However, it was clear to me that these comparisons did not extend into barriers that would prevent me from achieving an elevated status in life.[15]

Hence, when I first came to the United States, I just did not understand why the African Americans I encountered did not feel the same way I did; I believed in the principles of meritocracy—*just pull yourself up by the bootstraps*. Having lived here since 2000, however, I have come to understand that the comparisons that were so superficial in my social context (light/dark; good hair/bad hair) have deep historical, systemic, and structural roots that perpetuate marginalization and inequities in this context.

Even after moving to the United States, I spent most of my early years viewing my encounters and experiences through my majority lens perspective. However, after living here for more than seventeen years, after being married to an African American man who got tired of butting his head against the proverbial glass ceiling in corporate America and decided instead to become self-employed, after observing and experiencing racial injustices in white-dominated academia, after living in a predominantly white neighborhood, and after having my daughters be the only black students in their suburban classrooms, the lens with which I once viewed my experiences has bifurcated. I am now able to move in and out of majority/minority identity perspectives. The adoption of this multifocal lens is the part of my emerging identity that I guard most judiciously. At the same time, it is a lonely vantage point for people like me. We do not quite fit in with normative definitions of blackness, even as we most certainly are not part of the white majority culture.

However, I am finding that the adoption of this multifocal lens has uniquely positioned, and even challenged, me to switch places with *the other* in encounters that might be interpreted as racial microaggressions in the academy. For example, as I have reflected further on the previously described request to serve on the committee, I have tried to place myself in the position of that administrative leader. What if he had not even tried to include someone of color on the committee? Then there might have been an outcry of racial inequity. When he does make and extended effort to ask me to serve, I decline for sound reasons. When I ask other faculty of color to serve in my place, they decline for equally sound reasons. Thus, when this scenario is viewed from the perspective of the other, no one can be accused of doing the wrong thing. Yet the end result is still the same—lack of racial/ethnic diversity in the final faculty committee composition. What also remains is the hidden subtexts in these kinds of interactions—hallway conversations among faculty of color in hushed voices continue to detail the ways in which they are marginalized, and I suspect that closed door communications in predominantly white male presidential office spaces continue around issues of diversity and inclusion. Yet members of neither group are able to position themselves in the place of the other or to access relevant information to get a clearer understanding of the nuances of each other's perspective; both groups are limited by their own monolithic lens.

WHAT NOW?

After returning from the Multi-Ethnic Leadership Development Institute, I had an opportunity to process and apply some of the things I was learning about diversity and inclusion in Christian higher education. My university went through a major restructuring process later that year. Not to anyone's surprise, one of the recommendations going forward was to seek more intentional ways to address issues of diversity and inclusion on our campus. I was invited to speak with one of the vice-presidents about my experiences as a faculty member of color and to make recommendations regarding the way forward. Given the bifurcated lens that I bring to my understanding of issues around diversity and inclusion in Christian higher education, I welcomed the opportunity to talk candidly about my observations and experiences at the university.

However, as one who values and teaches about the importance of solid evidence in problem identification in the social sciences, I concede that everything I articulated there and here, though informed by my research, interactions, and personal experience, is still based on a singular perspective. Diversity and inclusion issues are broader than my focus on racial/ethnic and gender disparities. Hence my best recommendation for Christian higher education is that institutional leaders ground future planning on the results of a cultural audit in order to understand the climate in their own institutional context. This is a critical step in carefully and systematically diagnosing the existent challenges and opportunities, and in planning a strategic evidence-based course of action. Moreover, these data can prove useful for institutions to benefit from the advice offered by Bolman and Deal, who say leaders should learn "how to use multiple lenses to get a better sense of what they are up against and what they might do."[16]

Given my own experiences, an integral part of the process should be to create opportunities for faculty and administrators, students, and staff to uncover the subtexts of racial tensions that challenge our ability to unite around the common pursuit of quality Christian higher education. I challenge us all to step out of the comfort of our monolithic lens and to embrace the perspective of the other—because this is the space in which the real work of diversity and inclusion can begin.

FOR DISCUSSION

1. The author describes her family unit and commented: "I am aware that though we are all black, we are not all the same kind of black. In some ways, I think this variation among my own family circle is a good, though imperfect, analogy for beginning conversations about the multiplicity of black experiences in the United States." In what ways have you observed or experienced these differences on your campus or in your life experiences? From your perspective, are there certain implications of being aware of these differences?

2. Citing the work of Kimberlé Crenshaw on intersectionality, the author suggests "the combination of two or more socioidentities, the intersection, creates potent challenges for such persons as they navigate leadership positions in predominantly white spaces." To what extent have you experienced the challenges of such intersectionality? Can you identify specific ways in which we support our students in understanding and addressing such challenges?

3. Discuss how embracing the perspectives of others who are different from oneself (for example, age, gender, ethnicity) can potentially provide insights for better practice in interactions between students, between faculty and students, and/or between faculty and administrators in the academy.

4. The author advocates for viewing situations from the perspective of others in minority/majority relations. How practical is this advice given that many in positions of majority privilege have not themselves experienced the phenomenon of minority classification? How might any identified challenge be addressed to make such perspective taking possible?

5. Discuss practical steps that institutions can take to follow Bolman and Deal's advice to learn "how to use multiple lenses to get a better sense of what they are up against and what they might do" as it relates to the diversity and inclusion in the context of Christian higher education.

6. The author discusses the challenges of being overburdened as person of color in predominantly white institutions. What has been your experience in this regard—either for yourself or observed in the pressures faced by others? What has been the most helpful advice you have received in regard to this concern for being overburdened?

7. In this chapter, the author discusses the challenges of being overburdened as person of color in predominantly white institutions. Discuss strategies

that faculty of color can employ in such contexts to be strategic about self-care as well as having voices in predominantly white institutional contexts.

NOTES

1   Eugene Robinson, *Disintegration: The Splintering of Black America* (New York: Anchor, 2011).

2   Kathy-Ann C. Hernandez and Kayon Murray-Johnson, "Towards a Different Construction of Blackness: Black Immigrant Scholars on Racial Identity Development in the United States," *International Journal of Multicultural Education* 17 (2; 2015): 53–72, http://dx.doi.org/10.18251 /ijme.v17i2.1050.

3   Kathy-Ann C. Hernandez, Faith Ngunjiri, and Heewon Chang, "Exploiting the Margins in Higher Education: A Collaborative Autoethnography of Three Foreign-Born Female Faculty of Color," *International Journal of Qualitative Studies in Education* 28 (5; 2015): 533–51, doi: 10.1080/09518398.2014.933910.

4   Kimberlé Crenshaw, "Demarginalizing the Intersection of Race and Sex: A Black Feminist Critique of Antidiscrimination Doctrine, Feminist Theory, and Antiracist Politics," *The University of Chicago Legal Forum 1989* (1989): 139–67.

5   Kimberlé Crenshaw, "Mapping the Margins: Intersectionality, Identity Politics, and Violence against Women of Color," *Stanford Law Review* 43 (6; 1991): 1241–99.

6   Patricia Hill Collins, *Black Feminist Thought: Knowledge, Consciousness, and the Politics of Empowerment* (London: Routledge, 1990).

7   Hernandez and Murray-Johnson, "Towards a Different Construction of Blackness."

8   Ibid.

9   Eastern University, "Common Data Set 2014–15," accessed November 4, 2016, http://www.eastern .edu/sites/default/files/sites/default/files/offices-centers/ie/2014_CDS%281%29.pdf.

10 Debra E. Meyerson, "The Tempered Radical: How Employees Push Their Companies—Little by Little—to Be More Socially Responsible," *Stanford Social Innovation Review* Fall (2004): 13–22.

11 Debra E. Meyerson, *Tempered Radicals: How People Use Difference to Inspire Change at Work* (Boston: Harvard Business School Press, 2001).

12 Sheryl Sandberg, *Lean In: Women, Work, and the Will to Lead* (New York: Knopf, 2013).

13 John Fiske, *Power Plays, Power Works* (New York: Verso, 1993), 238.

14 Kirby Wilson, "Lack of Diversity Leads to Burden on Professors of Color," *The Chronicle of Higher Education*, accessed November 4, 2016, http://www.dukechronicle.com/article/2015/02/lack -diversity-leads-burden-professors-color.

15 Hernandez and Murray-Johnson, "Towards a Different Construction of Blackness," 53–72.

16 Lee G. Bolman and Terrence Deal, *Reframing Organizations: Artistry, Choice and Leadership* (San Francisco: Jossey-Bass, 2008).

Chapter Twenty-Two

NAVIGATING THE TRANSITION TO ADMINISTRATIVE LEADERSHIP

GLADYS ROBALINO, PhD

Messiah College, Chair of Modern Language Department

In March 2015, I received a surprising email from the dean of my school. He wondered whether I would consider attending a Multi-Ethnic Leadership Development Institute sponsored by the Council for Christian Colleges & Universities, to be held north of Seattle that June.

"I realize at this point you haven't had a lot of opportunity to move into leadership positions," the dean wrote in his email. "But both the provost and I have been impressed with your committee work, and I certainly think you have the skills to develop into a good administrator if that seems like a route you might want to pursue someday."

The prospect was both exciting and frightening for me. On the one hand, it was encouraging to think that the dean saw me as a prospective administrator for our institution. On the other hand, I wasn't sure if I wanted the extra workload or whether I was qualified for such a position. Yes, I had years of teaching experience, but I had not done any significant administrative work to that point.

As I considered his offer, the idea of assuming this kind of role seemed very daunting. Not only had I never aspired to it, but I was happily involved in my teaching and research. Perhaps I also perceived myself as too different from the norm for campus leadership possibilities for several reasons: I was one of the few international faculty members, a Latina, and a teacher and scholar who was Catholic in a mostly evangelical college. I was also a single woman at the time, in an environment that seemed to cater more toward those who were married with families.

Nonetheless, I accepted the dean's initial invitation to attend the June gathering. And less than a year after the Multi-Ethnic Leadership Development Institute, I was offered the opportunity to chair my department. Subsequently, my transition of shifting my self-identity from primarily faculty to serving as department chair, as recounted in the following pages, has been one marked with challenges and opportunities I could not have anticipated. Yet it has been one from which I have grown and benefited in numerous ways.

SEEING OURSELVES AS LEADERS

When I arrived at Cedar Springs Christian Retreat Center for the Multi-Ethnic Leadership Development Institute in June 2015, I had many questions: Why am I here? Is this really what I want? Shouldn't I be using my summer to secure another publication? What had I been thinking when I signed up for this?

Despite my doubts, I wanted to remain open to learning as much as I could. I wanted to prepare myself for what seemed an inevitable career move into administration for and within my college. It was a call to institutional service I knew I needed to take seriously. Before that time, I had not seen myself as an administrator; like many faculty members, I viewed administrative jobs as distractions from teaching and research. Indeed, advanced institutional service might seem more prestigious, but I knew that it could also be costly. Professors, after all, are trained to teach and do research, not to administer. The fear of being unable to perform well or of maintaining and mediating friendly relationships with colleagues and administrators was real. And such fears can keep even the best scholars from considering the option of broader institutional service.

For me, there were also other factors to be considered. As the only full-time Latina professor on our campus, I was aware that the gender issue was being addressed in positive ways in my institution: several women were (and still are) in administrative positions, including the president. Nonetheless, as I heard some of their personal stories on what it meant to juggle household and child-rearing responsibilities with the demands of administrative jobs, I understood the transition into administrative leadership is not easy for women, and even more challenging for women of color.

As a result, I spent the three months after receiving the email from my dean wondering whether this was an opportunity I wanted to pursue, and if so, whether I could meet his expectations. I doubted my capacity to become a leader. I dreaded assuming a position of authority over my peers, and I was terrified at the possibility of failure. And the more I heard seasoned attendees of the Multi-Ethnic Leadership Development Institute recount the challenges they faced, the less confident I became.

My turning point came when I read Sheryl Sandberg's book *Lean In*. It was the first in a series of reading assignments I had been given related to the various meetings and discussions that followed the Multi-Ethnic Leadership Development Institute. Sandberg addressed my concerns head-on when she noted that "fear is at the root of so many of the barriers that women face. Fear of not being liked. Fear of making the wrong choice. Fear of drawing negative attention. Fear of overreaching. Fear of being judged. Fear of failure. And the holy trinity of fear: the fear of being a bad mother, wife, and daughter."[1]

Then Sandberg pointed to the lower percentage of women in the workplace who aspire to leadership positions and tend to "characterize themselves [less] as 'leaders,' 'visionaries,' 'self-confident,' and 'willing to take risks.'"[2] She argues that women have traditionally been raised to opt for safer career choices that would allow them space for a family. The result is what she calls the "leadership ambition gap," a phenomenon that involves not just having fewer women in leadership roles, but fewer women who *want* to be in leadership roles. Women are often culturally conditioned to be less aggressive, less ambitious, less outspoken, and less bold—the precise characteristics that are commonly associated with leaders. And in my case, it seemed that my cultural background, which has even more fixed gender roles and expectations, amplified all of these characteristics.

Having been raised in Latin America in a Catholic family, I was brought up with fewer freedoms and more fears than my only male sibling. Fear becomes your own police and marker of boundaries, and fear factors into any decision being made. My husband points out how cautious I am at everything I do, how much I like to follow the rules, and how long I think before making a decision. This is good most times, but I have learned with him that never taking risks is a very limited life.

Sandberg's book made me aware of how much my inclination to stay "safe" spilled into my professional life. I felt safer staying with my teaching than taking an administrative role on campus. Sandberg challenged women to "lean in" to their professional potential, asking, "What would you do if you were not afraid?" The question pushed me to ask myself, *What if I was not afraid? Or what if I was and still dared to imagine taking the risk?*

Another book by Herminia Ibarra, titled *Act Like a Leader, Think Like a Leader*, also pushed me into new territory. As much as Sandberg's book had inspired me, the reality was that I had no management training. A year earlier, when the dean had offered to put my name on the candidate list for director of a unit, I considered that option but with a sinking heart. In the end, I thanked him and asked him not to include my name on the list to be considered. I had actually been on the committee that supported that department for several years (and still am) and knew the extent of the director's responsibilities reasonably well. I had worked closely with the previous director, an excellent leader who ran things very smoothly, and I could not imagine anyone filling his shoes—least of all me! I could not have seen myself juggling all that he did with such skill and grace.

But Ibarra's insights were helpful: nobody enters a new job already having mastered everything it entails; instead, most real leaders become leaders first (i.e., they begin acting as a leader must act) and gradually learn as they go by accepting the risks of the unknown and stepping into the responsibilities of the role. Ibarra refers to this as the "outsight principle," meaning "the only way to think like a leader is to first act [like one]."[3]

In other words, who we are now does not necessarily define who we can become. This is particularly so with faculty moving into administrative positions. Most do not have management training yet, but do have a good understanding of the problems faculty face, and of the relationships among faculty, the administration, and the students. When I began to realize that what mattered most was having an understanding of those dynamics, and that the managerial duties could be learned on the job, I could begin to imagine myself in an administrative role.

BEING SEEN BY OTHERS AS A LEADER

Because I had lived and worked most of my life in my home country of Ecuador, I had not realized the breadth of the roles I would come to play when I accepted a job as a Spanish language and literature professor at a predominantly white Christian liberal arts college. In fact, I had arrived being largely unfamiliar with the politics pervading most North American campuses. During my second year after arrival, I was invited to participate in the campus diversity committee. Soon other requests and invitations followed: advisor for the Latino students club, member of the Senate, member of the global engagement committee, and others. As one of the few faculty of color on campus, I have been included in many committees where diverse voices are needed. I was not expecting to be a voice for diversity, but I have now embraced this responsibility. I had not necessarily signed up to be the "designated" voice for diversity, but like many of the M-E LDI participants, I have come to understand the importance of having diverse voices in the discussions across our campuses. Yet despite the benefits of having such conversations, it can be intimidating to be the one to push for difficult conversations that need to happen. In fact, participating in several committees gave me the opportunity to find my voice, engage with others, and "act" as a leader even before "thinking" about becoming one. Ibarra's advice seemed to apply: "Plunge yourself into new projects and activities, interact with very different kinds of people, and experiment with unfamiliar ways of getting things done. Those freshly challenging experiences and their outcomes will transform the habitual actions and thoughts that currently define your limits."[4]

For me, the push of being one of the few faculty of color on campus was an important contributor to taking that plunge. Whereas previously I had felt uncomfortable or fearful of stepping on people's toes during conversations around cultural issues and diversity, I have learned to engage more sensitively. I have made an effort to understand better the context of our community and to imagine the kind of culturally appreciative environment that we hope to become. Yes, committee work can sometimes feel like a burden. It takes a lot of time, and it can be frustrating when things do not move at the pace we would prefer, but committee work can also be a great opportunity to meet other people on campus, to connect with kindred spirits, to get a better understanding of the institution as a whole, and to help guide the conversations to reflect a more inclusive vision.

The other positive aspect of participating in committees is that as we grow in understanding the politics of our workplaces and use our skills in the different roles we play, we become more confident about taking different responsibilities and connecting with people outside our departments. In fact, new responsibilities and new connections beyond our own offices can often help nurture new resources for understanding and action. Speaking directly to the importance of such intentional interactions, Ibarra wrote: "[Networking] can keep you informed. Teach you new things. Make you more innovative. Give you a sounding board to flesh out your ideas. Help you get things done when you are in a hurry and you need a favor. The list goes on."[5]

At my institution, my "unique" cultural and theological identity initially kept me from seeing myself as a potential leader, administrator, or voice for anything. I did not think I had anything to say that had relevance in the campus governing. Finding my voice and being aware of the contributions that I can make by participating on various key committees has shown me otherwise.

BUILDING THE PATH ON SOLID ROCKS (ALLIES, MENTORS, AND SPONSORS)

During the Multi-Ethnic Leadership Development Institute, we were asked to list the mentors and sponsors we presently had. I sat there for a while without being able to come up with anything. Finally, I jotted down a few names on my "mentors" list, but the space to list the names of my sponsors remained blank. I turned to my right to peek at my neighbor's list. She, like me, had few names listed. Then I turned to the neighbor on my left, observing that her page seemed to be too small to include all the names she was listing! I gave a big sigh and wondered what her secret was.

After attending the Multi-Ethnic Leadership Development Institute, one of our assigned tasks for the following academic year was to identify and develop at least one sponsor inside and/or outside our place of work. As I continued reflecting on why, how, and where to find sponsors and mentors, I realized that part of my problem was my attitude. I did have a number of allies, mentors, and sponsors both in my workplace and outside of it, but I had failed to understand the importance of their impact on my development; therefore, I had failed to nurture those relationships.

For instance, the person I consider my most important mentor was assigned to be in that role as I navigated my first year on campus. She teaches in the anthropology department, which is not even in the same school that I am in. During this assigned (formal) mentorship arrangement, we followed the program requirements: to observe each other's classes a few times and to share ideas over coffee. While I enjoyed this part of the experience, at the time I did not feel that I gained much from it.

Yet because we stayed in touch as friends and colleagues, I have come to her many times for advice on issues such as the tenure process, publication, teaching, and even the possibility of taking an administrative role. Her professionalism, scholarship, publications, and excellence in teaching model for me the qualities of the best mentors and colleagues. She fits all the categories of a mentor described by Sylvia Ann Hewlett in her book *Forget a Mentor, Find a Sponsor*: "[A mentor is an] experienced person willing to help and support you, builds your confidence and provides a sounding board, offers empathy to cry on, [and] expects very little in return."[6] Because developing leaders need input from experienced leaders, I came to understand the long-term value of that original mentoring match.

Something similar happened as I was trying to identify a sponsor. It took me a while to realize that my interaction with a sponsor had been there all along. My dean had been the one nudging me to be part of some committees and to take on special responsibilities. By asking me to make a presentation or devotional for a school meeting, he helped grow my confidence. He also sponsored my attendance in the Multi-Ethnic Leadership Development Institute and other professional development seminars, and eventually offered me the chair position when my predecessor had to take an extended personal leave. He believed in my potential, advocated for me, encouraged me to take risks, and still expects great performance and loyalty.[7] Sponsors such as my dean help potential emerging leaders see and understand the bigger picture of the mission and vision of the organization.

Before diving into these readings and conversations through the Multi-Ethnic Leadership Development Institute, I did not think of myself as one with leadership potential. Now I see that I have more to offer than I realized, and that I had more mentors and sponsors than I had recognized. My list continues to grow as I seek to create and nurture relationships that benefit our broader community life. Each has become a rock in my professional life and my voice for diversity across campus. I now more fully recognize the important work that must be embraced by people across Christian colleges and universities that proactively seek to live out a commitment to model the kingdom of God in all respects. With that goal in mind, I am excited about the prospects that have opened by adjusting my sense of self-identity to understand the potential role I have to contribute to the diversity agenda, while also serving as a role model and lending my voice to the broader work of my institution.

FOR DISCUSSION

1.   What keeps you from seeing yourself as a leader?
2.   What mentors and sponsors can you seek out inside and outside your place of work?
3.   What strategies can you utilize to nurture your mentor and sponsor relationships?
4.   What opportunities are available at your campus to help you train for leadership?
5.   In what capacities do you already see yourself as a leader in your community? Reflect on how this can help you become a leader in broader spheres of influence within your institution.

NOTES

1   Sheryl Sandberg, *Lean In: Women, Work, and the Will to Lead* (New York: Knopf, 2013), 24.
2   Ibid.,16.
3   Herminia Ibarra, *Act Like a Leader, Think Like a Leader* (Boston: Harvard Business Review, 2015), 5.
4   Ibid., 5.
5   Ibid., 71.
6   Sylvia Ann Hewlett, *Forget a Mentor, Find a Sponsor: The New Way to Fast-Track Your Career* (Boston: Harvard Business Review, 2013), 21.
7   Ibid., 21.

Chapter Twenty-Three

I DON'T BELONG HERE: A "CIRCLE" LEADER IN A "SQUARE" UNIVERSITY

RUKSHAN FERNANDO, PhD

Azusa Pacific University, Associate Dean of the School of Behavioral and Applied Sciences

Some men see things as they are and say, "Why?" I dream things that never were and say, "Why not?"
—Robert Kennedy

I was fortunate to attend the Council for Christian Colleges & Universities' (CCCU) Multi-Ethnic Leadership Development Institute program in June 2015. Set in beautiful Sumas, Washington, the program gave me the physical and intellectual space to retreat from everyday noise to reflect on my potential as an administrator and leader. The beauty of the location, the fellowship, and the hospitality I experienced gave me a much-needed safe space to consider the hills and valleys of both my past and future, as well as the next steps of my career. I had recently been promoted to a new position, and I knew that this role would give me a better understanding of the systemic institutional challenges administrators face.

The Multi-Ethnic Leadership Development Institute held many opportunities for meaningful conversation and breakthrough learning. After such a mountaintop experience, I expected to come crashing down to earth when I returned to campus and faced the deluge of adjuncts to interview, budgets to project, and forms to sign. My first day back, I walked into a meeting room lined with portraits of white men. While I knew that these were great men who had shaped the institution, their images presented me with a piercing question: How would I traverse the networks of family legacies, church affiliations, alumni connections, and cultural cues to negotiate my place in a significant and meaningful institutional role? Or, put simply, how would I maintain my own identity without losing myself to white male normality?

While colleges and universities across the nation have established efforts to provide equitable access to students from diverse backgrounds, there is still much work to be done to change the structural diversity that exists within higher education.

The same is true for the vast majority of member institutions that comprise the CCCU. While some colleges and universities in the CCCU have begun to attempt to deal with the structural issues of student homogeneity as a whole, less attention has been placed on developing a diversity pipeline for administrators of color.

As an administrator of color, I am situated in an institution that possesses its own dynamics, culture, and power structures. This is true of all institutions—not just mine or any other CCCU members. A resounding message hovers around me when I walk down halls lined with portraits reflecting a legacy of white male leaders: *I do not belong here.* I know this is not true, that I *do* belong here because God has led me here. Still the question—and images—confront me: What does it mean for a person of color to break the "portrait barrier" at a predominately white institution?

This chapter recounts my struggles and triumphs as I transition from faculty member to administrator. My narrative will provide the reader with a nuanced account of the ways that the intersections of race, ethnicity, national origin, and gender play a role in both advancing and impeding my calling to higher education administration. It's my hope that through my own narrative, current and aspiring leaders will be empowered to confront the structural challenges that have limited people of color from rising to the highest ranks of our institutions. While such challenges are nuanced and complex, I highlight four that impede the success of administrators of color: the intersectionality of race and gender, the difficulty of rural living, the invisibility of people of color in leadership, and the dilemma of the diversity silo.

THE INTERSECTIONALITY OF RACE AND GENDER

"I have walked that long road to freedom. I have tried not to falter; I have made missteps along the way," wrote Nelson Mandela. "But I have discovered the secret that after climbing a great hill, one only finds that there are many more hills to climb."[1] Mandela discovered that even after his release from prison and the dismantling of apartheid, another series of hills remained to be climbed as the president of South Africa. There had to be a long, arduous process of restorative and redistributive justice.

As a South Asian administrator, my hill to climb is frequently feeling that I am a "loner" in my institution. Just when I think I've established a legitimizing presence, another hill appears on the horizon that I must climb.

In our Christian institutions, the additional hills Mandela refers to represent structural processes where white males and females have privilege and unearned social capital due to the color of their skin. While I value growing gender diversity in leadership teams, the informal networks fostered by white female leadership sometimes feel akin to an "old white girls' club," creating a barrier for me as a man of color, and even more so for women of color. It is short-sighted to think that merely increasing the gender diversity in the ranks of administrative leadership will solve the structural diversity issues at our institutions. When the majority of leaders are from the white majority—men *or* women—CCCU institutions limit the range of perspectives needed to meet the complex issues facing Christian higher education in the twenty-first century.

Let me give you an example: as a social work educator, I am often in rooms filled with helping professionals. More often than not, I am the only male and the only person of color in these rooms. On many occasions, I experience passive aggressive behaviors such as gossip and receiving the "cold shoulder" from women at such gatherings. There have also been moments when some female leaders have questioned my passion and concerns for gender equity on campus because I express that both gender and racial diversity hold equal importance. While similar concerns are expressed about white men, questions surrounding my commitment to women in leadership are raised due to my South Asian background. In addition, I do not have access to social gatherings in predominantly female contexts where informal networking occurs. As a result, I often feel like an outsider while colleagues discuss female-oriented topics like mother-daughter relationships, makeup, and breast-feeding.

Even so, attempting to understand the experiences of women has been valuable, helping me empathize with faculty members who work in male-dominated disciplines. Because of the oppression that some of these women have experienced in a white male world, they have shared with me expectations that men of color will treat them worse due to stereotypes established by the mainstream media and the entertainment industry. For example, when I share about my background and the role my mother played as a school principal, board member, and community leader, many women have been surprised, admitting they expected a more simplistic, predictable personal narrative.

In other circumstances, I've experienced macro- and microaggressions from white female faculty and staff. Often assumptions have been made about how I should interact with others based on my culture of origin, and their limited understanding of South Asian culture. Such misunderstandings have led me to seek to educate, inform, and dialogue. As Frances Kendell wrote, "Without crucibles—transformative experiences through which an individual comes to a new or altered sense of identity—change does not occur."[2] Because it is easy for the majority to overlook and dismiss experience, marginalization, and oppression, white women must seek to more deeply understand the experiences of others who hold different racial identities.

The statistics related to demographics in the student population and in higher education leadership are worthy of note. A 2012 report issued by the American Council on Education on the American College President reported:

[W]hile college campuses have diversified the racial and ethnic makeup of their student bodies, the racial and ethnic composition of college and university presidents has changed very little. Between 1990 and 2009, the share of college students that were racial and ethnic minorities increased from 20 percent to 34 percent. Between 1986 and 2011, the racial makeup of college presidents only increased from 8 percent to 13 percent. Moreover, when comparing data from the two most recent president studies, racial diversity declined from 14 percent in 2006 to 13 percent in 2011.[3]

However, the report mentions that there has been slight improvement in gender diversity during this same period. While the increase of gender diversity in the presidency is a step in a positive direction, there must also be a rise of leaders who represent the intersectionality of ethnic identities. If diverse men and women of color in various areas of campus leadership are given the opportunity to work together with white men and women, the next generation of Christian leaders will more effectively be shaped.

RURAL LIVING: GREEN ACRES AND BROKEN EXPERIENCES

Many CCCU institutions are located in rural locations, which can pose a challenge for people of color. Some of these rural communities have histories linked to the Ku Klux Klan or are predominantly homogenous. For eight years, I worked at a CCCU institution in a small town, and it was an incredibly difficult place to live. Our car was egged repeatedly, we received threatening phone calls, and people drove back and forth past our house in pickup trucks hailing gun racks and confederate flags. I was run off the road several times and was followed regularly when shopping at the local grocery store and gas station. In public settings, we were often "otherized" by constant stares, and received questions about our biracial children's backgrounds, or general silent looks of discomfort by our presence.

One afternoon, I went to the pharmacy in my work clothes—a shirt and tie. When I took my items to pay, the cashier's mouth dropped open and she appeared to be paralyzed by my presence. Because we lived in a farming community, most men of color were migrant workers and did not hold white collar positions. My wearing a tie in her store seemed to debunk her racial categories and capabilities.

Growing up in this small town also began to take a toll on our daughter. One day, she lamented to my wife that she was always the only brown kid. In discussing her feelings with my wife, she finally insisted, "*Everyone* is white except me . . . even Jesus is white!" When people would say to us, "This is a great place to raise kids. Things haven't changed since the good ol' days," we'd ask ourselves, *Good ol' days for whom?*

Do such references to *good ol' days* harken back to times where majority groups had even more power, privilege, and social capital? If these surrounding communities aren't hospitable to diversity, how will CCCU institutions create safe spaces where people of color can thrive both professionally and personally? The "escape" that these communities provide from the changes in culture and the metropolis often negatively impact the diversity pipeline in higher education administration.

THE INVISIBILITY OF DIVERSE LEADERS

"*Dr.* Fernando—are you the associate dean?" The admission representative's tone communicated an attitude of surprise that *someone like me* was the associate dean. I nodded and entered the meeting, reminded that, once again, I didn't fit "the box" of what an administrator should look like.

While scholars have discussed the impact of microaggressions on students and faculty of color, administrators of color are often faced with subtle assumptions, negative jabs, and nonverbal messages. Too often, the unspoken metanarrative for many of our CCCU institutions is that to be the voice of the institution, one ultimately must be a white man or woman, able to nuance the cultural language of white "evangelical-ese." If our own employees expect homogeneity in leadership roles, how will Christian higher education attract majority-minority students who need to see themselves reflected in the leadership of our institutions?

Once, when I was meeting with members of faculty who serve on a council, one professor asked me: "Why are you interested in administration? I would imagine *someone like you* would be more interested in research." "What do you mean?," I replied. "I don't know, I just didn't see *you* as an administrator." As an administrator of color, I look forward to the days where faculty and staff will encourage and challenge me to be a leader on campus. On the other hand, when talking to my students about my own career path, they often ask why there are so few diverse leaders on campus. This has been an interesting contrast for me—my students expect and question the lack of diverse leadership on campus while *my own colleagues* are surprised when such diverse individuals take on such positions.

As leaders in our institutions, we want to listen to and consider all of our constituents—students, faculty, staff, the church, and so on. However, the difference in the response between my colleagues and students clearly reflects that we are out of touch with the reality that our students expect. As Soong Chan Rah asserts, if we don't diversify our leadership, Christian colleges will end up as irrelevant to mainstream society as the Amish community: living out an admirable mission, but one designed and organized for a different century.[4]

THE DILEMMA OF THE DIVERSITY SILOS

As an administrator of color, I sometimes hesitate to raise issues of diversity. I hesitate to be branded as the sole diversity champion or expert on campus. While I am passionate about issues of diversity and inclusion, my teaching and research background is in nonprofit management and leadership. Certainly, I have grown in the area of diversity and inclusion teaching and research, but it is not my primary area of expertise. In spite of this, I have frequently been asked to consider the role of chief diversity officer (CDO), even though I have no professional interest or scholarship in this area. Because of my racial and ethnic background, I have had to be intentional in not allowing my professional identity to be overshadowed by my ethnicity. For example, in one institution I visited, a leader approached me and inquired if I was interested in a newly created CDO position at the university: "Rukshan, you would make an excellent CDO. Unlike African Americans and Latinos, you don't bring anger and baggage into conversations about diversity. This would be helpful in shaping the future of our institution."

It seemed this leader saw my value to the institution solely through the lens of my skin color and ethnic background—at the expense of other people of color as well as my professional expertise. What was most discouraging about this interaction was that I had been working hard to engage in cross-department councils, program development, and other collaborations that were not diversity related. Yet he seemed to overlook this and instead perceived my value related primarily to my cultural identity.

PRACTICAL SUGGESTIONS FOR ADMINISTRATORS OF COLOR

The challenge of developing a leadership structure and culture that supports diversity is no easy task. As reflected in my personal experiences, leaders of color in today's Christian institutions need to be more effectively affirmed and supported in their struggle to thrive in communities that do not necessarily reflect their cultures or values. In recent conversations with administrators of color from across the CCCU, I have been struck by the deep commitment these leaders have to the religious identity and mission of their institutions. Their commitment to the Christ-centered missions of our institutions, framed within the diverse constellation of their racial and ethnic identities, provides a starting point from where institutional and individual shared values might be discovered. We must create an environment that honors the reality that many people of color are also committed to seeing Christian higher education thrive in the twenty-first century but who may see it differently than through traditional white eyes.

Based on my experiences as an emerging leader at a CCCU university, I offer the following list of practical suggestions for administrators of color.

Develop a Network Team

In her book, *Act Like a Leader, Think Like a Leader,*[5] Herminia Ibarra discusses the importance of a team's diversity in thought and perspective. It is easy to fall into "tribes" and engage with the people who think, behave, and act similarly. It is far more difficult to collaborate with people who have different skill sets and backgrounds. Professional teams should therefore consist of people from a variety of backgrounds and expertise, because diverse teams create more value for those involved and for the organization, avoid groupthink, generate career opportunities, and sense trends and access opportunities for the organization.[6]

Get a Sponsor

In the reading list at the end of this book, I recommend *Forget a Mentor, Find a Sponsor.*[7] Sylvia Ann Hewlett discusses the importance of sponsorship: a reciprocal relationship with the sponsor promotes the emerging leader with stretching assignments, greater organizational exposure, and consistent feedback. In return, the sponsor's own career is advanced through the exemplary work of the individual being sponsored.

In the past year, I've developed a relationship with two sponsors, one internal and one external. These individuals have been incredibly wise, frank, and encouraging, and have given me a platform from which I have continued to grow in my career as a higher education administrator within the context of predominately white Christian higher education institutions.

PRACTICAL SUGGESTIONS FOR CCCU CAMPUSES

If implemented, the following suggestions for CCCU institutions could provide helpful strategies for empowering current or future administrators of color.

Create a Plan for Leadership Development

Does your institution have a leadership development strategy and plan? If so, what are the metrics and benchmarks that define and articulate the faculty and staff who could be candidates for leadership positions in your campus? Is your institution's conceptual understanding and practical application based on practices, backgrounds, and behaviors that might be more closely associated with white, American, evangelical males and females?

Consider developing a plan with some significant players on your campus and gather multiple and diverse perspectives so that your institution does not have a cookie-cutter approach to determining and selecting leaders for the future. Moreover, this leadership development plan must identify the theological and institutional rationale for the need to develop a diverse leadership pipeline at the institution. If there are interested people of color on the list, invest in them—and communicate that you want to invest in them—in ways that allow them to flourish at your college or university. Don't just invite people to the table. Give them the power to determine what will be on the menu.

Parker Palmer wrote, "It seems I am in community when I feel seen, known, and respected . . . when I am taken seriously and appreciated, not just for the function I perform, but for whom I am as a person."[8] His words reflect the need for people of color to be seen and valued. They also affirm what I have seen in my fourteen years in Christian higher education, as faculty and staff of color have shared with me their aspirations to become leaders in their institutions. Many of them have expressed these sentiments with me: "I know that people were excited about my hire, but it was not because of my skills, competencies, and unique gifts. It's for the *function* or *role* that I fulfilled. What does that mean for my future here? I'm not just a pretty face who appears now and again in important meetings so that my chair or the board of trustees can say we are a diverse institution. *I want to make a difference here.*"

Just as instructors often take attendance at the beginning of a class and expect students to respond, "Present!," so do many future leaders of color feel they are the student named "Diversity." Once they say "Present!," they are not invited to participate for the rest of the class. In response to this reality, institutional leaders must be intentional and proactive in their diversity efforts across campus, from technology and faith integration to beautiful campus amenities and so on. Obviously, such concepts and products take time, resources, and strategic plans. Therefore, when capable faculty and staff of color are present, administrators need to surround them with opportunities that might "stretch" them and also send them a message that "we can't go on and be true to our mission without your leadership."

It is both a missional imperative and a market reality.

FOR DISCUSSION

1. When hiring, what specific steps are taken during the search to maximize the numbers of minority and female applicants?

2. When hiring, do you send position announcements directly to professional associations and departments at universities that are members of historically black colleges and universities (HBCUs), Hispanic serving institutions (HSIs), and tribal colleges and universities?

3. How often does your Board of Trustees interact, dialogue, and listen to administrators of color on your campus? What perspectives and insights might the board gain if this were to happen?

4. Has your cabinet, school, or department leaders identified women and people of color on campus who will be the future leaders of your institution?

5. Have you identified administrative sponsors on campus who can empower emerging diverse leaders on your campus?

6. People from different backgrounds bring new and different networks. How do these networks of communities and people increase your institution's social and cultural capital?

7. If you are an administrator of color, are you distinguishing between your own business and the baggage and work of others?

8. If you are an administrator of color, what lies or imposters are you believing? What are ways you can grow into your authentic selfhood?

9. As people of color on the campuses of predominately white Christian colleges and universities, how do we avoid attributing malice to that which cultural incompetency might explain?

NOTES

1 Nelson Mandela, *Long Road to Freedom: The Autobiography of Nelson Mandela* (New York: Little Brown & Company, 1995), 751.

2 Francis Kendell, *Understanding White Privilege: Creating Pathways to Authentic Relationships across Race*, 2nd ed. (New York: Routledge, 2011), 3.

3 B. Cook and Y. Kim, *The American College President 2012* (Washington, DC: American Council on Education), 1.

4 Soong Chan Rah, "The Next Evangelicalism," Keynote Lecture, National Student Leadership Conference, Taylor University, Upland, IN, February 2007.

5 Herminia Ibarra, *Act Like a Leader, Think Like a Leader* (Boston: Harvard Business School Publishing, 2015).

6 Kevin Holloway and Julian Barling, "Leadership Development as an Intervention in Occupational Health Psychology," *Work and Stress* 24 (3; 2010): 260–79. See also E. Holloway and A. Day, "Building Healthy Workplaces: What We Know So Far," *Canadian Journal of Behavioral Sciences* 37 (4; 2005): 223–35.

7   Sylvia Ann Hewlett, *Forget a Mentor, Find a Sponsor: The New Way to Fast-Track Your Career* (Boston: Harvard Business Review, 2013).

8   Parker Palmer, "The Quest in Higher Education," in *Creating Campus Community: In Search of Ernest Boyer's Legacy*, eds., W. McDonald et al. (San Francisco: Jossey-Bass, 2002), 183.

Chapter Twenty-Four

A LIFETIME IN SEARCH OF A SPONSOR

REBECCA TORRES VALDOVINOS, MEd

George Fox University, Director of the English Language Institute

"Tía? That means aunt, right?" The Sister from Sacred Heart of Mary asked the question in her New England accent. Dressed in her full habit, she looked down at the small seven-year-old Mexican American child. I looked up at her with amazement. She did not know that the women I was describing in the conversation about our family party celebrating my First Communion were my mother's sisters. At that age, I had no comprehension of the word "aunt"; I only knew "tía." This was my first awareness of being from a culture other than the majority white norm of the 1960s.

My ethnic identity has been a salient feature of my academic journey. I grew up in the barrio of East Los Angeles, the place of my birth. After twelve years of parochial school with the Sacred Heart of Mary religious order, I broke new ground for my family by going on to enter higher education. My SAT scores were far from what would normally be required, so Sister R[1] advised me not to pursue college based on her assessment that I did not have the aptitude for such a venture. She suggested instead that I take the domestic route of marriage and child rearing.

Granted, this *was* perceived to be an acceptable path within the Mexican American culture, where I had been taught that girls were not to be "over-educated" for fear of not being marriage material. So I held back any desire to achieve because to do otherwise would depict me as an "aggressive woman no man would want to marry." And I believed Sister R's words as truth.

Nonetheless, I went on to graduate with honors. I also married and ended up divorced. As a Mexican American single mother of four, I pursued an academic career, but my marital status created many challenges for me in academia, especially as I pursued leadership roles. I belonged to the generation at the end of the Civil Rights era when politicians were throwing money at the disenfranchised minority kids from the slums of urban areas. After attending the local community college, I graduated cum laude and transferred to the University of California at Santa Barbara with the benefit of a full-tuition scholarship. The "mentors" who existed in my low socioeconomic environment were my "tías," a cadre of employees in the service areas of the university. They worked long hours for very little pay or reward, apart from the joy of seeing girls like me advance.

As I have reflected on these challenges from my upbringing and university years, I now realize how they helped propel me toward success in my professional journey.

CHALLENGES: GOING IT ALONE

I wish I could say that I had mentors along my undergraduate path, but I can't. Like the type of young woman Sheryl Sandberg describes in *Lean In: Women, Work, and the Will to Lead*, I was afraid to be outspoken or even career-minded.[2] With "necessity as the mother of invention," I needed to reinvent myself in order to feed my four children. During my graduate studies at California State University, Los Angeles, my first mentor came into my life.

I was working on my master's degree in education when a professor took an interest in me. The professor had the power and influence on my life that was described in Sylvia Ann Hewlett's book *Forget a Mentor, Find a Sponsor*.[3] Unfortunately, all of the potential of this mentoring opportunity was largely missed, given that I did not recognize the importance of this relationship. I moved sixty miles away, and we had soon lost contact.

Sometime later, another professor—the chair of my graduate research committee—looked at my thesis and abruptly commented, "That's the problem with bilingual education; they don't teach you how to write." My chairperson was the antithesis of a sponsor; she completely undermined the passion in my heart to attain a graduate degree. I believed that professor's opinion of me, left my graduate program, and spent the next five years in a state of dejection. Eventually, however, I realized that her perception of my academic writing was harsh and untrue, and that realization led me toward another path of expertise.

I was not a product of the public school bilingual education system, nor was I bilingual, having spent all of my life speaking English. However, this event with my chairperson was not wasted; the experience actually influenced my future rise into leadership. Through the encouragement and impact of my former mentor, I came back six years later to complete my master's degree. The importance of this relationship reflects the power of having advocates, some of whom actually serve as sponsors. In her book, *Executive Presence: The Missing*

Link between Merit and Success, Hewlett describes a sponsor as someone who will catapult you in the right direction.[4] Although the influence of this professor opened the door for me to complete my degree, that is where the relationship stopped. During a second critical period of my personal journey, an opportunity for professional growth and enhanced self-confidence was missed because of my lack of direction.

In the *Forget a Mentor* book, Hewlett described a situation in which a young woman thought that getting ahead professionally "was all about performance"[5] and that if she just worked hard enough her superiors would notice her talent. I could identify, as this was my work ethic as well, but I learned that hard work did not necessarily open doors. Eventually, I landed a job in the Pacific Northwest as a full-time faculty member at a small community college in rural Lewis County. In that setting, I received mixed messages. I was told, "We hired you for your diversity and multicultural views as an educator." Yet in contrast to what had been communicated verbally, the subtle messages within the culture conveyed "This is a white male-dominated environment, and we would like it to stay that way."

Again I had no sponsors because the two women who had been my champions during the interview and hiring process—one on the selection committee, and the other the college president—both left the institution shortly after I was given the position. With no vision, I settled back into the accepted cultural norms for a Mexican American woman: I taught classes, went to school events, made meals, and took care of the day-to-day domestic needs of my growing children. Hewlett explains some of the dynamics behind the appearance that women lack vision, identifying three dimensions in particular: distraction, a tendency to be overburdened with demands, and lacking time to think about their future.[6] I did not have the luxury of time to discover my leadership potential, even though I was put in a leadership role. The lack of support for developing a leadership identity was both internal and external. For example, when I saw an advertisement for a leadership program offered by Harvard University, I went to my director and requested participation. It was denied. I never looked back; I merely accepted my invisible position at the college. Gradually, though, I began to understand a valuable lesson from that disappointing experience: it helped me recognize the importance of developing a relationship with those who have academic clout.

FINDING A NICHE

Confidence and sponsorship sprouted for me when I entered a new position that offered a different context for my work. After I had ten years of experience in higher educational under my belt, I was hired by George Fox University.

In that environment, which has been shaped by its "Friends" (Quaker) roots, my strength of "context" was activated in ways that proved to be beneficial to me both personally and professionally. Context is one of thirty-four "themes of talents" identified on the Clifton StrengthsFinder instrument. According to author Tom Rath's book titled *StrengthFinder 2.0*, a person who has context as a top strength is someone who uses experiences from the past and learns from them.[7] Exactly that perspective and ability has been my forte in my rise to leadership, but it's taken a lifetime of learning to reach the point where I am today.

One aspect of my academic cultural experience became an area of distinction for me, even assisting me in developing my "currency" or expertise.[8] Being a first-generation, college-educated Latina woman has given me a perspective that is different from the traditional white male view that permeates higher education. One life lesson in particular served me well in the teaching audition that was part of the hiring process for my position at George Fox University. The discouraging experience I'd had with my thesis chairperson led me to research about writing styles. In that process, I discovered studies on the theory of "contrastive rhetoric,"[9] on which I based my teaching audition lesson about the influence of culture on students' academic writing whose primary language or culture is not English.[10] As a result, I was able to highlight the value that I brought to the university, and it landed me not only the job but also the added position of serving as director of the English Language Institute.

THE POWER OF SPONSORSHIP

As I pursued more opportunities in higher education, I began to recognize professional relationships that could be nurtured to assist me in developing my leadership identity. The appointment as director was a pivotal one, opening new doors and helping me recognize the importance of establishing my role as a leader at the institution. Knowing I needed more "coaching" in this role, I sought out the former director and founder of the program. Because she had been granted emeritus standing by the university, I have the impression that my superiors looked favorably on the fact that I had reached out to request her tutelage, in addition to developing other strategic partnerships that would enhance my leadership of the English Language Institute.

The network of relationships that has supported my professional growth and understanding was further enhanced when I was encouraged to participate in the Multi-Ethnic Leadership Development Institute. Without knowing how this program would subsequently impact my life, I leaned into the opportunity and said, "Yes." As Hewlett points out in *Forget a Mentor, Find a Sponsor*, this is an important characteristic of people who are viewed as leaders.[11]

Even the process of applying for the Multi-Ethnic Leadership Development Institute reinforced for me some valuable professional lessons. Because the application process required two letters of recommendation, I was made more fully aware of the hierarchical support that existed for my potential expanded leadership within the university. The dean and provost were the two institutional leaders who provided these letters of endorsement for my application, and although I could not have known at that time, that tangible evidence of support was also the beginning of an important sponsorship relationship.

When I attended the four-day leadership development institute near Sumas, Washington, I was uncertain of the outcome. I knew that a variety of resource leaders with diverse backgrounds and titles would be coming from across the United States to help us understand the joys and challenges of senior-level leadership, drawing from their experiences. Yet as a faculty member in leadership, I was hesitant about my contribution to this group, because most of the participants were from the administrative side of higher education.

However, we were also given a small library of leadership books and articles, some of which would be discussed at the institute. Other resources were offered in the form of case studies, becoming familiar with our Clifton StrengthsFinder results, fireside chats in the evening in which senior leaders talked about their professional journeys, web links, and one-on-one interaction with a successful leader of color. In my entire career, I had never participated in anything as unique as Multi-Ethnic Leadership Development Institute. Whereas I had spent my professional life working in an environment of white dominance, the Multi-Ethnic Leadership Development Institute gave us the opportunity to spend several days learning from, and sharing with, a room of people who had similar backgrounds and experiences.

The four-day leadership development institute was just the beginning of my journey in establishing a sponsorship relationship with two people who are critical to my work at George Fox University: my dean and my provost. Many important leadership lessons were drawn from two of the books, both authored by Sylvia Ann Hewlett, that were featured at the Multi-Ethnic Leadership Development Institute: *Executive Presence* and *Forget a Mentor, Find a Sponsor.* After attending the institute, I signed up to participate in an optional collaborative research project that involved seventeen of the Multi-Ethnic Leadership Development Institute participants. The focus of the project was to explore the effectiveness of identifying and tapping into at least one "sponsorship" relationship during the following academic year. As part of the research project, we were encouraged to respond to two or three questions that were posted online monthly on a site that was private to our group, and we had monthly conversations with group members about the topics being addressed in the electronic posts. Various aspects of this research project, and the relationships that were maintained through it, contributed to my commitment to a more purposeful pursuit of advancement. Although in the past I would have been satisfied with and grateful for my position, now I also felt a responsibility to step up and think more broadly about how my talents and knowledge could contribute to my institution.

The first skill I needed to develop more intentionally was the art of actively listening. So I listened carefully when the provost commented about having a concern about retention of our first-generation and domestic English language learners. The provost asked me if the English Language Institute (ELI) could be utilized to fill an academic gap in the transition of these students to the demands of higher education. I recognized that here was an opportunity to bring my authentic self as a Latina to my cache of leadership strengths. I had read in *Executive Presence* about the need for a leader to be authentic.[12] In fact, Hewlett had stated in that book: "Among women of color, Hispanics were the likeliest to say they'd sacrificed authenticity in order to conform."[13] Now I had the opportunity to be my authentic self and assist the next generation in achieving their goals of obtaining a degree. Through the ELI, I took on the responsibility of creating a course to help with this transition.

In addition, in *Forget a Mentor, Find a Sponsor*, Hewlett pointed out the importance of "growing her sponsor's legacy."[14] By listening to the needs of the provost, I could contribute tangibly to the retention of Latino students while also addressing a concern of the provost, and fulfilling a need that was felt within the university. According to Hewlett, these kinds of quid pro quo dynamics characterize a sponsorship relationship, with both parties benefiting while advancing a common good.

Another example of how the sponsorship relationship with my dean influenced my professional contributions, all to the benefit of the university, related to being better prepared to serve international students. I learned from my previous mistakes to be visible and receptive to the priorities of my dean. Hence, when developing a pre–master of arts in teaching program that would focus on international students, I provided the recruiters with various assessment tools to diagnose students' academic language abilities. With the dean's endorsement, I also created and recruited talented faculty who could teach the specialized courses designed with these international education graduate students in mind.

This kind of proactive spirit in wanting to serve my dean, provost, and the university with all that I had to offer related to being more visible as a leader within the institution. However, the need to be viewed and respected as a leader in relation to external constituencies still needed to be addressed. As an initial step on that journey, I obtained a position on a professional board as the state's liaison to the national advocacy conference in Washington, DC. According to Hewlett's *Forget a Mentor, Find a Sponsor* book, intentional leadership requires a sustainable relationship with sponsors that will take the name of a university to national and global level.[15] Accordingly, I pursued opportunities to present at two national conferences about the Multi-Ethnic Leadership Development Institute research project. In both settings, I represented George Fox University as I related the impact of having two sponsors as a result of my involvement in this project. One of those presentations, at the 2017 Ethnographic and Qualitative Research Conference, focused specifically on the methodology used for our Multi-Ethnic Leadership Development Institute project (a collaborative autoethnography research approach). Additionally, I was accepted as a presenter at an international conference in Singapore, which took the name of my university to an international stage.

LESSONS LEARNED AND INCLUSION

According to Hewlett, building on the core values of loyalty, trust, and exemplary performance represents a cyclical relationship between sponsors and emerging leaders. Delivering on promises related to programs in my areas of responsibility, collaborating with colleagues, and ultimately reaching nontraditional students and helping them succeed in their university aspirations has become my trademark on the road to professional advancement. My experience can be replicated in many ways and in institutions across higher education, and particularly in Christian colleges and universities where human potential and gifting should be fully affirmed and embraced. Too often, individuals who have the potential to be leaders of color are unfamiliar with this path or may not even know where to start. In *Executive Presence*, Hewlett offered this counsel: "You've got to be proactive in asserting who you are, what you stand for, and how you'd like to be perceived."[16]

As a petite Mexican American woman in the latter years of my career, stepping into the identity of being a leader has sometimes been a challenge. Yet with the rise of women in corporate America, the time is right. The face of leadership is changing; women are becoming part of the landscape. Books such as *Lean In*, *Executive Presence*, and *Forget a Mentor, Find a Sponsor* are helpful resources that can challenge and encourage institutional leaders, including for human resources personnel, to take us seriously. Looking back over my more than thirty years of experience across a variety of West

Coast academic institutions, I am thankful to have found a platform and a niche. True, thirty years ago, I perceived my ethnicity to be a deterrent to advancement, but now that same ethnicity is something to be embraced and celebrated.

Additionally, there are accessible paths to leadership within the partnerships of sponsors. The Center for Talent and Innovation discovered the "sponsor effect" and documented the fact that when protégés of color had sponsors, they were more inclined to be on a leadership track. Those without sponsors were dissatisfied with their lack of progress.[17] Although I could relate to that sense of dissatisfaction, I had no idea how to get on the right track. I have learned to listen to my sponsors and produce results that are on their radar. Being at the right place at the right time is not enough. This is where some take a misstep on their path. My ethnicity had been a challenge because my culture and generation typically were not supportive of the concept of strong female leaders. Today, however, there is a new generation, one that is looking at the global market. With specified purpose, this path is open to new leaders to fill the top ranks. From my own experience, I now know that there is room for vision and the freedom to be our authentic selves, there is the possibility of advancement by taking strategic steps, and there is the need for each individual to advance the purposes of our institutions. And for many of us at midcareer or beyond, there is also the responsibility of serving as sponsors to the next generation.

FOR DISCUSSION

1. Did the author learn from only the beneficial experiences in her journey, or do you see the negative ones being just as enriching? Explain your answer with specific examples or quotes from this chapter.

2. From the author's journey toward a reciprocal sponsorship relationship, think about how you view your career journey in terms of purpose and direction. What relational investments have you attempted, or how will you be more intentional in pursuing your journey?

3. Discuss the pertinent relationships that have lead to your present position that may parallel the ones that were mentioned in the chapter.

NOTES

1   Name deleted for privacy.

2   Sheryl Sandberg, *Lean In: Women, Work, and the Will to Lead* (New York: Knopf, 2013), 8.

3   Sylvia Ann Hewlett, *Forget a Mentor, Find a Sponsor: The New Way to Fast-Track Your Career* (Boston: Harvard Business Review, 2013), 29.

4   Sylvia Ann Hewlett, *Executive Presence: The Missing Link between Merit and Success* (New York: Harper Collins, 2014), 12.

5   Hewlett, *Forget a Mentor, Find a Sponsor*, 16.

6   Ibid., 53.

7   Tom Rath, *StrengthsFinder 2.0* (New York: Gallup Press, 2007), http://www.strengthsfinder.com/home.aspx.

8   Hewlett, *Executive Presence*, 122.

9   Robert Kaplan, "Cultural Thought Patterns in Inter-cultural Education," in *Language Learning* (Hoboken, NJ: Blackwell Publishers, 1966), 1–20.

10 Ibid., 1–20.

11 Hewlett, *Forget a Mentor*, 128.

12 Hewlett, *Executive Presence*, 147.

13 Ibid., 150.

14 Hewlett, *Forget a Mentor*, 108.

15 Ibid., 93.

16 Hewlett, *Executive Presence*, 32.

17 Ibid., 166.

Chapter Twenty-Five

GOING TO THE NEXT LEVEL: OPPORTUNITIES AND CHALLENGES FACING AFRICAN AMERICAN WOMEN LEADERS IN THE ACADEMY

ROBERTA WILBURN, EdD, ThD

Whitworth University, Associate Dean for Graduate Studies
in Education and Diversity Initiatives

Gender, race, power, and identity are inexorably intertwined in academia.
The experiences of black women administrators and faculty attest to this fact.
Women in higher education look to new challenges but find countless frustrations
in actions and decisions that are treated as painful rites of passage rather than
as painless rights of way. Yet as much as we know that an institution that is dominated
by white males is filled with promises and perils, we do not always know how to navigate
the perilous waters. We must depend on the experiences of others for guidance.
—Phyllis Strong Green, *Black Women in the Academy: Promises and Perils*

I first read this quote in 2010 while doing research for a presentation on women of color in the academy that would be given at the Oxford Round Table in England. I thought to myself, *Wow—This statement describes my life story and there must be others who have had similar experiences.* There were so many times when I faced the frustration of being treated differently, but I could not exactly tell which one of the "-isms" was at work. The intersectionality of racism and sexism has definitely been a part of my world.

I remember an experience at one of the universities where I worked when a dean asked me to attend an event at another university in his place. After being at the function for a while, I was asked by an administrator from a sister institution who I was. When I explained that I was filling in for my dean, he promptly informed me that my dean would be doing things much differently than what I was doing, had he been there. His tone conveyed disdain and made it very clear that he did not feel I represented my dean well. I was taken aback by his comment and asked myself, *Am I being treated this way because I am a female, or is it because I am African American . . . or could it be because I am both?*

The convergence of sexism and racism impacts the professional realities of many women of color who pursue careers in academia. One might expect to find more equity and diversity among the administrative and faculty ranks in the hallowed halls of intellectual pursuits, yet research has documented the reality of a significant gap when it comes to women of color in regard to rank, authority, collegial acceptance, and support. Authors Kijana Crawford and Danielle Smith make this point in an article titled *The We and the Us: Mentoring African American Women in Higher Education*: "Although we have crossed the threshold of the twenty-first century, our college and university faculties and administrators still do not come close to reflecting America's racial and class diversity."[1] In spite of the stark reality of marginality, like many women of color who have managed to survive and thrive in higher education, I have endeavored to become a catalyst for sociopolitical change. However, when I look over the course of my thirty-five years in academia, it is clear that this hasn't always been the case. As I contemplate what is next in my professional career, it is also a time of reflection on how very far I've come.

Although some professionals would be considering retirement at this point in their career, I feel energized about more fully embracing the work that God created me to do. This energy comes from viewing the work that I do as a divine calling, even as I recognize that it will continue to be fraught with opportunities and challenges. I have come to a point where I have the ability to help change the landscape of higher education through championing the cause of equity, diversity, and inclusion. In the sections that follow, I want to present four lessons that I have learned on my leadership journey that might be beneficial to others: (1) harness the power of sponsorship, (2) advocate for yourself, (3) recognize the impact of intersectionality and multiple identities, and (4) draw upon your spiritual strength.

THE EARLY YEARS OF AN ACADEMIC CAREER

I have been fortunate to have worked in a variety of higher education institutions, including predominantly white institutions, historically black colleges and universities, secular universities, and Christian institutions at both the graduate and undergraduate level. From the beginning of my career, I have held positions that combined responsibilities that were both faculty and administrative in nature. Looking back, I wish that I had known then what I know now, including the power of sponsorship.

HARNESS THE POWER OF SPONSORSHIP

Prior to participating in the Council for Christian Colleges & Universities (CCCU) Multi-Ethnic Leadership Development Institute, I had not given much thought to the topic of mentoring. Having spent years as a counselor educator, I had thought about sponsorship only in regard to support given to recovering addicts participating in the twelve-step program. I have always considered myself to be a mentor to many, but I have never actively sought out a mentor, let alone a sponsor, to support my professional journey. However, after reading Sylvia Ann Hewlett's book, *Forget a Mentor, Find a Sponsor*, I realized that I have been blessed to have several mentors and at least one sponsor. Hewlett argues that mentors differ from sponsors in the following way: "Mentors give, whereas sponsors invest."[2] In fact, the kinds of investments made by a sponsor stretch beyond those of a mentor and include advocating for your next promotion, encouraging you to take risks, and always watching out for your best interests. Sponsors invest but also expect a return on that investment, which Hewlett describes as "stellar performance and loyalty."[3] When I considered this distinction, it became clear that my former supervisor was more than a mentor—he was actually a sponsor.

In what ways was this supervisor a sponsor? First, he believed in me when he hired me, even though I had no prior experience working at a Christian university. Second, he made sure that I felt welcomed and would be successful. Third, he advocated for me, gave me honest feedback, and always "had my back,"[4] another characteristic of sponsors that was identified by Hewlett. For example, I recall being concerned about my course evaluations when going through the promotion process. At the time, I was unfamiliar with research documentation that African American women were often given unfavorable evaluations by white students.[5] And specifically, my evaluations were a concern because I taught several diversity courses and, in that context, I sometimes challenged the traditional thinking of many of our white students, which led to some negative feedback. In discussing this matter with my supervisor, he not only gave me concrete suggestions but also went to the assistant vice-president of academic affairs, who was overseeing the evaluation process, and asked that those factors be taken into consideration. Subsequently, I received the highest possible evaluation scores that put me on the trajectory for a future promotion.

My sponsor was also instrumental in my professional growth and advancement. As a senior administrator, he was in a position to restructure the entire school of education and to create new positions. In changing the organizational structure, he created two new associate dean positions, one of which was designed specifically for me. This kind of proactive advancement of my career evidenced one of Hewlett's dimensions of sponsorship; she states that "sponsors, not mentors, put you on the path to power and influence by affecting three things: pay raises, high-profile assignments, and promotions."[6] As another example of sponsorship, this same academic leader recommended me for a very prominent position on a state board. As a result, I was appointed by the governor to become a state commissioner on the Washington Charter School Commission.

Although my former supervisor fulfilled all of the requirements Hewlett identified as characterizing a sponsor, neither of us at the time used the term or was intentional about establishing a sponsorship relationship. Being a participant in a collaborative research project related to sponsorship that emerged from the CCCU's Multi-Ethnic Leadership Development Institute led me to want to formalize our sponsorship relationship. Yet, despite having a level of comfort with someone serving in this role, it felt intimidating to approach him with this request. His affirmative response that he would be honored to be my sponsor was liberating for me and changed the dynamics of our relationship. From my side, I felt greater ease in setting specific goals regarding how I wanted him to help me reach the next professional level. In turn, he seemed to be more forthcoming with his advice concerning my career, and his level of support for my professional growth increased even more. In short, being intentional about sponsorship and formalizing that kind of synergistic relationship with my supervisor has proven to be invaluable to my leadership journey.

ADVOCATE FOR YOURSELF

Over the course of my career, I have had the opportunity to work at several historically black colleges and universities. Interestingly, I had more than one white supervisor while employed in these settings. Despite the fact that I always got along well with my supervisors, I occasionally found myself in professionally challenging situations. In one case, my supervisor would take all of the credit for projects that I had worked on, such as grant writing, locating funding, and the development of successful programs. Although senior faculty members are typically given top billing over junior faculty, my contributions to these projects were not acknowledged at all. When I decided to leave six years later, my supervisor also wanted to claim ownership of books I had written that were being sold to local public schools. This became a major issue of contention, because she wanted to continue reaping the proceeds and recognition for the publications. Looking back on these experiences, I realize that although she seemed to be supportive of me as a person, she did little to empower me as a developing professional. After conceding to her wishes many times, I finally decided to advocate for myself. We eventually reached a satisfactory resolution regarding the intellectual property of my books when I took the battle, along with all of the related documentation, to the chair of the department, who was an African American male.

Through this experience, I came to understand how helpful it can be for African American women who may lack support and/or authority to build alliances with African American men who can leverage their elevated status to achieve a desired end. In a chapter titled "Rites of Passage and Rights of Way," Phyllis Strong Green described having used a similar strategy in her professional career, noting "that minority males, including Latinos and Asian Americans, were for the most part my valued allies, serving as mentors, advisors, and advocates."[7] In my case, this male administrator reviewed everything objectively and released the books and ownership rights to me. It took a lot of courage to stand up for myself, but through this process I also came to recognize that there are times when it is important—especially for African American female administrators without visible advocates—to muster up the inner gumption and advocate for yourself.

RECOGNIZE THE IMPACT OF INTERSECTIONALITY AND MULTIPLE IDENTITIES

In talking to other African American women who work in Christian higher education, I have seen that the positive atmosphere in one department is not always manifested across the university. The same issues of racism and sexism that I experienced in several of the secular institutions where I worked were part of their experience in Christian colleges and universities. Indeed, there have been times when the intersectionality of racism and sexism converged to the point where I couldn't tell which was the predominate force operating. Phyllis Strong Green described a similar scenario: "In dealing with the equity or discrimination issues, black women sometimes find themselves in the double bind of not being clearly able to separate race from gender."[8] In my case, the "-ism" did not matter, because I still felt marginalized and therefore felt ineffective in doing certain aspects of my job. The challenges become even more complex in some situations, because we may be subjected to the compounding impact of the intersectionality of divergent identities. In fact, our multiple identities may be celebrated in one segment of the campus yet not throughout the institution more broadly.

The complexities are also real and deeply felt because African Americans who seek careers in higher education are often trailblazers and trendsetters in the field. This point was made in a report issued by the American Council on Education more than a decade ago:

> Women of color continue to make history as "firsts" in many contexts within higher education. While they are no longer among the few, they are still pioneers, and in their accomplishments they continue to pave

the way for others who see in their success possibilities for themselves. As leaders, they have influenced the direction in which their institutions develop, creating welcoming inclusive environments. Through their inspiration, motivation, and desire to serve, they have modeled for others the joys of leading of higher education.[9]

The challenges posed by being a trailblazer are common to women who advance into leadership, as well as to people of color. For example, the leader of a large multinational organization commented to me, "It is tiring to be the only one of anything, because you always have to be on." As a white female, this top administrator experiences a certain level of privilege, yet also has faced challenges as a result of her gender in a male-normed profession. When we look at the intersectionality of race and gender that many African Americans face in administrative leadership roles, the circumstances are compounded. This has been my experience on more than one occasion.

When I was working in a college on the east coast, for example, my all-white staff did not want to acknowledge that I had a doctorate with more professional preparation than they had, nor did they want to refer to me as "Dr." Later, when I began to think that I had overcome the major racial battles that had confronted me, my office was broken into. Personal items were destroyed and racial epithets were written on my office wall. I was no longer dealing with passive aggressive behavior and microaggressions, but blatant acts of racism targeted directly at me.

Isolation and lack of support during critical times like these are common themes among African American women administrators in higher education. The importance of building support networks is therefore evident, and those networks should be built long before they become necessary. Allies and supportive individuals would ideally come from within our institutions, but they may also need to come from our community, churches, and other social networks. Having others who can understand what it is like to be marginalized, oppressed, and face microaggressions in the workplace can be a source of encouragement.

DRAW ON YOUR SPIRITUAL STRENGTHS

When I had no mentor or sponsor and was facing challenges, I would call on the Lord because I knew he would never leave me or forsake me. At one point, I considered giving up my career in higher education altogether to go into full-time ministry. But then the Lord prompted me to consider a position at a predominantly white, Christian university in the Pacific Northwest. Little did I know that when I prayed the prayer of Jabez, asking God to enlarge my territory (1 Chron. 4:10), I would end up on the other side of the country, leaving my adult children and grandchild behind. With my husband as my only source of family support, I packed up my belongings and made a trip across the country that was, for me, an Abrahamic journey akin to coming into the promised land.

Upon my arrival, I found that I was the only African American faculty member or administrator on campus. In the school of education where I was called to serve, I felt fully embraced and valued. I found great comfort in being surrounding by fellow believers, in a place where I was respected and I could openly share my faith. As a result, I was able to flourish. Research has identified faith and spirituality to be important sources of strength for African Americans. Wilma J. Henry and Nicole M. Glenn advised that "spirituality may be employed as a connective strategy to assist Black women in overcoming the issues of isolation and marginalization they experience in higher education."[10] Similarly, Deborah Owens identified the centrality of faith as she interviewed African American women about their professional journeys in higher education, noting "each woman described her strong faith or spirituality as an important component of her life. Their faith/spirituality provided support, helped them to stay centered, and enabled them to persevere in the face of obstacles, both personally and professionally."[11]

Now that I have spent ten years in Christian higher education, I am feeling that still small voice of the Holy Spirit nudging me, letting me know that this assignment is coming to a close because God wants to take me to the next level. After being in this positive space, I am ready to see where God is leading next. I take with me lessons learned and new knowledge that will not only help me continue to be successful in higher education but also help other African American women who are following in my footsteps.

RECOMMENDATIONS/STRATEGIES FOR PREDOMINANTLY WHITE CHRISTIAN INSTITUTIONS

Christian universities have the potential to empower administrators and faculty of color by modeling respect, embracing diversity, and encouraging inclusion based on a Christ-centered mission. Women in higher education, and particularly those who are people of color, often encounter challenges as a result of the intersectionality of racism and sexism and other discriminatory practices. The following strategies can help people of color thrive on campuses where the dominant culture is white and often male-normed:

- Provide opportunities, either informally or formally, to connect women of color with others who have paved the way and been effective on your campus or at nearby institutions, allowing for the development of supportive peers and mentors that can contribute to having a sense of community.

- Identify white allies and people of color within your university who have a passion for helping newcomers acclimate and succeed. Providing opportunities for formal or informal mentoring, particularly during the early years on a campus, can be critical in learning the culture and navigating the political landscape.
- Facilitate training, or perhaps a small group discussion of Hewlett's "sponsorship" book, that enhances awareness and support for the sponsorship model and its importance in being proactive about professional advancement.
- Ensure that faculty development and student development training equips employees with understanding and pedagogical approaches related to topics such as diverse learning styles, non-Western perspectives, and understanding privilege and power.
- Tangibly demonstrate a commitment to building communities that model "a sense of belonging," including respecting a variety of worship styles and faith traditions. Ameliorating the sense that some community members are "insiders" while others are "outsiders" can allow all individuals to align with the spiritual dimension of campus life and service that is foundational to Christian institutions.

FOR DISCUSSION

1. How can your university intentionally empower faculty and administrators of color to develop leadership skills and opportunities to move into leadership roles?

2. In what specific ways is your institution supporting female faculty and administrators of color to be successful in their professional career? Do you have a retention plan in place to help support faculty and administrators of color? What are you personally doing to help faculty and administrators of color to feel welcomed and included within your Christian college community? If you are not doing anything, what are the barriers that are keeping you from being helpful in this way?

3. Are mentorship programs utilized to help faculty and administrators of color advance into effective leaders where you work? How can you use the Hewlett book and the sponsorship model to help faculty and administrators of color assume greater leadership roles in your institution?

4. If you are a person of color, have you had mentors or sponsors in your career? If you have not, do you think they would have been helpful in your work in higher education? What do you think you can do to cultivate a mentorship or sponsorship relationship with a senior-level professional in your institution to help advance your career? If you are a white person, have you ever mentored a person of color, and what was that experience

like? If you have not, what is keeping you from assisting a colleague in this way? What skills and experiences do you believe you have that would be helpful to a faculty or administrator of color?

5. If you are a person of color, have you had others to advocate on your behalf during your career in higher education? If you have, state whether this experience was beneficial to you or not. Give a rationale for your response. If you have not had someone advocate for you, describe a time when you had to advocate for yourself or a time when you wish you had someone to advocate for you in your career in higher education.

6. If you are a white person, have you witnessed a person of color at your school being marginalized or being a victim of microaggression? How did you respond to the situation? Did you advocate for the person of color or intervene in some way? State why or why not. What do you think you can do to advocate for a faculty or administrator of color who is being marginalized at your school?

7. If you are a person of color, have you used your faith/spirituality to help deal with difficult times during your professional career? In what ways was this helpful? How have you been supported by the Christian community in your institution? How would you like to be supported by the faith community?

NOTES

1   Kijana Crawford and Danielle Smith, "The We and the Us: Mentoring African American Women," *Journal of Black Studies* 36 (1; September 2005): 52, http://www.jstor.org/stable/40027321.

2   Sylvia Ann Hewlett, *Forget a Mentor, Find a Sponsor: The New Way to Fast-Track Your Career* (Boston: Harvard Business Review, 2013), 19.

3   Ibid., 21.

4   Ibid.

5   L. A. Crouther, "Results Matter: When the Other Teacher Teaches English in the Bluegrass State," in *Women Faculty of Color in the White Classroom*, ed. L. Vargas (New York: Peter Lang, 2002), 219–36.

6   Hewlett, *Forget a Mentor*, 22.

7   Phyllis Strong Green, "Rites of Passage and Rights of Way," in *Black Women in the Academy: Promises and Perils* (Gainesville: University of Florida Press, 1997), 155.

8   Ibid., 155.

9   Summit for Women of Color Administrators and Faculty in Higher Education, *Leadership through Achievement: Women of Color in Higher Education* (Washington, DC: American Council on Education, 2005), iii.

10 Wilma J. Henry and Nicole M. Glen, "Black Women Employed in the Ivory Tower: Connecting for Success," *Advancing Women in Leadership Journal* (2009), 1–18.

11 Deborah L. Owens, "Black Women in Higher Education: Negotiating the Cultural Workplace," in *Building Bridges for Women of Color in Higher Education: A Practical Guide for Success*, ed. Conchita Y. Battle and Chontrese M. Doswell (Lanham, MD: University Press of America, 2004), 85.

For Further Reading

Banaji, Mahzarin R., and Anthony G. Greenwald. *Blindspot: Hidden Biases of Good People.* New York: Delacorte Press, 2013.

Barber, Leroy. *Embrace: God's Radical Shalom for a Divided World.* Downers Grove, IL: InterVarsity Press, 2016.

Barndt, Joseph. *Understanding and Dismantling Racism: The Twenty-First Century Challenge to White America.* Minneapolis: Fortress Press, 2007.

Bonilla-Silva, Eduardo. *Racism without Racists: Color-Blind Racism and the Persistence of Racial Inequality in America.* 5th edition. Lanham, MD: Rowman & Littlefield, 2017.

Box, Kim. *Woven Leadership: The Power of Diversity to Transform Your Organization for Success.* Gold River, CA: Authority Publishing, 2011.

Bradley, Anthony B. *Aliens in the Promised Land: Why Minority Leadership Is Overlooked in White Churches and Institutions.* Phillipsburg, NJ: P&R Publishing, 2013.

———. *Black Scholars in White Space: New Vistas in African American Studies from the Christian Academy.* Eugene, OR: Wipf and Stock, 2015.

Brown, Michael, Martin Carnoy, Elliot Currie, Troy Duster, David Oppenheimer, Marjorie Shultz, and David Wellman. *Whitewashing Race: The Myth of a Color-Blind Society.* Revised edition. Berkeley, CA: University of California Press, 2005.

Chang, Heewon, Karen A. Longman, and Marla A. Franco. "Leadership Development through Mentoring in Higher Education: A Collaborative Autoethnography of Leaders of Color." In *Mentoring & Tutoring: Partnership in Learning,* 22, no. 4 (2014): 373–89.

Chang, Jeff. *We Gon' Be Alright: Notes on Race and Resegregation.* New York: Picador Press, 2016.

Chin, Jean Lau, and Joseph E. Trimble. *Diversity and Leadership.* Thousand Oaks, CA: SAGE Publications, 2014.

Clark, Christine, Kenneth J. Fasching-Varner, and Mark Brimhall-Vargas, eds. *Occupying the Academy: Just How Important Is Diversity Work in Higher Education?* Lanham, MD: Rowman & Littlefield, 2012.

Cleveland, Christena. *Disunity in Christ: Uncovering the Hidden Forces That Keep Us Apart.* Downers Grove, IL: InterVarsity Press, 2013.

Coates, Ta-Nehisi. *Between the World and Me.* New York: Random House Books, 2015.

Collins, Christopher S. and Alexander Jun. *White Out: Understanding White Privilege and Dominance in a Modern Age.* New York: Peter Lang, 2017.

Collins, Patricia Hill. *Black Feminist Thought: Knowledge, Consciousness, and the Politics of Empowerment.* New York: Routledge, 2008.

Collins, Patricia Hill, and Sirma Bilge. *Intersectionality (Key Concepts).* Cambridge, UK: Polity Press, 2016.

Davis, Jeff. *The First Generation Student Experience: Implications for Campus Practice, and Strategies for Improving Persistence and Success.* Sterling, VA: Stylus Publishing, 2012.

Delgado, Richard, and Jean Stefancic. *Critical Race Theory: An Introduction.* New York: New York University Press, 2012.

DiAngelo, Robin. "White Fragility." In *International Journal of Critical Pedagogy* 3, no. 3 (2011): 54–70.

Emerson, Michael O., and Christian Smith. *Divided by Faith: Evangelical Religion and the Problem of Race in America.* Oxford: Oxford University Press, 2000.

Emerson, Michael O., and George Yancey. *Transcending Racial Barriers: Toward a Mutual Obligations Approach.* Oxford: Oxford University Press, 2010.

Ginsberg, Margery B., and Raymond J. Wlodkowski. *Diversity and Motivation: Culturally Responsive Teaching in College.* Hoboken, NJ: Wiley, 2009.

Glaud, Eddie. *Democracy in Black: How Race Still Enslaves the American Soul.* New York: Broadway Books, 2016.

Gordon, Wayne, and John Perkins. *Do All Lives Matter: The Issues We Can No Longer Ignore and the Solutions We All Long For*. Ada, MI: Baker Publishing, 2017.

Harper, Shaun R., and Sylvia Hurtado. "Nine Themes in Campus Racial Climates and Implications for Institutional Transformation." In *New Directions for Student Services 2007*, 120 (2007): 7–24.

Harvey, Jennifer. *Dear White Christians: For Those Still Longing for Racial Reconciliation*. Grand Rapids: Eerdmans, 2014.

Hernandez, Kathy C., Faith W. Ngunjiri, and Heewon Chang. "Exploiting the Margins in Higher Education: A Collaborative Autoethnography of Three Foreign-Born Female Faculty of Color." In *International Journal of Qualitative Studies in Education* 28, no. 5 (2015): 533–51. doi: 10.1080/09518398.2014.933910.

Isenberg, Nancy. *White Trash: The 400-Year Untold History of Class in America*. New York: Penguin Books USA, 2016.

Joeckel, Samuel, and Thomas Chesnes. *The Christian College Phenomenon: Inside America's Fastest Growing Institutions of Higher Learning*. Abilene, TX: Abilene Christian University Press, 2011.

Jones, Robert P. *The End of White Christian America*. New York: Simon & Schuster, 2016.

Katongole, Emmanuel, and Chris Rice. *Reconciling All Things: A Christian Vision for Justice, Peace and Healing*. Downers Grove, IL: InterVarsity Press, 2008.

Keller, Timothy. *Generous Justice: How God's Grace Makes Us Just*. New York: Riverhead Books, 2012.

Kendall, Frances. *Understanding White Privilege: Creating Pathways to Authentic Relationships across Race*. Abingdon, UK: Routledge, 2012.

Kivel, Paul. *Uprooting Racism: How White People Can Work for Justice*. 3rd edition. Gabriola Island, BC, Canada: New Society Publishers, 2011.

Livermore, David. *Cultural Intelligence: Improving Your CQ to Engage Our Multicultural World*. Grand Rapids: Baker Academic Press, 2009.

McIntosh, Peggy, and Paula S. Rothenberg. *White Privilege: Essential Readings on the Other Side of Racism*. 5th edition. London: Worth Publishers, 2015.

McNeil, Brenda S. *Roadmap to Reconciliation: Moving Communities into Unity, Wholeness, and Justice*. Downers Grove, IL: InterVarsity Press, 2015.

McNeil, Brenda S., and Rick Richardson. *The Heart of Racial Justice: How Soul Change Leads to Social Change*. Downers Grove, IL: InterVarsity Press, 2004.

Moore, Eddie, Jr., Marguerite W. Penick-Parks, and Ali Michael, eds. *Everyday White People Confront Racial & Social Injustice: 15 Stories*. Sterling, VA: Stylus Publishing, 2015.

Morris, Monique. *Pushout: The Criminalization of Black Girls in Schools*. New York: The New Press, 2016.

Omi, Michael, and Howard Winant. *Racial Formation in the United States*. 3rd edition. New York: Routledge, 2015.

Park, Andrew Sung. *Racial Conflict and Healing: An Asian-American Theological Perspective*. Eugene, OR: Wipf and Stock, 2009.

Park, Julie J. *When Diversity Drops: Race, Religion, and Affirmative Action in Higher Education*. New Brunswick, NJ: Rutgers University Press, 2013.

Pope, Raechele, Amy Reynolds, and John Mueller. *Creating Multicultural Change on Campus*. San Francisco: Jossey-Bass, 2014.

Priest, Robert, and Alvaro Nieves. *This Side of Heaven: Race, Ethnicity, and Christian Faith*. Oxford: Oxford University Press, 2007.

Quaye, Stephen John, and Shaun R. Harper. *Student Engagement in Higher Education: Theoretical Perspectives and Practical Approaches for Diverse Populations*. New York: Routledge, 2014.

Rah, Soong-Chan. *The Next Evangelicalism: Freeing the Church from Western Cultural Captivity*. Downers Grove, IL: InterVarsity Press, 2009.

———. *Prophetic Lament: A Call for Justice in Troubled Times*. Downers Grove, IL: InterVarsity Press, 2015.

Rothenberg, Paula S. *White Privilege: Essential Readings on the Other Side of Racism.* New York: Worth Publishers, 2002.

Sanders, Cody J., and Angela Yarber. *Microaggressions in Ministry: Confronting the Hidden Violence of Everyday Church.* Louisville, KY: Westminster John Knox Press, 2015.

Shaules, Joseph. *The Intercultural Mind: Connecting Culture, Cognition, and Global Living.* Boston: Intercultural Press, 2015.

Shelton, Jason, and Michael Emerson. *Blacks and Whites in Christian America: How Racial Discrimination Shapes Religious Convictions.* New York: New York University Press, 2012.

Smith, Daryl G. *Diversity and Inclusion in Higher Education: Emerging Perspectives on Institutional Transformation.* Abingdon, UK: Routledge, 2014.

———. *Diversity's Promise for Higher Education: Making It Work.* 2nd edition. Baltimore: Johns Hopkins University Press, 2015.

Stanley, Christine A. "Coloring the Academic Landscape: Faculty of Color Breaking the Silence in Predominantly White Colleges and Universities." In *American Educational Research Journal 43, no. 4* (2006): 701-736. doi:10.3102/00028312043004701

Steele, Claude. *Whistling Vivaldi: And Other Clues to How Stereotypes Affect Us.* New York: W. W. Norton & Company, 2010.

Stevenson, Bryan. *Just Mercy: A Story of Justice and Redemption.* Reprint edition. New York: Spiegel & Grau, 2015.

Sue, Derald Wing. *Microaggressions and Marginality Manifestation, Dynamics, and Impact.* Hoboken, NJ: Wiley, 2010.

Tatum, Beverly Daniel. *Why Are All the Black Kids Sitting Together in the Cafeteria? And Other Conversations about Race.* Revised edition. New York: Basic Books, 2003.

Taylor, Keeanga-Yamahtta. *From #Blacklivesmatter to Black Liberation.* Chicago: Haymarket Books, 2016.

Terrell, L. Strayhorn. *College Students' Sense of Belonging a Key to Educational Success for All Students.* New York: Routledge, 2012.

Wallis, Jim. *America's Original Sin: Racism, White Privilege, and the Bridge to a New America.* Grand Rapids: Brazos Press, 2016.

West, Cornel. *Race Matters.* 2nd edition. New York: Vintage Books, 2001.

Williams, Damon A. *Strategic Diversity Leadership: Activating Change and Transformation in Higher Education.* Sterling, VA: Stylus Publishing, 2013.

Wise, Tim. *Color-Blind: The Rise of Post-Racial Politics and the Retreat from Racial Equity.* San Francisco: City Lights Books/Open Media Series, 2010.

———. *White Like Me: Reflections on Race from a Privileged Son.* 3rd edition. Berkeley, CA: Soft Skull Press, 2011.

Yancey, George A. *Compromising Scholarship: Religious and Political Bias in American Higher Education.* Waco, TX: Baylor University Press, 2011.

———. *Neither Jew Nor Gentile: Exploring Issues of Racial Diversity on Protestant College Campuses.* Oxford: Oxford University Press, 2010.

About the Contributors

Allison N. Ash is Dean of Student Care and Graduate Student Life at Wheaton College. Her prior experience includes working seven years in full-time church ministry in Michigan and Texas and serving as an administrator at Fuller Theological Seminary in Pasadena, California, where she also earned her Master of Divinity degree. She is the coauthor of several publications related to racial diversity in Christian higher education, including "Pathways to Success for Students of Color in Christian Colleges: The Role of Institutional Integrity and Sense of Community" and "The Paradox of Faith: White Administrators and Anti-Racism Advocacy in Christian Higher Education," both published in *Christian Higher Education*. Ash serves on a research team that explores the experiences of white administrators active in racial justice advocacy in Christian higher education institutions. She is currently completing her PhD in higher education from Azusa Pacific University and enjoys roasting marshmallows and going to parks with her husband and two young daughters.

Andrea Cook has been dedicated to higher education for forty years, holding positions at Judson Baptist College, University of Oregon, George Fox University, and Goshen College before assuming the role of Vice-President of Institutional Advancement at Warner Pacific. She was inaugurated as the College's seventh and first female President in September 2009. Cook holds a bacheor's degree in Elementary Education from Northwest Nazarene University and both a master's degree and a PhD in Educational Policy and Management from the University of Oregon. During her time at Warner Pacific, Cook has led the institution to embrace its urban identity. Through specially tailored programs, diverse, first-generation students are achieving their higher education goals, paving the way to a brighter future.

Kimberly Battle-Walters Denu is the Vice-President and Chief Diversity Officer at Azusa Pacific University. She has a master's degree in Social Work from Temple University, and a doctorate in Sociology, with an emphasis in race and family, from the University of Florida. Denu received a Fulbright Scholar award to teach and conduct research in South Africa and has published articles on African American issues, women, and family matters. Her book *Sheila's Shop: Working-Class African American Women Talk about Life, Love, Race, and Hair* was listed in a Los Angeles newspaper as one of the top ten African American books. She and her mother coedited a book entitled *Mothers Are Leaders* (ACU Press, 2014). In addition, Denu is an ordained minister who does ministry work around the globe.

Like a medical doctor who cures ailing patients, **Edwin F. Estevez** is passionate about healing the woes that leave organizations struggling to function at an optimum level. For more than twenty-two years, Estevez has delivered transformational growth to individuals, groups, and organizations by providing the remedy to complex problems. Employing big-picture analysis to enhance project and risk management efforts, Estevez understands how to change an organization's culture and help its people grow. The Dominican Republic native holds an undergraduate degree in Social Work from Greenville College and graduate degrees in Social Work, Education, and Administration, including a master's degree in Social Work from Washington University-St. Louis and a doctorate in Administration from St. Louis University. Before his current role as Senior Vice-President and Chief Operations Officer at Greenville University, Estevez also served as Provost overseeing Academics, Admissions, and Student Development.

As Associate Dean, **Rukshan Fernando** helps to manage the School of Behavioral and Applied Sciences at Azusa Pacific University in Los Angeles, California. Fernando has lived in the urban core of Colombo, Sri Lanka, the rural cornfields of Indiana, and in the dynamic metro regions of Washington, DC, and Los Angeles. These community contexts empowered him to pursue a life of reconciliation and restoration between and among people in Christian higher education, the local community, and the church. Fernando has also served as a consultant to World Vision Sri Lanka, the Department of Housing and Urban Development, and the Department of Treasury.

Leah Fulton is a Common Ground Consortium fellow at the University of Minnesota where she is pursuing a PhD in Organizational Leadership with an emphasis in Higher Education. Prior to full-time doctoral studies, she spent nearly eight years in Christian higher education with student development, including five years at Bethel University in Saint Paul, Minnesota. More than four years of Fulton's time at Bethel were spent as the Associate Dean of Intercultural Student Programs and Services where she provided oversight for a number of diversity initiatives, including the successful implementation of a campus cultural center and the Act Six Leadership program. Fulton's interests are related to organizational leadership, student success, culture, and women in the workplace. Her research has previously been published in the journal *Growth*.

Kathy-Ann C. Hernandez was born and raised on the twin island republic of Trinidad and Tobago. She is a professor in the College of Business and Leadership at Eastern University. Hernandez earned her doctorate in Educational Psychology from Temple University where she received the Marlene Smigel Korn Humanitarian Award (2004) for excellent contribution in teaching, scholarship, and/or service from the College of Education. Hernandez is a scholar/activist who has collaborated to conceptualize and lead several university-community partnership programs for underserved populations including the Bill Cosby Academic Posse Program and the Temple University After-school Program. Her research is focused on the Black Diaspora and the salience of race/ethnicity, gender, and social context in identity formation, leadership development, and social and academic outcomes.

Rebecca Hernandez currently serves as Associate Vice-President of Intercultural Engagement and Faculty Development at George Fox University. Previously, she served as a Center Director and Associate Dean at Goshen College from 2008 to 2014. Through her work in administrative roles in academia, government, and non-profit sectors, Hernandez has developed and advocated for policies and programs to serve diverse communities through health and education. She completed her BA at Southeastern College, MPA at Portland State University, and PhD in Human Development and Family Studies at Oregon State University. Hernandez grew up in Nampa, Idaho, where her family settled after working as migrant farmworkers. She enjoys travel, meeting new people, and spending time with her eighteen (and counting) nieces and nephews.

Shirley V. Hoogstra is the seventh President of the Council for Christian Colleges & Universities. In this role, Hoogstra combines her zeal for the rule of law and her passion for Christian higher education as she promotes the value and purpose of high quality, Christ-centered liberal arts education that shapes the heart, soul, and mind. For fifteen years, Hoogstra served as Vice-President for Student Life at her alma mater, Calvin College, which prepared her for many of the issues facing higher education today. She also has been a leader in the legal profession, having spent more than a decade practicing law as a partner at a firm specializing in litigation in New Haven, Connecticut, and serving as President of the New Haven Bar Association and Foundation.

Brian M. Howell came straight from his graduate program at Washington University in St. Louis to Wheaton College in 2001 to teach Cultural Anthropology. His graduate research on Philippine Protestantism became the foundation of his first book (*Christianity in the Local Context*, 2008), but it was his participation in a multicultural congregation in St. Louis that did the most to push forward his interest in race, equality, and education. While at Wheaton, Howell wrote two other books (*Short Term Mission*, 2012, and *Introducing Cultural Anthropology* [with Jenell Williams Paris], 2011), in addition to articles and book chapters addressing questions of culture, Christianity, conflict, race, and identity. Howell has three children and lives in Wheaton, Illinois, with his wife, Marissa Sabio.

Jeanette Hsieh is Provost Emerita at Trinity International University in Deerfield, Illinois. Previously at Trinity, she served as Interim President, Executive Vice-President/Provost, the Susan Stover Chair for Leadership, and Professor of Education. The Jeanette Hsieh Chair for Educational Leadership was given in her honor and is occupied by the Director of the PhD (Educational Studies) program at Trinity Evangelical Divinity School. Prior to Trinity, Hsieh chaired the education departments at Wheaton College (Wheaton, Illinois) and Judson University (Elgin, Illinois). She also served as President of the Illinois Association of Colleges for Teacher Education and the Illinois Association for Teacher Education in Private Colleges. Hsieh served on the boards of David C. Cook Ministries, Illinois Association for Supervision and Curriculum Development, Ecker Center for Mental Health, and Wheaton College.

Lisa Ishihara has held the role of Director of Chapel Programs at Biola University since 2008. She earned an undergraduate degree from California State University at Fullerton in Business Administration and a Master of Divinity and a Master of Arts in Spiritual Formation and Soul Care from Talbot School of Theology. As a member of the Evangelical Spiritual Directors Association, she has led prayer services and soul care retreats and worked as a speaker and spiritual director. Prior to campus ministry, she worked in the church for ten years and as an Executive Team Leader for the Target Corporation. She is ordained in the Free Methodist Church and loves her multigenerational church. In her free time, she enjoys sharing a good meal with friends and family and traveling to beautiful places.

Alexander Jun is Professor of Higher Education at Azusa Pacific University. He has published extensively on college access for disenfranchised students, and he conducts research on equity and justice in higher education. He is the author of *From Here to University: Access, Mobility, and Resilience among Urban Latino Youth* (2001). A TED speaker and international scholar, Jun was a Global Fellow with the Center for Khmer Studies (CKS) in Cambodia and International Research Fellow with the National Centre for Student Equity in Higher Education (NCSEHE) at Curtin University in Perth, Australia. Jun is Associate Editor of *The Journal of Behavioral and Social Sciences*. His latest book with coauthor Christopher Collins is entitled *White Out: Understanding White Privilege and Dominance in the Modern Age* (2017).

Glen K. Kinoshita currently serves as the Director of Imago Dei Initiatives at Biola University. In this role, Kinoshita seeks to enhance cultural competency and cultivate inclusive excellence throughout the Biola community and beyond to honor the Image of God in all of us. He previously served for twenty-two years as the Director of Multi-Ethnic Programs. Kinoshita's professional background includes diversity training for both secular and Christian institutions, serving ethnically and socioeconomically diverse student populations, and creating learning communities for staff and faculty to engage on topics of diversity. He is the founder and current director of the national SCORR conference (Student Congress on Racial Reconciliation) and has produced several documentary films and articles on enhancing diversity within Christian institutions.

Karen A. Longman is the PhD Program Director and Professor of Doctoral Higher Education at Azusa Pacific University. She also serves as a Senior Fellow of the Council for Christian Colleges & Universities (CCCU), where she worked for nineteen years as Vice-President for Professional Development and Research. In 2016, Longman's contributions to Christian higher education were recognized through receiving the John R. Dellenback Global Leadership Award. Longman is coediting *Christian Higher Education: An International Journal of Research, Theory, and Practice* and an eight-volume book series being sponsored by the International Leadership Association focused on Women and Leadership—the first volume is titled *Women and Leadership in Higher Education*. She holds a PhD in Higher Education from the University of Michigan.

Aisha Lowe is a passionate educator who has dedicated her life to improving education for youth and communities. Lowe serves as Associate Professor of Education at William Jessup University, where she oversees the thesis research of future teachers in training. She also serves as the Associate Dean of the Office of Academic Research, leading the university's Strategic Academic Research Plan and academic grant making. Lowe uses her research on effective strategies for educating students of color to help K–12 and college faculty identify and combat their own implicit biases, and create classroom environments of acceptance and belonging to fully support students and maximize their academic outcomes. Lowe received her bachelor's degree in Psychology, her master's in Sociology, and her PhD in Education from Stanford University.

Michelle R. Loyd-Paige completed her graduate work at Purdue University, earning both a master's and a doctoral degree in Sociology. Currently serving as the Executive Associate to the President for Diversity and Inclusion at Calvin College, Loyd-Paige is responsible for leading deep, meaningful, and pervasive change in the way the college understands and practices diversity and inclusion. Prior to her current role, Loyd-Paige—a tenured member of the Department of Sociology and Social Work at Calvin College— taught classes on diversity for twenty-two years and served for nine years as the Dean for Multicultural Affairs at Calvin College. Her work outside the college includes chairing the CCCU Commission on Diversity and Inclusion and serving as a college representative to the West Michigan President's Compact.

Pete C. Menjares is Senior Fellow for Diversity with the Council for Christian Colleges & Universities and currently serves at Vanguard University of Southern California as Senior Director of the Institute for Faculty Development. With over two decades of leadership in the CCCU, he has held various roles as a tenured faculty member and administrator at Biola University, as the eleventh president of Fresno Pacific University, and member of the Board of Trustees at Seattle Pacific University. His commitment to diversity and racial harmony is rooted in an understanding of God's kingdom as inclusive and just; he continues to serve as a resource to presidents, boards, campus leaders, faculty, staff, and students across the CCCU who seek to nurture communities of intercultural learning.

Kristy Paredes-Collins is the Dean of Enrollment Management at Pepperdine University, where she leads a team of forty individuals in the Offices of Admission, Financial Assistance, and International Student Services. Prior to serving in this role, she held a variety of admission-related roles, as a doctoral writing consultant, Special Assistant to the Provost at Azusa Pacific University, and as Associate Editor for the journal *Christian Higher Education*. She earned a BA and an MA from Pepperdine and a PhD in Higher Education from Azusa Pacific University. Paredes-Collins's scholarly research focuses on the intersection between spirituality and diversity in Christian higher education. Paredes-Collins and her husband, Chris, live in Malibu, California, with Mateo and Adela, their two beautiful children via the miracle of adoption.

David L. Parkyn has dedicated his professional career to teaching undergraduates and leading institutions of higher learning. A graduate of Messiah College, he holds a master's degree from Gordon-Conwell Theological Seminary and a PhD in higher education from Boston College. Early in his career, Parkyn held faculty appointments at Endicott College and Messiah College. Subsequently, he was Executive Assistant to the President and then Senior Vice-President at Messiah College. After serving as Provost at Elizabethtown College, he began an eleven-year tenure as President of North Park University in Chicago. Raised in Guatemala as the son of church workers, Parkyn's scholarly interests include the intersection of religion and politics in Latin America, and religious folk art in Guatemala. He also writes and speaks frequently on topics related to higher education.

Yvonne RB-Banks recently served as Dean for the Center of Academic Programs for Support Services and was in an administrative post from 1998 to 2015 at the University of Northwestern. Prior to that, she worked for sixteen years in K–12 public education. Her international travels, speaking engagements, various publications, board affiliations, and scholarship center on themes related to educational equity, inclusion, and leadership. She is a founding member of the Minnesota Chapter of the Association of Black Women in Higher Education, a rich resource for mentoring new scholars. Serving with the Coalition to Increase Teachers of Color and American Indians (MN) allows her to work as a core advocate. She consults on projects related to educational reform and follows her teaching passion, doing so in both traditional and online settings.

Gladys Robalino is an Associate Professor at Messiah College. She holds a BA in Linguistics from the Pontificia Universidad Católica del Ecuador, an MEd from Universidad Tecnológica Equinoccial (Ecuador), an MA in Hispanic Studies from McGill University (Canada), and a PhD in Spanish Literature from Vanderbilt University. Her doctoral dissertation on the plays of Ruiz de Alarcón studies colonial voices in seventeenth-century Mexico. She has published scholarly articles in *Bulletin of the Comediantes*, *Alarconiana*, and *Comedia Performance*. Robalino's teaching and research interests are on sixteenth-century chronicles of discovery and conquest as well as seventeenth-century theater and novels with a particular focus on transatlantic themes, identity, and gender issues. She currently chairs the Modern Languages Department at Messiah College.

Jennifer W. Shewmaker is Professor of Psychology and the Assistant Provost for Teaching, Learning, and Inquiry at Abilene Christian University in Abilene, Texas. She graduated with her bachelor's in Psychology from Abilene Christian University and her PhD in Psychology from Texas Woman's University. Shewmaker is a nationally certified school psychologist who has worked with hundreds of families, children, teachers, and community organizations in her career. She is a graduate of the HERS Leadership Institute, the American Psychological Association's Leadership Institute for Women, the CCCU Women's Advanced Leadership Institute, and the Center for Courage & Renewal's Academy for Leaders. Shewmaker is a cofounder of the ACU Master Teacher Program, helping faculty use research-based teaching practices and peer observation to promote greater student learning.

Rodney Sisco, Director of Multicultural Development at Wheaton College, has consistently provided leadership in Wheaton's developing diverse community. He has served on the Racial Harmony Commission of the CCCU, the Board of the National Christian Multicultural Student Leaders Conference, and the Diversity Taskforce of the Association of Christians in Student Development (ACSD). Presently, he serves on the Executive Committee of ACSD, where he was recognized with the Jane Higa Award for Racial Harmony. Sisco is a transformational leader with a history of leadership in increasingly complex situations, bringing a global perspective including strategic planning, diversity and inclusion, leadership, and communication. He has developed a reputation for guiding and leading people to excel and to develop their own unique abilities. He and his wife, Hasana, run the PennaSis Group.

David F. Turk has been Provost and Vice-President of Academic Affairs at Nyack College since 2003. A "lifer" at the College, Turk has also served as Director of the Higher Education Opportunity Program, Head of the English Department, and Vice-President of the NYC Campus. He did his undergraduate work at Nyack and received his MA and PhD in English and American Literature from New York University. Having taught a wide range of literature classes at Nyack and having directed over twenty plays and musicals, Turk continues to teach and even direct occasionally. He frequently leads book discussions at public libraries near Nyack and has lead a number of site team evaluation visits for the Middle States Commission on Higher Education. Currently, he serves the CCCU on the Diversity Commission. With his wife of forty-three years, Dr. Vara Neverow, Turk enjoys hiking, gardening, and traveling to world cities.

Rebecca Torres Valdovinos is currently Director and Assistant Professor for the English Language Institute at George Fox University in Oregon. Her career has spanned the West Coast states for the past thirty years in education. She was born in the *barrio* of East Los Angeles, which shaped her understanding of the urban experience. She started as a preschool teacher with LA's county Parks and Recreation Department. Her undergraduate degree is from the University of California at Santa Barbara. She has received a number of teaching credentials from California, Oregon, and Washington. Valdovinos's graduate work in teaching started at the University of Southern California and was completed at California State University Los Angeles. She has been an international TESOL presenter in Asia, including conference presentations in Singapore and Mainland China.

Sarah Visser serves as Vice-President for Student Life at Calvin College. A 2001 Calvin graduate, Sarah spent more than twelve years working in higher education institutions in southern California, serving in both faculty and administrative roles. She completed her PhD in higher education at Claremont Graduate University, where her research focused on diversity and change, exploring how institutions build capacity in the area of diversity. She has a passion for engaging scholarship and praxis related to social justice issues, with specializations in organizational culture, gender studies, and identity development. Sarah and her husband of sixteen years, Matt, reside in Grand Rapids, Michigan, with their three children, Emma, Max, and Adelyn.

Roberta Wilburn is the Associate Dean for graduate studies in Education and Diversity Initiatives at Whitworth University. In addition to setting the vision and mission for eleven graduate programs in Education, Wilburn develops and coordinates diversity initiatives across the School of Education. She has held a variety of positions, including Chair of the Division of Education, Director of International Studies, Founder and Director of Global Village Child Development and Family Studies Center (a laboratory school), and Coordinator for Early Childhood Education. Her research interests are aligned with her career's focus on diversity, equity, and inclusion in the context of leadership development, counseling, and education.

As Assistant Director of Residence Life, **Kevin Williams Jr.,** until recently, oversaw the Special Interest Houses and the SALT House through the Student Affairs division at Messiah College. He enjoys new initiatives and helping to shape and determine direction for projects and research. Williams taught a class called "Engaging Harrisburg" in which he helped students engage the city through the lens of the kingdom, not just the media. He served on Messiah College's grant team through the Office on Violence Against Women. Williams and his family love road trips, movies, and telling jokes. Upon the conclusion of writing his chapter, Kevin made a job transition and will now serve as Director of Residence Life and Restorative Justice Coordinator at Bluffton University in Ohio.

ENDORSEMENTS

"What is taught (content) matters greatly, but so does who teaches it and what experience they bring (voice). Diversity matters because education, deep and broad education, is worth it. I'm excited to support the release of this new and much-needed study on the value of racial diversity in the future of Christian higher education."

—**Ken Wytsma**, President, Kilns College, Founder of The Justice Conference, author of *Pursuing Justice*, *The Grand Paradox*, and *Create vs. Copy*

"This book brings together a diverse set of voices and is filled with truth, grace, conviction, and hope. *Diversity Matters* invites readers to assess both their personal diversity journey as well as their institution's history and diversity efforts. As a consultant with colleges and universities for many years, I am confident that *Diversity Matters* is a significant and timely new resource that will contribute to ensuring that campuses more fully reflect the values and commitments of the Kingdom of God. I highly recommend it!"

—**Brenda Salter McNeil**, President, Salter McNeil & Associates, author, *Roadmap to Reconciliation*

"This book is a breath of fresh air in Christian education. It represents the stories of experienced educators of color along with others who share their desire to see Christian colleges flourish—the work of diversity being at the center of this flourishing."

—**Leroy Barber**, The Voices Project, Board Chair Mission Alliance

"Compelling. I was immediately swept into the first person honest accounts of pursuing diversity in Christian higher education. Courageous leadership in following the teachings of Scripture to shape the future of our nation. Convicting but at the same time instructive in developing a diverse campus of faculty, students, and staff. The principles are applicable beyond higher education. A seminal book!"

—**Jo Anne Lyon**, Ambassador, General Superintendent Emerita, The Wesleyan Church

"For years we have worked with Christian colleges and universities, looking for ways to faithfully serve the increasingly diverse landscape of Christianity in America. *Diversity Matters* is an answered prayer. This tome masterfully weaves together the biblical and theological imperatives on diversity with the practical lessons of university leaders charting the way forward. This is a must-read for twenty-first-century Christian educators and visionaries."

—**Rev. Dr. Gabriel Salguero**, President, National Latino Evangelical Coalition, Pastor, Calvario City Church

"Ask a leader about diversity and you might hear a vision; ask a colleague, she may provide a thoughtful proposition; ask a friend, he may tell you a story. Compile several together and you have elements to drive a transformative movement. In this book, leaders provide a compelling vision, colleagues give helpful instruction, and friends relate persuasive stories that prompt action. We must get better at engaging with diversity. I will use this volume in my leadership for that purpose."

—**Dr. Edee M. Schulze**, Vice-President for Student Life, Westmont College, and President of the Association for Christians in Student Development (ACSD)

"I have no doubt that people who read this volume will be blessed, challenged, helped, stretched, encouraged, and perhaps even disappointed at the state of things. They will find much with which they agree and from which they can learn while also being pushed to reflect on a number of diverse perspectives that dot the chapters throughout this volume. The editors who envisioned and orchestrated the writing of this book are to be commended for fostering these serious conversations. All readers will want to celebrate the call to authentic racial reconciliation while offering gratitude for the guidance that is provided regarding genuine kingdom diversity."

—**David S. Dockery**, President, Trinity International University

"Diversity is an essential component of any healthy university; but at a Christ-centered university, it is even more essential. Diversity is not just an educational value; it's a biblical priority. But growing in this area is easier said than done. That's why we need resources to help us to better embody the biblical value of diversity."

—**Barry H. Corey**, President of Biola University, author of *Love Kindness: Discover the Power of a Forgotten Christian Virtue*

"*Diversity Matters* is a groundbreaking and revolutionary book that shatters the myth of 'one way (teaching style, chapel services, student events, etc.) fits all' in Christian higher education institutions. Engaging biblical principles, using practical application tools, and affirming personal experiences from this book will revolutionize your campus culture, nurture a revival climate, and reveal the greatest assets on a college and university campus. I challenge each administrator to make *Diversity Matters* a non-negotiable read for your campus community."

—**Doretha O'Quinn, PhD**, Provost and Vice-President for Academic Affairs, Vanguard University, author of *Silent Voices, Powerful Messages*

"Christian universities should be known for reconciliation. More often, they are places of pain for persons of color and justice-minded whites. Powerful contributions from so many voices within Christian higher education make this volume a treasure trove of case studies, curricular/cocurricular initiatives, and lessons in resilience. Scholarly and accessible, thorough and concise, practical and inspirational, the Gospel and the future demand that this book is a must-read for all Christian institutions and organizations."

—**Curtiss Paul DeYoung**, CEO, Minnesota Council of Churches, formerly professor of Reconciliation Studies, Bethel University

"At a critical juncture in Christian higher education, *Diversity Matters* introduces voices vital for us to hear. Multifaceted narratives—deeply personal yet broadly communal—give form to the complexities of race and ethnicity. With clarity and grace, these voices offer practical wisdom and future directions marked by urgency and redemptive hope. I highly recommend this book to academic administrators and faculty as a valuable conduit for increasing understanding, action, and systemic change within our institutions."

　　—**Janet Sommers**, PhD, Senior Vice-President for Academic Affairs, professor of English & Literature, University of Northwestern - St. Paul

"In a hurting world and polarized society, Christian higher education should be distinctive, especially in matters of diversity. In the many stories and reflections provided in this volume, there is ample evidence of missteps and failures. But this chorus of diverse educational leaders presents a gift to help us move forward in ways that will not only allow faith based colleges and universities to better reflect the calling of Scripture, but also influence congregations and communities that their graduates will lead."

　　—**Dr. Steven Timmermans**, Executive Director, The Christian Reformed Church in North America

"*Diversity Matters* requires critical reading by any individuals, leaders, or institutions truthfully addressing their need to increase awareness, sensitivity, cultural competency, and appreciation of diverse populations. This vital resource is particularly insightful and relevant for educational Christ-centered institutions still grappling with how to accept and embrace diversity. This powerful book will have a profound impact on any institution truly committed to fulfilling a leadership role of enhancing the understanding, discourse, and interactions of its constituents."

　　—**Dr. Cheryl T. Chatman**, Executive Vice-President and Dean of Diversity, Concordia University

"I have long felt that if anyone should be leading the movement of diversity and inclusion on college campuses, it should be Christian universities. Ironically, in recent years, most of my time has been spent working with secular universities across the country and globe and have watched what seemed to be greater progress in their diversity efforts. But how refreshing and encouraging to read about the level of commitment and demonstrated progress being made in the Christian higher education community. This book is a must-read and rightfully repositions Christian institutions to lead the way, offering hope and powerful lessons to both Christian and secular institutions alike."

　　—**Dr. Sandra Upton**, Vice-President, Educational Initiatives, Cultural Intelligence Center